[illegible]ler™
Search & Rescue Training for the Field Responder

Alliance for Emergency Response Instructors & Examiners

Dion Petaros (EDITOR),
Wes Podboy, James Keck,
Gary Jenkins, and Julie Petaros

AERIE PUBLICATIONS • *Lake Dallas, Texas*

SARResponder: Search & Rescue Training for the Field Responder

AERIE Publications
201 S Shady Shores #13
Lake Dallas, TX 75065

ISBN: 978-0-9894449-2-7
Library of Congress Control Number: 2015934028

Cover and text design by John Reinhardt Book Design

Printed in the United States of America

To all the unpaid Search & Rescue professionals. You endeavor, every day, to improve your capabilities to perform your duties. You respond without hesitation, putting yourself in harm's way with no thought of compensation or reward. It is with great awe that we humbly dedicate this book to you.

Acknowledgments

One would think that completing subsequent books in a series would become easier with each one. Procedurally, that may be so. But without the team of my fellow authors, contributors and colleagues providing their great insight and knowledge the journey to completing this book would have been impossible. To them I owe a greater debt than could ever be repaid. Once again I cannot imagine a more professional publishing team, especially John Reinhardt and Kathleen Strattan, without whom this book would not be the quality publication it has become. They again demonstrated unlimited patience, guidance and assistance even when pressured with seemingly unrealistic time constraints and deadlines. Without you, this endeavor would simply not have been possible. And lastly, but not least, to all those in the SAR community who encouraged AERIE to create this book. You asked that we provide you with additional knowledge to prepare you to perform your duties. What you didn't realize is how much you inspire us just knowing you are out there serving your fellow citizens.

Dion Petaros
April 2015

Contents

Introduction

The fact that you are reading this book is a testament to your dedication to caring for your fellow man. That devotion to service is, unfortunately, becoming rarer in our society that increasingly focuses on the "me." It is for you this book has been written.

This book is the second in a series developed to educate individual responders with the knowledge and skills required to function professionally in a Search & Rescue incident. As with all scholarly endeavors, it is imperative that you establish a proper foundation by starting at the beginning. In order to fully understand the concepts presented here, we strongly urge you to review the lessons in the first book of the series, *SARAware*™. Without that foundational knowledge, you will find understanding the information in this book very difficult. Since all the preparation and foundational information is presented in the *SARAware*™ text of this series, we will not revisit that material. While all the *SARAware*™ concepts are vital to functioning in a SAR incident (and again we recommend you study that information first or revisit it if you have already studied the *SARAware*™ text), we will begin presenting new and follow-on concepts pertinent to responders pursuing careers as *ground searchers* and other specialty SAR field responders. It is also critical that you supplement your study of this book with participation in the practical training of the skills described in this book. It is essential that you participate in such training with qualified and experienced Instructors. Otherwise applying improper techniques or *learning bad habits* will make it that much more difficult for you to become competent in performing your duties.

As the name implies, our goal for this text is to prepare the responder to function in the field, performing field search tactics. Such responders are frequently called *field operators*. We will use the terms *field operator* and *field responder* interchangeably, but always referring to those performing field search tactics away from the Command Post and/or Base, regardless of the SAR environment involved.

January 2015
Lake Dallas, TX

Human Physiology & Fitness

1

Objectives

Courtesy of FreeDigitalPhotos.net

- Describe the need for proper physical preparedness in SAR
- Discuss the human energy cycle
- Explain the heat production and loss process, including the role of the circulatory system
- Differentiate ways the body loses heat, including:
  - Radiation
  - Conduction
  - Convection
  - Evaporation
  - Respiration
- Describe hydration and electrolyte requirements
- Discuss nutritional requirements, including differences in diverse SAR environments
- Describe the physical conditioning requirements for SAR field responders
- Explain the "SAFE" components of a SAR ready exercise program
- Describe the concept of "Mental Fitness" as it applies to SAR

Being a Search & Rescue Field Responder is hard work. These individuals deal with Psychological Stress and high levels of Physical Exertion on a regular basis. Making it even more difficult to prepare is the fact that there is no prior notification of when the responder will be called to engage in activities resulting in stress and exertion. The SAR field responder must participate in an ongoing program of physical and mental preparation combined with an understanding of how the body works to maximize the training plan results and mitigate external influences reducing effectiveness. Above all, our plan to remain healthy and fit at all times must be a *whole person* concept that includes mental fitness and physical fitness. The first step will be to gain a basic knowledge of human physiology. The second will be to develop an understanding and plan for fitness.

> Understanding Human Physiology and Maintaining Physical & Mental Fitness are essential concepts because there are lives at stake—Yours, Your Teammates' and the Subject's!!

Merriam Webster defines Physiology as a branch of biology that deals with the functions and activities of life or of living matter (such as organs, tissues, or cells) and of the physical and chemical phenomena involved. You must have a basic understanding of human physiology so you will understand how your body works, what helps your body function effectively, and what inhibits your body's ability to perform crucial SAR tasks.

Fitness is defined by The American Heritage Medical Dictionary as the state or condition of being physically sound and healthy, especially as the result of exercise and proper nutrition and a measure of the ability of a person to perform certain tasks. Our discussion of SAR fitness will include both physical ***and*** mental fitness.

Food and Nutrition—The body uses the foods that we intake to create energy and maintain body thermal homeostasis (temperature balance). The three main nutrients used for energy are **carbohydrates, protein, and fats**, with carbohydrates being the most important source. Your body can also use protein and fats for energy when carbs have been depleted. When you eat, your body breaks down nutrients into smaller components and absorbs them to use as fuel. This process is known as metabolism. Carbohydrates come in two types, simple and complex, and both are converted to sugar (glucose). The body breaks the sugar down in the blood and the blood cells use the glucose to provide energy. Complex carbohydrates such as high-fiber cereals, whole-grain breads and pastas, dried beans, and starchy vegetables are the best type of foods for prolonged energy because they are digested at a slow, consistent rate. Complex carbohydrates contain fiber, which takes a longer time to digest in the body as it is absorbed slowly. Complex carbs also stabilize your body's sugar level, which in turn causes the pancreas to produce less insulin. This gives you a feeling of satiety and you are less hungry. Also important in a healthy, energy-producing diet is protein (preferably chicken, turkey, pork tenderloin, and fish), legumes (lentils and beans), and a moderate amount of healthy monounsaturated and polyunsaturated fats (avocados, seeds, nuts, and certain oils). And don't forget hydration!

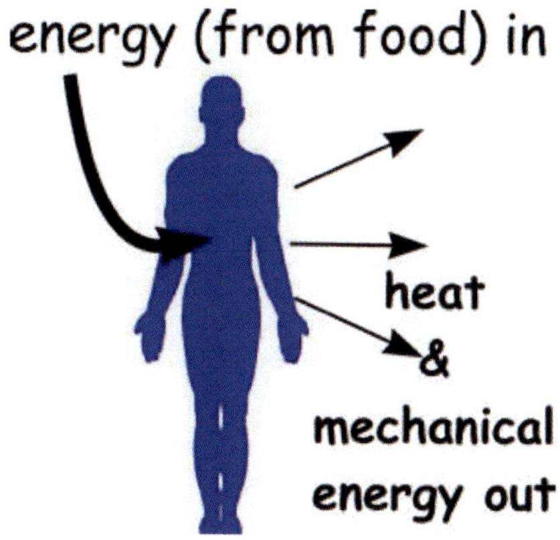

Simple carbohydrates, on the other hand, should be limited. Ranging from candy and cookies to sugary beverages and juices, simple carbs are broken down and absorbed quickly by the body. They provide an initial burst of energy for 30 to 60 minutes, but are digested so quickly they can result in a slump afterward.

Adequate fluids are also essential for sustaining energy. Water is necessary for digestion, absorption, and the transport of nutrients for energy. Dehydration can cause a lack of energy. While some newer studies vary on how much water is required on a daily basis, the average person needs to drink six to eight 8-ounce glasses of water each day. We will cover hydration in more detail, later in this chapter.

You should also avoid alcohol and caffeine. Alcohol is a depressant and can reduce your energy levels, while caffeine usually provides an initial two-hour energy burst, followed by a crash.

Nutritionists have set minimal daily standards of caloric in-take, which vary by person, to keep us healthy. The calorie charts below outline the general calorie intake requirements. As we noted, engaging is SAR field operations will be physically stressful and will require higher amounts of energy. You should plan accordingly. Be careful to not fall into a useless effort to just eat twice as much because your calorie needs for the day are doubled. Unless you are already involved in a daily fitness program that includes a nutrition plan, you will have no foundation from which to increase or decrease your caloric intake. Additionally, since you will not likely have much advanced notice of the deployment, timing the increase in caloric intake is all but impossible.

> It is imperative that you apply the concept of good nutrition EVERY DAY! Do not ignore good nutrition and then try to "catch up" when you're called to deploy.

When evaluating the charts below, remember the projected caloric needs reflect that required to maintain your present weight. After consultation with your physician, you may determine that you need to lose (most of today's western society!) or gain weight. Your caloric intake must be adjusted accordingly.

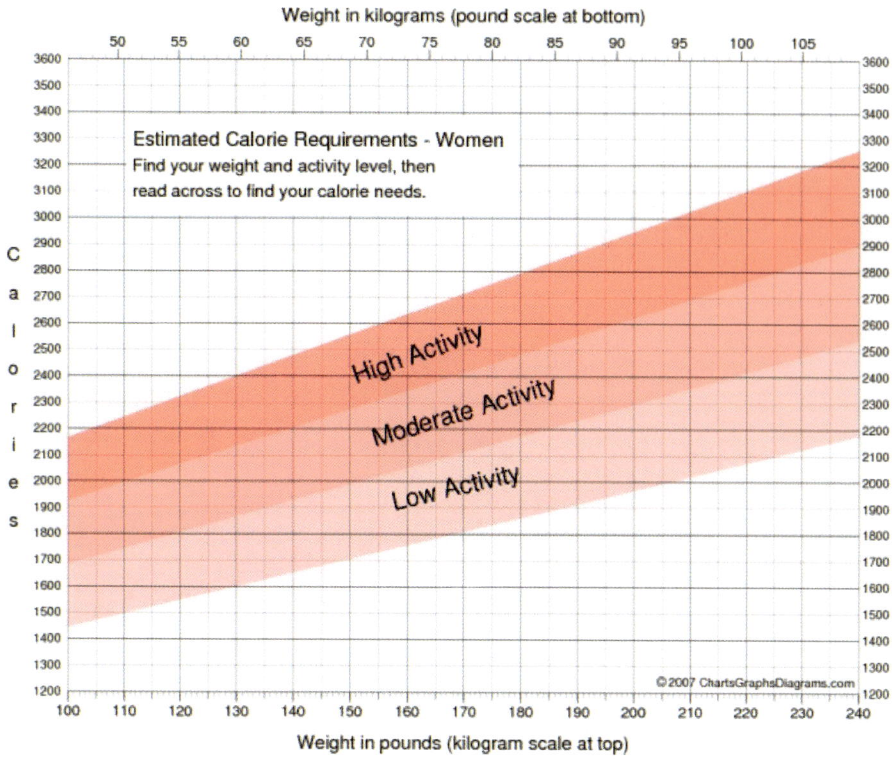
Weight in kilograms (pound scale at bottom)
Estimated Calorie Requirements - Women
Find your weight and activity level, then
read across to find your calorie needs.
High Activity
Moderate Activity
Low Activity
Calories
Weight in pounds (kilogram scale at top)
©2007 ChartsGraphsDiagrams.com

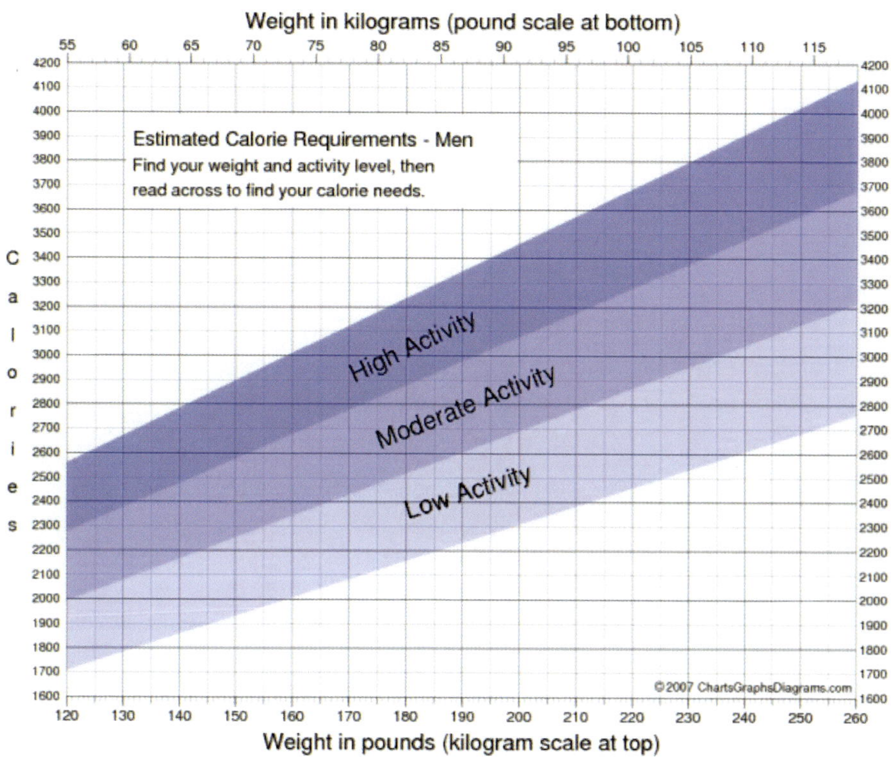
Weight in kilograms (pound scale at bottom)
Estimated Calorie Requirements - Men
Find your weight and activity level, then
read across to find your calorie needs.
High Activity
Moderate Activity
Low Activity
Calories
Weight in pounds (kilogram scale at top)
©2007 ChartsGraphsDiagrams.com

Maintaining Thermal Homeostasis

While the production of body heat may be viewed as a by-product of creating energy, maintaining core body temperature, within a very narrow range, is critical to warm-blooded animals. Should your core temperature fall outside this acceptable range it is unlikely you will be able to perform your SAR duties and might possibly suffer long-term harm or even death.

As warm-blooded animals, humans possess a formal regulatory system that maintains the body temperature at about 98° Fahrenheit (37° Centigrade), regardless of environmental fluctuations. Since the body constantly produces heat through the creation of energy and mechanical movement, heat must be transferred from the body to the environment or prevented from being transferred to the environment, to maintain a constant temperature. Thermal equilibrium is the balance between the rate of heat production and the rate of heat loss.

The body's primary method of regulating its temperature involves finely adjusting the flow of heated blood (circulatory system) between its core (brain, heart, lungs) and periphery (skin, arms and legs). The determining factor is always the temperature of the core. If the core temperature is falling, blood is shunted away from the periphery back to the core, thus preserving heat. If the core temperature is increasing, circulation to the periphery is increased to remove excess heat.

This aspect of circulation should not be confused with glucose transport. As we noted in the nutrition discussion, carbohydrates are converted to glucose and transported to the body's cells via the blood. This glucose is then "burned" by the cells to create energy. As higher levels of energy are required during exercise, blood flow to muscle tissue is increased to provide the additional glucose required.

The human body can also absorb heat from the environment. Think about being outdoors on a hot sunny day. The ability to block this environmental heat, and conversely prevent heat loss on a cold day, is essential when performing our SAR field assignments. Our primary external method of temperature control is through the clothing we wear. This will be discussed in detail in Chapter 3, but leads us to review the concept of heat gain/loss through environmental interface.

Concepts of heat loss through environmental interface

A study of physics shows us that there are five primary means of body heat loss through environmental means. These include: Radiation, Conduction, Convection, Evaporation and Respiration.

- Radiation—The heat generated from within the body is given off to the surrounding atmosphere. Infra-red photography of the human body shows how there is a layer of warm air (warmer than the surrounding air temperature) immediately adjacent to the body.
- Conduction—Outdoorsmen jokingly refer to this as "cold butt syndrome." Body heat is lost through contact with a colder surface. Sitting on a cold surface will eventually cause your buttocks to feel cold as your body cannot generate heat quick enough to equal the loss. An important note on the difference between radiation loss through air and conductive loss in water—you will lose heat 25 times faster through immersion in water than exposure in air.
- Convection—This method of heat loss is due to movement of air (or water) that increases dissipation of heat from the body surface. If you blow (even gently) on exposed skin, that patch of skin will feel cool. The greater the air currents the greater the heat loss.

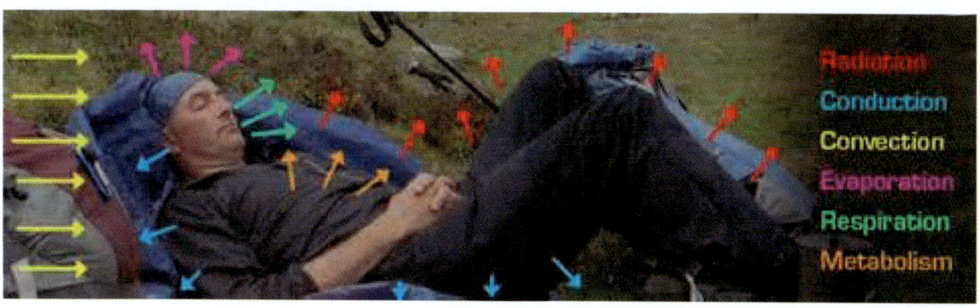

Courtesy of www.backpackinglight.co.uk

- Evaporation—Heat loss through evaporation occurs when liquid is converted to a gas. Human sweat is the primary example of evaporation. The process of sweat evaporating from your skin (or clothes), causes a loss of heat even when the atmospheric temperature is higher than the skin.
- Respiration—As you breathe in cold air it is warmed before it gets to your lungs. You then breathe out warm air and you are effectively losing heat every time you breathe. There is nothing we can do about breathing. We have to do it to stay alive! In comparison with the other mechanisms of heat loss, however, heat loss through breathing is relatively insignificant.

Hydration

Water is essential for proper body function. Hydration is important because the body is comprised mostly of water, and the proper balance between water and electrolytes in our bodies really determines how most of our systems function, including nerves and muscles. The human body may be able to survive as long as a month without food but only a matter of days without water. And your cognitive functions may degrade even more quickly from only slightly reduced levels of hydration.

Dehydration occurs when water loss exceeds water intake, usually due to exercise or disease. Mild dehydration is characterized by thirst and general discomfort and usually resolves with oral hydration. Most people can tolerate a three to four percent decrease in body water without difficulty. A five to eight percent decrease can cause fatigue and dizziness. Over ten percent can cause physical and mental deterioration, accompanied by severe thirst. A decrease more than fifteen to twenty-five percent of the body water is invariably fatal.

So how much water should the average person drink each day? We've heard for years that we need to drink eight, 8-ounce glasses of water a day. Before you start chugging, is it true? Recent studies indicate there is no scientific evidence whatsoever for that rule. While it's certainly not a harmful rule, there is no scientific rationale behind it.

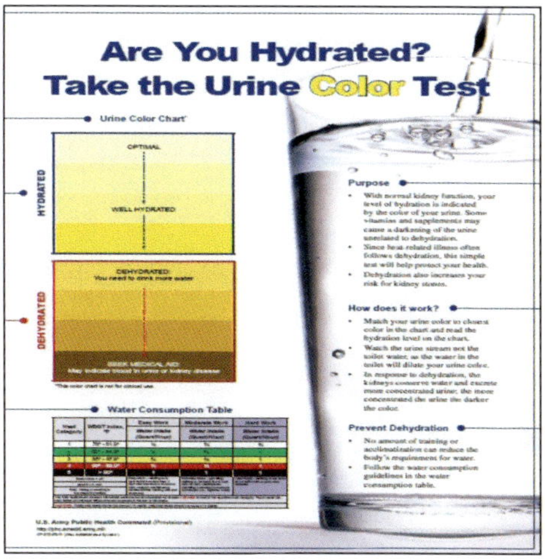

U.S. Army Public Health Command

But there is a simple guideline... You should be drinking enough so that you urinate every two to four hours, and that the urine is a light color.

There is also much discussion on what types of fluids are valid considerations for hydration. For many years we excluded drinks with caffeine, such as coffee and soft drinks. Contrary to the myth, yes, coffee counts when you're tallying fluid intake. "There is no truth to the idea that coffee makes you dehydrated. That is a pervasive myth," says a spokesman for the American College of Sports Medicine (ACSM). "The diuretic effect of the caffeine of soda and coffee is mild compared to the amount of fluid they contain."

There has also been much discussion on whether you should drink plain water or "sports drinks" that claim better results. Originally, we feared that consuming sports drinks would create an electrolyte imbalance resulting in excessive electrolytes including hypernatremia (too much sodium). Recent studies now show many of the (manufacturers') claims have some basis in fact.

When you sweat, you probably know you lose more than just water -- you also lose electrolytes, particularly sodium, the most critical electrolyte lost and a key component of the hydration process. When exercising intensely for longer than approximately 45 minutes, it's important to consider replacing what you lose in sweat to maintain proper hydration.

However, a sports drink containing too little sodium will not promote optimal rehydration. When selecting a sports drink for intense exercise, look for at least 70 mg of sodium per eight-ounce serving, which is what the National Athletic Trainers' Association (NATA) suggests to help stimulate thirst, increase voluntary fluid intake, maintain fluid balance and ensure sufficient hydration.

Besides sodium, a properly formulated sports drink should also include the right amount of carbohydrates (the primary and most important energy source for the body during exercise) to fuel working muscles, fight fatigue and provide sweetness. Sports drinks with a carbohydrate level of about six percent (approximately 14-15 g of carbohydrates per eight oz. serving) have been demonstrated by research to promote rapid fluid absorption and supply enough energy to allow active individuals to maintain their physical performance.

Keep in mind that if a sports drink contains too much carbohydrate (above 18 grams of carbohydrates per eight oz.), it will hinder fluid absorption. If the drink is too dilute (not enough carbohydrates) then you'll get the fluid you need, but without the appropriate amount of energy needed to fuel working muscles.

Energy drinks are not suitable for hydration during exercise. The amount you would need to consume for proper hydration could become counterproductive due to the overabundance of caffeine consumed. A recent report to make this connection concluded that energy drinks can cause "angina, cardiac arrhythmia (irregular heartbeat) and even sudden death." This finding confirms that of a similar report from a year ago, and reaffirms that energy drinks should be imbibed with caution—and most probably in moderation, and almost definitely not right before or during any sort of trying physical activity. (Devon Jackson, *Outside Magazine*, October 2014)

Exercise, such as field searching, will require additional fluid intake to balance fluid loss. But how much is necessary to replace the fluid loss? Another of the myths of hydration recommended "prehydrating" in preparation for exercise. More recent studies measured athletic performance of three different groups. The first group simply drank according to thirst levels, the second drank moderate amounts of water pre-emptively and the third drank large amounts of water pre-emptively. The study showed no significant differences in core body temperature (dehydration reduces blood volume levels which impairs temperature control) or athletic results. The only difference came from the high rate of intake causing stomach distress alleged to excessive intake of fluid. Based on this study, it appears that fluid intake, based on thirst levels, should be done to maintain fluid level rather than prevent fluid decrease.

Nutrition for field responders

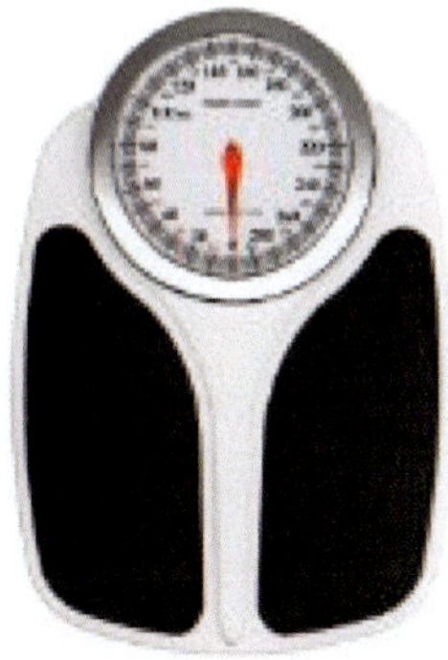

A nutrition plan is an important part of your overall fitness program. Getting to and maintaining your optimal weight is essential to performing your best every day, and especially when called in service to those in need. There are three principles of proper nutrition, which include variety, balance, and moderation. Adding a variety of foods to your diet is essential to ensure eating from the five major food groups. Remember, no one food supplies all the nutrients the body needs. A balanced diet supplies the nutrients and calories the body needs if eaten in appropriate amounts. Serving sizes differ for individual needs based on age, gender, and activity level. Many people, looking to lose weight, believe they have to deprive themselves of their favorite foods, but choosing certain foods in moderation is key to successful long-term weight management. Consulting your physician before beginning a weight management program is important to good health and preventing unwanted negative effects.

Here are some suggested guidelines to begin a weight management program:

- Set a realistic initial weight goal. If you and your physician agree you should lose weight, a reduction in body weight of approximately 10% in the first six months and keeping it off for one year is reasonable.
- Monitor your eating habits by keeping a food journal for a period of one or two weeks to familiarize yourself with your eating habits: how much you are eating, where, why, with whom, and what mood are you in when you eat. You can keep

track by using smart phone apps (many are free) available at your "app store."

- Do not starve yourself. Avoid rapid weight loss and its dangerous side effects such as light headedness. Consider starting with a 25% reduction in caloric intake from your current levels.
- Use the Food Guide Pyramid, below, to plan your meals so that you select foods from all six food groups.
- Read the **Nutrition Facts Food Labels** found on pre-prepared foods. Pay special attention to the fat, sodium, and carbohydrate content when shopping, especially if your family history includes cardiovascular and/or diabetes risk factors.
- Choose protein sources from plants and lean sources of meats. A good rule of thumb in selecting meats with less fat is to look for the words "round" or "loin" when shopping for beef, and the words "loin" or "leg" when shopping for pork or lamb. Remember, when shopping for poultry, white meat has less fat than dark meat.
- Choose a diet rich in soluble fiber including oat bran, legumes, barley, and most fruits and vegetables. 20 to 35 grams of fiber daily are recommended.
- Watch serving sizes and avoid going back for seconds.
- Adopt healthy meal preparation techniques to reduce sodium, fat, and sugar.
- Plan in advance when dining out. Treating yourself to a nice restaurant meal is appropriate. But thinking ahead of what to eat can prevent a binge that will undo your good work.
- Limit your consumption of alcohol. It provides empty calories.

Good nutrition provides more than energy, structural components, vitamins and minerals. There are other substances in the foods that you eat that have become better known over the last few years. For example, antioxidants help protect your body from damage that comes from the sun, pollution, smoke, and poor dietary choices. They are found in the phytochemicals of fruits and vegetables, as well as some vitamins and amino acids. A healthy diet will give your body the right amount of energy, enough raw materials and all of the "little helpers" you need to stay healthy.

Another source of information for nutritional planning is a federal government website www.choosemyplate.gov. This website provides numerous articles, videos and sources for nutrition, fitness and health considerations. A suggested 2000 kilo/calorie daily diet, from this website, is included below.

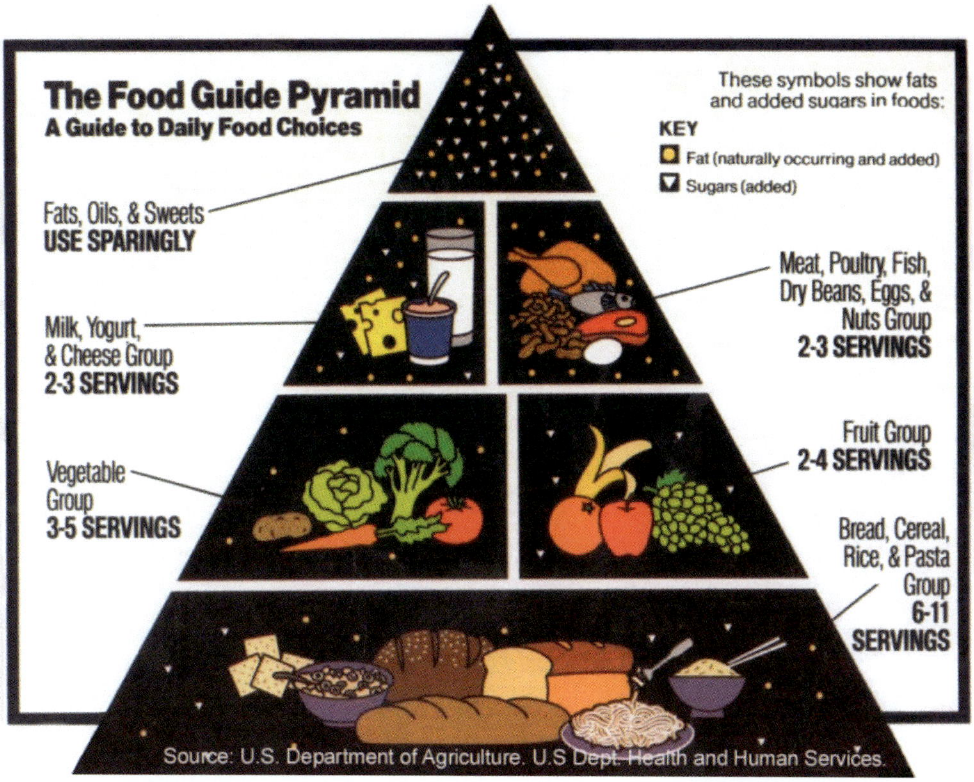

Table 1	
MyPlate Recommended Daily Amounts for a 2,000-Calorie Diet	
Food Group	Daily Average Over 1 Week
Grains	6.2 oz. eq.
Whole grains	3.8 oz. eq.
Refined grains	2.4 oz. eq.
Vegetables	2.6 cups
Vegetable subgroups (amount per week)	
Dark green	1.6 cups
Red/orange	5.6 cups
Starchy	5.1 cups
Beans and peas	1.6 cups
Other vegetables	4.1 cups
Fruits	2.1 cups
Dairy	3.1 cups
Protein foods	5.7 oz. eq.
Seafood	8.8 oz. per week
Oils	29 grams
Calories from added fats and sugars	245 calories

Implementing a fitness exercise program

Functioning as a field responder requires you to be in good shape and maintain a high level of fitness. You do not want to become a victim yourself, fall behind the rest of the team or be unable to perform the necessary activities required for search & rescue of a subject in need. Long-term motivation will be the key for many to staying fit. January is the big sign up month for memberships at fitness gyms. Everyone wants to lose those pesky additional pounds they put on during the holidays or there is that New Year's resolution concept. Things go great for 4-7 weeks, then that newness wears off and you start skipping a day here and there. Then you find out that you didn't really lose all the weight that you had envisioned. Next you get more frustrated and just give up.

So once you and your physician agree on your ability to embark on an exercise program, you must determine the goals to meet. One challenge for SAR field responders is the lack of standard fitness requirements. Many teams have no requirements for any physical fitness. This borders on criminal negligence and could result in litigation from field responders injured or falling ill attempting to perform duties they are unfit to do so. Litigation could also result from victims or their families finding that operations were hampered by field responders unfit for duty. If your resource does not have (minimally) an annual fitness testing program, consider helping them start one or implement your own program.

Physical fitness needs for SAR field responders vary from those of our Public Safety colleagues, but therein could lie a basis for beginning. As members of the SAR community, we constantly interface and work alongside members of Law Enforcement, Fire Service and Emergency Medical Services. As those individuals are required to meet the fitness requirements of their departments, gaining their respect will involve demonstrating our commitment to a similar fitness requirement.

Many of these departments use a national fitness standard in the form of Cooper Physical Fitness Test—Age Adjusted. A full copy of the 2007 version of that document is included in the Appendices. While each team and individual should decide their own need, exceeding the 50th percentile requirements of the Cooper Physical Fitness Test is considered to be a minimal goal for SAR field responder. This is an excerpt of the 70th percentile requirements:

70th percentile	Male	Male	Male	Male		Female	Female	Female	Female
Age	20–29	30–39	40–49	50–59		20–29	30–39	40–49	50-59
Vertical jump (inches)	22.5	22	18	16		16.3	14.9	12.3	
1 min sit ups	45	41	36	31		41	32	27	22
300 m run (sec.)	52	53	61	70		60	68	75.3	
1 min push ups	41	34	26	21		24	18	14	
1.5 mile run	10:49	11:09	11:52	12:53		12:51	13:41	14:33	16:26

So a fitness program should include activities that will prepare the responder to meet the testing activities in standards such as the Cooper testing requirements. But there are additional considerations that SAR field responders should include in developing their program. These additional components can be found in the acronym SAFE (Strength, Agility, Flexibility, and Endurance).

While we use this acronym as an aid to remembering these concepts, the priority a field responder should place on these components is reversed. Therefore, Endurance should be your primary concern, followed by Flexibility, then Agility and finally Strength.

- Endurance—There are two forms of endurance important to field responders. The first is cardiovascular endurance which is body's ability to keep up with exercise like running, jogging, swimming, cycling, and anything that forces your cardiovascular system (lungs, heart, and blood vessels) to work for extended periods of time. Together, the heart and lungs fuel your body with the oxygen needed by your muscles, ensuring that they have the oxygen needed for the work they are doing. Improving your cardiovascular endurance involves determining an appropriate target heart rate for your age, weight and current fitness state. Then exercise (walking, running, swimming, biking, etc.) to sustain that target heart rate for 30 minutes. Doing this exercise 3-5 times weekly will increase your cardiovascular fitness.

  The second form of endurance is muscular endurance. This is the ability of your muscles to perform contractions for extended periods of time. Rather than just lifting or carrying something for a few seconds, the muscles are used for minutes at a time.

The way to increase muscular endurance is to train with light weights, working in the 20—25 rep range. Working with lighter weight will train the muscle fibers needed for muscular endurance, and the higher rep range leads to a longer period of exercise.

- Flexibility—Flexibility is one of the most important, yet often overlooked, components of physical fitness. Without flexibility, the muscles and joints would grow stiff and movement would be limited. Flexibility training ensures that your body can move through its entire range of motion without pain or stiffness.

For a very basic test of your flexibility, lean forward and try to touch your toes. Those with good flexibility will usually be able to touch their toes, while those with limited flexibility will not. The sit and reach test (sitting on the floor and reaching toward your toes) is another good way to assess your flexibility. The more flexible you are, the closer you will come to touching your toes and beyond. Practicing proper stretching as part of your exercise routine is key to improving flexibility. Some suggestions for stretching:

1. **Stretch after your workout**—Studies have shown that stretching before exercise doesn't reduce our risk of injury or soreness. In fact, stretching cold muscles could possibly lead to injury. If your goal is to increase flexibility, it's best to stretch after your workout when your muscles are warm and pliable. Set aside at least 5 minutes to enjoy this part of your workout.
2. **Stretch the muscles you worked during your workout**—If you don't have much time, focus on your major muscles or the muscles that tend to be the tightest such as the hips, quads, hamstrings, calves and chest.
3. **Don't bounce**—When doing static stretches, don't bounce. Hold a comfortable position until you feel a *gentle* pull on your muscle. It shouldn't hurt and bouncing could cause you to pull a muscle.

4. **Hold each stretch for 15-30 seconds** to get the most flexibility benefits.
5. **Stretch throughout the day**—Stretching when you're warm can increase flexibility, but stretching throughout the day can also help you reduce tension and stress.

- Agility—is the ability to change the body's position efficiently, and requires the integration of isolated movement skills using a combination of balance, coordination, speed, reflexes, strength, and endurance. Agility is the ability to change the direction of the body in an efficient and effective manner. There are numerous exercises demonstrated on the internet that can help improve your agility. One of those, involving two techniques, is described below:
    - Agility ladders (speed ladders)—a flat "ladder" device that is lying on the ground, or tape on the floor or carpet 14" apart. There are dozens of drills and demonstrations on the internet. You can walk through the drills to start out and for a lower impact workout. 2 common drills are:
        1. **Forward Running, High-Knee Drill:** *This drill is great for improving foot speed and coordination for all types of people that are trying to improve their agility. Walk (initially with knees low) and build up to running with high knees, forward through the ladder, touching every ladder space. Land on the balls of the feet and drive forward with your arms.*
        2. **Lateral Running, Side-to-Side Drill**: *The lateral movement of this drill is great for everyone and improves knee and ankle stability as well. Keep a low center of gravity and step side-to-side through the ladder one foot at a time. Touch in each space in the ladder with both feet. Land on the balls of the feet and repeat right to left and left to right.*

- Strength—To the field responder, muscular strength is the least important component of a physical fitness program. Still, muscular strength can be an asset. Muscular strength is the power exerted, for short periods of time, to move heavy objects.

The best way to increase muscular strength is to train with heavy weights. The technique uses repetitions in the 4—6 or 12—15 ranges. The heavier the weight, the fewer reps you should perform!

Mental Fitness

The final concept involved in preparing ourselves as field responders is the idea of mental fitness. Being psychologically prepared to perform our duties is every bit important as the physical preparation. In training and when responding, the body is asked to push physical limits of endurance, power, speed, and strength. Similarly, the mind is asked to push mental barriers, such as focus, composure, determination, and handling the stress of life and death response. Examples of traits that need to be learned or developed include:

- Ability to not fixate on fear
- Ability to accept pressure to perform
- Ability to manage stress & anxiety
- Ability to compartmentalize personal challenges away from your SAR duties
- Ability to allow psychological relaxation upon demand (e.g. after your assignment)
- Ability to function within team environments
- Adaptability to fluid performance demands
- Commitment and ability to set goals
- Composure, emotional control
- High self-confidence (obtained through effective training)
- Ability to remain focused on task
- Passion and compassion (for the mission and the subject)
- Positive attitude and mindset
- Responsibility (to yourself, your team, your agency, and the subject and their family)

- Ability to develop and implement personal plans (fitness, equipment, being a competent resource)
- Above normal work-ethic
- Ability to grieve appropriately (the right time and the right place)

How does a responder develop mental fitness? The mental training process typically involves the following four steps:

- *Education*: Learning about mental fitness principles and strategies.
- *Self-Awareness*: Increasing responders' self-knowledge by helping them reflect on responses related to their best and less than best performance situations, experiences, and perspectives. Topics can be briefly mentioned during the event debriefing and in the After Action Report.
- *Implementation*: Challenging resources to apply newly acquired knowledge of searching or a rescue, strategies, and lessons learned in the performance of their task or assignment.
- *Evaluation:* Inviting responders, and external observers (such as people in ICS positions), to evaluate mental fitness capacities and identify key lessons that can be applied to future missions.

Some final thoughts on mental fitness...

All of us need to periodically de-stress. This is an increasing challenge, during long term incidents, to care for responder mental well-being. We have implemented a combination of informal and formal programs to assist our personnel.

Informally, we must make sure to give our responders adequate breaks to break their focus on the incident. It is this intensity that, while desirable when performing our SAR duties, causes high levels of psychological stress when not allowed to dissipate. When engaged in a field assignment, Unit Leaders must ensure their personnel get frequent breaks. Physical exhaustion will exacerbate mental fatigue.

This combination will debilitate a responder and possibly cause long term stress disorders if not alleviated early and frequently.

From a more formal perspective, there is a system of *Critical Incident Stress Management* (CISM). Critical incidents are traumatic events that cause powerful emotional reactions in people who are exposed to those events. The most stressful of these are line of duty deaths, co-worker suicide, multiple event incidents, delayed intervention and multi-casualty incidents. Every profession can list their own worst-case scenarios that can be categorized as critical incidents. Emergency services organizations, for example, usually list the *Terrible Ten*. They are:

1. Line of duty deaths
2. Suicide of a colleague
3. Serious work related injury
4. Multi-casualty / disaster / terrorism incidents
5. Events with a high degree of threat to the personnel
6. Significant events involving children
7. Events in which the victim is known to the personnel
8. Events with excessive media interest
9. Events that are prolonged and end with a negative outcome
10. Any significantly powerful, overwhelming distressing event

Once incident management recognizes the existence of a critical incident stress environment, a three level system of intervention is implemented. The three levels are: defusing, debriefing and follow-up.

- Defusing—A defusing is done the day of the incident before the person(s) has a chance to sleep. The defusing is designed to assure the person or people involved that their feelings are normal, to tell them what symptoms to watch for over the short term, and to offer them a lifeline in the form of a telephone number where they can reach someone whom they can talk to. Defusings are limited only to individuals directly involved in the incident and are often done informally, sometimes at the scene. They are designed to assist individuals in coping in the short term and address immediate needs.

- Debriefing—Debriefings are usually the second level of intervention for those directly affected by the incident and often the first for those not directly involved. A debriefing is normally done within 72 hours of the incident and gives the individual or group the opportunity to talk about their experience, how it has affected them, brainstorm coping mechanisms, identify individuals at risk, and inform the individual or group about services available to them in their community. The final step is to follow up with them the day after the debriefing to ensure that they are safe and coping well or to refer the individual for professional counselling.

Although many have co-opted the debriefing process for use with other groups, the primary focus in the field of CISM is to support staff members of organizations or members of communities which have experienced a traumatic event. The debriefing process (defined by the International Critical Incident Stress Foundation [ICISF]) has seven steps:

1. Introduction of intervener and establishment of guidelines
2. Invite participants to introduce themselves (while attendance at a debriefing may be mandatory, participation is not)
3. Report details of the event given from individual perspectives
4. Relate emotional responses given subjectively with personal reaction and actions
5. Follow with a discussion of symptoms exhibited since the event
6. Conduct instruction phase where the team discusses the symptoms and assures participants that any symptoms (if they have any at all) are a normal reaction to an abnormal event and "generally" these symptoms will diminish with time and self-care

7. Follow with another brief period of shared informal discussion regarding resumption of duty where individuals are returned to their normal tasks

The intervener is always watching for individuals who are not coping well and additional assistance is offered at the conclusion of the process.

- Follow-up—The important final step is follow-up. This is generally done within the week following the debriefing by team members. A determination can then be made if additional counseling is indicated.

Summary

Preparation for participation as a SAR field responder is a *whole person concept*. It begins with an understanding of how our body and mind work. Then we must develop and implement programs to enhance our physical and psychological being. Finally, we must maintain these programs as a lifestyle. Only then will we be perpetually prepared to answer the call of our fellow citizens in need.

References

Centers for Disease Control and Prevention - Disaster Mental Health for Responders: Key Principles, Issues and Questions, www.cdc.gov

Fitness Magazine—Various references www.fitnessmagazone.com

Outside - Various references www.outsideonline.com

Medical Reserve Corp—PSYCHOLOGICAL FIRST AID Field Operations Guide (FOG) www.medicalreservecorps.gov

Tactical Education & Medical Solutions, LLC—Various discussions Brent Cusher, www.tacticalmedicteam.com

The Cooper Institute—Physical Fitness Testing; Age Adjusted www.cooperinstitute.org

U.S. Army Public Health Command—Various Discussions http://phc.amedd.army.mil

Wikimedia Foundation/Wiktionary—Various Information Used in this Book (2012)
The Free Online Dictionary, http://en.wikipedia.org/wiki/Wiktionary
Fitday.com—Various discussion and references (2013)
www.fitday.com, Internet Brands Inc.
Ask the Trainer.com—Various discussions and references (2015)
Mike Behnken, www.askthetrainer.com
Sports Fitness Advisor—Various discussions and references (2015)
Sporting Excellence Limited, Merseyside, England
WebMD—Various discussions and references (2015)
WebMD LLC
Livestrong.com—Various discussions and references (2015)
Demand Media Inc.

Personal Survival Concepts & Techniques

2

Photograph by Dan Saelinger

Objectives

- Define the concept of survival
- Explain the concept of comfort zone and how it affects your ability to respond to a survival event
- Differentiate between short term and long term survival
- Describe the "Rules of Three" as it applies to the necessities of life
- Explain the four stages of response to life-threatening situations
- Describe ways to control fear
- Explain the acronym STOP and its benefit to the survival process
- Describe some priority actions necessary for outdoors/wilderness survival including:
  - Improvised Shelter Construction
  - Firecraft
  - Signaling
  - Water Acquisition and Treatment

Defining Survival

To begin a discussion of survival, we must first agree on what that actually is. Merriam-Webster defines survival as: the state or fact of continuing to live or exist, especially in spite of difficult conditions. We can certainly see how a subject lost in the wilderness would encounter such "difficult conditions" making survival unlikely without appropriate training. But even in an urban environment an injured person who cannot care for themselves may also find they are in a situation requiring survival skills. Studies have shown, however, that lost and missing subjects who do not employ these survival concepts have an extremely high mortality rate, especially after 72 hours without water and shelter. It is unlikely that a SAR field responder will need to exercise the skills presented in this chapter, when participating in a SAR incident. Field resources are never deployed "solo." Understanding the concepts required to survive without all the conveniences of modern society, might just save that same responder when they encounter such a situation without benefit of a team of colleagues. This knowledge might also give the responder insight into the plight of the subject(s) they seek.

Comfort Zones

All of us go about our everyday lives content to have our basic life needs fulfilled without any struggle. We know that flipping a switch will give us light. If we are cold, we raise the thermostat a few degrees. When we're hungry or thirsty, we go to the refrigerator or drive to a local restaurant. All this convenience keeps us in a *comfort zone*. This comfort zone works fine until we are confronted with a stressful situation that exceeds the limits of our personal comfort zones.

When considering our reactions to being placed in a life-threatening situation, the ultimate stressful event, our comfort zone will dictate our response. For most subjects encountering a life-threatening or survival occurrence, their immediate reaction is one of incomprehension and, frequently, panic. Remember the current state of our comfort zone gave us no warning of impending danger. We are completely surprised to find ourselves in this predicament and have no preparation to counteract its impact.

If we want to deal with stressful events in a more efficient manner, we need to *expand our comfort zones*. How can we acquire this higher level of stress tolerance? The most successful approach is a two stage process. Stage one is education and training. Stage two is experience.

In order to accommodate stress-laden environments we begin by learning about those environments. It is important to study the causes of the danger or risk. These studies should include the origin of the risks and whether they can be prevented or the results mitigated. As part of and after these studies, it is essential to practice the skills used in preventing the danger or those used to minimize the negative outcomes caused by the event. So just having knowledge of the stressful situation is not enough. We must acquire skills to overcome it.

The second step in expanding our comfort zone is gaining experience. Once we learn about the stressful situations we may encounter, and the skills needed to deal with them, we must apply the knowledge and practice the skills. Repeated practice will ingrain the proper actions and provide for a more "automatic" response when our rational thought process may be impaired by the stress encountered. The more we practice, the more proficient we become and the better our response to these events.

Short Term vs. Long Term Survival

Our next consideration is to categorize types of survival situations. There are two broad categories of survival. They are *Short Term* and *Long Term* survival. For our purposes, a short term survival occurrence is that situation requiring an individual to provide and care for themselves, without external assistance or any items other than what they might be carrying, for a period of seventy-two hours or less. As responders, we train to prepare ourselves for a short term survival event. Since we understand the clues that field responders are seeking and management analyzes in order to locate lost and missing subjects, we should be able to assist the searchers in finding us in less time than seventy-two hours. If only we could teach these skills to the broader public, we might have a greater opportunity to locate and extricate subjects, lowering the mortality and morbidity rates.

As we can discern, long term survival events are those lasting longer than seventy-two hours. Should we find ourselves in this situation, we will need to expand upon the concepts and skills employed in short term survival. When we present those short term techniques, you should also be considering how they could be adapted for the occurrence of a survival event lasting longer than seventy-two hours. The only additional requirement for long term survival is the need to acquire enough food sources for extended nutritional support.

Necessities of Life

When studying how to survive without the support found in our society, there are some elementary understandings we must observe. It is essential that you obtain the knowledge of human physiology. You must then take that knowledge and apply it to the concept of *body management*. As you continue your research into proper body management remember it also includes mental acuity. Survival requires a *whole person* approach. Without concern for the ability to support intellectual function the subject will perish even with all necessities provided for physical function.

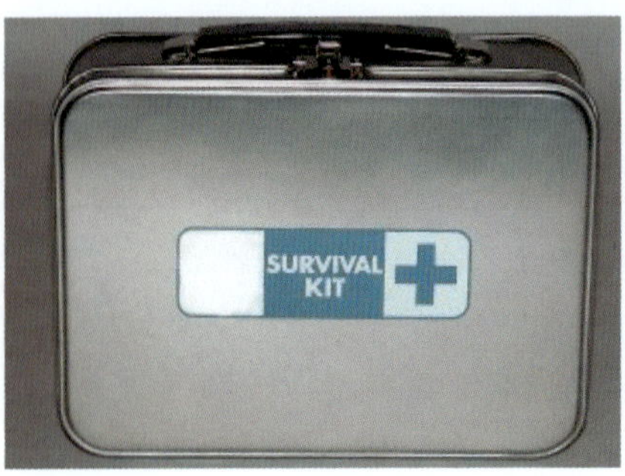

So what should one be concerned about, if confronted with a life-threatening survival situation? There is a body of knowledge developed by survival experts from the military and civilian outdoors community that presents a list of the *necessities of life* and the time periods in which the "survivor" must fulfill them. Among those experts, this list is known as the *Rules of 3s*. These "rules" are listed in order of time priority. In order to properly address a survival event, they should be accomplished/provided for in the order presented:

1. 3 Seconds: Positive Mental Attitude
2. 3 Minutes: Air (or more specifically—Oxygen)
3. 3 Hours: Shelter
4. 30 Hours: Rest
5. 3 Days: Water
6. 3 Weeks: Food/Nutrition

Let's take a look at each of these necessities in more detail:

1. Positive Mental Attitude: Though most individuals will ignore this necessity it is the most important of all. If a person does not have the mental strength (or will) to survive, they will not survive. Wikipedia describes it this way: "Positive mental attitude (PMA) is the philosophy that having an optimistic disposition in every situation in one's life attracts positive changes and increases achievement. *It employs a state of mind that continues to seek, find and execute ways to win, or find a desirable outcome, regardless of the circumstances. It opposes negativity, defeatism and hopelessness.*" If you don't believe you will survive, your belief will become a self-fulfilling prophecy.
2. Air/Oxygen: Most everyone has heard that "brain death" occurs within four to six minutes of the brain being denied oxygen. It is important to understand that is the concept of brain death. We must concern ourselves with the occurrence of *diminished brain capacity*. That is moment when our intellectual functioning decreases to the point where we are no longer making appropriate assessments and decisions. This can occur well in advance of brain death. For the

purpose of survival discussions, it is nominally stated at "about" three (3) minutes.

3. Shelter: Did you know that subjects have been found deceased, from "exposure" to the elements, in temperatures as warm as seventy degrees Fahrenheit/twenty-one degrees Celsius (70° F/21° C)? If you become wet, even in these warm temperatures, you could suffer decreased mental/physical function or even death. The main goal of accessing shelter is to maintain the body core temperature of approximately ninety-eight point six degrees Fahrenheit/thirty-seven degrees Celsius (98.6° F/37° C). Simply acquiring additional or dry clothing can be viewed as providing shelter. For more examples of shelter, we'll address locating or constructing improvised shelters later in this chapter.

Photograph by Philip Werner

4. Rest: Stressful situations are tiring. Increased metabolic rates combined with physical exertion are going to "wear you out." As it may be difficult to restore energy levels, we must look for ways to conserve energy. Building shelter, locating water, creating signaling systems, are all going to require energy. We must also look at the physiologic benefits of rest. During rest/sleep the body rids itself of wastes that, if allowed to accumulate, will degrade physiologic function. Finally, consider the psychological benefits of rest. We have time to calm ourselves, reflect on the situation and plan the actions necessary to survive.
5. Water: Looking back to the chapter on human physiology you will remember that your body consists of fifty to seventy percent (50—70%) water. Even slight losses in water content will significantly degrade the body's ability to function. As we discussed, if you are experiencing thirst, you are already mildly dehydrated. The dehydration will only get worse without immediate and substantial intervention. Dehydration will dramatically impact the body's

heat transfer process and will adversely affect your ability to stay warm, or "cool off." It is essential you locate reliable sources of water prior to getting dehydrated. While three days without water will certainly result in the subject's inability to care for themselves, even shorter periods of time without water will make it less likely the subject can perform the tasks necessary to ensure survival.

6. Food: In the short term (72 hour) survival event, it is likely that you will not require any food or nutritional support at all. Man does not need a daily intake of two thousand (2000) calories to survive! In fact, there are verified accounts of people surviving for six to eight (6-8) weeks without eating. It is true that you will experience hunger during the seventy two (72) hour survival event, but it will not affect your ability to perform the tasks necessary for survival. Should the survival period extend beyond the initial short term event, it will be necessary to secure food sources.

One final consideration to resolving a survival event is creating *signals* to alert searchers to your location. We can become so involved in performing the survival tasks listed above that we forget our primary goal of removing ourselves from the environment causing the stress of survival. There is much discussion on where signaling fits in the above list. We recommend that you begin your signaling efforts as early as possible, but certainly within the first twenty-four (24) hours of requiring assistance. Whether you rest first or develop your signaling process will depend on your physical needs, but if you want to be found and removed from the danger, you should assist searchers by having means of signaling.

Response to Life Threatening Events

We have repeatedly noted the role of psychology/mental attitude in coping with survival situations. Psychologists have studied human reaction to emergencies and have developed four stages of response to such events. Let's review those stages:

1. Alarm
2. Reaction
3. Response
4. Rest

1. Alarm: It frequently begins as that feeling of uncertainty. Something doesn't seem right. In fact, your comfort zone limits are already being challenged. If the stimulus remains, the feeling of uncertainty progresses to a state of alertness/watchfulness. Apprehension and nervousness may grow as the subject begins to imagine possible negative outcomes.
2. Reaction: This stage is more properly named *body reaction*. Once your conscious mind confirms the danger, or you have progressed to an irrational fear, the brain triggers your body's fight-or-flight response. This is an instinctive, immediate reaction to danger that prepares your body to help defend itself by fighting or escaping.

   The brain's hypothalamus initiates the body's fight-or-flight response by simultaneously activating both the sympathetic nervous system (which triggers the nerves) and the adrenal-cortical system (which dumps hormones into the bloodstream). The action of the sympathetic nervous system causes the body to become tense and very alert. Meanwhile, the hypothalamus alerts the pituitary gland to activate the adrenal-cortical system, which releases about 30 different hormones to prepare the body to handle the threat.

   The hormones released into the body during a fear response cause the following physical reactions:

- Increase in heart rate and blood pressure
- Dilated pupils
- Constriction of veins in the skin, which causes the chilly sensation often associated with fear

- Increased blood glucose
- Tensing of muscles and goose bumps
- Relaxation of smooth muscles
- Shutting down of nonessential systems such as digestion and the immune system
- Difficulty concentrating on small tasks

Once the threat diminishes, the body releases the hormone cortisol to calm itself back down to normal. The entire fight-or-flight cycle is part of a defense mechanism that has developed over thousands of years. Without it, one of your direct ancestors may not have been able to defend themselves or escape from predators or enemies.

3. Response: Now your body is prepared to take action. Those actions will be decided by your preparation to encounter stressful situations. It is here that your knowledge, training and proficiency will determine whether you respond rationally and appropriately or if you will respond irrationally (panic for example), or perhaps not at all.

   If you have been expanding your comfort zone and preparing for stressful (and perhaps, life-threatening) situations, your response will likely be thoughtful and systematic. Should you not be prepared, it is likely you will respond with disbelief and in a disorganized manner. At the extreme, you will be panic stricken with any/all the accompanying characteristics. These can include: nausea, vomiting, trembling, crying, fainting, fleeing/running, remaining frozen in place, etc.
4. Rest: Once the threat diminishes, the body releases the hormone cortisol to calm itself back down to normal. You have just experienced significant levels of psychological stress and physical exertion (even if you remained frozen in place, your body has expended large amounts of energy). Whether you make a conscious decision or not, your body will require and seek a period of rest.

One concern to be aware of during this stage is the onset of psychological shock. The symptoms can include: anger, irritability, confusion, difficulty concentrating, feeling disconnected, numb, sad or hopeless or combinations of these. Someone who has experienced a life-threatening event would do well to seek counseling to mitigate the immediate and long term psychological effects of the event.

Fear

After discussing comfort zones and response to life-threatening events it is appropriate to extend the discussion to controlling fear. The venerable Mark Twain once said, "Courage is resistance to and mastery of fear — not the absence of fear." So whether we need to act courageously or simply perform tasks rationally, we must learn to control the fear we will encounter in our lives. Let's consider a logical scheme to control fear.

Acknowledge you are experiencing fear: This may sound like a contradiction, but accept that you are afraid. This doesn't mean you can't cope with the danger, just that you are fearful. The process of admitting this fear may allow you to think clearly and focus on the cause of the fear. This focus is the first step to a methodical approach to resolving the threatening event.

Don't dwell on the fear: If you remain fixed on the peril, you cannot develop a response to overcoming the danger. You've acknowledged your fear, now move on to dealing with the problem.

Focus on getting through the event: This is where your training can be implemented. Formulate a plan to respond to the threat. Consider the steps/tactics that must be performed to overcome the danger. Establish contingencies to counter unexpected occurrences while dealing with the original threat.

Turn the fear into a motivator: Let the fear remind you that you have prepared for situations like this one. You have exposed yourself to stressful events to expand your comfort zone. You have learned the typical responses to life-threatening events. You have trained in skills required to perform tasks to overcome obstacles. You have practiced those skills and participated in exercises simulating events like this. You are ready to challenge this situation. We don't mean become suicidal and charge blindly into the breach. But you can tell yourself to stand up to the fear and move on.

When encountering a stressful or life-threatening event remember the acronym S.T.O.P. This will help you relax and concentrate on resolving the situation.

Stop and Sit: When you realize that you're afraid, faced with a difficult situation, or unsure of how to find your way past an obstacle, stop and take a moment to collect your thoughts. Take a deep breath. Controlling your breathing will help you relax and focus.

Think: Take a mental inventory of your options before you make any moves and think about the possible repercussions of each of them. Prioritize your separate needs, such as attending to an injury before choosing a plan of action.

Observe: This sort of goes along with the previous item, but what in your immediate area is noteworthy, useful for purposes of building a fire or shelter, or pose a risk? What is the weather like? Is there anything or anyone who can render assistance?

Plan: Once you have collected yourself and considered your options, you will create a plan of action for yourself and execute it. In going through this process and not resorting to panic, you have already done yourself a major favor.

With your positive mental attitude, training, a sound plan and the realization that you have the tools to overcome the situation, you will prevail.

Photo courtesy of freedigitalphotos.net

Concepts of Improvisation

Let's start by defining what it means to *improvise*. Merriam-Webster lists a number of definitions, but the one most applicable to us is: *to make or fabricate something out of what is conveniently on hand.* Our ancestors were masters at creating whatever they needed using materials found in their environment. Unfortunately, this is a talent we have lost. In our modern society, we rarely require more than one application out of any product. Think of how often you will drive to a store to purchase an item simply to have a different color, size or design. When we consider a survival situation where we cannot visit our local "big-box" store to get what we need, will we be able to construct what we need with materials on hand? Do you at least have some basic survival gear in a "fanny" or back pack? You don't need to carry much, but the heart of improvisation lies in being able to craft multiple applications of each item you carry.

Just as with general survival concepts, there are some general principles of improvisation to help you regardless of the item you are attempting to improvise. While we can be overwhelmed with a list of items we need to "build", start with a strategy. What are my immediate goals/objectives? What actions (tactics) do I need to take to meet my goals? What items do I need to find or create to aid in performing the tactic? Survival and survival improvisation must be approached as a series of small, achievable steps. Listed below are the main tenets of survival improvisation:

- Determine the "big picture" scenario confronting you
    - Apply the Necessities of Life to your needs
    - Which priorities will you need to satisfy, in order
- Develop a Plan
    - Keep it simple
    - Establish goals to ensure survival and extraction from the environment
    - Determine the tactics (small steps) to achieve the goals
    - Consider materials on hand to serve as alternatives to needed items not available
- Implement the Plan
    - Safety is still a primary consideration
    - Apply contingency actions for unsuccessful tactics
- Assess the success of the actions against the goals of the Plan

Now that we have an understanding of the concepts of survival and survival improvisation, let's discuss some specific tasks that will have a significant effect on the likelihood of survival and removal from the perilous environment. Specifically, we'll address: *Improvised Shelters, Firecraft, Signaling and Water Acquisition/Treatment.*

Improvised Shelters

Shelter is all about maintaining body core temperature. As you learned in Chapter 1, there is a very small range of tolerable body core temperatures supportive of life. The goal of seeking/improvising a shelter is always to maintain body temperature in that range. While shelter is one of the highest priorities in the list of Necessities of Life, it is only one. So it is necessary to properly plan to address shelter needs to respond in a timely manner, with a minimum amount of energy expenditure. Considering such planning, we categorize shelters in three categories regardless of Urban or Wilderness environment:

1. Immediate Action Shelter: This is shelter that can be accomplished in a few minutes. It can be as simple as putting on additional clothing or donning a trash bag!
2. Temporary Shelter: This is shelter that can be accomplished in less than 60 minutes. Generally, it will be found or constructed in the natural environment or in the gear you carry. Examples would be trees, caves, vehicles, existing structures, ponchos, tarps, etc. With some planning and consideration, this category may be the shelter that lasts until a rescue is affected.
3. Long-Term Shelter: This shelter will require more extensive planning and effort. Its purpose is to accommodate the "inhabitants" for longer than 72 hours.

Immediate Action
PHOTO BY MOUNTAINSURVIVAL.COM

Short Term
PHOTO BY SURVIVALCOMMONSENSE.COM

Long Term
PHOTO BY JOE O'LEARY

In the Urban, Suburban and Rural environments we can usually make use of existing structures. Depending on the gear you carry, it is the Wilderness environment that typically challenges us to construct shelter. So let's discuss some types of shelter you can construct in the Wilderness environment.

1. Natural shelters
    a. Rock formations (overhangs)
    b. Trees (tree den, tree shelter)
    c. Caves

2. Debris shelters
    a. Lean-to shelter
    b. Double Lean-to A-frame
    c. Wickiup
    d. Wigwam
    e. Half Tepee

3. Poncho / Tarpaulin or sheeting shelters
    Materials that can be used are: (canvas, plastic, ponchos, mylar emergency blanket, trash bag)
    a. Lean-to
    b. Double lean-to (a-frame)
    c. Jungle A-Frame

4. Snow Shelters
    a. Snow caves
    b. Snow trench
    c. Quinzhee/Quinzee hut

5. Pit Shelters

PHOTO BY BRIAN MERRILL

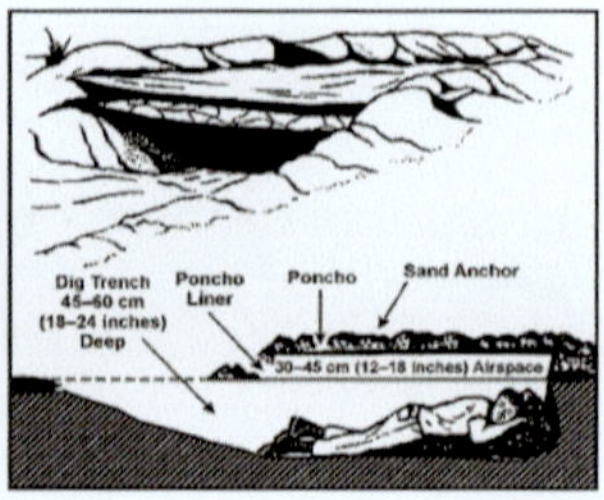

Let's discuss one general consideration for wilderness shelters. That is the issue of location. The choice of location for a shelter must take into account a number of options:

1. *Safety:* As with every task we perform, safety must be our first and foremost concern. You should use your situational awareness to consider these and other risk factors:
    - Dead Trees and Limbs—Beware of any object that could fall on you causing injury or damaging your shelter. You should perform a reconnaissance far enough from the shelter to see if any deadfall will cause damage to other trees resulting in danger to you or your shelter.
    - Flooding—What will happen to your location in the event of rain? You must consider any water runoff or drainage. If runoff is likely to come into/past your shelter, and you can't relocate your shelter, you will have to build a channel to divert the water. In desert or arid regions, the dry wash you are in could become a raging torrent

without any notice from a storm miles away, that you won't even know is happening.

- Avalanche or Rockslide—If you are in hilly or steep terrain, you should seek or construct shelter with consideration of the possibility of a rockslide or perhaps even an avalanche. Should there be any location or natural barrier offering protection from this danger you must take advantage of it.
- Wildlife, Insects and Poisonous Plants—While this may appear to be common sense, you must inspect the area within and around your shelter for these plants and signs of wildlife and insects. Besides the discomfort they can cause, there is real concern for injury and illness that would seriously compromise your ability to survive.

2. *Signaling*: Remember that beyond your initial survival, your goal is to be rescued. It is essential that you assist those searching for you. This can be especially difficult if you are in a heavily wooded area and your shelter is constructed of natural materials. Evaluate what materials you have with you that might be spotted by searchers. Decide if you can (safely) keep fires burning so that rescuers might notice the smoke during the day and the firelight at night. If you plan on carrying a tarp or poncho for shelter, make sure it is a bright color that will stand out in the environment you will be traveling through.
3. *Temperature Control*: This is not as simple as it appears. If you need to stay cool during the day, you must determine if that location will be suitable during the cooler temperatures at night. Consider if a change in wind direction can be accommodated in this location. The best option may be to seek or construct a shelter where you can vary the amount of air to control heat transfer. In colder climates choose a location that provides shelter from the wind and has fuel available for your fire, with water nearby. In warmer environments a breeze is necessary along with a water supply. The need for a fire, in warmer weather, will be

contingent on your signaling plans along with the energy required to gather the fuel necessary. In warmer weather you may be inclined to stay close to a water source, but be conscious of both wildlife and insects. They will be seeking water also.

Firecraft

Photo courtesy of FreeDigitalPhotos.net

When confronted with a survival situation, the ability to start a fire can make the difference between living and dying. Additionally, fire fulfills many needs. It provides heat for comfort and body temperature control. It not only cooks and preserves food, it also provides warmth in the form of heated food that saves calories our body normally uses to produce body heat. Fire can be used to purify water, sterilize bandages, signal for rescue, and provide protection from animals. Fire can also be used to produce tools and weapons. Equally important, fire can be a psychological boost by providing peace of mind and companionship.

We can see the great benefit of having a fire in a survival event. But it takes skill to properly build, light and sustain a fire when we don't have access to all the assets available at our local market. It still makes sense to always carry some aids in our pockets or pack. As we present this section, you will be made aware of many small items that will assist you in creating fire.

Success in any undertaking requires an understanding of the basics. Firecraft is no different. The first step in successfully building a fire is revealed in the *Fire Triangle.* The three sides of the triangle represent *oxygen, heat,* and *fuel.* If you do not mix them properly the fire will not light. If you remove any of these the fire will go out. The correct ratio of these components is very important for a fire to burn at its greatest potential. The only way to learn to balance the ratio is to practice with various "ingredients" in varying conditions.

These three components are simple to understand, but there are two common misunderstandings in their regard. Oxygen, in the air, is common enough. Most individuals, however, believe that oxygen burns. That is not true. Oxygen, or any other oxidizer, by itself is not flammable. Instead the oxygen molecules interact with the gaseous molecules of the fuel source and ignite when the proper heat level is applied to the mixture. The second mistakenly held belief is that the fuel itself burns. Fuel (in a nongaseous state) does not burn directly. When you apply heat to a fuel, it produces a gas. This gas then combines with oxygen, and again, the mixture burns.

A simple example is a wooden match. Heat is generated by friction when running the match over a coarse structure. This heat releases molecules from the chemical substance on the match head to mix with oxygen in the air. Once the temperature is high enough, and the ratio of fuel to oxygen is correct, we see a flame/fire. Hold the match up to eye level, parallel to the ground, and look closely. The wood is not burning. The flame is actually just above the match. As the chemicals in the wood of the match are heated up, they evaporate to a gaseous state and combine with oxygen to continue the flame. The "wood" turns black as the chemicals are depleted, leaving only charcoal.

Beyond this science we need the skills required to create a fire. Let's discuss the steps to do so. We'll begin with the broad phases of *Preparation, Construction, Ignition, Maintenance* and expand upon the tasks required for each.

1. **Preparation:** This is the most important phase of the entire process. Understanding that the need to create a fire may be urgent, skipping any of this process is likely to reduce your chances of having a successful fire.
    a. *Site Selection*—Your first decision is where you can safely locate your fire. Determine where you can build this fire and be able to contain it. Will the wind blow sparks igniting nearby tinder or melting your plastic tarp? Are there low hanging branches that will heat up and ignite?

Can you gain the fire's warmth without being overcome by smoke? The next step in site selection is to identify a location consistent with the main purpose of your fire.

If your primary purpose is signaling, you will need to choose a site that will be visible at long distances at night and one that will allow significant smoke rise during the day. If your primary purpose is warmth you need to determine where you will locate your shelter or sleeping area. Then you can locate your fire in relation to your shelter to provide the most warmth. You might even decide to build a number of small fires around your shelter to provide warmth on all sides.

b. *Site Preparation*—Preparing your site builds on the concepts presented above. If time and energy levels allow, you should clear and prepare an area large enough so there are no fire safety concerns even if you are distracted from monitoring your fire. Determine how big your fire pit should be based on the reason for building a fire. Cooking fires tend to be small, while warming fires will be somewhat larger. Should you be needing warmth, you will get better results from building a few smaller fires that you can sit or lie between, rather than one large one.

Begin by clearing the area directly in your fire pit and at least two to five feet beyond the planned fire ring. You should remove all flammable material (leaves, pine needles, twigs/branches, etc.) from this area. Beware of any tree limbs overhead. Next build a ring of rocks or dig a fire pit that's several inches deep using a log, shovel or hand trowel. Constructing a ring of stones will insulate the fire. Make sure you leave the ring slightly open at the end into the wind, to ventilate the fire. If the ground is wet or covered with snow, build a platform, in your fire ring/pit, out of green logs and cover them with a layer of earth or stones. Consider building a fire wall with logs or rocks on the opposite side of where you will sit or lay to reflect the fire's heat towards you.

Now it's time to gather your fire materials. There are three types/sizes of fuel necessary for your fire: *Tinder, Kindling* and *Sustaining Fuel.*

Tinder: Tinder is dry material that ignites with little heat—a spark starts a fire. This is extremely thin, flammable matter. You will need a large amount of tinder to be successful. In fact, your supply of tinder should be at least equal to the amount of kindling you gather. The tinder must be absolutely dry to be sure just a spark will ignite it. This is a list of materials suitable for use as tinder:

- *Birch bark*
- *Shredded inner bark from cedar, chestnut, red elm trees*
- *Fine wood shavings*
- *Dead grass, ferns, moss, fungi*
- *Straw*
- *Sawdust*
- *Very fine pitchwood scrapings*
- *Dead evergreen needles*
- *Punk (the completely rotted portions of dead logs or trees)*
- *Evergreen tree knots*
- *Bird down (fine feathers)*
- *Down seed heads (milkweed, dry cattails, bulrush, or thistle)*
- *Fine, dried vegetable fibers*
- *Spongy threads of dead puffball*
- *Dead palm leaves*
- *Skin-like membrane lining bamboo*
- *Lint from pocket and seams*
- *Charred cloth*
- *Waxed paper*

- *Outer bamboo shavings*
- *Gunpowder*
- *Cotton (especially soaked in lighter fluid, kerosene or Vaseline)*
- *Laundry Lint (cotton only)*

Kindling: Kindling is readily combustible material that you build into the fire structure and add to the burning tinder. Again, this material should be absolutely dry to ensure rapid burning. Kindling increases the fire's temperature so that it will ignite less combustible material. To raise the fire's temperature to that level will require significant amounts of kindling. Examples of material suitable for use as kindling are:

- Small twigs (less than ½ inch in diameter)
- Small strips of wood
- Split wood
- Heavy cardboard
- Pieces of wood removed from the inside of larger pieces
- Wood that has been doused with highly flammable materials, such as gasoline, oil, or wax

Sustaining Fuel: Fuel is less combustible material that burns slowly and steadily once ignited. This is the mainstay of your fire. Since this fuel burns slowly, you will not need as much, initially. Once your fire is burning successfully enough to ignite and keep this material ablaze, you will be able to gather additional quantities without your fire extinguishing. Examples of sustaining fuel include:

- Dry, standing wood and dry, dead branches
- Dry inside (heart) of fallen tree trunks and large branches
- Green wood that is finely split
- Dry grasses twisted into bunches

- *Peat dry enough to burn (this may be found at the top of undercut banks)*
- *Dried animal dung*
- *Animal fats*
- *Coal, oil shale, or oil lying on the surface*

A final consideration on the topic of preparation. You must make sure that all of your ignition and fuel materials are present in quantities beyond your expected need. Once you have lit your fire it is essential to have all materials at hand and organized such that you can add precisely what is needed at the time, in the proper quantities. For example, if you don't have enough tinder to successfully ignite your kindling, your fire will extinguish. That will cost you valuable time in your survival event, forcing you to gather new materials and start your fire building again.

2. **Construction:** Now that you have prepared your site and gathered the required components, you can begin to build or *lay* your fire. Instructors in outdoor skills agree that you will achieve greater success if you actually build a structure for your fire, rather than haphazardly throw material onto a pile. With the exception of a *pyramid* fire structure, the process will begin with placing tinder in the center, at the base, with kindling arranged in a manner that will allow ignition of the tinder, and eventually the kindling, without smothering the tinder. This typically involves *leaning* the kindling upward allowing natural convection to carry the heat up to the kindling and igniting it. When using a pyramid structure you will place the tinder and kindling on top of the highest level causing the fire to burn downward. The most common structures used in *laying* a fire are: *Lean-to, Tepee, Pyramid, Log Cabin* and *Star.*
   - Lean-To: A quick and easy structure to build. The most common challenge is burning up all the tinder without catching the kindling because too much air space is left open.

- Push a green stick into the ground at a 30-degree angle with its tip pointing in the direction of the wind.
- Put tinder underneath and lean sticks of kindling against the main stick.
- Light the tinder and add more kindling as needed.

- *Tepee:* Often considered the most useful and easiest to light. This style produces a fast flame and quickly falls into itself in a pile of coals. The heat is directed up to a single point and is useful for boiling water in a single pot above the teepee. The key is to stick a few sticks into the ground to supply support for the rest of the kindling.
  - Place your tinder bundle on the ground or on a small piece of bark.
  - Stick three or four kindling twigs in the ground to form a teepee above the tinder.
  - Lean small kindling twigs against the downwind side of the tinder. Leave an opening on the upwind side all the way to the center tinder where you can light the fire.
  - Continue to lean twigs around the teepee structure.
  - Work your way up to pencil-sized sticks, leaving plenty of air space between sticks.
  - Poke three or four pencil-sized sticks into the ground forming a larger teepee structure.
  - Lean some smaller sustaining fuel pieces against this support structure.

- Have additional small sustaining fuel and kindling ready in case it is needed.
- Once the teepee collapses, sustaining fuel can be laid around it building a *log cabin* or just to crisscross on top of the flames.

- *Pyramid:* This structure is frequently used for warmth overnight. Since it burns downward, it can be left on its own with no attention necessary, if you have built it large enough.
    - Place 2 small logs or branches on the ground so that they're parallel to each other. Then, put a solid layer of small logs or branches on top of them in a perpendicular direction.
    - Add 3 or 4 more layers, each time alternating the direction, and each layer being smaller, and using smaller material, than the one before.
    - Now build a *Tepee* with tinder and kindling on the top of your pyramid.
    - Light the Tepee, on the *top* of the pyramid, on fire. The flame will naturally travel down toward the base.

- *Log Cabin:* A Log Cabin structure is similar to the structure of a pyramid, but with a Log Cabin lay, the starter fire (Tepee) is built inside the Log Cabin. It is good to know the Log Cabin structure, because it can be a lifesaver in foul weather. The Tepee fire in the center aids in drying the walls, while the walls and "roof" provide good rain protection to the internal fire. It becomes a symbiotic relationship that can greatly help you through a cold and wet night.
    - Lay a small teepee fire.
    - Lay two larger pieces of sustaining fuel parallel on opposite sides of the teepee.
    - Lay two slightly smaller pieces of sustaining fuel parallel on the other two opposite sides. Leave a space under the upwind piece through which you can reach the tinder to light it—you might need to fashion a mini-torch and stick it in to light.
    - Continue to lay smaller and shorter pieces to form a cabin or pyramid shape.
    - Have extra kindling ready to drop into the top or through the spaces on the sides to feed the internal fire until the outer walls catch fire.

- *Star Fire:* This structure is an ideal fire lay for conserving scarce fuel. Another advantage is that its low flame makes it safer than other fire lays for using inside a shelter.
    - Make a small Tepee fire and arrange logs around the outside pointing inwards. You can use any number of logs to form the points of a star. The logs can be of any length, avoiding the need to cut them up.

- As the ends of the logs burn down each log is pushed towards the center as the ends are consumed. You can keep this fire burning with little maintenance; just push one of the longs inwards occasionally.

3. **Ignition:** We finally made it to the point where we're ready to light our fire. Remember to always light your fire from the upwind side. This will allow the wind to assist in igniting your fire and keep any smoke or debris blowing away from you. Now you must determine what you will use to ignite your tinder. Igniters provide the initial heat required to start the tinder burning. They fall into two categories: *modern methods* and *primitive methods.*
    - *Modern Methods:* These are all those devices, frequently "store bought" that you are used to having around your house. Keeping a few on your person or in your pack will make it much easier to light your fire. The best plan is to have a number of different types to provide options based on conditions.

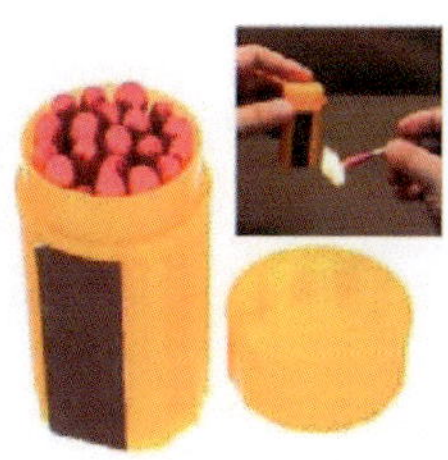

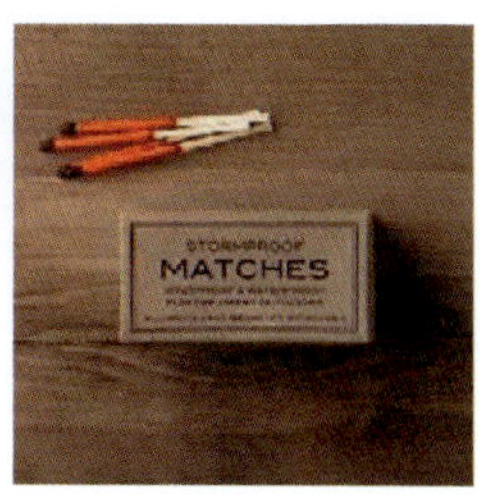

- *Matches*—In today's technological world this device is frequently overlooked. Matches still work in survival events provided you understand and plan for certain limitations.

Outdoor skills instructors strongly recommend you use/carry *strike anywhere* matches, kept in a waterproof container. These matches have a typical red or green head, but with a white tip that will ignite when rubbed on a coarse surface such as a rock or zipper. Varieties include longer burning models giving you a better chance to get the tinder lit. Even when using strike anywhere matches, it is recommended you keep an extra striker or flint strip in your waterproof container.

- *Convex Lenses*—You may have experimented with this method as a young person. Focusing sunlight through the lens onto any surface will heat that surface. Use this method only on bright, sunny days. The lens can come from binoculars, a camera, telescopic sights, or magnifying glasses. Angle the lens to concentrate the sun's rays on the tinder. Move the lens up and down to make the "heat" spot as small as possible. Now hold the lens over the same spot until the tinder begins to smolder. Gently blow or fan the tinder into a flame and apply it to the fire lay.
-

- *Lighters*—There are two main types of lighters typically used to ignite tinder. The first uses butane as its fuel source. These lighters are inexpensive (in the disposable variety), small and lightweight. They are advantageous in igniting tinder in windy conditions with just a small amount of shielding.

Butane lighters also come in a refillable style. The refillable models are typically more expensive and may encounter leaking issues upon being refilled.

The second type of lighter uses (liquid) lighter fluid as its fuel. It is somewhat more expensive than the disposable butane type, but is "refillable" using easily found lighter fluid. This type of lighter is frequently referred to as a "Zippo", but it should be noted that Zippo® is a brand of this type of lighter. This type of lighter is frequently marketed as windproof, but it still requires some shielding from strong breezes.

As with any mechanical devices, lighters can fail or break. Additionally, many lighters do not work well when wet. The "prepared" responder will always have multiple ignition sources immediately available.

- *Ignition Aids*—Keeping with our goal of preparing you as a field responder, you should be aware that devices and materials exist to assist you in igniting your fire. It is worthwhile to consider carrying these easily acquired, lightweight items as part of your ready gear.

  Igniting your tinder can be difficult with either a match or lighter. Lighting a candle to use to ignite the tinder frequently makes the job much easier. Of course, a long burning candle can also be a source of light and warmth (inside a shelter).

  Items that can serve as tinder, especially in unfavorable weather conditions, or assist in burning the tinder hotter include: commercially available *fire sticks*, *solid fuel tablets* and *magnesium starters*. As an additional benefit, magnesium starters frequently come complete with flint and a steel striker. The flint and steel will produce sparks, typically much hotter than a match. This combination provides you with a fourth possible ignition device.

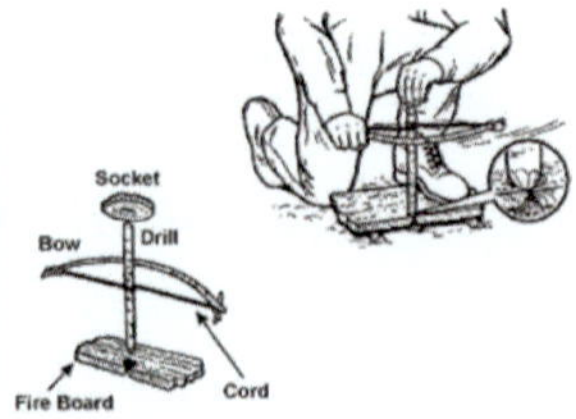

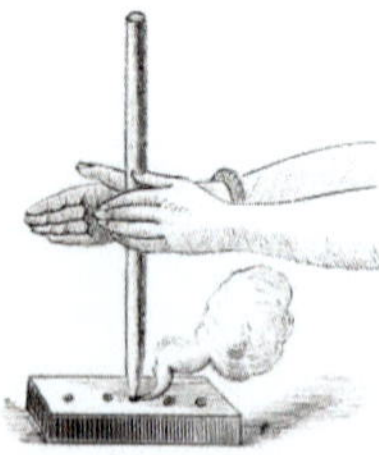

- *Primitive Methods:* We would never expect a trained responder to conduct a search tactic without being prepared with appropriate gear to prepare and start a fire. Should you find yourself without such devices, as during an unpredicted disaster or emergency, there are methods of constructing ignition devices from materials found naturally in wooded areas. If you might find yourself in such a situation, we recommend you prepare by researching primitive methods of fire starting such as: *Fire-plow, Bow and Drill, Hand Drill, etc.*

Signaling

If you are lost and want to be found, you will have to assist the searchers in finding you. The means of assisting them is by *signaling*. If you have located the subject of your search incident and have summoned rescuers to extract the subject, you may have to assist them in getting to your location. You can facilitate their arrival by signaling. In this section, we will discuss the techniques of signaling without electronic technology. Of course, it would be much easier with radio or telephone, but these devices you already know how to use. The question to be answered is whether you can signal for help when modern technology fails or is unavailable.

There are two main ways to get attention or to communicate--visual and audio. The means you use will depend on your situation and the material you have available. Whatever the means, always have visual and audio signals ready for use. And remember, whether visual or audio methods are employed, the international signals for distress always occur in threes (3s)!

When most of us encounter a dangerous situation our first reaction is to "call for help." This makes sense in an environment with lots of people around to hear the call. While, given appropriate circumstances, there is the need to understand and perform audio signaling, in preparing to travel areas where there are not many responders to hear us, your first consideration should be for visual signals.

Visual Signaling—When thinking of ways to communicate visually with search resources it is always best to use multiple means. The most common methods are: *signal fires (including smoke), signal mirrors, signal panels & signs* and *hand/body signals.*

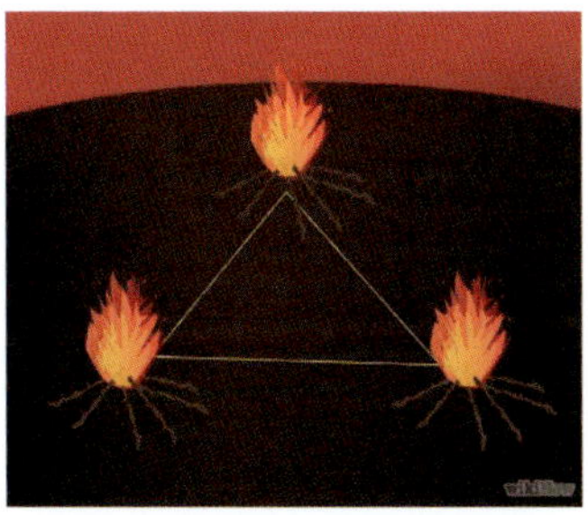

We've spent a great deal of time discussing how to create a fire. But you will need a few additional considerations to use fire as a signal: When possible, create three fires in a triangular layout with the fires approximately 80 feet/25 meters apart. An open field location is best for this method. If you can't create a triangle, a straight line of three fires is best. Finally, if you can't construct three fires, build the biggest fire possible to be visible for long distances, at night.

During the day, flames from your signal fires will not be very visible. You will need fires that generate a great deal of smoke. This requires very hot fires. They need to produce a 'thermal punch' to send smoke above any tree tops. After building large, hot fires, throw living/green, leafy or evergreen boughs on the top to create thick white smoke. On a cloudy day, you can use old rubber debris to produce black smoke.

- Signal mirrors are an extremely effective method to get the attention of rescuers. While we typically think of using these devices to signal aircraft, they can be used to signal ground resources also. The flashes can be seen for upwards of ten (10) miles!

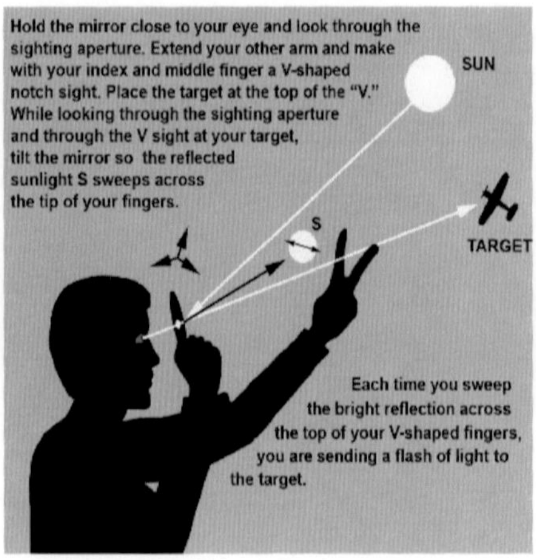

Whether you are planning to continue your training to become a field responder or just enjoy a day hike, acquiring a signal mirror is a wise investment. There are numerous commercially produced versions available at your favorite outdoors retailer that remain very inexpensive. If you prefer the "do it yourself" version, old CDs or DVDs work very well.

The first step to use a signal mirror properly is sighting it.

1. Hold your mirror surface towards the target that you are trying to signal in one hand close to your face.
2. Put your other hand in front of you in an outstretched fashion.
3. Move the mirror to focus the reflection of the sun onto your hand.
4. Keeping the reflection on your "target hand", move your target hand so the intended target is in the "V" of your fingers. This places the reflection (*flash*) on the target.
5. Sweep flash across the target in a series of three.

Creating a *sign* using man-made or natural materials, or even scratching out letters in the dirt can also be an effective means of alerting search resources to your location. As with all daytime signals, these signs must be large enough to be seen at great distances. They must also contrast with the colors of the natural environment in order to stand out in that environment. And remember... bigger is better in this instance! Let's look at ways to create a "billboard" to attract attention.

If you are fortunate enough to be carrying a military issue VS-17 signal panel, you are well prepared! Simply lay this panel on the ground for aircraft to spot, or hang from a tree for ground resources to see. These panels are visible from great distances and are colored to contrast with most urban and wilderness environments.

A less expensive option is a blue plastic tarp. This material will contrast well in the wilderness environment and possibly in the urban environment. With multiple uses, such as using it for shelter, the tarp is a wise choice to carry in your ready pack. For signaling, you can cut strips of the tarp to form words (e.g. HELP, SOS) to get the attention of search resources.

Another method of signaling with words uses materials found in your environment. In the wilderness, tree limbs and other deadfall can be used to spell out words in a clearing. In the urban environment, building materials and debris can be used. Regardless of environment, look for items that will stand out in contrast with the surroundings and that will create a sign large enough to be seen at large distances.

One final method of creating a sign is to "scratch" or dig in into snow, dirt or sand. In these areas, you can tramp, dig or scratch the ground to form letters or symbols. Then fill the depression with contrasting material (twigs or branches). The graphic "SOS" at the beginning of this section is a good example. In brush-covered areas, cut out patterns in the vegetation or sear the ground. In tundra, dig trenches or turn the sod upside down.

There is a standard chart of signals to aircraft. While many pilots will not be familiar with the actual meaning of your symbols, they will recognize that the sign is man-made and should send help to that area. This graphic lists the symbols you can use to communicate with aircraft:

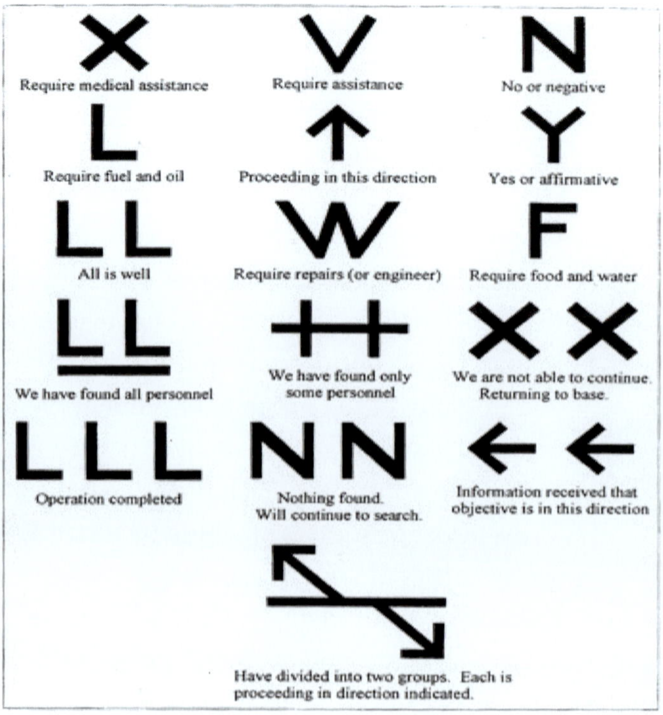

- When considering hand or body signaling, we are still confronted with the need to "stand out." One way is to don clothing that will contrast in color with the natural environment. When participating in a SAR event as a field responder, you should always be wearing outer garments that are very visible even in heavily vegetated or urban areas. In this case you are already prepared.

If you are signaling aircraft it may be best to lie on the ground and "wave" using arms and legs. This is similar to making "snow angels." Studies done in the desert southwest show significant improvement of being spotted, by helicopter, when laying on the ground making this type of movement. The likelihood of being detected increased by 21% over standing while waving arms!

Attempting to signal ground resources is best done standing. Again you should try to be as visible as possible. Stand in front of a "background" that will contrast with your clothing color and be as active as possible. Also remember that horizontal "lines" stand out in contrast of the vertical lines created by trees and shrubs.

One additional concept on visual signaling. If you became stranded using a vehicle, **stay with the vehicle**, unless safety reasons require you to move. Vehicles are much easier to detect by air or ground resources. You can flash lights and turn up the radio for as long as you have power. If you have to leave your vehicle, it is best to leave a note with explanations of your situation and the direction in which you departed.

Audio Signaling—Sound carries great distances and can be used to attract attention. While shouting can help, whistles, and gunshots are some of the better methods you can use to signal your presence to rescuers. As with our visual signals, audio signals should be produced in a series of three.

Whistles are inexpensive devices that will broadcast your position over as much as 1.2 miles/2 kilometers. Even in the urban environment whistle blasts are likely to get attention. There really is no excuse for not having a whistle in your pack, as they are light and take up virtually no space. Again, follow the rule of threes when signaling. The added benefit of a whistle is that it requires little effort (as opposed to prolonged yelling) and it will never run out of power. Even if you are completely incapacitated, as long as you are lucid enough to put the whistle in your mouth you will be able to signal with it.

If you happen to have a firearm with you, three gunshots is also a signal for assistance. Please consider the safety issues with discharging a firearm. Even in the wilderness environment you must be aware of where the bullet is going to travel/fall. In the urban environment it will be nearly impossible to discharge a firearm without harming someone else. Of course, this will probably get authorities to locate you fairly quickly!

Water Acquisition and Treatment

Photo courtesy of freedigitalphotos.net

We have already established the importance of water to life. In a survival event acquiring potable water is essential. In recent years the recommended amount of water required by an adult has been under scrutiny by many scientific groups. Estimates currently range from ½ oz. per pound of body weight to a flat 100 oz. These estimates do not include consideration for level of activity/exercise or climatic conditions. One additional discussion among these scientists is whether your hydration requirements apply specifically or whether all fluids, including caffeinated and alcoholic beverages, can be included in these estimates. Since it is unlikely you will find significant quantities of coffee, cola, and cocktails during your survival event, we will ignore this part of the discussion and assume we are seeking and treating water.

Water Acquisition—Water intake should never be rationed. If you become thirsty you must drink. The key to hydration then becomes replacing your water supply. Where to look for water sources will depend on the environment in which you find yourself. In the urban environment you will likely encounter numerous sources of water, both flowing and stagnant. The major task in the urban environment will be purification. In the wilderness environment you may need to seek out water sources not readily apparent. If you find yourself in arid conditions, not even true desert, knowledge of water catchments and sources could truly make the difference between life and death. The U.S. Army created the following table to assist.

Environment	Source of Water	Means of Obtaining and/or Making Potable	Remarks
Frigid areas	Snow and ice	Melt and purify.	Do not eat without melting! Eating snow and ice can reduce body temperature and will lead to more dehydration. Snow and ice are no purer than the water from which they come. Sea ice that is gray in color or opaque is salty. Do not use it without desalting it. Sea ice that is crystalline with a bluish cast has little salt in it.
[redacted]			
At sea	Sea	Use desalination kit.	Do not drink seawater without desalting.
	[redacted]		
	Rain	Catch rain in tarps or in other water-holding material or containers.	If tarp or water-holding material has become encrusted with salt, wash it in the sea before using (very little salt will remain on it).
	[redacted]		
	Sea ice		See remarks above for frigid areas

Environment	Source of Water	Means of Obtaining and/or Making Potable	Remarks
Beach	Ground	Dig deep enough to allow water to seep in; obtain rocks, build fire, and heat rocks; drop hot rocks in water; hold cloth over hole to absorb steam; wring water from cloth.	Alternate method if a container or bark pot is available: Fill container or pot with seawater; build fire and boil water to produce steam; hold cloth over container to absorb steam; wring water from cloth.
[redacted]			
Desert	Ground · at foot of concave banks of dry river beds · at foot of cliffs or rock outcrops · at first depression behind first sand dune of dry desert lakes · wherever you find green vegetation	Dig holes deep enough to allow water to seep in.	In a sand dune belt, any available water will be found beneath the original valley floor at the edge of dunes.
	[redacted]		
	Cacti	Cut off the top of a barrel cactus and mash or squeeze the pulp. CAUTION: Do not eat pulp. Place pulp in mouth, suck out juice, and discard pulp.	Without a machete, cutting into a cactus is difficult and takes time since you must get past the long, strong spines and cut through the tough rind.

Environment	Source of Water	Means of Obtaining and/or Making Potable	Remarks
Desert (continued)	Depressions or holes in rocks		Periodic rainfall may collect in pools, seep into fissures, or collect in holes in rocks.
	[redacted]		
	Fissures in rock	Insert flexible tubing and siphon water. If fissure is large enough, you can lower a container into it.	
	[redacted]		
	Porous rock	Insert flexible tubing and siphon water.	
	[redacted]		
	Condensation on metal	Use cloth to absorb water, then wring water from cloth. Following are signs to watch for in the desert to help you find water:	Extreme temperature variations between night and day may cause condensation on metal surfaces. - All trails lead to water. You should follow in the direction in which the trails converge. Signs of camps, animal droppings, and trampled terrain may mark trails. - Flocks of birds may circle over water holes especially at dawn and sunset.

Water Purification—It is not enough to simply find water. In the United States and many other countries, it is nearly impossible to access water from natural sources that is not tainted with chemicals, viruses, bacteria, etc. Even water taken directly from a natural spring will need to be purified.

Photo courtesy of freedigitalphotos.net

Contamination in water sources can be generally grouped in six categories: *Microorganisms, Disinfectants, Disinfectant Byproducts, Inorganic Chemicals, Organic Chemicals* and *Radionuclides.* Examples of each category follows:

- *Microorganisms*—Cryptosporidium, Giardia Lamblia, Coliforms, Viruses. The risk to individuals in survival events is for the gastro-intestinal upset. These organisms frequently cause vomiting and diarrhea. Either symptom will contribute to the onset of dehyration and restrict the individuals ability to perform physical exercise.
- *Disinfectants—Chlorine* and *Chloramines.* These contaminants will also cause gastro-intestinal distress. Additionally, they can cause eye and nose irritation.
- *Disinfectant Byproducts*—Bromate, Chlorites. Typically the dangers from contact with or drinking of these contaminants are long term. Unless you are planning to spend the rest of your life in this predicament, this type of contaminant does not pose a risk.
- *Inorganic Chemicals*—Antimony, Arsenic, Barium, Chromium, Copper, Lead, Selenium and Thallium. Some of these chemicals cause gastro-intestinal distress. Some of them will cause cardiovascular issues such as elevated blood pressure. Some will cause numbness in hands and feet. Chromium can cause allergic dermatitis. All these issues would be serious from someone confronted with a survival situation.
- *Organic Chemicals*—Many of these chemicals are found in hazardous levels in water sources. While this presents serious

problems for society, the medical problems caused by this category of contaminants are long term in nature.

- *Radionuclides*—These contaminants are radioactive materials. Fortunately, their typical levels of concentration, commonly found in water, are low enough to not present immediate health problems. Long term exposure is where the hazard exists at these levels.

There are numerous methods of "treating" water found outside of government purified sources. These include: *Boiling, Filtration/Purification Pumps, Purification Drops & Tablets* and *Evaporation/Distillation.* You should note, however, that there are no reliable improvisational means to remove chemicals. It has been reported that devices using *activated charcoal* will remove some chemical pollutants. Scientific studies on this are in short supply, but there is some evidence that activated charcoal does remove commonly found chemical contaminants. You will still need to assure your device also filters and/or purifies the water as activated charcoal will not. Let's further discuss some of these methods of treating water.

Boiling—The easiest way to purify water is to boil it, provided you have the equipment to do so, plus a campfire or camp stove. Bring water in a pot over a high heat until you have the water boiling fervently (rolling bubbles), and let the water keep boiling for at least ten minutes. Then let it cool down before drinking. Boiling kills most microorganisms including: bacteria, viruses and parasites.

Filtration/Purification Pumps—There are many devices that filter or purify water to differing levels. The market for portable water filters and purifiers is, well, flooded. There are dozens of products to choose from, but they all basically work the same -- water is pumped in one end, goes through a series of filters and treatments and then out the other end. Some of them work by hanging a bag from a tree and letting gravity do its thing, and some have hand pumps. Some are battery operated and some are built into the center of a water bottle, using suction (as through a straw) to move the water through the filter.

There is a difference between filters and purifiers. They both get rid of dangerous bacteria, but purifiers take care of viruses as well. The purifiers use chemical agents in addition to the regular filtration system. Most filters use a core made from ceramic, carbon or fiberglass. Purifiers have an additional chemical layer of iodine resin. Even when using this type of device, you should avoid water from areas where there's been obvious human or animal traffic

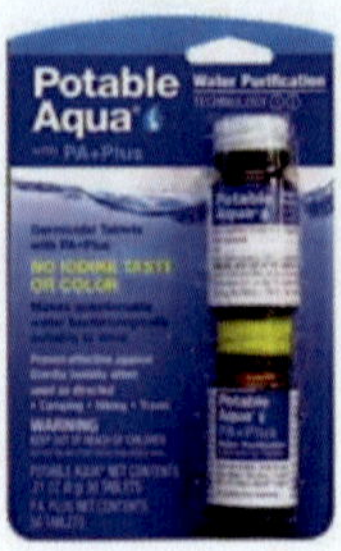

Purification Drops & Tablets—A simple and inexpensive, but not necessarily the best tasting, method of purifying wild water is by dropping in a couple of purification tablets or drops. The most common chemical used is iodine, but chlorine or potassium permanganate are also effective. These commercially available products are lightweight and convenient, but it is important to follow the manufacturer's instructions to assure complete purification. If the taste is a problem, you can mix the now purified water with powdered mixes to improve the taste.

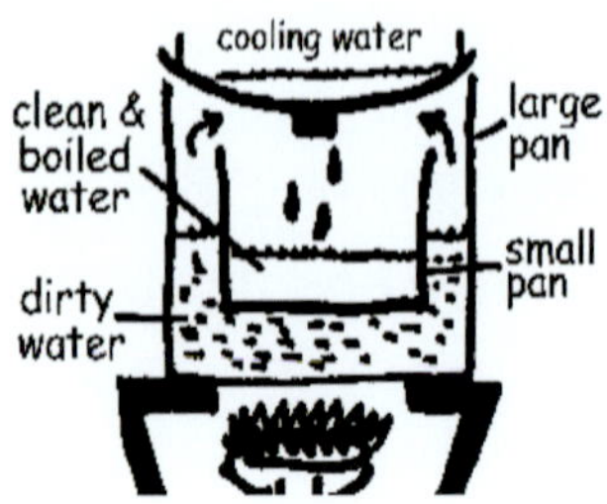

Evaporation/Distillation—Evaporation techniques typically combine boiling the water with capturing the steam and condensing back to (now pure) liquid state. This graphic shows an efficient set-up for this process. The key is to use an inverted lid or cover to run the condensed steam down into the "inner" (smaller) container. That way you will recover all the clean water.

Distillation is a similar process to evaporation that combines water acquisition resulting in "clean" water. An example of this process is the *solar still*. This is a tedious process, generating only about one quart per day, so if it is the only option for acquiring and treating water you should create numerous stills. The process of building a still is:

1. A hole is dug or scooped in the ground in a sunny position. The hole should be about 3' [90 cm] across and 15" to 18" [38 to 45 cm] deep or deeper if possible.
2. Line the hole with green material such as shrubs or succulent herbage, if it is in the vicinity, and pack it down. It may be necessary to weigh the material down with a few flat stones.
3. In the center of the hole, and in the deepest part, a container is placed to catch the moisture collected by condensation.
4. Lay the sheet of plastic to cover the top of the hole, and weigh the edges with stones and use some of the earth scooped from the hole to seal the edges lightly.
5. Place a stone in the center of the upper side of the plastic sheet above the approximate center of the water container to weigh it down to just over the container. Weigh the plastic down so the "point" is just a few inches/centimeters above the container that will catch the water.

Moisture in the soil, and in the greenery placed in the hole will be drawn off by the heat of the sun and condense on the underside of the plastic. Condensation results because the air above the plastic is considerably cooler than the air on the underside of the plastic. The condensed moisture will collect into droplets, coalesce and trickle down the underside to the lowest point where it drops off into the container.

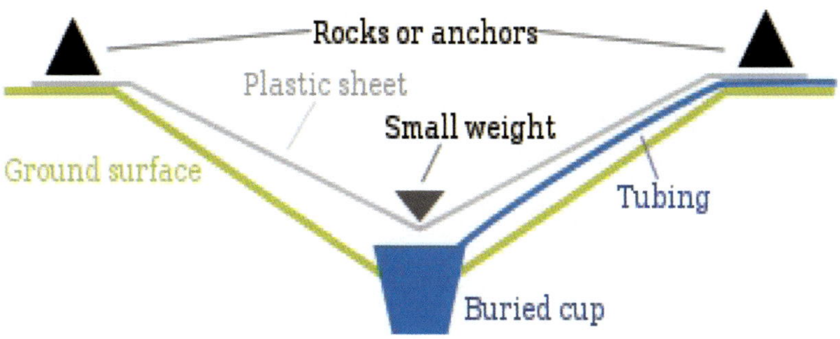

Summary

The concepts we have presented in this chapter are just the beginning. In subsequent chapters we will discuss additional challenges we may encounter when traveling in the wilderness or simply unable to access the conveniences of our modern society. For now we want to emphasize again, you must become proficient in these skills. If you have not practiced them repeatedly, you will be subjecting yourself to very difficult trials if confronted with a survival situation.

References

Merriam-Webster, Inc. (2014)
www.merriam-webster.com

wikipedia.org, (April 2014)
Wikipedia Foundation, Inc., San Francisco, CA 94105 USA

Survival, FM 3-05.70 (May 2002)
United States Army, John F. Kennedy Special Warfare Center and School, Fort Bragg, NC 28310

Camping & Wilderness Survival, The Ultimate Outdoors Book (1999 ed.)
Paul Tawrell, *Paul Tawrell*, Shelburne, VT/Green Valley, ON Canada

curiousity.discovery.com (July 2011)
Discovery Communications, LLC, New York, NY

Wilderness Survival for Dummies (2009)
John Haslett & Cameron M. Smith, *Wiley Publishing Inc.*, Hoboken, NJ

Wilderness Survival Shelters
Robert Munilla, www.practicalsurvivor.com

SAR Clothing—The First Line of Defense

3

Objectives

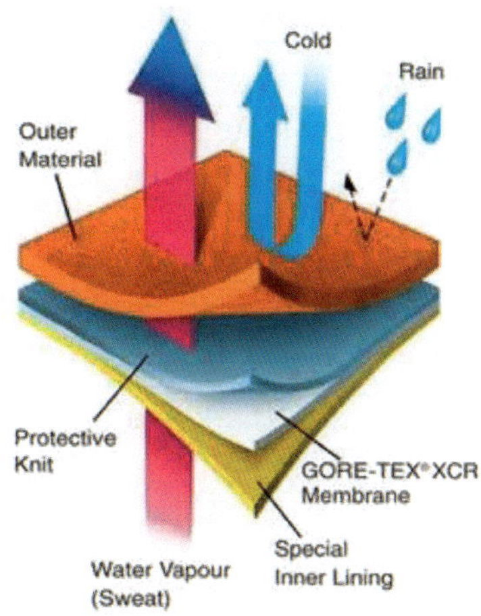

Courtesy of www.gore-tex.com

- Describe the natural, synthetic and artificial fibers used in SAR clothing
- Explain the advantages and limitations of the natural, synthetic and artificial fibers in SAR clothing
- Describe the features of SAR clothing construction as it applies to heat transfer
- List and Explain the five layers of SAR clothing, and the advantage of layer dressing
- Describe the accessories to protect head, hands and feet
- Discuss critical features and construction of SAR footwear

As you have been dressing yourself for many years, you may wonder why we would dedicate a chapter to clothing concepts. There are two main reasons. The first has to do with the subject of our searches. The number one killer of humans, in the outdoors, is hypothermia. While our subjects may not have the knowledge and training to seek or construct improvised shelter, having the correct clothing for the environment (weather and terrain) might just keep them alive long enough for us to find them or perhaps even prevent them from becoming debilitated to the point of requiring rescue.

The second reason for our discussion of clothing relates to your ability to perform your duties as a field responder. If you do not properly regulate your body comfort through the proper use of clothing systems, your focus will shift from the subject to your discomfort. Being hot, cold, wet or stiff from bulk will distract your attention from the task at hand. Should this discomfort become extreme, there are health and safety issues that begin to involve your team, distracting them from performing their duties. These issues could even result in your team aborting its assignment to extract you from the environment causing your difficulties. Once again, to the detriment of our subject.

As noted above, the concept of clothing in the outdoors, whether in the urban or wilderness environments, should be one of a complete system. And like any system, there are foundational concepts that must be reviewed. With clothing systems, that foundation is with the very fabric used in the construction of the clothing.

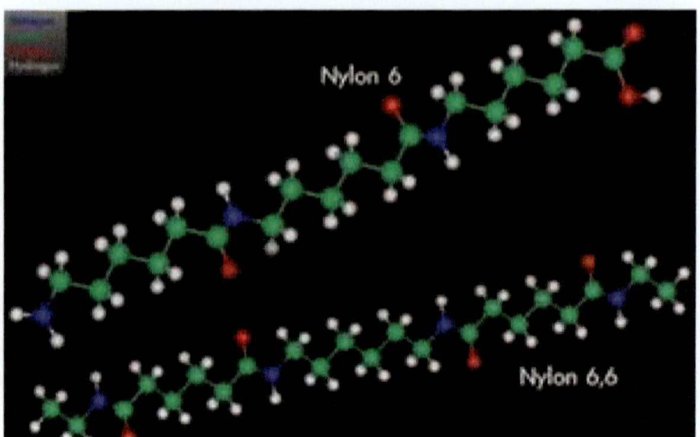

Courtesy of Wikipedia.com

Historically, clothing is and has been made from many materials. These materials range from grasses to furs to much more elaborate and exotic materials. Some cultures, such as the various people of the Arctic Circle, until recently, made their clothing entirely of prepared and decorated furs and skins. Other cultures have supplemented and replaced leather and skins with cloth.

When we look at the fibers used to construct clothing, we encounter two main categories. The first group contains those fibers discussed above, from the natural world. We classify these fibers/materials as *natural*. These include sources that have been used by mankind for millennia, such as cotton, wool, silk, down, and animal hide. The second group owes its existence to modern chemistry and forms the man-made category we know as *synthetic*. This group includes fibers such as nylon, polyester, polypropylene, spandex and a number of others you likely know of by their brand names.

Natural Fibers—Let's begin discussing those fibers found in nature. We'll limit discussions to the types most often used in clothing favored by SAR field responders.

- Cotton—Cotton has been used to make clothing for thousands of years. In fact, some cotton fabric has been dated to 5000 BC. But it was the invention of the cotton gin that made wide scale production of cotton garments possible. As we discuss the characteristics of cotton it is important to note that cotton fibers are *hydrophilic*. This means that cotton readily absorbs and retains water.

  COURTESY OF WWW.COTTON.ORG

  First, a look at the advantages of fabric made from cotton: cotton is hypoallergenic and therefore suitable for people with allergies, asthma and sensitive skin. It is also breathable, making cotton cool to wear in summer. With its hydrophilic properties, it quickly absorbs perspiration. Then, as the moisture evaporates from the fabric it cools the wearer. It is also an excellent insulator which keeps the wearer warm in colder weather. Wearing cotton is comfortable because the fiber is soft and because it is usually spun tightly; the fabric won't irritate the wearer's skin or generate static electricity. Garments made from tightly spun cotton fibers can also provide some protection from wind and rain. Cotton garments are also a good investment as they can be long-lasting when properly cared for. Additionally, cotton does not melt when burned so it won't stick to a victim's skin.

As for the disadvantages: That same hydrophilic property that keeps you cool in the heat can cause you problems in cold weather. If cotton gets wet in cold weather, either from external sources or perspiration, its tendency to retain moisture will rapidly induce hypothermia by forcing the wearer to attempt to heat the fabric to cause evaporation.

- Wool—Wool is another fiber that dates to ancient times. Archaeology shows wool fabrics in use around 4000–3000 BC. In medieval times wool became an important industry and by the Renaissance it had become the basis for the wealth of many of the great banking system families, like the Medici. When considering the characteristics of wool, we look at the feature of being *hygroscopic*. This is similar to hydrophilic, but differs due to the physical structure of the wool fiber. While wool can absorb large amounts of water (as much as one-third its own weight) it's fibers are hollow, so it gives up moisture quite easily.

The capacity to absorb makes wool a "temperature regulator" because it can protect the body in both cold and warm conditions. Wool always absorbs moisture from the atmosphere of greater humidity and releases it to the drier environment as it creates a balance in moisture conditions. This characteristic makes wool a versatile all-season fabric.

Wool absorbs perspiration; thus it keeps a layer of dry air next to the skin which, in turn, helps to hold in body heat. As wool absorbs atmospheric moisture, the hydrogen bond of water is broken and chemically reacts with molecules of the wool to generate heat.

Wool garments are therefore regarded as good protection against hypothermia... a condition that occurs when sudden drastic lowering of body temperature causes the body to lose heat faster than it can be produced. Wool does not lose its insulating ability when wet. Equally important, wool does not freeze solid when wet in extreme cold.

The same principle of moisture contact on the skin acts to protect against hot weather as well. The body cools itself naturally with the evaporation of perspiration. Wool expedites this process by absorbing perspiration and keeping the same dry air next to the skin. This is why wool clothing is worn throughout the desert regions of the world where it's hot during the day and cool at night.

Wool is fire resistant. Instead of burning freely when touched by flame, wool chars and stops burning when it is removed from the source of fire. Wool is self-extinguishing. It will not support combustion; this is why wool blankets are recommended for use in extinguishing small fires.

There are a few disadvantages to wool:

- Cost—A fine wool sweater may cost two to three times more than one constructed of synthetic fibers. If paying the extra cost for wool, apply it to classic wardrobe staples that will last a long time, such as outerwear, and perennial accessories like scarves and light layers. For trendy items you will discard at the end of the season, opt for less expensive fibers to avoid frustration when the garments go out of style.

    - Comfort—Some varieties of wool can be very itchy to sensitive skin. Lower quality woolens are composed of shorter, coarser fibers with many more ends to stick out and cause irritation. For a more comfortable wear, opt for sweaters crafted from softer wools like Merino.
    - Difficulties of care—Wool can be easily stained in the course of daily wear. It also tends to absorb odors from cooking, cigarette smoke and long-term storage. To protect your fine wool clothing from damage, avoid wearing against your bare skin, promptly spot clean any stains, and make sure to store in a well-ventilated area. Wool garments will shrink when washed and dried by machine. To safely clean fine woolens, gently wash them by hand or take them to the dry cleaner. This unfortunately means spending more money and time as compared to a less sensitive fabric.
- Silk—As with our previous natural fibers, silk has also been used since ancient times. The production of silk originates in China in prehistoric times. The Crusades brought silk production to Western Europe, in particular to many Italian states, which saw an economic boom exporting silk to the rest of Europe. Changes in manufacturing techniques also began to take place during the Middle Ages, with devices such as the spinning wheel first appearing. During the 16th century France joined Italy in developing a successful silk trade, though the efforts of most other nations to develop silk industries of their own were unsuccessful. The Industrial Revolution changed much of Europe's silk industry. Due to innovations in spinning cotton, cotton became much cheaper to manufacture and therefore caused more expensive silk production to become less mainstream.

Courtesy of www.pattayamail.com

Silk has the property of being a very flexible material. For example, a silk scarf can readily be pulled through a wedding ring, and it will quickly retake its original shape without a lot of wrinkling. It is light in weight, and it can be easily folded. This gives it an appeal over other fabrics that are more stiff and rigid. In addition, silk holds its structural integrity and will not rot. Silk is also more heat resistant than many other fabrics, including wool, for example, and is actually rather difficult to burn.

One remarkable property of silk is its high tensile strength and its fibers will not easily be torn or damaged. It is also an elastic material that can be stretched and then will recover to its original size unless stretched beyond 20-25% of its original length. It has been used in the past in making guy ropes to take advantage of this characteristic.

Silk clothing keeps one cool in the summer, and it provides surprising warmth in the winter and is often used as an insulation layer in different types of clothing or even in sleeping bags. Silk can absorb a fairly significant amount of moisture before it feels wet.

The advantages of silk are:

- Silk can absorb up to a third of its weight in water before it feels wet.
- Silk is breathable. It keeps you cool on hot days and through warm nights.
- Silk regulates body temperature, and preserves your body heat in the cold.
- Silk has impressive moisture wicking properties, keeping you dry and comfortable in any climate, year-round.
- Silk naturally repels mold & mildew.
- Silk is hypoallergenic, and won't irritate sensitive skin.
- Silk is lightweight and soft, making it easy to layer under daywear.
- Silk doesn't create static, so it does not cling or crease easily.

- Silk fibers are naturally elastic, and can stretch up to 20% without breaking.
- Silk fabrics make ideal base layers, and are available in light, mid & heavy weights.

The disadvantages of silk are:

- Cost—Silk is one of the most expensive fabrics on the market. Compared to cotton or nylon, silk is pricey. Silk garments cost significantly more than cotton counterparts because of the fabric's elegant appearance and the difficulty in its manufacture. Silk is considered a luxury product; expect to pay more for it.
- Difficulty of care—Silk is more difficult to care for than other fabrics. Dry cleaning is generally the preferred method for cleaning silk. If you plan to hand wash, test a small area first. Hand washing each garment separately using a silk-specific detergent or mild soap is advisable to keep silk looking fine. Silk cannot be bleached or soaked in prewash products. All silk items must be air dried and steam ironed on a low setting. Wringing or twisting silk garments can ruin and permanently damage the clothing. Although silk is valued for its delicacy, that same delicacy is considered a disadvantage of the fabric. Silk fades easily in direct sunlight, so a new garment dried outside can look old and worn. The fabric has a tendency to develop a yellow color over time and is particularly prone to perspiration stains. Traveling with silk garments can be impractical because silk wrinkles easily and requires a steam iron. Silk is also water absorbent, so liquid stains are obvious.

- Down—For our final discussion of natural fibers/materials, let's consider down. The down of a bird is a layer of fine feathers and clusters underneath the tougher exterior feathers. Down used for insulation is made up of a combination of down feathers and clusters. The down feather has a short or vestigial rachis (shaft), few barbs, and barbules that lack

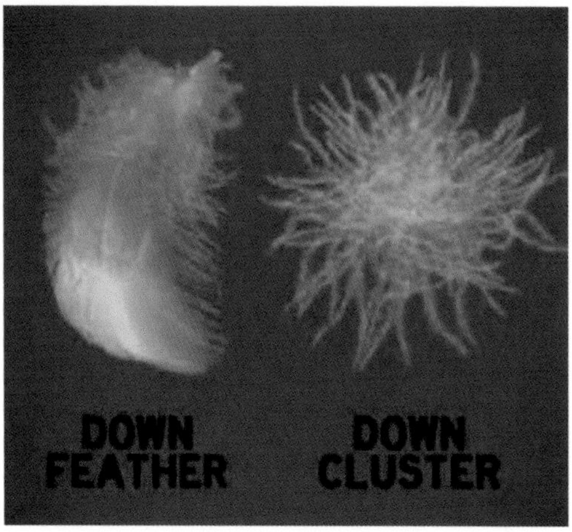

Courtesy of www.ymmreviews.com

hooks; it is the simplest of all feather types. Down clusters are tiny, fine, fluffy feathers from the birds' undercoat, which has no quill shaft. Higher quality down has a higher ratio of clusters to feathers. A product is required to contain at least 75 percent down clusters to be labeled as down. Typically, down will be used as an insulator in garments or outdoor gear. Down is used in combination with feathers in most clothing and gear. As trapped air provides the best form of insulation, you can imagine the benefits of down with its ability to trap air within the down and standard feathers.

When we evaluate the effectiveness of down as an insulator, we use the concept of loft. Loft is the "fluffiness" of the insulation and directly related to the insulation's ability to trap air. The higher the down to feather ratio, the more loft or "fluffiness" your insulation will have. Loft is measured in fill power, which can range from about 500 to 900. The higher the fill power the more air an ounce of the down can trap, and thus the more insulating ability an ounce of the down will have. High lofting down can create a very light, yet warm garment. Lower lofting down can be just as warm, but more fill is needed and the garment becomes heavier and less comfortable.

So when we consider the advantages of down we consider:

- Ounce for ounce, down is warmer than synthetic insulation. No manmade fiber matches down's warmth-to-weight ratio.
- Down retains its shape and loft well. With proper care, it can last for decades. Few synthetics can beat down's longevity.

- Down is highly compressible and lightweight. Although synthetic insulation has come a long way, it still doesn't hold a candle to down's ultralight weight and amazing compressibility.

As for the disadvantages of down, we must consider:

- Unlike synthetic fibers, down loses its insulating power when it becomes wet and takes a long time to dry out, especially in a humid climates.
- Cleaning down gear requires special care. Harsh detergents and other chemicals will break down its natural loft and luster. Only very mild detergents or down-specific cleaning products should be used. Down-insulated items should never be put in the drier.
- Although it's not a problem for many people, down is not hypoallergenic. Although the down may not cause an allergic reaction itself, lower quality down can harbor dust particles, debris or other non-down materials, causing a reaction in sensitive people. However, high-quality down is cleaned very well according to strict industry standards, and is less likely to cause issue. If you're prone to allergies, it's wise to invest in only high-quality down products, or go with synthetic.
- Costs is another big factor. Down insulation can be significantly more expensive than synthetic. If you're on a strict budget or don't plan on using your gear often, synthetic may be a better choice.

Synthetic fibers—The term "synthetic" is not accurate in all cases. There are natural fibers that are modified through chemistry included in this category, as well as fully manmade (known as *artificial)* fibers. As a group, they are very diverse, but the leading reasons for their creation, for use in garments, is to control water repellency, heat/air transfer ("breathability") and insulation (air trapping).

Sir Joseph Swan invented the first synthetic fiber in the early 1880s. His fiber was drawn from a cellulose liquid, formed by chemically modifying the fiber contained in tree bark. The first successful commercial process was developed in 1894 by English chemist Charles Frederick Cross. This fiber was named the fiber "viscose", because the reaction product of carbon disulfide and cellulose in basic conditions gave a highly viscous solution of xanthate. The first commercial viscose rayon was produced by the UK company Courtaulds Fibers in 1905. The name "rayon" was adopted in 1924, with "viscose" being used for the viscous organic liquid used to make both rayon and cellophane. Rayon and acetate are both synthetic fibers, but not truly artificial, being made from wood.

Nylon, the first artificial fiber, was developed by Wallace Carothers, an American researcher at the chemical firm DuPont in the 1930s. It soon made its debut in the United States as a replacement for silk, just in time for the introduction of rationing during World War II. Its novel use as a material for women's stockings overshadowed more practical uses, such as a replacement for the silk in parachutes and other military uses like ropes.

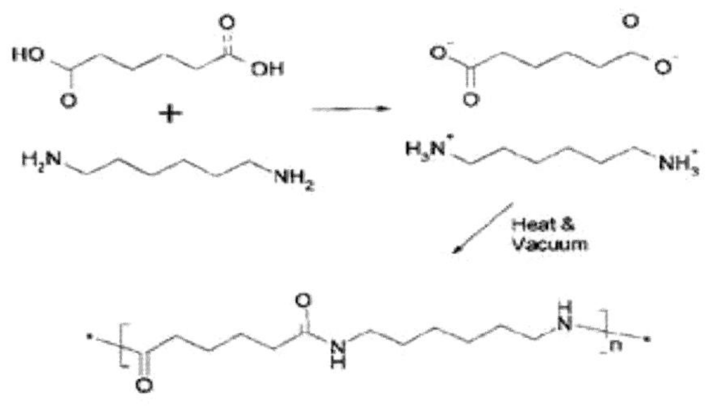

Courtesy of www.fibersource.com

Let's continue our review with some characteristics of specific artificial fibers. We'll start at the beginning with nylon.

- Nylon—Since its development in the 1920s, nylon has been in high demand. By the end of World War II nylon accounted for 25% of the entire fabric fiber market, mostly at the expense of cotton. Much of this success can be attributed to the advantages nylon presents:
    - Durability: its high tenacity fibers are also used for seatbelts, tire cords, ballistic cloth and other uses.
    - High elongation: Nylon fibers stretch very well.

- Excellent abrasion resistance: You will learn later that nylon is the choice for modern rope making.
- Highly resilient (nylon fabrics are heat-set): Nylon has a high melting temperature and will not burn.
- High resistance to: insects, fungi and animals molds, mildew, rot and many chemicals.

Naturally there are some disadvantages to nylon, especially over some of the newer artificial fibers:

- Impervious to water penetration: Since nylon does not let water pass through (*wicking*), moisture such as perspiration stays on the surface. This would keep the wetness next to the skin.
- Nylon melts: While the melting temperature may be high, when it is achieved (as through proximity to a campfire or sparks) nylon will melt onto the skin and requires medical intervention to remove. It will also become misshapen in high heat, as in a dryer.
- Needs UV stabilization: Nylon can be damaged by sunlight.

• Polyester—The first *polyester* fiber was introduced by John Rex Whinfield and James Tennant Dickson, British chemists working at the Calico Printers' Association, in 1941. They produced and patented the first polyester fiber which they named Terylene, equal to or surpassing nylon in toughness and resilience. After DuPont acquired to rights to polyester/Terylene, they refined it and developed it (further) in the 1950s. It was renamed Dacron at that time. Many of its characteristics are similar to the advantages presented by nylon:

- Polyester fabrics and fibers are extremely strong.
- Polyester is very durable: resistant to most chemicals, stretching and shrinking, wrinkle resistant, mildew and abrasion resistant.
- Polyester is hydrophobic in nature and quick drying. It can be used for insulation by manufacturing hollow fibers.
- Polyester retains its shape and hence is good for making outdoor clothing for harsh climates.
- It is easily washed and dried.

The disadvantages are also very similar to nylon:

- Impervious to water penetration: Since polyester is hydrophobic, it does not let water pass through (*wicking*), moisture such as perspiration stays on the surface. This would keep the wetness next to the skin. One difference between nylon and polyester is that polyester manufacturing can be altered to give it the ability to wick moisture.
- Melting characteristic: While the melting point of polyester is higher than nylon, polyester can melt when exposed to high temperatures.
- Needs UV stabilization: Like nylon, polyester can be damaged by sunlight unless treated during the manufacturing process.

Polyester is frequently blended with other materials in manufacturing fabric. Blended and other variations of polyester can frequently be found as insulation in SAR clothing and gear. Brand names of polyester insulation that may be familiar include: Polartec®, PolarGuard®, Hollofil® and Quallofil®.

- Polypropylene—Polypropylene is an artificial fiber/fabric that is very popular with SAR responders and is commonly known as "polypro." The history of polypropylene began in 1954

WWW.WITHFRIENDDSHIP.COM

when a German chemist named Karl Rehn and an Italian chemist named Giulio Natta first polymerized it. Polypropylene has been used for the fabrication of cold-weather base layers, such as long-sleeve shirts or long underwear. Polypropylene is also used in warm-weather clothing, which transports sweat away from the skin. More recently, polypro has replaced polyester in these applications in the U.S. military. Let's review the positive characteristics of polypropylene:

- Polypropylene has a higher melting point than the other plastic fibers we have discussed (320°F or 160°C).
- Polypropylene does not absorb water, so it dries out very quickly.
- It allows passage of water to promote wicking of perspiration away from the skin.
- New versions do not retain odors and wash in regular home washing machines.
- Polypropylene is lightweight and very flexible.
- It is resistant to mold, bacteria and other noxious elements.
- Polypropylene has the highest insulation property of any of the artificial fibers.
- It is inexpensive.

When compared against the other artificial fibers we have reviewed, polypropylene has no disadvantages. The major consideration is to ensure that polypro garments are not subject to heat in excess of 320°F/160°C. This lack of disadvantages is likely the main reason polypro is so widely used SAR field responders, especially for under-garments.

Heat Transfer—the reason for clothing

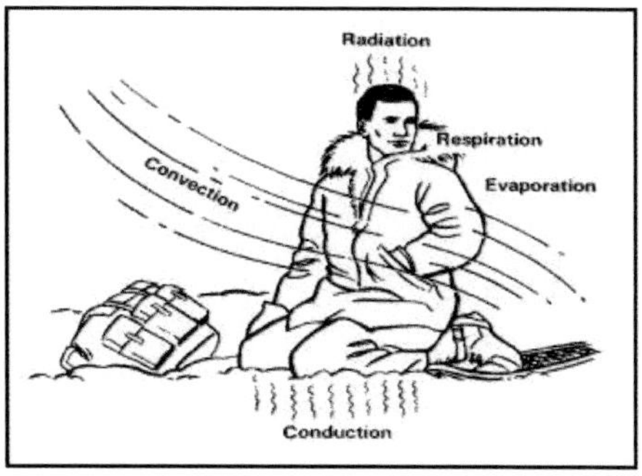

The reason we wear clothing is for *thermoregulation*. In other words, we seek to control our body temperature by controlling the amount of heat retained or released by using clothing. This concept is paramount to our dis¬cussions of clothing concepts.

Retention or release of heat by clothing is dependent on three elements and one set of features: trapped air space, air transfer, moisture and garment construction. Regulating each of the three elements, in combination with proper garment construction, keeps us cool in hot weather and warm in cold weather.

- Trapped air space—The quantity or thickness of the "dead" air space controls the insulating affect. As previously noted, trapped air is one of the best insulators. The thicker the layer of trapped air (between the skin and the environment) the warmer the body temperature will remain.
- Air transfer—The greater the exchange of air from inside our clothing to outside our clothing, the more heat is released. In warmer temperatures large volumes of air exchange will keep us cooler, along with wicking of perspiration to be evaporated. In colder climates that same air exchange can quickly result in rapid heat loss, possibly leading to hypothermia.
- Moisture—Once again, we look to control heat loss. Heat loss in water occurs 24 times faster than in air. In warm conditions, the evaporation of moisture from our clothes helps to keep us cool. In cold weather, wet clothing results in rapid and extreme heat loss that can result in debilitating hypothermia in minutes.
- Garment Construction—When we review how a garment is constructed, we consider a number of features:
    - Fabric—Based on our discussion of fibers and fabric, which is the better choice for the conditions expected. Do we need

a fabric that will allow large amounts of air exchange or one that will keep large amounts of air trapped? Is moisture repellency more important than breathability?

- Seams—Seams need to be constructed so as to not allow water/moisture to seep through. This is especially important on outer layers. For jackets and other outer garments, seams should be *taped* and *sealed*. This will prevent water from leaking though the seam without having to decrease the breathability of the garment by "waterproofing" the entire vestment.
- Vents—Most modern (outdoor recreation) outer garments have vents that will increase air exchange in areas of high body heat. The challenge is to ensure that these vents close properly to prevent air exchange, when that ventilation is not required, and not lessen the water resistance of the garment.
- Openings—There are two types of openings on garments. They are those that can be fully closed, typically used to don or remove a garment, usually by buttons or zippers, and those that accommodate body parts such as sleeve cuffs (hands and wrists) and collars (head and neck). As with seams, closures must be constructed such that they prevent air exchange and water seepage when closed. On outer garments, this is usually accomplished be using a process to waterproof zippers and installing a flap on the inside or outside of the zipper.

Openings on sleeve ends and at the collar have similar requirements. When we need to dissipate body heat they should open in a manner to release only the amount of air exchange required. When conditions require the trapping of air to retain heat, there should a method of closure that will stop the air exchange and limit the entrance of water (as in rain) without constricting blood flow. (Of course restricting blood flow at the neck might cause enough difficulties on its

Courtesy of www.velcro.com

own such that neither cold nor moisture is worrisome!) This opening and closing of these apertures is frequently effected by zippers (as described above) or Velcro, or a combination of the two. But beware of malfunctioning zippers and Velcro when they get dirty or covered in ice.

Dressing in Layers

In addition to regulating heat exchange and moisture control via garment construction, we can truly manage our defensive clothing system by using a method of layering various clothing to gain the maximum benefit of different types of garments and the flexibility of adding or removing layers as necessary.

To maximize flexibility, a layered clothing system consists of five levels. With today's modern fabrics it is possible to derive the same effect using only three or four layers, but we'll discuss all five separately. Then you can choose what works best for you. The five layers include: the underneath, the wicking, the "clothing", the insulation and the shell layers.

- The Underneath Layer—This is more commonly known as underwear and socks. We normally think this layer's main purposes are comfort and discretion, but an important consideration is the ability of perspiration to pass into and be removed from this layer. Frequently this layer will be of a cotton fabric, but be cautious of environments that would result in the cotton becoming wet with perspiration and having no way to dry out. This wet layer, against the skin, for long periods of time could cause enough discomfort to limit the responder's ability to perform their duties. Think irritation of sensitive body parts and illness/injury to the feet.

  Socks—You may recall our discussion, in Chapter 2, of foot problems brought on by wet and cold conditions. Developing any discomfort, or worse, involving the feet is a sure way of stopping a responder from completing their assignment. If this occurs in the field, it could even involve reallocation

Courtesy of www.rei.com

of resources away from searching for the subject to extricating the debilitated responder. Let's review this important topic a bit further.

First, let's get one major point covered. Wearing two pair of socks is always recommended, regardless of the weather. Avoid cotton for socks. When your feet perspire the cotton will stay wet and lose any insulating value. For the thin inner layer, consider socks made of polypropylene, silk or even nylon. These fabrics will wick the perspiration away from the skin, keeping your feet dry. For the outer layer consider using a wool blend. Examples are acrylic yarns, merino wool/nylon, etc. This outer layer will absorb the moisture away from the inner layer and allow it to be evaporated. This combination will keep your feet either cool or warm, as appropriate, and dry.

WEAR TWO PAIR OF SOCKS!!

1. KEEP FEET WARM/COOL & DRY
2. AVOID BLISTER FORMATION

The additional advantage of two layers of socks is reducing or eliminating friction against the skin. When wearing only one layer of socks, the sock will move back and forth in the boot as the responder walks. This creation friction on the skin and will inevitably lead to the formation of blisters.

- The Wicking Layer—This layer is frequently combined with the underneath layer, forming a *base layer* combining the features of both. If kept as a separate layer, the function of this layer is to remove moisture from the underneath layer so that fabric next to the skin is kept dry. Considering the wicking ability versus the disadvantages of fabrics used in the wicking layer, SAR field responders generally choose synthetic/artificial fibers for this layer:
    - Polypropylene has been used as a base layer material for decades. It's lightweight, breathable and dries very quickly. Many people still wear polypropylene long underwear. However, some

people dislike the texture of the material, so polyester has generally become more popular. Polypropylene is also more susceptible to retaining odor than other synthetic and natural fibers.

- Polyester is probably the most common material used to make base layers today. It's breathable, moisture-wicking, fast-drying and affordable. Polyester may be blended with other fibers. Spandex adds enhanced stretch. Nylon adds durability. One drawback to polyester is that it may eventually begin to retain body odor, although some brands add an antimicrobial treatment to help maintain freshness.
- Silk is a natural, lightweight, breathable and moisture-wicking material that is very effective for making base layers. Although silk is very soft and comfortable against the skin, it's not as durable as polyester or polypropylene. It's also more expensive to produce. Silk base layers may require special laundering, so it's important to check the label before you pop them in the washer or drier.
- Merino Wool base layers have become increasingly popular in outdoor sports, starting around the late 1990s. Superfine New Zealand merino wool from brands like Icebreaker® and SmartWool® is warm, breathable, moisture-wicking and fast-drying. Unlike regular wool, merino wool is soft and quite comfortable against the skin. It's also naturally odor-resistant and biodegradable, which makes it a popular alternative to polyester. Merino wool is more expensive than most synthetics, however.
- Cotton is a comfortable material for general wear, but is not ideal for outdoor recreation. Cotton fibers dry very slowly compared to the other fibers mentioned above. This means that once you start sweating, your cotton base layer will most likely remain damp until you change clothes. If you stop moving in chilly weather and your base layer is damp, you'll probably experience a chill.

- The Clothing Layer—This layer includes all the normal pieces of clothing we typically wear, such as shirts, pants and even some insulating garments like vests and sweaters. Depending on the requirements of the weather and environment, this layer may be combined with the insulating layer and called the *mid layer*. While almost any fabric can be used in the clothing layer, even cotton if the conditions are warm enough for this to be the "outer layer", there are three predominant materials used here:
    - Polyester clothing/mid layers are always a good choice because they wick moisture and dry quickly.
    - Merino wool provides the same benefits as regular wool, without the scratchy, itchy feeling. Merino wool garments make excellent clothing/mid layers.
    - Nylon is used for its lightweight, breathable and quick-drying characteristics. A long-sleeved nylon shirt can be a good mid-layer for hiking or backpacking when worn over a short-sleeved base layer. Nylon is more durable than polyester and is sometimes blended with other materials to enhance durability.

  A few more considerations in our review of the clothing layer—If this layer is to be worn as "outer wear", color can also be important. Dark colors absorb more of the Sun's radiant energy and work well in the cold weather. Conversely, light colors are effective in warm weather as they reflect more of this same energy. Additionally, in warmer weather, it is recommended to wear looser or even baggy (without causing difficulty moving) clothes. This allows movement of air across the skin resulting in cooling via evaporation and convection. Effective wearing of baggy clothing in hot weather is amply demonstrated by desert cultures in North Africa and the Middle East.
- The Insulation Layer—As previously noted, this layer can be combined with the clothing layer if conditions are conducive. But it can also be combined with or serve as the *shell* or outer layer. If worn separately, the purpose of this layer is to assist

in maintaining warmth. As we have learned the best way to retain heat is to create trapped air space. That is the goal of the insulation layer, to provide space for dead air insulation. Fibers and fabrics used in this layer include most of the natural and artificial ones, including:

- Wool is the traditional insulation/mid layer material with several good properties: it has good insulation even when wet, absorbs moisture but does not feel wet even when it holds significant moisture, and transfers moisture.
- Fleece made from polyester or other synthetics has many of the features of wool, but is lighter. It provides good insulation even when wet, absorbs very little moisture, and dries quickly. Although no longer commonly used in the industrialized world, natural sheepskin fleece could also serve the insulation/mid layer function.
- Down has a very good warmth to weight ratio, and can be packed down (squeezed) to take very little room. On the downside, it is expensive, makes a thick garment, dries slowly, loses its insulating properties when wet or compressed, and stops lofting properly after being washed several times.
- Synthetic Fiberfill such as polyester fiber is used similarly to down, but does not have as good a warmth to weight ratio. However, it is less expensive, provides good insulation even when wet, dries quickly, and absorbs very little moisture. There are brands of very fine fiberfill like Thinsulate®, PrimaLoft® or Thermolite®, that provides multiple times the warmth for a given thickness.
- Cotton, as with the underneath layer, is a cheap alternative, but a reasonable choice only when low insulation and moisture transfer is needed. Most people involved in outdoor activities would agree that cotton is a very poor material to wear in the outdoors because you MAY need to insulate yourself and, unless you are not moving, you WILL need moisture transfer.

- The Shell Layer—The outermost clothes are called the shell layer, but only if they block wind or water, or have good mechanical strength. Ideally the shell layer lets moisture through to the outside (that is, is breathable), while not letting wind and water pass through from the outside to the inside. While this is enabled to some degree by modern materials, even the best and most expensive materials involve a slight trade-off between breathability and water- and wind resistance.

  When we discuss water resistance in outerwear, we have come to accept that outer garments protect us from external water (e.g. rain, snow, etc.) while allowing moisture wicked away from the body to flow out through the shell, in three different varieties. These shell garments can be *waterproof, non-breathable* or *waterproof, breathable* or finally *water resistant, breathable.*

  - Waterproof, non-breathable: Old-school rain jackets and rain pants made of a durable, polyurethane-coated nylon are a good example of non-breathable waterproof outerwear. These provide the highest level of weather protection, but also don't allow internal moisture vapor to escape. For this reason, non-breathable waterproof jackets and pants are usually only used by off-shore fisherman and deck workers that require a significant level of water protection on rough, stormy seas.

Courtesy of Carhartt

  - Waterproof, breathable: Waterproof breathable shells like Gore-Tex® by Gore, MemBrain® by Marmot and Dry. Q® by Mountain Hardwear provide the best protection in moderate to extreme conditions. In order to qualify as waterproof, a shell must have a membrane and be fully seam-sealed.

However, no waterproof breathable shell is going to be "completely waterproof." With enough water pressure, even the best jacket will leak eventually.

- Water resistant, breathable: Jackets and pants labeled water-resistant and breathable provide good protection in mild to moderate weather. They are known as *soft* shell, vs the *hard shell* (waterproof) garments. Most have a DWR (durable water repellent) coating to shed light rain and snow. Soft shells and waterproof jackets that are not fully seam-sealed fall into this category.

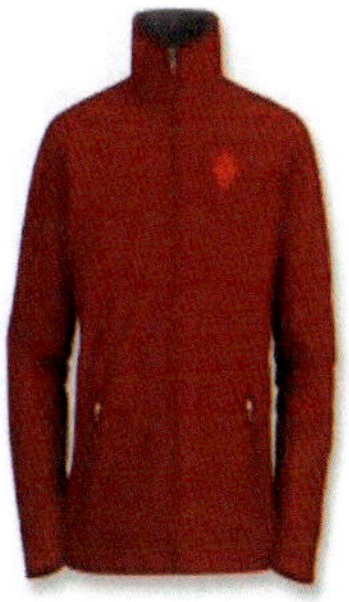

Courtesy of Black Diamond

The term soft shell is increasingly used to describe garments that combine partial or full water resistance with partial or full wind breaking ability. Soft shell fabrics come in numerous varieties with many garments offering a combination, such as a wicking layer. In many cases insulation is combined in an attempt to replace several layers with a single highly flexible one. One of the most unique characteristics of the woven softshell fabrics is the combination of windproofness, a high level of water resistance, and stretch -- in many cases four-way stretch.

Extremity protection

Since we are discussing protecting ourselves through the use of clothing systems, we must include discussion of our extremities. Specifically, let's review how we protect our hands, head and feet.

- Hands—There are two main goals in protecting our hands. The first is to protect them from injury such as lacerations, punctures and abrasions. In SAR operations, this type of protection is usually achieved through the use of leather gloves. Generally, these gloves are lightweight and flexible. Unfortunately, they provide little or no thermal protection and should not be relied upon

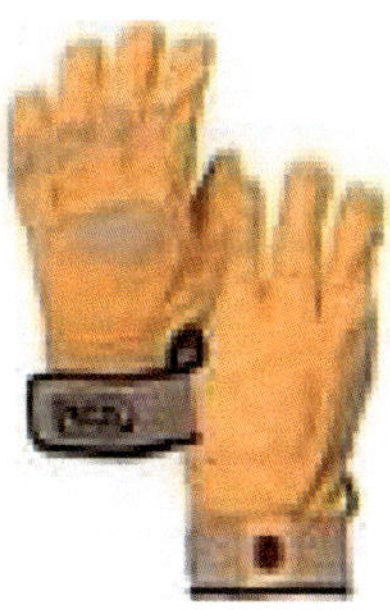

Courtesy of Petzl

for protection from the cold. An example of this type of glove is the glove used for working with ropes, sometimes called rappel gloves. They can provide adequate protection against hand injury caused by tree branches, thorns and in some cases, sharp tools like knives. Leather gloves can also assist in keeping toxic or biological agents from contacting the skin, Gloves can also assist in protecting the *chain of custody* when handling evidence.

The second protection necessary for our hands is *thermal* protection. Our fingers are especially sensitive to cold and will quickly lose dexterity if the temperatures become extreme. In cold weather we must achieve thermal protection combined with injury protection.

To accomplish this, we can use gloves with a durable outer shell and an effective insulating layer (e.g. Thinsulate®). Unfortunately, this type of glove severely reduces dexterity. If we have to remove the glove to perform a function requiring higher levels of dexterity, we will lose all protection, both thermal and injury. While mittens provide greater thermal protection than gloves, the loss of dexterity prohibits the use of mittens except as an outer layer to be removed when use of our fingers is required.

A better method might be to employ a layered system as we do with the rest of our garments. There are numerous varieties of thin, insulating type gloves, frequently referred to as *liners*. For harsh work such as SAR, these liners are usually made of synthetic/artificial fibers, but are also found constructed of natural fibers. Some examples are "polypro", Thinsulate®, silk and wool. An advantage to these types of material is that they will retain much of their insulating and heat retention quality when exposed to rain and snow if the outer glove has to be removed.

For a shell layer there is the option of using mittens or gloves made of durable fabric to provide injury protection. This layer should include a mechanism to reduce air exchange via the wrist opening. Velcro straps are an effective method.

Remember to keep the Velcro clean of dirt, snow and ice or it will lose its ability to "close."

- Head—As with our hands, we need to provide both thermal and injury protection. When we consider protecting our head from temperature extremes, remember that the "unprotected" head is responsible for one-third to one-half of the body's heat loss in cold weather and the body's heat gain in hot weather. This heat exchange does not only occur via the top of the head. We must also consider protecting the face, ears, neck, etc.

EYE PROTECTION IS ALWAYS REQUIRED, REGARDLESS OF WEATHER CONDITIONS. DEBRIS, TREE BRANCHES, INSECTS AS WELL AS BIOLOGIC AND CHEMICAL SPLASHES CAN ALL INJURE YOUR EYES AND POTENTIALLY CAUSE BLINDNESS. ALWAYS WEAR SAFETY GLASSES OR GOGGLES WHEN PERFORMING SAR FIELD DUTIES.

In hot weather, choose a hat that will allow a great deal of air exchange while providing maximum sun protection. Choosing a light color will also help reflect the Sun's radiant heat. A baseball cap or even a "boonie" is generally not enough. You will need a hat with a wide enough brim to shade your face, ears and neck. Additionally, during daylight, you will need tinted eye protection that is 100% UV blocking.

In colder weather, there are many choices for head cover. They include hats, hoods and balaclavas among others. If you choose a hood as an outer layer with an insulating layer/hat underneath, be sure the hood falls into one of the three shell layer categories for water resistance. The insulating layer should be of fibers that will wick moisture away from the head and provide sufficient insulating value. If you choose one head garment (no layering), make sure it has all the features of the layered system combined. And as we discussed previously, you must make provision for face, neck and ear protection. This is just as critical, or perhaps more so, in cold weather operations.

feet measured by a footwear professional. That person can also discuss the particular structure of your feet and can make recommendations for specific models of footwear, or accessories and modifications, to make the footwear suit your feet and not vice versa. Once you have proper fit worked out comfort becomes much easier to achieve.

The first step in attaining comfort in our footwear is to determine the environment and use of the footwear. This does indeed mean you will have more than one pair of shoes/boots for your SAR duties. The pair you wear during an urban environment incident are not likely suitable for wear in a mountainous, wilderness environment.

The urban environment will require comfortable walking shoes that offer a bit of support and good traction. Walking up and down hills in the wilderness environment will require a boot. Preferably one that offers significant stability and support. The wilderness boot should be high enough to limit ankle twisting and padded enough so we don't notice the jagged landscape. The tread pattern must be deep enough to provide good traction even on loose soil and scree. All of which is likely excessive for wear in that well developed urban environment.

Comfort also extends to temperature and moisture control. Just as with the rest of our clothing systems, we must consider the insulation level in our footwear. For use in cold temperatures, many models of footwear now utilize insulation layers such as Thinsulate®. To promote breathability while maintaining water resistance, modern footwear is using fabrics like Gore-Tex®.

Construction features are also important to deliberate. Is it important for the tongue to be laterally attached to the upper to prevent water from entering the footwear? Do we require lace hooks instead of eyeholes, for ease of tightening laces while walking up or downhill and then loosening them on level terrain? Is a padded collar necessary to prevent debris and water from entering the boot and to reduce friction around the ankle area? These features and more must be evaluated against the intended use of our footwear.

When we assess the use of footwear in brushy, snowy or wet terrain, consider using gaiters. Snow, water, dirt and pebbles have a way of sneaking into even the most waterproof of boots. To prevent this, put on some gaiters. Gaiters cover the vulnerable tops of your footwear, including the laces, as well as the lower pants leg to fully protect your feet from the elements. Just as with all of our clothing systems, there are features and construction factors to consider based on the anticipated use of the gaiters.

The right pair of gaiters depends on the kinds of activities you have planned and the conditions you expect. The main types:

- Trail gaiters: These lightweight, breathable gaiters offer basic protection against rocks, grit and light rain while on mild-weather excursions.
- Alpine gaiters: These are designed for all-around hiking, snowshoeing, mountaineering and cross-country skiing. They offer added protection against rock abrasion and water.
- Expedition gaiters: These provide heavy-duty protection and add insulation for extended mountaineering trips in harsh conditions. Most feature a waterproof, breathable fabric for superior comfort and protection.
- Women's gaiters: While these can fall in any of the above categories, women's styles are typically shorter in height and have a bit more top girth to specifically accommodate a woman's calf.

Gaiters are typically available in two height categories. Choosing the correct height category depends on the amount of protection you require.

- Low gaiters are ankle high, about 8 to 12 inches tall. These are best for less-than-extreme conditions when you just need to keep trail debris and rain out of your boots.
- Regular gaiters are calf high, around 15 to 18 inches tall. These are designed for rugged conditions such as searching in deep snow, wet brush or in bad weather.

Gaiter construction is relatively standardized with some features varying based on price-value points purchased.

- Entry system: Gaiters are usually opened and secured by front rip-and-stick fasteners (VELCRO® brand or similar), although a few models feature a sturdy zippered entry. Older models tended to be rear entry, which offered less convenient on/off access.
- Top closures: Basic gaiters are typically cinched with toggles and elasticized drawcords; some models are a bit fancier and feature a dedicated top strap with cam buckle.
- Instep straps: These secure the lower edge of your gaiters around your boot insteps. Basic gaiters come with simple lace straps. Premium gaiters feature beefier leather/synthetic straps for extra durability.

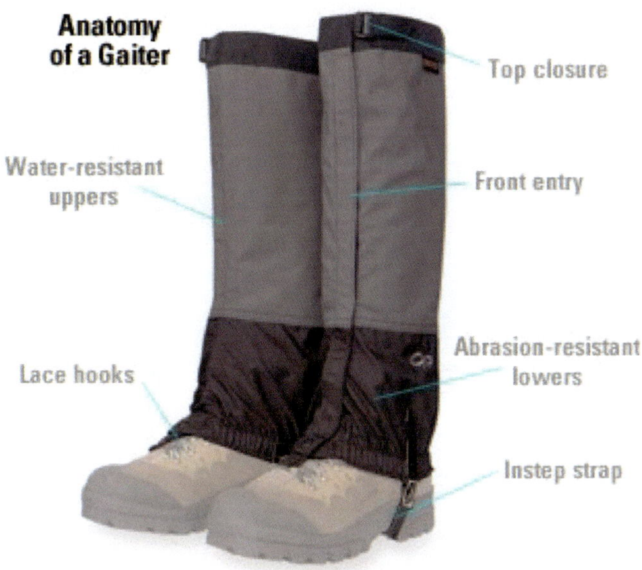

- Lace hooks: Offered on some styles, these let you attach your boot laces to your gaiters for added security.

Much like with outerwear, fabrics help define the level of gaiter performance you're going to get. Most gaiters feature a lower section that is abrasion-resistant to fend off scrapes and an upper section that is waterproof or highly water-resistant. Here's a breakdown of the most common fabrics:

- Gore-Tex®: This well-known laminate provides superior waterproof, windproof protection and breathability. It's ideal for tromping through wet or snowy conditions.
- Cordura® nylon: This super-rugged fabric is designed to withstand the abrasion of ice, rocks and the occasional nick of crampon points.
- Coated nylon: Basic gaiters are very light and are usually made with polyurethane-coated nylon. If a short day hike or fast-packing through talus, sand and wet brush is on your agenda, this type of fabric will work just fine.
- Schoeller® fabrics: This family of soft-shell fabrics offers flexibility and stretch as well as excellent weather protection

Summary

This knowledge of clothing systems is an additional component to assist you in preparing to safely engage in search & rescue field work. Selecting the right clothing for the mission will allow you to comfortably conduct your search assignments in some of the most extreme environments and weather you can imagine. Our ability to do so is essential as the subject may not survive our waiting for more favorable conditions before entering the field.

References

Wikipedia – The Free Encyclopedia, Various Discussions and Information (2015)
Wikimedia Foundation Inc., San Francisco, CA

Camping & Wilderness Survival, The Ultimate Outdoors Book (1999)
Paul Tawrell, *Paul Tawrell*, Shelburne, VT/Green Valley, ON Canada

www.textilehelpline.com – Solutions for Students, Various Discussions and Information (2015)

www.rei.com – Numerous Articles (2014)
Recreational Equipment, Inc., Sumner, WA

www.sierratradingpost.com – The Buying Guides (2015)
Sierra Trading Post, Cheyenne, WY

4 Safety Concepts for Field Responders

Objectives

Photo by Nancy Antosh

- Discuss the basic rules of SAR safety regardless of operating environment
- Describe some specialized SAR environments and their safety considerations
- Discuss lightning safety concepts
- Discuss prevention, diagnosis and field treatment of cold injuries including:
  - Chilblain
  - Frostnip
  - Frostbite
  - Immersion Foot
- Discuss prevention, diagnosis and field treatment of heat injuries (Hyperthermia) including:
  - Heat Cramps
  - Heat Exhaustion
  - Heat Stroke
- Explain the occurrence of Acute Mountain Sickness and its field treatment

- Describe prevention, diagnosis and field treatment of the following safety issues:
  - Blisters
  - Snake Bites
  - Insect Bites & Stings
  - Poisonous Plant Contact
- Discuss additional safety considerations pertinent to Urban Environment operations

> !!!!
> NOTE: You should always research the most current recommendation on prevention and treatment of hazards and safety issues!

The basic rules of SAR safety

SAR (Search & Rescue) safety is vitally important throughout the mission and actually is an important component of training, pre-planning, and mobilizing—all of which occur long before you arrive at the scene.

When you arrive at the incident, and receive a briefing, there are several basic rules of SAR safety regardless of the operating environment that must be included in either a general or tactical briefing. These basic safety rules of SAR include:

- The individual SAR Team member must be mentally and physically prepared for the search, rescue or recovery.
- The individual SAR Team member must be trained, experienced and equipped for the mission.
- The team, resources and equipment must be prepared to respond.
- There must be an effective ICS in place for the mission to be safely executed.
- A Safety Officer and a Safety Plan must be in place as soon as practical.

- Situational awareness must be a top priority for everyone's safety. This is as important during mobilization as during demobilization.
- Technical and specialized tasks must be performed by the appropriate technical team.
- Once the subject is found. Do No Harm!!! This is strongly emphasized in the Emergency Medical Services training and actual patient treatment!
- Preplan and ensure the safety of everyone else (family, friends, general public, support agencies like the American Red Cross, Salvation Army, Church groups, vendors, law enforcement, military, etc.).
- Recovery of a deceased subject is not an emergency—perform it extremely safely after a thorough risk analysis.

Photo by Rachel Schooler of Rachel Schooler Photography

Often overlooked but of the highest level of importance is being mentally prepared to participate in a SAR incident. This requirement applies whether the incident currently focuses on a potential live find or a recovery. One way to become mentally prepared is to be properly educated and certified while continuing to attend regular training. That will familiarize you with your responsibilities as well as the flow of a SAR incident. This, in turn, will greatly reduce your stress levels while on-scene. Examples of additional methods of mental preparation include attending a crime scene preservation class or other classes where pictures of injured and deceased subjects are shown. Of great benefit would be to attend a Critical Incident Stress Management (CISM) or Psychological First Aid. Such a course will prepare you to recognize signs of destructive levels of stress in you and your colleagues. That knowledge will allow you to decline further participation when those high stress levels are reached or support your teammates when you identify signs they have reached such levels of stress. Safety begins with knowing when you and your colleagues are psychologically prepared to begin and continue participation in a SAR event.

Being physically prepared to respond is also paramount to your safety. If you become exhausted you are more likely to become injured. Once a responder is injured, the focus shifts to the injured responder and detracts from the ability to locate and assist the missing or lost subject(s). There are several methods to stay physically fit. First, consult with your physician. You need to become aware of any limits to participation in the high levels of physical exertion required in Search & Rescue field operations. Then develop your personal program for becoming and staying fit. Being a SAR Field Responder is a 24/7/365 responsibility. There is no opportunity for an "out of shape" or overweight participant. Determine if your team has any physical fitness testing requirements (if not consider joining another team!). A good example is the Cooper Physical Fitness Test program used by many Law Enforcement and Fire Service Departments as a guideline. Then talk with a personal trainer or fitness professional about a workout plan designed for your goals and your team's requirements. Remember, physical fitness is a lifestyle choice, not a one-time effort.

Once you are prepared and you have the proper gear (see Chapters 3 & 5) you are ready for the response phase. Consider safety in traveling to and from an incident. One advisable training course is an emergency vehicle driving class or a defensive driving class. Even though some of the material covered in an Emergency Vehicle Driver Training (or an EVOC course), such as driving with lights & siren may not apply, there are many topics that will be useful. The defensive driving class such as the ones offered through the National Safety Council, are not only a good refresher since you last took your drivers education class but it will allow you to obtain a discount through many car insurance companies. A state fire or EMS agency may offer free classes.

Different SAR environments and their unique hazards

PHOTO BY ELIZABETH KECK

Wildlife considerations in the Wilderness

In the wilderness environment you may encounter various animals that pose a danger to you, your team (including your animal partners) and the subject. Knowing and understanding the fauna you might encounter in your search area is a major safety consideration. Animal life you may come upon includes bear, mountain lions/cougar/puma, and panther (considered *"Apex Predators"*), wolves, alligators, dogs (wild or feral), coyotes, wild pigs or hogs, Gila monsters (which grow up to 65 inches and are the only poisonous lizard in the US) as well as other animals that are not normally dangerous but may become so because of injury or disease (including rabies). Many of these "harmless" creatures can become a threat when they perceive a threat to themselves or their young. Some examples include domesticated canines and felines, birds of prey (raptors), skunks (plus their spray), farm animals (territorial males, protective females), rats, bats, bobcats, mountain goats, Rocky Mountain bighorn sheep, deer species (moose, caribou, elk, etc.), bison, snakes, alligator snapping turtles (seriously!), etc. Some will be more likely to attack your animal resources than humans so you must be prepared for both situations. Obviously some encounters will be extremely rare so preplan for the most likely scenarios (bison in National Parks & Refuges, Coral snakes & alligators in the Southeast US, panthers in FL, Gila monsters in the SW, etc.). You can research how to handle encounters by obtaining information from The National Park Service, State Park offices, Federal or State Wildlife Agencies, National Geographic, the BART (Basic Animal Rescue Training) organization, and specialized Animal Rescue Teams within the MRC (Medical Reserve Corp), etc.

Illegal/Criminal Activities in any environment

Criminal activities such as stills, marijuana plots, stolen property caches, poaching locations, etc. could all have booby traps, up to and including Improvised Explosive Device (IED), and even armed guards, willing to shoot to protect their actions from detection. Remember, to the criminal, you represent law enforcement!

Clandestine drug lab sites such as Methamphetamine (meth) labs are especially dangerous. Meth is a powerfully addictive stimulant with inherent physical and physiological dangers. Drug labs also present an explosive risk as the chemicals used to create many of these illegal drugs are extremely volatile. The health hazards from coming into contact with the drugs is also a risk to the field responder. Unknowingly entering a building or makeshift shelter can acutely expose SAR personnel to hazardous substances used in the illegal drug production. Exposure to these substances can occur from simple contact with surfaces, walking in liquid you think is just water, inhalation of volatile air emissions, and spills/fires/explosions that the searcher initiates. The hazardous materials can not only cause negative health effects but can contaminate equipment that must be properly decontaminated. This "decon" is technically difficult to perform and the only safe way to prevent bringing the chemicals home to your family is to dispose of them properly! Some suspect locations may have to be searched at a later time after sampling and analysis have been performed by a Drug Lab Cleanup Contractor. A visual inspection from a safe distance, uphill, and upwind may be your only option. Awareness training to protect you and your animal resources from these environments can be obtained through your local fire department, law enforcement agency, drug task force, military resources such as a Civil Support Team, etc.

In many environments we will have the need to work with armed law enforcement. There will be occasions where the circumstances of the lost or missing subject leads incident management to believe there is a threat to responders that requires armed assistance accompany field SAR resources. Examples of such situations include—responding to a callout where unknowns exist such as the mental status of the subject, the intent of the subject to be found, armed or unarmed abductors, probability of dangerous animals or illegal activities in the search area, searches where the lead agency is law enforcement, etc. Classes are available for civilians to assist them in understanding how to work with armed resources. In these cases you will likely be dealing with a crime scene. A class in crime scene preservation is not hard to schedule and is a standard requirement for many SAR teams. Contact your local law enforcement agencies to inquire about these classes.

Confined Space Hazards

Natural or man-made confined spaces and hazards such as caves, caverns, mines, wells, oil/gas/water drill rigs/ storage tanks/settling ponds, farm equipment, dilapidated structures, and grain elevators are potentially dangerous to SAR personnel. OSHA, or MSHA for mines, regulations require that specialty responders have confined space entry and rescue training with immediate technical rescue availability, including air monitoring equipment, respiratory protection, and proper Personal Protective Equipment (PPE). This is just the minimum required before entering common confined spaces. Other unusual hazards exist for the other listed examples such as collapse, chemical contamination, lacerations and punctures from rusted or contaminated objects, falls into lower level chambers or rooms, engulfment hazards, and explosion from organic material stored in silos, etc. This is a perfect example of an environment that requires specialty/technical training and should never be attempted by the Search & Rescue field responder unless they have the training, equipment and support to do so.

Urban environment consideration

The Urban Environment and the Urban/Wildland interfaces present settings such as homeless camps, military installations, airports, commercial or homeowners' private property, questionable structural integrity of old or damaged buildings, illegal dumps or legal dumps on private property (unstable objects, snakes and animals, bio-hazards such as animal carcasses, etc.). All of these are unique locations that require knowledge and careful planning to be searched safely. Experts on each of these settings should be consulted and remain on-scene to assist incident management in reducing the risk(s) encountered.

PHOTO COURTESY OF TAMMY ROBERTSON

Summary of environmental hazards

The lost or missing subject location could be a crime scene, may have biohazards of some kind, or may have physical danger (terrain hazards, animals, etc.). Universal precautions must be used when uncovering suspicious debris or soil piled up and for assisting authorities with a deceased subject. Typical PPE would include safety glasses, nitrile gloves, face mask, disposable suit or uniform with body substance isolation layer that will be decontaminated after exposure—at a minimum.

Dealing with Extreme Weather

Extreme weather (or even normal weather if you aren't prepared for it) can range from annoying to deadly. Consider in your preplan or your Incident Action Plan just how you would manage each expected situation during mobilization. You must pre-plan for severe weather that occurs during an actual SAR mission or training—and when to suspend the mission for different scenarios. Changing weather conditions are normal, rather than the exception, during Search & Rescue incidents. In the *SARAware*™ text we discussed the ICS position of a Safety Officer. One of the major tasks of the Safety Officer is to monitor the weather forecast and not wait for severe weather to cause an unsafe condition. Your local Emergency Management office and severe weather spotters can assist. Suspend the SAR mission before the situation becomes critical! Examples of severe weather you could encounter include:

It is possible to lose enough heat through your head that blood flow to your extremities is shunted to warm your core. So if your feet are cold...put on a hat!

Courtesy of Petzl

When we add injury protection into our plan there is only one option—a safety helmet. There are many manufacturers, styles and colors to choose from. But the important factor is to make sure that the helmet is certified by the manufacturer to meet ANSI Z89 Type II standards. This certification ensures a certain level of puncture protection, as well as top, front, back and side impact protection. Without the certification, there's no guarantee the helmet will protect you when you need it.

Proper fit is extremely important if the helmet is to protect as advertised. You cannot buy a larger size to accommodate an insulating hat for use in cold weather. The better option is to find a close fitting and thin insulating hat that will provide thermal protection, yet allow you to utilize the proper fitting helmet for injury protection. In milder/cool weather, a bandanna or motorcycle style "do-rag" might suffice. In colder weather a thin polypro "watch cap" or small beanie style works well.

- Feet—If you have taken care of your entire body, but have neglected your feet, you will be unable to perform your search duties in short order. Much attention has been given to this subject. We've discussed foot injury and illness in the chapter on survival and the proper use of socks in this chapter. Additional information will be provided in the next chapter on safety. For now, let's consider footwear, or as applicable to the SAR field responder...the jeeps on your feet.

Courtesy of Vasque

While we will discuss a number of factors that affect our footwear, the single most important one is proper fit. If at all possible, it is strongly recommended you have your

Blizzards—occur from falling snow or a ground blizzard where the wind stirs up snow on the ground. Low or zero visibility in blizzard conditions is the risk. Field resources caught outdoors in a blizzard must seek or construct shelter, stay or get dry, stay hydrated, and discontinue SAR tasks until the blizzard conditions subside.

Derechoes—large clusters of thunderstorms that produce widespread (**tens of miles wide and several hundred miles long)** wind damage with speeds from 50 to 100+ mph. Most thunderstorms present one or more dangers to field responders. Seek or build a shelter and see the section on lightning hazards.

Flooding—can be flash flooding or slowly rising. Swiftwater Rescue Awareness Training is useful for all SAR Teams as you could run into flooding conditions any time you are present on a SAR incident. Avoid overnight stays in low lying areas since flash floods can originate from many miles away and give no warning of their arrival. Seek higher ground immediately when water starts to flow or rises.

Haboob (huge, intense, violent dust storms)—can cause navigation & breathing issues, suspend ops. Proper respiratory protection must be added to SAR packs if this can probably occur in your area. Look for a NIOSH-Approved N95 Particulate Filtering Facepiece Respirator (medical approval is required).

Hail storms—which can be deadly and are another good reason for carrying helmets. Seek shelter under trees, rock outcroppings, caverns, etc. and put on your helmet or cover yourself with your pack.

OSHA *Extreme Heat Guide* (excerpt)—Staying cool and making simple changes in your fluid intake, activities, and clothing during hot weather can help you remain safe and healthy.

Heat waves—can be deadly and are another good reason to be proficient with night searching & tracking. Refer to the Heat Index Chart in the Heat Stress section for

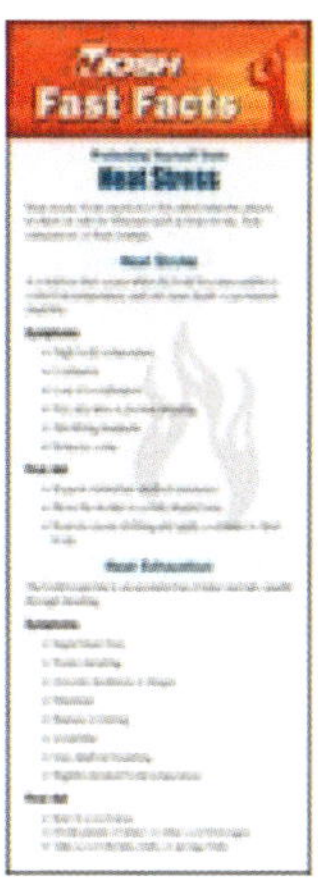
NIOSH Fast Facts

Heat Stress

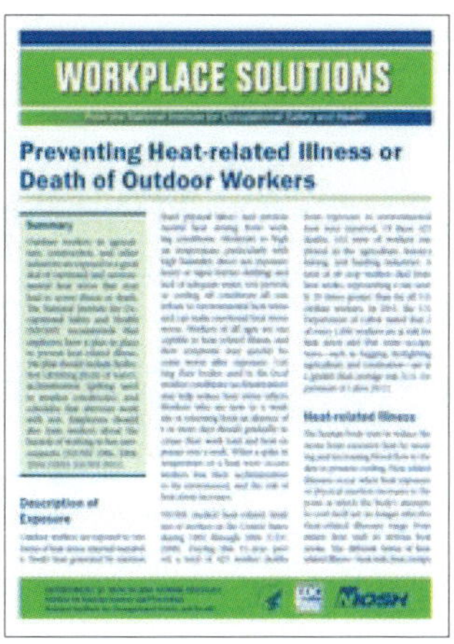
WORKPLACE SOLUTIONS

Preventing Heat-related Illness or Death of Outdoor Workers

Summary

Description of Exposure

Heat-related Illness

Examples of OSHA & NIOSH documents available online

dangerous heat and humidity ranges. Seek shade or at least wear a wide brimmed hat that has a high SPF rating and is light in color, stay hydrated.

High winds/squall—can make travel to the scene & search travel dangerous, causing tree limbs to fall, and other hazards. Your team SOG (Standard Operating Guidelines) must include guidelines for high winds which can be deadly. Standard fleet guidelines can be used such as when to suspend travel with or without a trailer. If you can't walk upright without leaning into the wind you might have to suspend tactical operations. Flying issues will also have to be addressed in the pre-plan and the Incident Action Plan.

Hurricanes—can cause heavy rain, flooding, tornadoes, logistic & transportation issues. Since they can be predicted several days in advance, the resulting severe weather (which can affect you from several hundred miles away) must never just surprise you—and result in the endangerment of responders.

Photos from the Weather Channel

Courtesy of Coal County Task Force, OK

Ice storms—can cause slip & fall hazards, hypothermia, transportation of equipment and supplies problems, and travel issues for responders.

Lightning storms—can cause serious injury or death and major property damage to command post, etc.

Snow storms—if you train & respond in warm climates, use caution when deciding if you should participate in SAR missions that would include searching, planned overnight stays or survival situations in cold weather (without cold weather training and equipment). Be especially careful in late Spring or early Fall when severe winter weather can occur. Plan for the worst weather you can reasonably expect. Use the same reasoning for the opposite situation, such as SAR in the extremely hot climates, like the desert during the summer.

Tornadoes and waterspouts (waterspouts are weak tornadoes that form over warm water)—there are no suitable shelters in the wilderness except a deep cave (not just a cavern). This would be a major disaster if the weather was not being watched closely and the mission was not suspended in time. Lay in a low area or depression while covering your head with your helmet, hands, or pack since flying debris from tornadoes causes most deaths and injuries.

Torrential rains and cloudburst (> 4" in 1 hour)—poor vision, routes blocked by flooding, swiftwater dangers, and hypothermia risks. Make sure you have proper rain gear and a pack cover or dry bags. Alternate evacuation routes, swiftwater awareness training, and hypothermia prevention knowledge could become lifesaving issues.

Tsunamis—can occur when SAR activities include the coast. Monitor NOAA's Tsunami Warning Center and follow recommendations or evacuation orders from officials. PFDs (Personal Flotation Devices) must be addressed in pre-plans and SOGs (Standard Operating Guidelines) when working around water (both stationary bodies and flowing water).

The secondary effects of ice storms and other weather issues include falling limbs and power lines, increased survival issues for the lost person and responders, and all around stress on the ICS.

Special outdoor hazards

Avalanche zones—good example of where even searchers, not just technical rescue teams, need advanced technical skills. There is really no good way to counter an avalanche. Avoidance is the key. You must obtain hands-on avalanche forecasting and rescue training before entering this type of area.

Volcanic activity (mainly the NW & Western US and Hawaii)—lahars (mud & debris flow) and landslides can occur even when a volcano is not erupting. Other windblown volcanic gases from far away include carbon dioxide, sulfur dioxide (which forms acid rain), hydrogen sulfide, hydrogen, and fluorine. Carbon dioxide is heavier than air and can be trapped in low areas in concentrations that are deadly to people and animals. Fluorine can poison livestock grazing on ash-coated grass and also contaminate domestic water supplies. The USGS Volcano Hazards Program monitors this type of activity. Obey recommendations and evacuation orders promptly.

Wildfires (sometimes with firenadoes)—make sure bases & camps operate safely so you're not the cause. ICP gear should include extinguishers & shovels. Be sure to clear fuel away from fire pits and parking areas and have a fire department brush truck standing by. Training in wildfire firefighting awareness would be good to know for base or camp issues or if encountered in the wilderness. There must be no fires allowed during high winds or burn bans (which can vary from one county to another)! There are several agencies and websites to obtain information from such as the Forestry Service and FIREWISE (which also offers online training—http://learningcenter.firewise.org/Firefighter-Safety/).

Photo from Wikipedia

A fire whirl (or fire devil) with flames in the vortex

Solar flares—can cause GPS & radio communication issues which would be a significant safety issue. SOGs should include backup communication in case of any disruption to the Radio Communication Plan (ICS 205 form) whether it's from solar flares, dead batteries, dropped radio, etc. HAM radios or State or County radios may be the primary radios; FRS, GMRS, or cell phones may be the secondary radios; in an emergency, messages may have to be relayed by horse or ATV or even Morse code. You can use flashes of light (sweep the beam quickly across the target for a "dot", and slowly for a "dash"). Learn basic Morse code or at least SOS: dot dot dot dash dash dash dot dot dot (... --- ...). You can also use a blinking light, horn honking, whistle blowing, or just yelling. Relying on alternative communication must be carefully evaluated because the safety of the team will be at stake. If you have a good size group of experienced searchers then the decision to continue may be the right choice if a child is probably alive but may not survive the night because of the weather. There are many scenarios and the information given during a pre-deployment brief must include what to do if communication is lost.

Earthquakes—which can start rockslides, mudslides, avalanches, cause branches or heavy snow buildup in trees to fall, are mainly encountered in the western states. They are difficult, if not impossible, to predict. The field responder must be educated and trained in operating with the expected hazards caused by earthquakes—after the main tremors subside. Situational awareness must be a high priority!

Water feature issues—water filled surface mines or quarries, deep or polluted bodies of water, swift water (creeks, rivers, runoff, etc.). Stay a specific distance away from water hazards based on your SOG and consider wearing PFD during specific activities (searching within ten feet of deep and moving water for example, etc.). Contact agencies with swiftwater rescue teams or swiftwater rescue training companies for recommendations. There are also bogs, swamps, and marshes which can be all over the US not just the Florida Everglades.

Terrain issues

Photo courtesy of Jim Delbridge

Beware of animal dens, snake holes, sink holes, slippery rocks at the top of cliffs and waterfalls, etc. Also remember to be aware of steep embankments as part of a cityscape or naturally occurring banks or cliffs near flowing water. These features can be a major issue for you and your team and a catastrophe if you are evacuating a patient! Keep your situational awareness high and appoint a scout to move ahead of a patient to find terrain hazards.

Other issues include dead branches hanging in trees ("widow makers"), plants/bushes/trees with thorns—such as the Blackjack that has three inch long very sharp spikes, trees with broken off branches that can be deadly (or a major eye hazard) if trips or falls occur near them.

There is also the under-rated hazard of quicksand which is not that uncommon along rivers. There are specific techniques for surviving an encounter with anything similar to quicksand such as those found on Discovery Channel's "Man vs. Wild," (Bear Grylls gets stuck in **quicksand** in the Moab Desert in Utah). Even WebMD.com has the usual advice (don't thrash around and have plenty of people to pull you out). "Yell, reach, throw, row, and then go", outlines what rescuers are taught for water or ice rescue and can be a helpful sequence of steps for quicksand rescue (except the "row" part).

Rock slides and mud slides can occur spontaneously. They can also be triggered as the result of earth tremors, rain, human or animals walking across a slope, helicopters running while loading or unloading, and vehicle traffic above the slide area. Hazards such as these are hard to pre-plan for but must be identified during scene size up before you enter a new area or begin rescue operations. This hazard identification must occur whether it's an avalanche zone or a water hazard. One way to accomplish this is to look at your surroundings (360 degrees). Look up and look down just as you would while searching for clues. The next step is to ask yourself what could probably go wrong! The last step is then to develop a plan of action so you do not encounter the hazards. This may be as simple as selecting a different route or as complex as requiring a technical rescue team to complete the task.

Tides or strong surf, tidal waves, and rip currents near the ocean can be very dangerous and require specialized training and equipment to work anywhere near.

A surface quarry or underground mine, excavations, caves, caverns, and sink holes all have the hazards of mild to deadly injuries from falls, toxic atmospheres, and crush injuries or suffocation from a collapse. Avoid these areas, warn others of their existence (on the radio and during debriefing), and mark them if at all feasible.

Other miscellaneous situations such as air operations; parking areas, driving routes, staging areas; canine, equine, ATV areas; and areas around generators have their own set of hazards. These hazards include struck-by, carbon monoxide, fires, shock hazards, fuel or oil spills, noise, animal aggression, etc.

There are many sources of information on preparedness, how to survive an event, and how to recover from an event and offered by FEMA, State Emergency Management, American Red Cross, CDC & NIOSH, OSHA, National Weather Service, and other response agencies.

Lightning Safety

One common type of weather issue that SAR teams must be prepared for during training and actual missions is lightning. We have all watched in amazement at the wonderful flashes of light in the sky. But when it is close, it is time to take heed. If you can hear thunder, you are close enough to get struck.

To determine if a storm is moving toward or away from you, you can use the 5-second rule. When you see the flash, count the seconds (use your favorite method) until you hear thunder. Every 5-seconds equals about one mile. When the storm is 6-10 miles away (less than 50 seconds between lightning and thunder), is when you must begin preparations and seek shelter.

While there are many responses you can take when there is lightning, the only recourse that you can take to truly protect yourself in lightning is to get inside a substantial building (with grounded wiring and plumbing) or a vehicle. Familiarize yourself with additional steps to follow, when you are on a SAR operation and, shelter is not available:

- Avoid open fields, the top of a hill or a ridge top.
- Stay away from tall, isolated trees or other tall objects. If you are in a forest, stay near a lower stand of trees.
- If you are camping in an open area, set up camp in a valley, ravine or other low area. However try not to set the tent in the lowest spot as you might get a small stream running through the tent if it rains or if enough rain falls you have to worry about flash flooding (the rain may occur miles away and not reach you till the middle of the night. Remember, a tent offers NO protection from lighting.
- Remain out of water, and away from wet items (such as ropes) as well as metal objects (hiking poles, fences and telephone poles). Water and metal are excellent conductors of electricity. The current from a lightning flash will easily travel for long distances, even underground.
- Avoid proximity (remain a minimum of 15 feet) to other people.
- Right before lightning strikes, your hair may stand on end because of the large amount of positive charges that are building up on the ground and objects that stick up above their surroundings.
- The charge coming up from these objects eventually connects with a negative charge reaching down from the clouds and zap—lightning strikes!
- When all else fails: Crouch down. Put feet together. Place hands over your ears to minimize hearing damage from thunder. Do not lie flat on the ground.

(LEFT) PHOTO COURTESY OF SCOTT JENKINS
(RIGHT) PHOTO BY AMY JENKINS

In the mountains, storms can come up on you in a matter of a few minutes as they will roll up over a mountain top without you seeing them. You generally have more time to react on flatter land, but you still may be in the trees and not be able to get a true gauge on the weather.

> **A note to mountain environment recreationalists and SAR responders**
>
> While hiking mountains in excess of 10,000 feet, a good rule of thumb is to be close to the top by 11:30 am so you can make a good judgment call on whether to proceed as you should plan for thunderstorms every day. Even when the clouds roll in and there are no signs of rain, the clouds are charged with electricity (this can occur even on the plains). The author has talked to many experienced hikers/responders who relate stories in which their hair has "stood up" while on the mountain. This means there is a significant amount of electricity in the air, ready to discharge, posing a significant danger to you.

While responders typically operate in an urgent mode (with lots of adrenaline flowing!), they need to take a little more time around lightning and other such perils be sure that they remain safe and do not become a victim themselves. A general rule of thumb is to wait 30 minutes after hearing the last clap of thunder before leaving your safe shelter. However, this time frame can be reduced if one can confirm that the lightning is moving away and is a safe distance from you.

Cold Injuries

The number one cause of outdoor fatalities is hypothermia. Whether you are engaged in a wilderness or urban environment you must properly prepare to work outdoors in a "cold" environment. This is a concern for responders, both in the field and at the support locations. As with any hazard, prevention is the best medicine. But

Photo courtesy of Gary Jenkins

since you have taken on the responsibility to serve your fellow citizens, you will likely have to work in extreme temps on both ends of the spectrum. Let's consider risks associated with operating in cold conditions. Being cold is not much fun. Knowing what your individual tolerance is will be the first step for determining requirements for personal comfort in keeping warm. Many environments present wide ranging temperatures that can fall dramatically and quickly. This is often encountered at night. Even with mild temperatures during the day, you may encounter hazardous, even deadly, cold temperatures after the sun sets. Altitude can also present extreme temperature changes.

REMOVAL FROM THE ENVIRONMENT IS THE PRIMARY ACTION TO BE TAKEN IN ALL COLD INJURIES.

Some cold-related risks in the field include: chilblain, frostnip, frostbite and immersion foot. Again, prevention is the best medicine. Removal from the environment is the primary action to be taken in all cold injuries. For short-term exposures, being sure that you can cover all exposed skin is critical in preventing frostnip and frostbite. This is even more critical if wind is expected. The wind will accelerate heat loss, thus it makes those sensitive areas like the tips if the ears, nose/cheek and hands more vulnerable. If you are planning to search in cold conditions, you should consider carrying ski goggles, double layered gloves and a heavy, full-face balaclava in order to cover those tough areas that generally are not covered.

Chilblain (also known as pernio) is the painful inflammation of small blood vessels in your skin that occur in response to sudden warming from cold temperatures. Their occurrence can vary from person to person and there is no one cause other than the area being cold. Chilblain can cause itching, red patches, swelling and blistering on extremities such as toes, fingers, ears and nose. The best primary treatment is remove the patient from the cold environment and to warm the area slowly. Chilblain may improve on its own, especially as the weather gets warmer. Chilblain usually clears up within one to three weeks, though it may recur seasonally for years. Treatments typically consist of lotions and medication. While Chilblain doesn't usually result in permanent injury, it can lead to infection, which may cause severe damage if left untreated.

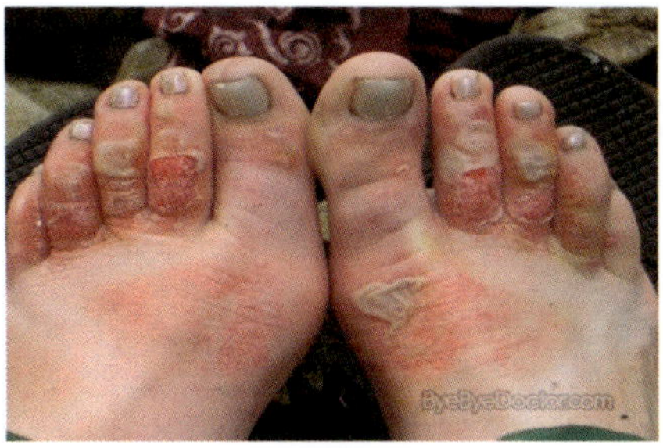

PHOTO COURTESY OF BYEBYEDOCTOR.COM

Frostnip usually affects skin on the face, ears, or fingertips. Frostnip may cause numbness or blue-white skin color for a short time, but normal feeling and color return quickly when you get warm. The skin and tissue under the skin is still warm and no permanent tissue damage occurs. Treat frostnip by coming in out of the cold. Don't rub the affected area so as not to injure the fragile skin. As the skin warms, it may turn red and feel painfully prickly.

Frostbite is freezing of the skin and the tissues under the skin due to exposure to temperatures below freezing. Frostbitten skin looks pale or blue and feels cold, numb, and stiff or rubbery to the touch. Pain may be severe as the frostbitten skin rewarms. Swelling and blisters are common after rewarming. Medical treatment for frostbite includes relieving pain and quickly rewarming the frostbitten area. This can help prevent problems such as infection, dead tissue, or amputation of the frozen part. Immediate treatment should include:

- Move the person to a warm place.
- Remove wet clothing, as well as jewelry that might constrict injured areas.
- If it doesn't delay getting medical treatment, wrap the affected parts in sterile dressings, carefully separating fingers and toes.
- Bring the person to an emergency room.

Immersion foot (trench foot) is a cold injury that occurs gradually over several days of exposure to cold, but not freezing, temperatures. The name comes from World War I troops who developed symptoms after standing in cold, wet trenches. Signs and symptoms of trench foot include:

- Red skin that turns pale and swollen.
- Numbness or burning pain.
- Leg cramps.
- No actual freezing of the skin.
- A slow or absent pulse in the foot.
- Development of blisters or ulcers after 2 to 7 days.

While not immediately life threatening, action must be taken and the responder removed from the field. First aid for trench foot includes rewarming the affected areas, relieving pain, and preventing longer term issues such as infection or even gangrene.

In cool or colder weather conditions, extra caution should be taken in areas with streams or lakes that might be frozen over. Just stepping in a small stream and getting your foot wet might very well end your day. Do not always take the shortest route over a frozen stream (even only 6-10 feet wide (2-3 meters). Seek another crossing, even if it means a considerably longer trek. You do not know how thick or strong the surface is. Frozen lake crossings should never be made unless it can be confirmed by locals knowledgeable of the recent weather and the lake itself. Crossing high mountain lakes in the winter is not likely to be a problem, but might be depending on the temperature trends that season. However, the month before and after the deep winter temperatures are especially dangerous. Temperature variations can make the lakes and streams appear frozen solid,

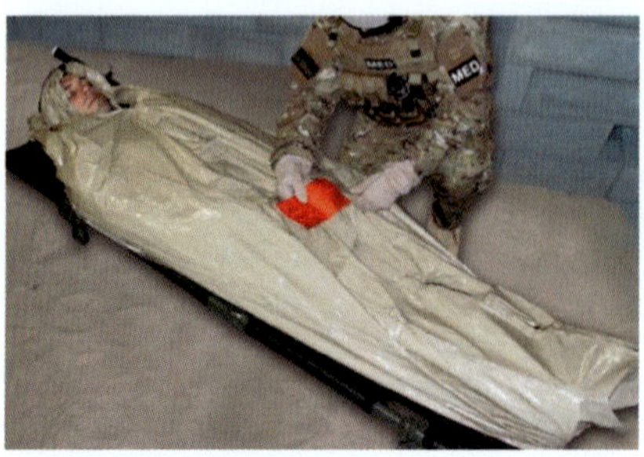

Tactical Medical Solutions Helios System

NAR (North American Rescue) Hypothermia Prevention & Management Kit

but the ice may not support your weight. In other than mountainous terrain, temperatures may be cold enough to freeze ponds and lakes, but again may not be thick enough to support crossing.

Remember, rule number one for treating cold injuries is removing the victim (even responders) from the cold environment. One piece of portable equipment effective for moderate or severe cold weather emergencies is a hypothermia treatment kit. These types of kits can prevent a cold weather injury from getting worse or can help prevent a patient from going into shock, while transporting or awaiting transport of the victim. Two examples are shown below.

General safety practices and not so common issues

Fording streams and creeks is a safety risk frequently encountered by SAR field responders. If you are using a typical SAR ready pack during a tasking, and need to cross streams or perform other activities in which you might fall (e.g. going down a steep incline), undo your waist and chest straps so that you can release yourself from the pack in order to not roll down the mountain or have the pack drag you under water.

Clothing and temperature protective gear is another significant safety consideration. As we discussed in Chapter 3, with this equipment, finding the right combination of insulating material type and amount (thickness) is a very individual choice. There is a tradeoff between natural material (wool and down) and synthetic (polypropylene, polyester pile, etc.) in weight, bulkiness, how they react to moisture, etc. Another factor is your potential length in the field and general weather conditions. If you are in a higher moisture (humidity, rain) area like the far northwest, you will have problems drying out your down gear, as well as everything else when (not if) it becomes damp or worse. In the dryer climates such as Colorado and Utah, you can lean toward down insulation unless you sweat excessively, then always go for synthetic.

If you are searching or overnighting in an environment with large or apex predators you need to employee safety techniques to avoid attracting these predators. Traveling in "bear country" is a good example. Food protection actions are mandatory in this environment.

A Better Way to Hang: The PCT Method

A system that combines the "bear" essentials for hanging a bear bag using the PCT method: here, an ultra light 600 ci food storage sack made with no-see-um mesh and sub-one-ounce silicone coated nylon (lined with an odor proof zip closure bag) and a rock sack of the same material, combined with 40 feet of Spectra rope, and a micro wire gate carabiner can weigh as little as three ounces.
(Photo: Bozeman Mountain Works UrsaLite Bear Bag Hanging System)

Affectionately known by the lightweight hiking underground as the "PCT Method" (presumably because it was first used by long distance hikers on the Pacific Crest Trail), a bear bag hanging method exists that is lighter, requires less rope, offers the benefits of counterbalancing, is easier to set up, and offers simple and quick hanging and retrieval of your food.

You can make your own system quite easily by assembling the following components:

- Food storage bag
- 40 feet of hanging rope
- Keychain carabiner
- Small stuff sack for a rock ("rock sack")
- Pencil-sized twig about 4-6 inches long.

Using 1.4-oz silicone-coated nylon waterproof stuff sacks for the rock sack and food storage bag, 1/8" parachute cord for the hanging rope, and a two-inch carabiner from Wal-Mart, you can achieve a system weight of about five or six ounces.

The system is used as follows:

1. Tie one end of the rope to the draw cord of the rock sack.
2. Tie a loop (e.g., bowline) into the other end of the rope and clip the carabiner through it.
3. Insert a rock into the rock sack, cinch it closed, and throw it over a branch that is 15-20 feet high.
4. Remove the rock from the rock sack.
5. Attach the food sack draw cord to the carabiner.
6. Clip the rock sack end of the rope through the carabiner so that it can run freely.
7. Pull the rock sack end of the rope until the food bag is at the height of the branch.
8. Take the twig and reach as far as possible up the rock sack end of the rope (for the average man, this is about six feet) and tie a clove hitch around the twig.
9. Let the rock sack end of the rope go, until the twig catches on the carabiner and keeps the food sack in place, at least 10 feet above the ground.

This system leaves extra rope hanging freely below the food bag, and unlike conventional hanging systems where the spare end of the rope is tied to a tree trunk, eliminates the possibility of an animal untying or chewing the rope in efforts to bring the food bag down.

In addition, the PCT Method requires less skill, and thus, is faster to deploy than the counterbalance method. Finally, the PCT Method requires a system of equipment that is lighter than the counterbalance method because it uses less rope and only one food storage sack.

First you must secure all food in containers that capture the food odor. Specially designed containers are the best method, but they are heavy, bulky and moderately expensive. Typically you will not be able to use them while engaged in a search tactic, but they may serve you well in Base. Make sure there are no compelling smells coming from your pack! In the past we would recommend "hanging" your food stuffs while camped. This is no longer the preferred technique unless you can employ a method colloquially called the PCT (ostensibly because it was first used/developed by hikers on the Pacific Crest Trail). If you plan to camp (or if the base is located in an area frequented by "problem" bears) you should study this simple method for storing your food outside your shelter. A quick summary of this technique is found in a textbox in this Chapter. Remember, scent is not only from food. It can be from items like tobacco, soap, balms and creams, and even insect repellent.

A frequently overlooked safety concern is responder medical conditions. Teammates, and equally importantly, Incident Management must be aware of any responder issues. Additionally, information on required treatment for such conditions needs to be available to Incident medical personnel. The problem of readily available medical information can be solved by giving each resource a form to fill out and keeping it on yourself in a specific location, supplying an incident ID card with a place on the back to write important personal information on it, or using one of the emergency medical triage information systems available. There is an advantage of using a system like the PMK Rescue Solutions "Treatment Application Band." If there is a medical issue, the patient information is readily available, and the same tag is already set up to write in additional information in case of a medical incident or accident. Information on the Rx-T.A.B. is shown here.

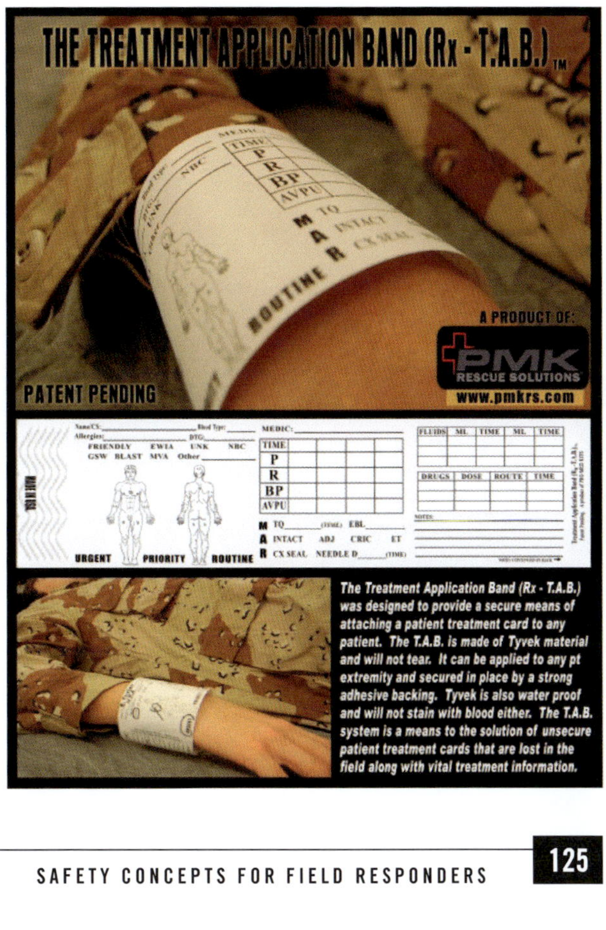

Photo from Dave Cruz of PMK Rescue Solutions

Heat Stress—heat cramps, heat exhaustion, heat stroke, hyperthermia

While the treatments for all of the heat related conditions are similar (rest and cool down), how this is accomplished will vary as to the severity of the condition. The more severe the condition, the greater the need to implement faster recovery systems to prevent further injury. Hyperthermia is a collective term that means the body temperature is elevated due to failed thermoregulation that occurs when a body produces or absorbs more heat than it dissipates. Extreme body temperature elevation then becomes a medical emergency requiring immediate treatment to prevent disability or death.

Heat Cramps

Heat cramps are painful, involuntary muscle spasms that usually occur during heavy exercise in hot environments. The spasms may be more intense and more prolonged than are typical nighttime leg cramps. Inadequate fluid intake often contributes to heat cramps. Muscles most often affected include those of your calves, arms, abdominal wall and back, although heat cramps may involve any muscle group involved in exercise. If you suspect heat cramps:

- Rest briefly and cool down
- Drink clear juice or an electrolyte-containing sports drink
- Practice gentle, range-of-motion stretching and gentle massage of the affected muscle group
- Don't resume strenuous activity for several hours or longer after heat cramps go away

Heat exhaustion

Heat exhaustion is one of the heat-related syndromes, which range in severity from mild heat cramps to heat exhaustion to potentially life-threatening heatstroke.

Signs and symptoms of heat exhaustion often begin suddenly, sometimes after excessive exercise, heavy perspiration, and inadequate fluid or salt intake. Signs and symptoms resemble those of shock and may include:

- Feeling faint or dizzy
- Nausea
- Heavy sweating
- Rapid, weak heartbeat
- Low blood pressure
- Cool, moist, pale skin
- Low-grade fever
- Heat cramps
- Headache
- Fatigue
- Dark-colored urine

If you suspect heat exhaustion:

- Get the person out of the sun and into shade.
- Lay the person down and elevate the legs and feet slightly.
- Loosen or remove the person's clothing.
- Have the person drink cool water or other nonalcoholic beverage without caffeine.
- Cool the person by spraying or sponging with cool water and fanning.
- Monitor the person carefully. Heat exhaustion can quickly become heatstroke.

Heatstroke

Heatstroke is the most severe of heat-related problems, after heat cramps and heat exhaustion. Heatstroke often results from exercise or heavy work in hot environments combined with inadequate fluid intake.

Young children, older adults, people who are obese and people born with an impaired ability to sweat are at high risk of heatstroke. Other risk factors include dehydration, alcohol use, cardiovascular disease and certain medications.

What makes heatstroke severe and potentially life-threatening is that the body's normal mechanisms for dealing with heat stress, such as sweating and temperature control, become inadequate. The main sign of heatstroke is a markedly elevated body temperature generally greater than 104 °F (40 °C)—with changes in mental status ranging from personality changes to confusion and coma. Skin may be hot and dry—although if heatstroke is caused by exertion, the skin may be moist.

Other signs and symptoms may include:

- Rapid heartbeat
- Rapid and shallow breathing
- Elevated or lowered blood pressure
- Cessation of sweating
- Irritability, confusion or unconsciousness
- Feeling dizzy or lightheaded
- Headache
- Nausea
- Fainting, which may be the first sign in older adults

If you suspect heatstroke:

- Remove the victim from the heat, minimally into a shaded area.
- Lay the person down and elevate the legs and feet slightly.
- Loosen or remove the person's clothing.
- Have the person drink cool water or other nonalcoholic beverage without caffeine.
- Cool the person by spraying or sponging with cool water and fanning.
- Monitor the person carefully. Heat exhaustion can quickly become heatstroke.

Passive cooling techniques, such as resting in a cool, shady area and removing clothing can be applied immediately. Active cooling

Heat Index Chart

Temperature	% Relative Humidity: 15	20	25	30	35	40	45	50	55	60	65	70	75	80	85	90
110	108	112	117	123	130											
105	102	105	108	113	117	122	130									
100	97	98	102	104	107	110	115	120	126	132						
95	91	93	95	96	98	100	104	106	109	113	119	124	130			
90	86	87	88	90	91	92	95	97	98	100	103	106	110	114	117	121
85	81	82	83	84	85	86	87	88	89	90	92	94	96	97	100	102
80	76	77	78	78	79	79	80	81	82	83	84	85	86	87	88	89

Legend

80-89 degrees	Fatigue is possible with prolonged exposure and/or physical activity.
90-104 degrees	Sunstroke, heat cramps and heat exhaustion are possible with prolonged exposure and/or physical activity.
105-129 degrees	Sunstroke, heat cramps and heat exhaustion are likely. Heat stroke is possible with prolonged exposure and/or physical activity.
130+ degrees	Heatstroke/sunstroke is highly likely with continued exposure.

Heat Index Chart. http://www.tvweather.com

methods, such as sponging the head, neck, and trunk with cool water, remove heat from the body and thereby speed the body's return to normal temperatures. Drinking water and turning a fan or dehumidifying air conditioning unit on the affected person may improve the effectiveness of the body's evaporative cooling mechanisms (sweating). Use the Heat Index Chart above as a guide to predict possible Heat Stress conditions. Your Doctor may need to advise you of specific personal issues you need to be concerned about based on your medical and physical condition.

Altitude Sickness

Altitude Sickness (AS) is a condition that occurs with a combination of low oxygen pressure at altitude. There are many other names such as acute mountain sickness (AMS), hypobaropathy and "the altitude bends" or soroche. AS is the first phase of the body letting you know that there is a problem. If time at altitude is continued, high altitude pulmonary edema (HAPE) affecting the lungs or high altitude cerebral edema (HACE) affecting the brain, can develop and both can be fatal. Medication is available for these last two medical conditions, but you should consult a physician about altitude sickness if you have the if you have a potential to spend a significant amount of time at moderate or high altitude.

AS is a fairly non-specific condition that generally occurs over 8,000 feet (2,438 meters) above sea level. No one gets this on an airplane since the cabin is pressurized. However, prior to modern planes, pilots had to be careful at altitude.

When rescuers are sent from lower elevations, say Houston to Denver, caution must be taken. It may take a few days to fully acclimate. There are many people that suffer mild cases of AS just coming to Denver. While there is no conclusive medical evidence, there has been some correlation to staying fully hydrated prior to and continuing through your stay at altitude, and not contracting AS.

Acquiring the bends while scuba diving has been more dramatized on TV, but it is essentially the same as when ascending in altitude on land. The rate of ascent, physical fitness, hydration as mentioned before, true altitude and one's individual susceptibility are all factors. Even people that live in Denver (5,280 feet/1609 meters above sea level) can have problems in the mountains while skiing or climbing 14ers (peaks higher than 14,000 feet/4267 meters in elevation).

Symptoms will vary from person to person along with the severity and can include:

- Lack of appetite, nausea, or vomiting
- Fatigue or weakness
- Dizziness or lightheadedness
- Insomnia
- Pins and needles
- Shortness of breath upon exertion
- Nosebleed
- Persistent rapid pulse
- Drowsiness
- Excessive flatulence
- General malaise
- Peripheral edema (swelling of hands, feet, and face)

Ascending slowly is the best way to avoid altitude sickness. This does not just mean doing this from the car or trailhead. An example of this is a person who lived in Atlanta and wanted to do some winter mountaineering in the Colorado mountains. The trip started with a drive from Atlanta to Denver in two days and ascending the next day to 10,000'. After snow shoeing about 1.5 miles, they started to set up camp and this one person was a little lethargic and decided to rest. After his nap, he was a little worse and it was decided that they needed to descend before they could not get themselves back without help. While the hike out in the moonlight was a great experience, it reminded them that the potential is always there for altitude sickness. Many people with experience doing Colorado 14ers have succumb to mild cases of altitude sickness and have needed to cancel their trips.

Hikers climbing Mt. McKinley (20,320') in Alaska have to spend 2-3 days at base camp (7,000') before ascending. Additionally, the assault on this high peak has to be slow and steady. When I summited Mt. McKinley, it took us four days to travel 10 of the 15 miles up the glacier and we spent five nights at the 14,000' camp just to acclimate.

A general rule of thumb on avoiding altitude sickness is to avoid strenuous activity such as skiing, hiking, etc. in the first 24 hours at altitude. Alcohol and sleeping pills are respiratory depressants, which slows down the acclimatization process and should be avoided. Alcohol also tends to cause dehydration and exacerbates AMS. Thus, avoiding alcohol consumption in the first 24–48 hours at a higher altitude is best.

The drug acetazolamide (trade name Diamox) may help some people make a rapid ascent above 9,000 ft., and it may also be effective if started early in the course of AMS. Acetazolamide can be taken before symptoms appear as a preventive measure at a dose of 125 mg twice daily. Prior to the onset of altitude sickness, ibuprofen is a suggested non-steroidal anti-inflammatory and painkiller that can help alleviate both the headache and nausea associated with AMS.

The above information is for altitudes above 8,000'. For extended stays at these altitudes you should conduct your own research and obtain advisement from expert resources.

Prevention, diagnosis and field treatment of some common safety issues

Surprisingly, one of the biggest issues in preventing field responders from conducting their duties is Blister! Blisters are fluid filled bumps that look like bubbles on the skin. They can occur for several different reasons. They can be an indicator a medical condition has developed that can range from minor to serious. Some of the more common blisters, how to prevent them, and how to treat each one in the field are shown in the following chart:

CAUSE OF BLISTER	*PREVENTION*	*FIELD TREATMENT*
Friction	Wear proper fitting boots and a liner sock & PPE such as gloves. Check for hotspots.	Doughnut shaped moleskin. See note below.
Burns (heat)	Wear leather gloves, avoid hot objects (generators, stoves), don't stand too close to fires	Remove heat source, cool the burn with water (not ice) wrap the burn loosely with a non-adherent gauze bandage or cool compress.
Burns (sun)	Wear clothing with a good SPF rating, cover exposed skin with sunblock	Same as Burns (heat)
Burns (electricity)	Do not use damaged equip. & use GFCIs (lighting, RVs, generators, power lines, etc)	Remove from source, call 911, check ABCs, cool with water, use non-adherent gauze bandage
Burns (chemicals)	Avoid contact with objects in dumps & structures (meth labs, etc) without proper PPE	Remove contaminated clothes & chemicals by flushing with water, apply dry sterile dressing but no ointments
Cold injury	Wear proper clothing, avoid long exposures, check skin for redness, numbness or tingling	Remove from cold environment, apply dry sterile dressing
Spider bites	Wear gloves or avoid likely locations (stacks of material or tall grass)	Wash with soap & water, cool skin to reduce swelling, cover with clean dressing

> Note: We DO NOT recommend puncturing blisters. You are better served by using moleskin or even duct tape to protect a blister from irritation. Use these materials with a hole in the center, the height of the blister, while surrounding the blister all the way. In the event the blister is keeping you from traveling to safety and it has to be drained, use extreme caution to prevent infection. Clean/sterilize a safety pin with an alcohol prep pad; carefully puncture edge of blister; press fluid out towards the hole; wash area with soap & water; apply antibiotic ointment & clean bandage. Return to base and report to the on-site medical team. End your direct involvement with field operations or switch to IC position if approved by medical.

Critters!

Common US Snakes

While it is more likely you will be struck by lightning than sustain a snake bite, some discussion is pertinent since field responders have no choice but to operate in environments where they are apt to encounter snakes. And remember almost all snake bites, but there are only four types of venomous snakes commonly found in the US.

Photo by U.S. Fish and Wildlife Service

Copperheads (so named because their heads are a copper color)

The average length of adult copperheads is 30 inches (76 cm). They have an unmarked copper-colored head, and reddish-brown, coppery bodies with chestnut brown cross bands that constrict towards the midline. Copperheads are social snakes and can be found close to one another near denning, sunning, courting, mating, eating, and drinking sites. Males are aggressive during the spring and autumn mating seasons. Copperheads have been reported to climb into low bushes or trees after prey or to bask in the sun. They have also been seen voluntarily entering water and swimming on numerous occasions.

Overall, this species inhabits the Florida panhandle north to Massachusetts and west to Nebraska. Copperheads inject prey with a hemolytic venom (causes the breakdown of red blood cells). Adult copperheads are primarily ambushers. The copperhead bites then releases immediately to allow the venom to take effect, then later tracks its prey. They are most active April through October, diurnal in the spring and fall, and nocturnal during the summer. The lifespan of the copperhead is up to 18 years.

Coral Snakes (Red on yellow—color pattern).
Photo by U.S. Fish and Wildlife Service

Coral snakes live in the wooded, sandy, and marshy areas of the southeastern United States, and spend most of their lives burrowed underground or in leaf piles. When threatened, a coral snake will curl the tip of its tail to confuse its attacker as to which end is its head. There is little or no pain or swelling at the site of the bite, and other symptoms can be delayed for 12 hours. However, if untreated by antivenin, a neurotoxin begins to disrupt the connections between the brain and the muscles. This can cause slurred speech, double vision, and muscular paralysis, eventually ending in respiratory or cardiac failure. Coral snakes are extremely reclusive and generally bite humans only when handled or stepped on. They must literally chew on their victim to inject their venom fully, so most bites to humans don't result in death. In fact, no deaths from coral snake bites have been reported in the U.S. since an anti-venom was released in 1967. The Coral snakes are sometimes confused with the nonvenomous Scarlet King Snake. The old rhyme "red on yellow, kills a fellow—red on black, a friend of Jack" helps to remember the difference.

Water Moccasins are nicknamed Cottonmouths because the inside of their white mouth looks like "cotton." They average 50–55 inches in length. The adult snake's skin is usually dark tan, brown, or nearly black, with vague black or dark brown cross bands. Juvenile Water Moccasins have a bold cross banded pattern of brown or orange with a yellow tail. They do not scare easily and will defend themselves when threatened. Fortunately, these snakes are not aggressive by nature. Typically they would rather flee than fight. Water Moccasins are frequently found in or around water such as wetlands, rivers, lakes, etc., in the southeastern states. They are primarily active at night using heat-sensing pits between their eyes and nostrils. They are able to detect temperature differences of as little as 1.8° F (1° C) higher or lower than that of the background. The pits allow the snakes to strike very accurately at the source of heat, often its prey or perceived aggressor. The sensory apparatus is most efficient at night when the target (such as a night searcher/tracker) is much warmer than the surrounding air. Because they spend much of their time in water, and water draws away heat more quickly than air, they must somehow maintain a high body temperature, particularly for their digestive metabolism. This is accomplished partly by basking in the sun. These snakes can cause very severe and even sometimes fatal damage when they bite. But again, this is very uncommon because the Water Moccasins are

Photo by U.S. Fish and Wildlife Service

Water Moccasin (or Cottonmouth)

normally not very aggressive creatures. The venom of this snake is hemotoxic. This means that the venom breaks down and destroys blood cells and other tissues and reduces the ability of blood to coagulate or clot. This results in a hemorrhage throughout any portion of the circulatory system that is penetrated by the venom.

Rattlesnakes

There are 36 species of rattlesnakes throughout North and South America (the Eastern Diamond-backed Rattlesnake is shown below left and the Western Diamond-backed Rattlesnake below right). Rattlesnakes are the largest of the venomous snakes in the United States. Rattlesnakes use their rattles or tails as a warning when they

Rattlesnakes

Photo from the Smithsonian National Zoo   Photo from the Arizona Game and Fish Dept.

feel threatened. Rattlesnakes may be found sunning themselves near logs, boulders, or open areas. These snakes may be found in most rural and wilderness SAR habitats including the mountains, prairies, deserts, and beaches. They can accurately strike at up to one-third their body length. The Western Diamond-backed Rattlesnake grows up to 66 inches long and is responsible for more bites and deaths to humans than any other rattlesnake species in U.S. Thirteen species of rattlesnakes live in Arizona and according to Arizona Poison Centers less than 1% of rattlesnake bites result in human deaths.

Snake Bites

The normal actions to stay safe from hazards do not always work for Search & Rescue. We can't avoid an area where snakes may be because the search subject could be in that location. A SAR team must instead take precautions in case of an encounter with many types of hazards from the animal kingdom. Part of your pre-planning must include common hazards such as snakes. Some suggestions for actions before, during, and after a snake encounter include:

- Preplan for snake encounters and the proper treatment that will be needed.
- Find out what proper medical resource are available in the area for you, your canine, or your horse.
- Cover the hazard in briefings (risk of encounter, prevention & response to bites).
- Add reminders of what to do and what not to do on documents given to deployed resources.
- Effective situational awareness must include hazards as well as clues.
- Log sightings and report during debriefing.
- Snakes can be active at night and during warm weather.
- Snakes can be in or near the water, hiding in debris, basking in the sun, etc.
- If you see a snake, stop, back away from it slowly, and don't start blindly running away.
- Avoid stepping over objects without first looking or probing with your tracking stick, etc. The preferred method is to step onto the obstacle and look over the other side before stepping down.

The ability to identify venomous snakes is thought by some to be only an additional benefit since any snakebite can become infected and you shouldn't wait for symptoms of venomous bites to start appearing. If you are bitten, you can try to remember the color or markings, but do not try to capture or kill it (one thing worse than a snake bite is a second snake bite)!

Some suggestions for PPE include heavyweight long pants and shirts, regular tall boots or snake boots, leather or puncture resistant specialty gloves, snake gaiters or snake chaps (plus they provide an extra barrier to ticks, chiggers, anything sharp), tracking stick or hiking pole. Remember that all gaiters and chaps are not specifically made to protect against snake bites.

Signs or symptoms associated with a snake bite may vary depending on the type of snake, but may include:

- A pair of puncture marks at the wound
- Redness and swelling around the bite (remove rings even if you were not bitten on the hand)
- Severe pain at the site of the bite
- Nausea and vomiting
- Labored breathing (in extreme cases, breathing may stop altogether)
- Disturbed vision
- Increased salivation and sweating
- Numbness or tingling around your face and/or limbs

The above list and several other types of injury or illness should make you think about the ever present possibility of a carryout and plan ahead.

The following steps should be taken if you are bitten by a snake:

- Follow your teams SOPs (Standard Operating Procedures), information given at your briefing, or the ICS Medical Plan depending on team member's certifications/equipment/ expertise/time, etc.
- Provide medical attention as soon as possible. Don't wait for signs/symptoms to appear!
- Try to remember the color or markings of the snake, which can help with treatment of the bite. But understand that it is unlikely any medical facility you travel to will administer anti-venom. All anti-venom is snake specific and the facility would have to be very sure which venomous snake bit you and then have to have all the possible types of anti-venom in inventory. Chance are they are simply going to treat the wound and provide antibiotics for infection.
- Keep still and calm. This can slow down the spread of venom.
- Inform your IC. Log the event, treatment, baseline vital signs, and changes in all relevant signs & symptoms until the patient is transferred to appropriate medical personnel.

- Sit or lie down with the bite below the level of the heart.
- Wash the bite with soap and water.
- Cover the bite with a clean, dry dressing.

DO NOT perform any of the following:

- Do not pick up the snake, bother it in any way, try to trap it, or try to kill it.
- Do not wait for symptoms to appear if bitten, immediately seek advanced medical treatment.
- Do not apply a tourniquet (thought by some to just allow concentrated damage).
- Do not make incisions over the wound with a knife (more problems from the injuries & infection than the bites).
- Do not suck out the venom with your mouth.
- Do not apply ice (which can damage tissue) or immerse the wound in water.
- Do not drink alcohol as a painkiller, to calm nerves, or anything else.
- Do not drink caffeinated beverages.

Bites and Stings from Insects, Arachnids, and Centipedes

- Insects include mosquito, bees, wasps (yellow jackets), hornets, fire ants
- Arachnids include scorpions, spiders, ticks, mites (chiggers, etc.)
- Centipedes (1/4–12 inches and over 3000 species) have one pair of legs per body segment

This group of creatures can have a wide range of effects on humans from itching to potentially lethal anaphylactic shock. Thousands of people are stung by insects each year, and as many as 90–100 people in the United States die as a result of allergic reactions. This number may be underreported as deaths may be mistakenly diagnosed as heart attacks or sunstrokes or may be attributed to other causes.

It is important when performing risk assessments, from pre-planning through demobilization, that you include the exposure to insects, arachnids, and centipedes. The information must include their risk of exposure, how someone can protect themselves from stings and bites, what they should do if they are stung or bitten, and identification (but only if the treatment can benefit from the identification and only if the action can be undertaken in complete safety).

Mosquitos

Mosquito bites can be more than just itchy and annoying. They can cause you to get sick. The most effective way to avoid the worst diseases, like West Nile virus in the United States, is to prevent mosquito bites. Be aware of the West Nile virus activity in your area and take action to protect yourself and your family. Almost 40,000 people in the U.S. have been reported with West Nile virus disease since 1999, and of those over 17,000 have been seriously ill and more than 1600 have died. Many more cases of this illness are not reported to CDC.

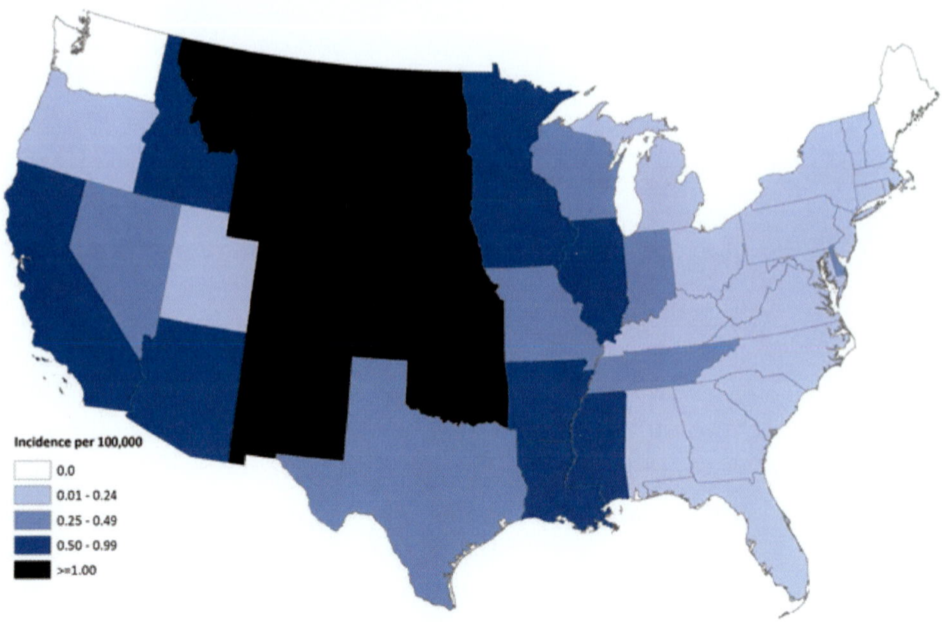

This map shows where West Nile virus is a problem (courtesy of www.cdc.gov)

Anyone living in an area where West Nile virus is present in mosquitos can get infected. West Nile virus has been detected in all lower 48 states (not in Hawaii or Alaska). Outbreaks have occurred every summer since 1999. Though anyone can get infected with West Nile virus, there are people at higher risk for severe disease. People over the age of 50 are at higher risk for encephalitis. The reasons one person becomes severely ill and another doesn't aren't entirely known.

Most people (70-80%) who become infected with West Nile virus do not develop any symptoms. About 1 in 5 people who are infected will develop a fever with other symptoms such as headache, body aches, joint pains, vomiting, diarrhea, or rash. Most people with this type of West Nile virus disease recover completely, but fatigue and weakness can last for weeks or months.

Less than 1% of people who are infected will develop a serious neurologic illness such as encephalitis or meningitis (inflammation of the brain or surrounding tissues). The symptoms of neurologic illness can include headache, high fever, neck stiffness, disorientation, coma, tremors, seizures, or paralysis. See your healthcare professional if you think you have the symptoms of West Nile infection.

Insect repellent

No one is safe from mosquito-borne diseases, but there are steps you can take to help prevent such virus infections.

1. **Apply insect repellent** on clothing before you go outdoors. Use an Environmental Protection Agency (EPA)-registered insect repellent. One such repellant is Permethrin®. This chemical can only be used on clothing. Permethrin® sprayed on clothing provides protection through several washes. **Don't use Permethrin® directly on skin!**
2. **Apply insect repellent** on your skin before you go outdoors. There are two frequently used chemical repellents. The first one is DEET. It is available in varying strengths and should be used in as low a concentration as possible while still effective in keeping insects from biting. Since DEET is neuro toxic, low doses are imperative. Effects of long term use of

DEET is still not known. Picaridin® is the second most used chemical repellent. Picaridin® only comes in one strength, approximately 10%.

3. **Cover up!** Wear long sleeve shirts and long pants and socks while outdoors to prevent mosquito bites.
4. **Avoid mosquitos.** Mosquitos are more commonly encountered (and are more active) between dusk and dawn. Limit the amount of time you spend outdoors during these hours. But mosquito bites are also possible during daytime hours. So any time you are outdoors, be sure to wear repellent and protective clothing.
5. **Consider mosquito control program techniques.** Mosquito control methods depend on the time of year, the type of mosquitos to be controlled, and the habitats where the mosquitos live. Methods can include eliminating mosquito larval habitats and applying insecticides to kill mosquito near command posts, bases, and camps.

Insect repellents

Look for these active ingredients recommended by CDC and EPA:

- DEET
- Picaridin®
- IR3535
- plant-based oil of lemon eucalyptus

Bees, wasps or hornets

Encounters with these insects can be particularly onerous. They are very similar, being in the same order and sub-order. Hornets are the largest members of the wasp family. For our purposes, we will consider them jointly. In most species the males do not have stingers. Though they may present their "tails" in a menacing manner when provoked, they cannot sting. Females may have either a smooth or barbed stinger. In the case of humans, being stung with a barbed stinger usually results in the stinger being torn from the insect and remaining in the skin. This is the origin of the legend that a "bee

Honey Bee
COURTESY OF WONDERVILLE.COM

Wasp
COURTESY OF HTTP://WWW.MIKESPESTCONTROL.NET

can only sting once." Whether an insect can sting multiple times, or not, is dependent on the type of stinger. Normally bees and wasps are not aggressive towards humans but can become very aggressive when threatened or agitated. An example of a very aggressive species is the Yellow Jacket (wasp). As with many other species, the Yellow Jacket will emit pheromones while stinging. This will bring many others into the attack.

Prevention and Reaction

- Wear light-colored, smooth-finished clothing.
- Avoid perfumed soaps, shampoos, and deodorants.
- Don't wear cologne or perfume.
- Avoid bananas and banana-scented toiletries like sunscreen, lip balm.
- Wear clean clothing and bathe daily. Sweat may anger bees.
- Wear clothing to cover as much of the body as possible.
- Avoid flowering plants when possible.
- Keep work areas clean. Social wasps thrive in places where humans discard food.
- Remain calm and still if a single stinging insect is flying around. Swatting at an insect may cause it to sting.
- If you are attacked by several stinging insects at once, run to get away from them. (Bees release a chemical when they sting, which may attract other bees.)
    - Go indoors.
    - A shaded area is better than an open area to get away from the insects.

    - If you are able to move out of the area, do not attempt to jump into water. Some insects (particularly Africanized Honey Bees) are known to hover above the water, continuing to sting once you surface for air.
- If a bee comes inside your vehicle, stop the car slowly, and open all the windows.
- Those with a history of severe allergic reactions to insect bites or stings, etc. must carry an epinephrine auto injector (EpiPen®) if prescribed by your Doctor. There are several methods to track resources that have allergies or medical issues and still maintain required privacy, including
    - Medical identification bracelet or necklace
    - A team or Agency in charge distributes a short form and selects a common place to store the documents on each individual (badge or ID holder, right front pocket, etc.)
    - Medical stickers for helmets, etc. They can be applied to a piece of plastic with a hole punched in it to attached it to a necklace, zipper pull, etc. (QRide Advanced Emergency ID, etc.)
    - Self disclosure to the ICS medical unit
    - These methods also allow you to communicate medical issues if you are unconscious, disoriented, or are having an allergic reaction

Emergency Medical Treatment

If someone is stung by a bee, wasp, or hornet:

- Have someone monitor the victim to be sure that they do not have an allergic reaction.
- If symptoms develop, assist the victim within the limits of your training or certification.
- Wash the site with soap and water.
- Remove the stinger using gauze wiped over the area or by scraping a fingernail over the area.
- Never squeeze the stinger or use tweezers.
- Apply ice to reduce swelling.

- Do not scratch the sting as this may increase swelling, itching, and risk of infection.
- Depending on the severity of the reaction—immediately notify who your team reports to within the ICS, prepare to wait for advanced medical assistance, leave the search area and go to a pickup point, etc.

Fire Ants

Imported fire ants first came to the United States around 1930. Now there are five times more ants per acre in the United States than in their native South America. The fire ants that came to the United States escaped their natural enemies and thrived in the southern landscape. Fire ants both bite and sting! They are aggressive when stinging and inject venom, which causes a burning sensation. Red bumps form at the sting, and within a day or two they become white fluid-filled pustules.

Courtesy of www.orkin.com

Preventing Fire Ant Stings and Bites

Take the following steps to prevent fire ant stings and bites:

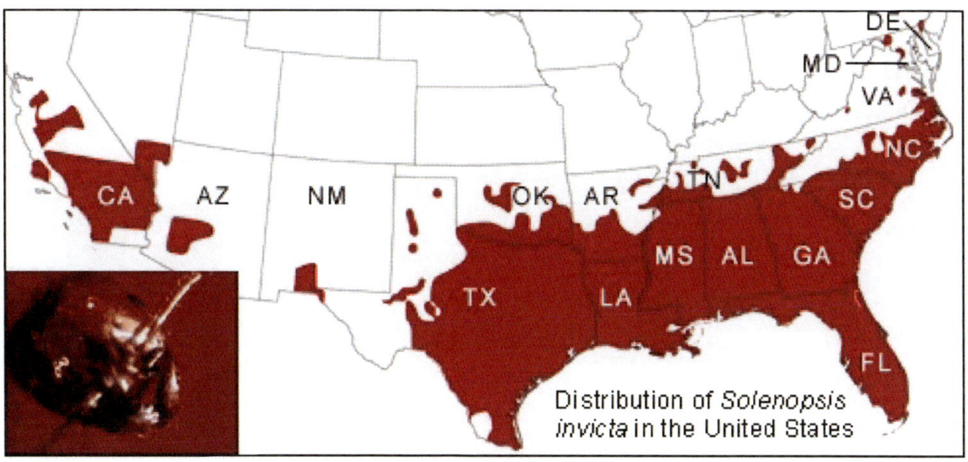

Graphic courtesy of http://evolution.berkeley.edu/evolibrary/article/_0_0/fireants_02

- Do not disturb or stand on or near ant mounds.
- Be careful when lifting items (including animal carcasses) off the ground, as they may be covered in ants.
- Fire ants may also be found on trees or in water, so always look over the area before entering.

Those with a history of severe allergic reactions to insect bites or stings must carry an epinephrine auto injector (EpiPen®) if prescribed by their doctor and must have a method to communicate their allergy if they can't speak.

Take the following steps if you are stung or bitten by fire ants:

- Rub off ants briskly, as they will attach to the skin with their jaws.
- Antihistamines may help.
- Follow directions on packaging.
- Drowsiness may occur.
- Take the patient to an emergency medical facility immediately if a sting causes severe chest pain, nausea, severe sweating, loss of breath, serious swelling, or slurred speech.

Spiders

Most all spiders are capable of causing an irritating, if not outright painful, bite. Whether you are indoors or outdoors it can be difficult to avoid accidental encounters with spiders. But our real concern lies with those spiders whose bite might be venomous. Venomous spiders found in the United States include the black widow, brown recluse, and hobo spiders. These spiders occasionally find their way inside structures or buildings. Spiders are usually not aggressive and most bites occur because a spider is trapped or unintentionally contacted. It is important for all responders, whether assigned to field operations or management and support in base, to educate themselves about their risk of exposure to venomous spiders. Responders must know how they can prevent and protect themselves from spider bites, and what they should do if they are bitten.

Types of Venomous Spiders—Black Widows, Brown Recluse Spiders, Hobo Spiders

Black widow spiders are found throughout North America, but are most common in the southern and western areas of the United States. They are identified by the pattern of red coloration on the underside of their abdomen. They are usually found in workplaces containing undisturbed areas such as woodpiles, under eaves, fences, and other areas where debris has accumulated. They may also be found living in outdoor toilets where flies are plentiful.

Black widow spiders build webs between objects, and bites usually occur when humans come into direct contact with these webs. A bite from a black widow can be distinguished from other insect bites by the two puncture marks it makes in the skin. The venom is a neurotoxin that produces pain at the bite area and then spreads to the chest, abdomen, or the entire body.

The ***brown recluse spider***, also known as the violin spider, is most commonly found in the Midwestern and southern states of the United States. It is brown in color with a characteristic dark violin-shaped (or fiddle-shaped) marking on its head and has six equal-sized eyes (most spiders have eight eyes). Brown recluse spiders are usually found in secluded, dry, sheltered areas such as underneath structures logs, or in piles of rocks or leaves. If a brown recluse spider wanders indoors or in your tent, they may be found in dark areas, shoes, etc.

The brown recluse spider cannot bite humans without some form of counter pressure, for example, through unintentional contact that traps the spider against the skin. Bites may cause a stinging sensation with localized pain. A small white blister usually develops at the site of the bite. The venom of a brown recluse can cause a severe lesion by

destroying skin tissue (skin necrosis). This skin lesion will require professional medical attention.

Recent studies have begun to question the toxicity of hobo spider venom. Comparisons of venom from US found spiders against that of European found spiders (where they are not considered venomous) show very little difference. Additionally a number of studies show that there are virtually no cases of venomous spider bites, resulting in necrosis, where the offending spider has been caught and shown to be a hobo spider. But as the CDC still includes this species as a venomous spider found in the USA, we will include it here. The ***hobo spider*** is found throughout the Pacific Northwest. It is large and brown with a distinct pattern of yellow markings on its abdomen. Unlike many other similar looking spiders, hobo spiders do not have dark bands on their legs. To catch their prey, hobo spiders build funnel webs in holes, cracks, and recesses. They may be found in the outdoors in fallen trees, trash piles, etc. Hobo spiders do not climb like most spiders but are fast runners. These spiders are much more likely to attack if provoked or threatened. The bite of a hobo spider may go unnoticed; however a moderate to severe, slow-healing wound will develop.

Symptoms

Symptoms associated with spider bites can vary from minor to severe. Although extremely rare, death can occur in the most severe cases. Possible symptoms resulting from a spider bite include the following:

- Itching or rash
- Pain radiating from the site of the bite
- Muscle pain or cramping
- Reddish to purplish color or blister
- Increased sweating

- Difficulty breathing
- Headache
- Nausea and vomiting
- Fever
- Chills
- Anxiety or restlessness
- High blood pressure

Recommendations for Protecting Responders

Protect responders from dangerous spider bites by training them on:

- Their risk of exposure to spiders
- How to identify spiders
- How to prevent exposure to spiders
- What they should do if they are bitten by a spider

Prevention

Responders can take the following preventive steps:

- Inspect or shake out any clothing, shoes, towels, or equipment before use.
- Wear protective clothing such as a long-sleeved shirt and long pants, hat, gloves, and boots when handling stacked or undisturbed piles of materials.
- Minimize the empty spaces between stacked materials.
- Remove and reduce debris and rubble from around the outdoor work areas.
- Trim or eliminate tall grasses from around outdoor work areas.
- Store apparel and outdoor equipment in tightly closed plastic bags.
- Keep your tetanus boosters up-to-date. Spider bites can become infected with tetanus spores.

First Aid

Responders should take the following steps if they are bitten by a spider:

- Stay calm. Identify the type of spider if it is possible to do so safely. Identification will aid in medical treatment.
- Wash the bite area with soap and water.
- Apply a cloth dampened with cold water or filled with ice to the bite area to reduce swelling.
- Elevate bite area if possible.
- Do not attempt to remove venom.
- Notify your supervisor.
- Immediately seek professional medical attention.

Posting information at the Command Post and mentioning precautions at briefings is a very good idea.

Ticks

Ticks are small arachnids, the same family as spiders. Like all arachnids, adult ticks have eight legs. Ticks are ectoparasites (external parasites). They survive on the blood of mammals, birds, and sometimes reptiles and amphibians. Ticks extract the blood by cutting a hole in the host's epidermis, into which they insert their hypostome, in order to keep the blood from clotting by excreting an anticoagulant or platelet aggregation inhibitor. Ticks are vectors (carriers and transmitters) of a number of diseases, including Lyme disease, Q fever, Colorado tick fever, Rocky Mountain spotted fever, and tick-borne meningoencephalitis.

Photo courtesy of www.scs-mall.com

Ticks find their hosts by detecting animals' breath and body odors, or by sensing body heat, moisture and vibrations. They are incapable of flying or jumping, but many tick species wait in a position known as "questing." While questing, ticks hold onto leaves and grass by their third and fourth pair of legs. They hold the first pair of legs outstretched, waiting to climb on to the host. When a host brushes the spot where a tick is waiting, it quickly climbs onto the host. Some ticks will attach quickly while others will wander looking for thinner skin like the ear, genitals and parts of the scalp. Depending on the species and the life stage, preparing to feed can take from ten minutes to two hours. On locating a suitable feeding spot, the tick grasps the skin and cuts into the surface.

Prevention

Preventing tick bites is performed in a manner similar to that of preventing mosquito bites:

- Determine the likelihood of encountering ticks where you will be operating.
- Wear protective clothing such as a long-sleeved shirt and long pants, hat, gloves, and boots. Be sure to tuck pants legs into boots, as temperature conditions allow. Hats with wide brims are better than "ball caps." Insect netting over the hat and covering the face and head down to the collar of the shirt/jacket is recommended in areas of heavy tick concentrations.
- Treat all outer-clothing with Permethrin® based insect repellent. **Do not allow the Permethrin® to come in direct contact with the skin**.
- Apply DEET or Picaridin® based insect to your entire body (skin), avoiding orifices and eyes. In this case use of the strongest concentration of DEET (without causing any irritation or reaction) is recommended.
- Conduct frequent "tick checks", including "buddy checks" (looking over each other for ticks).
- Remove clothing immediately upon returning from the outdoors. If the clothing

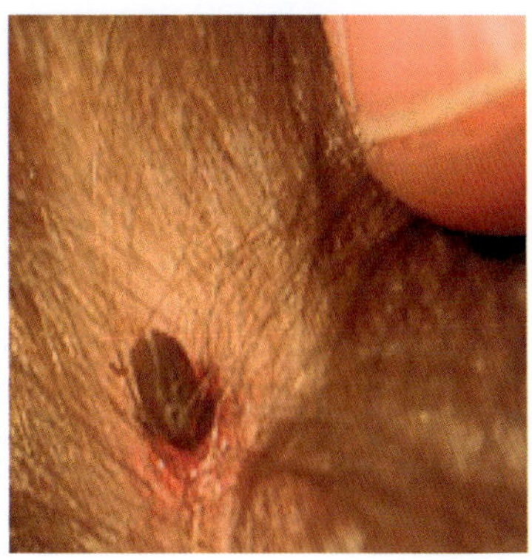

Photo courtesy of www.scs-mall.com

cannot be immediately laundered, store it in tightly closed plastic bags.

- Conduct body checks for any ticks that may have gotten under clothing.

Removal

In the event you suffer a tick bite, and the tick is still present/attached to the skin, it will be necessary to remove the tick. You will undoubtedly have heard numerous "old wives' tales and urban legends" on methods to remove ticks, but most experts agree there is really only one good way to remove a tick. In general, the best way to remove an adult tick is mechanically. To facilitate prompt removal, fine-tipped tweezers can be used to grasp the tick as close to the skin as possible and detach it by applying a steady upward force without crushing, jerking or twisting, in such a way as to avoid leaving behind mouthparts or provoking regurgitation of infective fluids into the wound. Proprietary tick removal tools are also available. It is important to disinfect the bite area thoroughly after removal of the tick. The tick can be stored and, in case of signs or symptoms of a subsequent infection, shown to a clinician for identification purposes together with details of where and when the bite occurred. If the tick's head and mouthparts are no longer attached to its body after removal, advanced medical procedures may be necessary to remove any parts that have been left behind.

Poisonous Plant Contact

Many native and exotic plants are poisonous to humans when ingested or if there is skin contact with plant chemicals. However, the most common problems with poisonous plants arise from contact with the sap oil of several ever-present native plants that cause an allergic skin reaction—poison ivy, poison oak, and poison sumac.

Poison ivy, poison oak, and poison sumac release an oil called urushiol when the leaf or other plant parts are bruised, damaged, or burned. When the oil gets on the skin an allergic reaction, referred to as contact dermatitis, occurs in most exposed people as an itchy

Poison Ivy

Poison Oak

Two Types of Poison Sumac

IMAGES COURTESY OF WWW.POISON-IVY.ORG

red rash with bumps or blisters. When exposed to 50 micrograms of urushiol, an amount that is less than one grain of table salt, 80 to 90 percent of adults will develop a rash. The rash, depending upon where it occurs and how broadly it is spread, may significantly impede or prevent a person from performing their assignment. Although over-the-counter topical medications may relieve symptoms for most people, immediate medical attention may be required for severe reactions, particularly when exposed to the smoke from burning these poisonous plants. Burning these poisonous plants can be very dangerous because the allergens can be inhaled, causing lung irritation. Examine the wood you gather for fires used to provide warmth, for cooking, for signaling, etc. to be sure no poisonous plants are attached.

Those involved in Search & Rescue, whether in the field or at IC, may be exposed to poisonous plants. Those responders that are in close proximity to forest fires or smoldering fires after a disaster are at additional risk because they could potentially develop rashes and lung irritation from contact with damaged plants or from burning poisonous plants. It is important to know about the risk of exposure to poisonous plants, how you can prevent exposures and protect yourselves, and what you should do if you come in contact with these plants.

U.S. Geographic Distribution—

One or more of the most common poisonous plant species are found throughout the United States (except Alaska and Hawaii). These plants can be found in forests, fields, wetlands and along streams, road sides, and even in urban environments, such as parks and backyards.

Poison Ivy

Poison Ivy can be found all across the United States, except California, Alaska, and Hawaii.

Maps in this section courtesy of U.S. Department of Agriculture

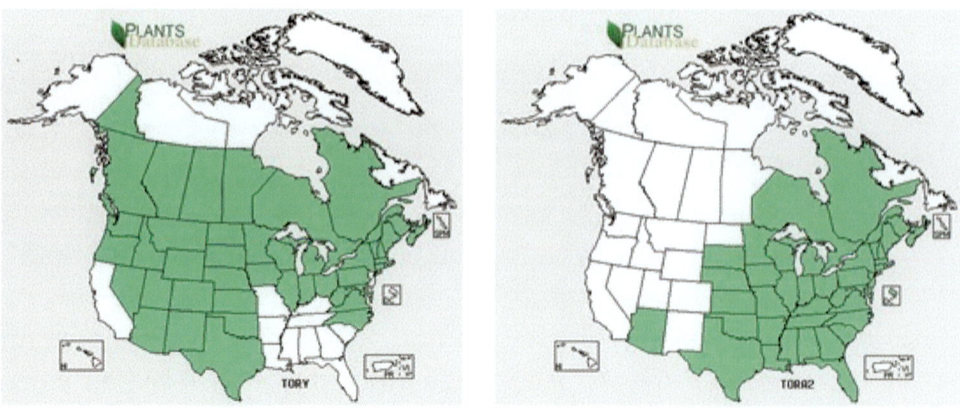

Western poison ivy (left); Eastern poison ivy (right)

Poison Oak

Poison Oak can be found primarily in the Southeast and the West Coast of the United States.

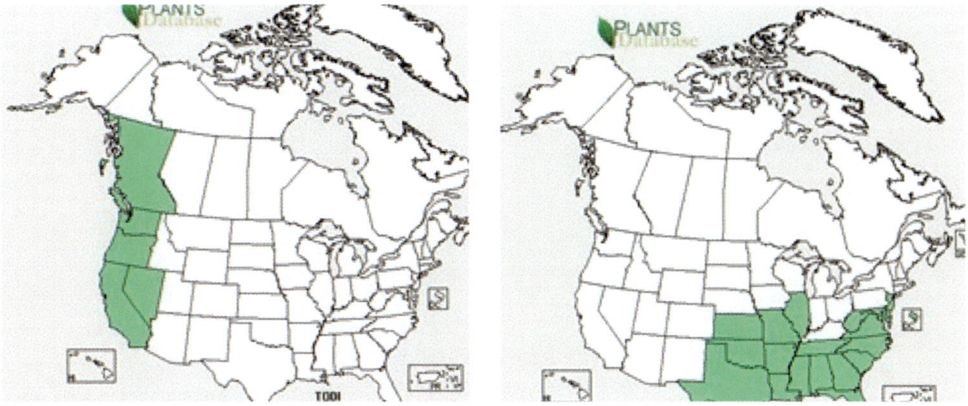

Pacific poison oak (left); Atlantic poison oak (right)

Poison Sumac

Poison Sumac is abundant along the Mississippi River and boggy areas of the Southeast United States.

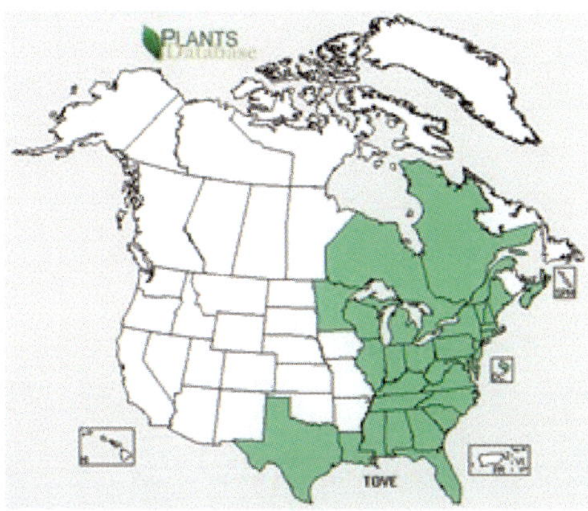

Plant Identification

The old saying "*Leaves of three, Let it be!*" is a helpful reminder for identifying poison ivy and oak, but not poison sumac which usually has clusters of 7–13 leaves. Even poison ivy and poison oak may have more than three leaves and their form may vary greatly depending upon the exact species encountered, the local environment, and the season. Being able to identify local varieties of these poisonous plants throughout the seasons and differentiating them from common nonpoisonous look-a-likes are the major keys to avoiding exposure.

Poison Ivy

Photos courtesy of U.S. Department of Agriculture

- Eastern poison ivy is typically a hairy, ropelike vine with three shiny green (or red in the fall) leaves budding from one small stem
- Western poison ivy is typically a low shrub with three leaves that does not form a climbing vine
- May have yellow or green flowers and white to green-yellow or amber berries

Poison Oak

Photos courtesy of U.S. Department of Agriculture

- Typically a shrub with leaves of three, similar to poison ivy
- Pacific poison oak may be vine-like
- May have yellow or green flowers and clusters of green-yellow or white berries

Poison Sumac

Photos courtesy of U.S. Department of Agriculture

- Woody shrub that has stems that contain 7-13 leaves arranged in pairs
- May have glossy, pale yellow, or cream-colored berries

Exposure

Responders may become exposed to urushiol through:

- Direct contact with the plant
- Indirect contact, such as touching tools, search canines or equines, or clothing that have urushiol on them
- Inhalation of particles containing urushiol from burning plants

Symptoms

Signs or symptoms associated with dermal contact with poisonous plants may include:

- Red rash within a few days of contact
- Possible bumps, patches, streaking, or weeping blisters (blister fluids are not contagious)
- Swelling
- Itching

Recommendations for Protecting Responders

You should know about:

- Your risk of exposure to poisonous plants
- How to identify poisonous plants
- How to prevent exposure to poisonous plants
- What to do if exposed to poisonous plants.

Prevention

Responders can prevent contact with poisonous plants by taking these steps:

- Wear long sleeves, long pants, boots, and gloves.
  - Wash exposed clothing separately in hot water with detergent.
- Barrier skin creams, such as a lotion containing bentoquatum, may offer some protection before contact.
  - Barrier creams should be washed off and reapplied twice a day.
- After use, clean tools with rubbing alcohol (isopropanol or isopropyl alcohol) or soap and lots of water. Urushiol can remain active on the surface of objects for up to 5 years.
  - Wear disposable gloves during this process.
- Do not burn plants that may be poison ivy, poison oak, or poison sumac.
  - Inhaling smoke from burning plants can cause severe allergic respiratory problems.

First Aid

Responders who have come in contact with poisonous plants should:

- Immediately rinse skin with rubbing alcohol, specialized poison plant washes, degreasing soap (such as dishwashing soap) or detergent, and lots of water.
  - Rinse frequently so that wash solutions do not dry on the skin and further spread the urushiol.
- Scrub under nails with a brush.
- Apply wet compresses, calamine lotion, or hydrocortisone cream to the skin to reduce itching and blistering.
  - Follow the directions on any creams and lotions. Do not apply to broken skin, such as open blisters.
  - Oatmeal baths may relieve itching.
- An antihistamine such as diphenhydramine (Benadryl) can be taken to help relieve itching.
  - Follow directions on the package.
  - Drowsiness may occur.

- If responder's children come in contact with work clothing contaminated with urushiol, a pediatrician should be contacted to determine appropriate dosage of medication.
- In severe cases or if the rash is on the face or genitals, seek professional medical attention.
    - Call 911 or go to a hospital emergency room if the responder is suffering a severe allergic reaction, such as swelling or difficulty breathing, or has had a severe reaction in the past.

The Medical Unit must be prepared for this possible issue by stocking proper soap, brushes, anti-itch cream or medications. They must also be prepared to detain responders in rehab until monitoring is complete for even moderate reactions if there is any question as to how severe an anaphylactic reaction may be. Report issues to the Safety Officer so an emphasis can be placed on the prevention and treatment of poisonous plants during meetings and briefings.

Eating plants during a SAR Tactic

There should never be a situation during a SAR mission that you will need to decide which plants you can eat to survive. Numerous poisonous plants appear similar to edible plants, so be cautious. Additionally, you will find incorrect – dangerous – information about poisonous plants such as "it's safe to eat what the animals eat". Such myths need to be ignored since animals can eat plants that are poisonous to humans. Another piece of misinformation is that if you boil a plant, the toxins will be destroyed or removed. The truth is that boiling doesn't remove all toxins in all plants.

If you aren't 100% sure of what a plant is, don't touch it or eat it. Eating the wrong plant can kill you! Nausea and vomiting, diarrhea, abdominal cramps, depressed heartbeat and respiration, headaches and hallucinations are all symptoms of poisoning. Consult several reliable sources for the plants in your area since information differs from one source to another. A course with field trips is recommended over just reading a book. Don't take a chance on turning the search or rescue focus from the victim to the Responder!

Urban Search & Rescue

Urban Search and Rescue (US&R) involves the location, rescue (extrication), and initial medical stabilization of victims trapped in confined spaces. Structural collapse is most often the cause of victims being trapped, but victims may also be trapped in transportation accidents, mines, mud slides, sink holes, collapsed trenches, and volcano activity.

Photos courtesy of www.fema.gov

As you might determine from the above description "true" US&R is best left to the trained professionals. It is likely, however, that missing and lost person SAR responders will frequently be called upon to assist in locating subjects in an urban area that does not involve collapsed structure or confined space searches. **Once again, leave specialty search tactics to the trained professionals!** In the last decade the most frequent subject type involved in a search & rescue incident has been the dementia victim (e.g. Alzheimer's sufferer). This has been followed by missing/lost children. When considering these types of subjects it is easy to see that we will often find ourselves called to search for them in urban (high density) and suburban (medium density) environments. You must be aware of safety concepts when operating in higher density structure and population areas.

Hazards

Let's look at some hazards almost certain to be encountered when searching in the urban environment:

- Traffic—It is easy to become so focused on the search tactic that the responder blocks out the presence of motor vehicles operating in the search area. With myriad alleys, garages, and lanes, vehicles can rapidly appear without warning or notice.
- Construction Sites—Numerous hazards will be encountered here. Holes, dangerous tools, sharp materials, "hazmat" type substances, etc. must be planned for and considered by the responder prior to and while operating in the search area.
- Culverts—These hazards are best left to professionals unless you can simply look through (end to end) the culvert or drain. If the responders elect to enter one they must protect themselves from hazardous debris, dangerous animals and insects, toxic gases and injuries sustained from operating in tight settings.
- Crime & Drug Related Activities—The best way to protect the responder is simply to not operate in areas known to have crime and/or drug activities ongoing. If it is necessary to enter or search in areas where criminal activity is expected, the search unit MUST be accompanied by Law Enforcement Officers.
- Low/High Angle Terrain—When responders operate in an urban environment they will frequently encounter sloping terrain. Consider the slope of the ground on the side of an interstate highway. Falls resulting in serious injury could easily happen while trying to descend from the road level. If descent is successfully achieved, will the responder be able to ascend without assistance? In many cases this type of terrain (search) should be left to resources trained and equipped to operate in this terrain environment.
- Private Property—This challenge can be encountered in any environment, but is certain to be a factor in urban and

suburban environments. The same basic rules apply: The field responder is not allowed to enter property without permission of the owner unless there is obvious exigent circumstances where the subject will suffer serious injury or death unless immediate access and rescue is made. Even when the responder can see the subject on the property, it is better to have law enforcement accompany the unit onto the property if the owner cannot be contacted quickly enough.

Summary

Field responders must be trained and practiced to safely operate in any environment. They must also be properly equipped to react to safety issues that will be encountered. Complacency must not be tolerated. It is easy to overlook safety factors, especially when operating in the familiar environment of the city/town we live in or the woods we recreate in. That is when injury, illness and even fatalities will occur. Safety in all environments is our first priority and requires unending vigilance.

References

National Geographic-Various information on snakes http://animals.nationalgeographic.com/animals/reptiles/eastern-coral-snake/

Smithsonian National Zoo-Various information and Discussions http://nationalzoo.si.edu/

Arizona Game and Fish Department-Various information and Discussions www.azgfd.gov

FEMA URBAN SEARCH & RESCUE (US&R) 2014 http://www.fema.gov/urban-search-rescue

Tactical Medical Solutions Helios System www.tacmedsolutions.com

North American Rescue, LLC Hypothermia Prevention & Management Kit www.narescue.com

PMK Rescue Solutions. Treatment Application Band. Contact: Dave Cruz www.promedkits.com

Mayo Clinic-Various medical treatments
National Weather Service-Various information on weather
NOAA, National Oceanic and Atmospheric Administration-Various information on weather
University of Virginia, Climatology offices-Various information on weather
Web MD-Various discussions of medical treatments
Centers for Disease Control and Prevention-Various information and discussions
www.cdc.gov, Atlanta, GA
The Handbook for Managing Land Search Operations (2001)
Robert "Skip" Stoffel, *ERI Publications & Training*, Cashmere WA

SAR Ready Pack—The House on Your Back & Other Outdoor Gear

5

Objectives

Courtesy of The North Face

- Determine the importance of the SAR Ready Pack relative to safety and comfort away from Base
- Describe the different types (construction) of packs and appropriateness for use in SAR
- Differentiate between Urban, 24 Hour, 72 Hour and Base Packs
- Discuss typical contents of a 24 Hour (non-urban) Ready Pack
- Discuss natural and synthetic shelter material and construction, including those carried in Ready Packs
- Explain the benefits and limitations of different pack hydration systems
- Describe the different fuel types and construction of stoves suitable for SAR field use
- Discuss the use of headlamps and flashlights and the limitations of each.
- Discuss additional field gear, including:
  - Compasses
  - Multi-Purpose Knives
  - Repair Supplies/Gear
  - Hygiene and Sanitation
  - First Aid Supplies

The Importance of the SAR Ready Pack

Being prepared is a key responsibility of the Search & Rescue Field Responder. Carrying the appropriate equipment, whether or not it is needed, is also key to safety and comfort in the field. It may be tempting to leave your pack behind, to lessen the load or to depend on the contents of someone else's pack, but nothing will prepare you for the unexpected except your own equipment. SAR Field Responders are responsible for providing their own equipment and for ensuring their own safety. The SAR Ready Pack recommendations in this chapter have been developed to assist you in assembling your own pack which will provide you with the essentials you may need in the event of a delay or emergency in the field.

The contents of the SAR Ready Pack are intended to provide you with shelter, food, water, fire and emergency medical care in the field—a virtual house on your back. Safety is first, but many of the items in the back will assist with your comfort as well. It is essential that you carry everything that you need, but it is also important not to carry too much. The physical and emotional strain on field responders is immense, even without the added burden of a much too heavy pack. The recommendations in this chapter have been developed to provide with you the essentials, but not excess, making it even more important that all field responders are prepared with their own equipment. One more thought before proceeding…Look for items with more than one use. This will help keep your pack lighter and more compact.

The SAR Ready Pack—The Backpack

The SAR Ready Pack can be one of many types of packs/backpacks. The standard recommendation is that it is of an internal frame construction with a capacity of 1800—3000 cubic inches. However, different types and sizes of packs work well for different types and sizes of people. It is important to research the different types and sizes of packs, try several on, and find one that FITS. Fit is one of the most, if not the most, important features to consider when choosing a pack.

Courtesy of REI, Inc.

If the pack doesn't fit, the field responder will be distracted, uncomfortable and under additional physical stress. A pack that does not fit can cause rubbing, chafing and blisters in a number of areas.

An internal frame is recommended as this type of pack provides for freedom of movement and good balance. The fit is close to the back with a low center of gravity. External frames may also be used, however, they tend to be rigid and inflexible. External frames are most useful for carrying extremely large loads. Remember, the most important feature to consider when purchasing a pack is fit.

Some of the features to consider when purchasing a pack include:

- Weight—the weight of your pack is important. If the pack feels heavy when empty, you may want to consider a lighter choice.
- Ease of access to your supplies—pockets, pouches, loops and zippers are different from bag to bag. Find one that makes it easy for you to organize, find and retrieve your supplies.
- Straps and Pads—a variety of straps are available to aid in your comfort and the distribution of weight from your pack:
  - Padded shoulder straps
  - Sternum Strap
  - Waist or hip suspension straps
  - Side compression straps
  - Lumbar pad
- Waterproof or non-waterproof—you may choose a waterproof pack, a

Courtesy of REI, Inc.

pack with an integrated rain cover, or you may prefer a non-waterproof pack that you can slip a trash bag over to keep dry, if needed.

- Adjustable torso length—assists in providing an exact fit
- Back panel mesh—aids in ventilation
- Internal or External Hydration—hydration sleeves or bladders are a convenient way to carry and access water. Pockets designed for water bottles should be included.
- Rip-stop material—prevent loss of your essentials with fabric that will not easily rip or tear. Double-stitching and other reinforcing material are also helpful.
- Loading method—does the pack load from the top or the panel (front or sides)
- Color—pick a color that enhances your ability to be seen from afar. Lime green, yellow and orange may not be your favorite colors, but they are wise choices for a pack color. These colors can be seen from far away and do not easily blend into the surroundings.
- Men's/Women's—many packs are designed specifically to fit men or women.
- Price—the backpack you choose can be an investment, or it can be chosen on a budget. Invest in the pack that is right for you and has the right fit. It is one of the most important pieces of equipment you will carry. A good pack will last for many years.

The SAR Ready Pack—A Pack for Different Purposes

The SAR Ready Pack described in this chapter and outlined in Appendix is a 24-hour pack. It is intended to provide for your needs should you be delayed in the field for a period of up to 24 hours. Your pack is not intended to provide for anyone but yourself. Each SAR Field Responder is responsible for their own safety, their own pack, and the contents of their pack. The 24-Hour SAR Ready Pack is the most common type of pack you will carry. The 24-Hour Ready Pack can be adapted for other purposes as well.

The SAR 24-Hour Ready Pack can be supplemented with additional supplies to make a 48-hour or 72-hour pack. By adding, food, water, additional clothing and medical supplies, you can easily adapt your 24-hour pack to serve longer periods of time. If your field work will take you far from your base camp, or lead you into possible severe weather conditions, you may consider a 48-hour or 72-hour pack. Under most circumstances, 24-hour Ready Pack will be sufficient. The SAR Ready Pack can easily be improvised to accommodate different circumstances and missions.

All SAR Ready Packs should contain at least the minimum equipment required to meet medical and survival needs for the Field Responder. A first aid kit should be part of any Ready Pack. The rest of the contents of a Ready Pack can be adapted for time, use and mission. An Urban Ready Pack will contain much of the same equipment as the 24-Hour Ready Pack, but not all the items and not necessarily the same quantities. The Urban Ready Pack is typically smaller and lighter than the 24-Hour Ready Pack. If you are searching in an urban environment, you may want to use the same pack but remove non-essential items. For instance, in the urban environment you may choose to depend on matches and leave a fire flint behind. For a wilderness pack, both matches and an alternate fire source would be essential. It is key to know your environment, your personal abilities and always consider the unexpected when removing any contents from your SAR Ready Pack. The items you remove could be the ones you needed most—you never can be overly prepared, but you can quickly get into a hazardous situation if you are under prepared.

When you have completed a mission, some of your resources will be depleted—certainly water and food, even on the shortest of missions. It is important to have a reserve of extra supplies available at base camp, your car or another accessible location, so that you may restock your SAR Ready

Pack between missions. For this purpose, you may want to consider a Base Pack. A Base Pack is exactly that—a pack that remains at base with extra supplies that can be used to replenish or supplement your SAR Ready Pack. A large duffle bag or army-type backpack are useful for this purpose. Knowing what is in your pack and having your pack ready to go at all times is the Field Responder's responsibility. The Base Pack assists in preparedness. The Base Pack should contain extra water, food, medical supplies and clothing at the very least. Extra clothing should include clothing for all types of weather and seasons. It is impossible to predict when you may get hot or cold, not matter where you are. Always be prepared for rain and lots of it—just when you think it will never rain, you will certainly find yourself in a deluge. You may also want to consider essential items such as extra batteries, replacement flashlight, extra safety goggles and an extra pair of shoes. At the end of every mission, your SAR Ready Pack should be prepared and ready to go for the next mission.

The SAR Ready Pack—What to Pack

The SAR Ready Pack Minimum 24 Hour Personal Equipment List can be found in the Appendix section. The list defines the items you are required to have in your pack at all times. All SARResponder™ Field exams require a pack check to ensure you are carrying the minimum equipment. If you are missing even one item, say a safety pin, you will fail that portion of the field test. The equipment list was created to provide you with the minimum amount of supplies you will need to manage an emergency situation. By omitting items from the list, you are putting yourself and others at risk. Some of the items on the list are discussed in other chapters. Pay special attention to the chapters in this book on clothing and safety. The clothing you pack and wear may be the difference between being miserable and being comfortable.

For convenience, you may want to organize your consideration of ready pack items in broad categories. While we will discuss some specific items in this chapter, this list will give you a reference to start the discussion on ready pack contents:

- **Storage**—In this category we list the pack itself, plus items such as resealable storage bags for safe-keeping (keeps items clean and dry until use) and evidence collection, as well as, lawn/leaf bags which can be used as emergency shelter.
- **First Aid and Personal Medications**—This will be among your most often used category. Remember, it will be used to care for you in the event you are injured or become ill. Your teammates' supplies are for their use, not yours!
- **Personal Clothing and Protection**—Remember this is your "first line of defense" against environmental conditions. Choose wisely!
- **Water and Hydration Systems**—These survival items include water bladders (e.g. Camelback®), Drinking Bottles, Purification Methods, etc. Don't leave home without them!
- **Tracking and Clue Gear**—Items such as Tracking Stick, Measuring Device, Pad & Pencil, Flagging Tape, etc.
- **Lighting Systems**—Flashlights, Headlamps, Lanterns, Light Sticks, etc.
- **Fire and Cooking Gear**—Fuel, Firestarter Materials, Stoves, Candles, Utensils (especially a multi-purpose knife), etc.
- **Rope Systems**—See Chapter 12 for details, but this gear serves numerous purposes.
- **Navigation Gear**—Compass, GPS, Pace Counter, Grid Reader, Distance Ruler, etc.
- **Comfort Items**—Toilet Tissue, Moist Wipes, Sunscreen, Lip Balm, Insect Repellent, Food & Snacks.

Now let's look at some of the specific items that you should consider including in your pack:

Personal Medical Kit

The medical supplies you carry in your pack may be one of the most important items you carry. Field Responders searching in urban and wilderness environments are subject to small cuts and bruises from the most benign of situations. Thorns, nails, barb wire, and staples

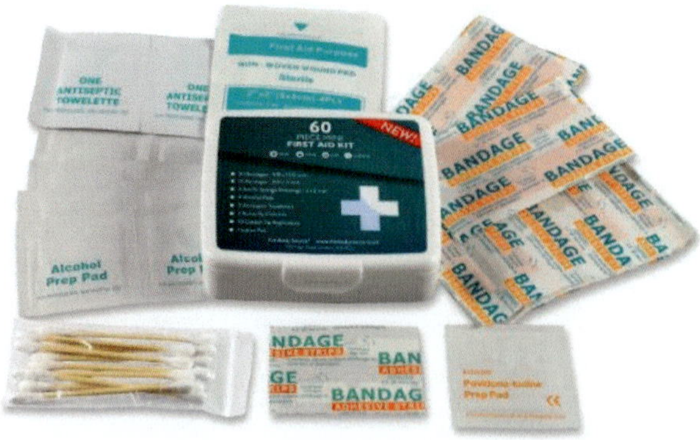

COURTESY OF AMAZON.COM

are common items that can create a bothersome wound at base camp or in the field. The moleskin in your first aid supplies will provide you with relief from painful blisters. Even if your boots are well-worn and fit nicely, in wet, hot or very long periods of walking, anyone is subject to the unexpected blister. A bad blister can inhibit your ability to search if not treated quickly.

Gauze, tweezers, sterile dressing, antiseptic ointment and bandages will all assist you in treating and protecting cuts and abrasions. It is tempting to purchase a pre-packed first aid kit that will contain most of the items you require. Pre-packaged kits, however, tend to be very expensive. You can buy full-size packages of all of the items without spending more or much more than a kit with the bare minimum supplies. Remember, your personal medical kit will have to be replenished frequently, as you use items in the kit. Having the full size packages of all of the items will allow you plenty of supplies for restocking. You may already have many of the items in your medical kit at home. Use what you have and conserve your dollars for more expensive investment items like a good pack and a good pair of boots.

The personal medical kit requires you to carry medicine such as aspirin, antacid tablets, antihistamine and any personal medication that you require over a 24-hour period. If you are allergic to certain plants or insects, such as poison ivy or bees, you will want to consider carrying an emergency allergic reaction kit (i.e. an epinephrine injection pen). An emergency allergic reaction can be life-threatening and distract from the search mission resources deployed for the mission. Being prepared may save yourself and the search mission itself. All of the medications you carry in your medical kit have expiration dates. Be mindful of the expiration dates and replenish expired supplies. If you challenge the SARResponder™ 2 certification exam, you will not pass the pack check with expired supplies in your pack, besides the risk of using ineffective medications.

Personal SAR Equipment—Clothing and Body Protection

Included in the SAR Resource Minimum 24 Hour Personal Equipment List are items required in order to ensure a high degree of safety in the field. These items include clothing, safety goggles, flagging tape, headlamp, flashlight, knife, rainsuit, gaiters, gloves, sunglasses, whistle and much more. Providing yourself with adequate protection in field will help prevent injury and discomfort. Refer to Chapter 3 for more detailed information on SAR clothing

Eye protection is recommended at all times, and mandatory at night. Field Responders have a lot to focus on during a search—direction, wind, location, time, team members, etc.—you never know when the unexpected branch will jump out and poke you in the eye. Daytime eye protection should include safety wear that protects your eyes from the sun. 100% UV protection is required for your SAR Ready Pack. Your fashion shades may not provide enough coverage around your eyes nor the required UV protection. It is important to select eye protection that protects your eyes from all directions and provides UV protection. Standard construction-type safety goggles available at home improvement stores are perfectly acceptable for day or night use. For the daytime, find a similar type of tinted glasses/goggles that will protect your eyes from all directions. They should provide 100% UV protection. If you wear prescription eyeglasses or contacts, you will need to have those available as well. Instead of investing in prescription safety glasses, consider wearing your glasses under your safety goggles or switch to contacts.

Head protection may include a hat to help shield your eyes from the sun or a helmet for searching buildings, rubble piles, or any situation in which something falling on your head or injury to the head is a concern. In colder weather, a hat to keep your head and ears

warm is essential. Your personal equipment should include several types of head gear and extras. On a windy day, losing a hat is a high probability. Wearing the right equipment in the right situation is key to keeping safe. In some areas, netting that goes over your hat or person may also be used to assist in combating insects.

Most agencies now require field responders to use ANSI compliant helmets. A wide variety of models are available, providing mission based flexibility and environmental based comfort. Head injuries are the leading cause of fatalities in falls and accidents. Take precautions and always wear a helmet when on a SAR tactical assignment.

Personal SAR Equipment—Shelter

The contents of the SAR Ready Pack must include materials you will need to build an improvised shelter in the event you need to protect yourself and/or a subject from the elements. Wind, rain, sun, cold and snow are all problematic when extended amounts of time are spent in the field. You may need to build a shelter for sleeping, protecting a subject from the elements or for waiting out the weather. The SAR Resource Minimum 24 Hour Personal Equipment List requires an 8x10 plastic or nylon tarp. Tarps, along with a number of ties from rope, paracord or wire ties can make an adequate shelter. Plastic tarps are inexpensive, but less durable than a ripstop nylon coated tarp. Plastic tarps may easily tear from branches, wind or blowing debris. A nylon-coated tarp is preferred. Nylon-coated tarps are durable and can withstand rips, tears and wind. Some tarps come with grommets which make them even more durable, but heavier.

Courtesy of Kelty

While the equipment list only requires an 8x10 tarp, many backpacker supplies manufacturers today are making high-quality backpacking tarps. These tarps will cost you much more than a generic 8x10 tarp, but they are lightweight and often made of coated polyester, rip-stop nylon or other high quality materials. Backpacking tarps often come with stakes, tie-downs and a storage bag, making them very convenient. Some of these types of tarps require poles, which are often sold separately. Consider the weight of your Ready Pack before investing in poles for your tarp. Trees, branches, and other items found in the wilderness can be used to assist you in building your shelter without the use of poles.

Many search missions may take you far away from home and require you to spend several days at or near Base Camp. Your Base Camp Ready Pack should include some type of shelter you can rely on in the event you have to stay overnight. Your car is always an option for shelter and sleeping, but there is no guarantee that your car will be at Base Camp. For this reason, consider investing in a tent of some sort. Tents are not practical for Ready Packs as they tend to be heavier, bulkier and more expensive than tarps. However, at Base Camp a tent would be welcomed. Most tents require the use of poles which can be heavy and bulky. Some tents are designed to be used with trees or even backpacks as supports. Some factors to consider when purchasing a tent include:

- Warmth—size, fabric and design all impact the warmth of a tent. Generally, the smaller the tent, the warmer it will be. Double-walled tents provide the best insulation, making them warmer than single-walled tents.
- Weight—the total weight of a tent includes the tent, pegs, rope, poles, rainfly and any other features specific to the tent. The type of fabric can greatly impact the weight of a tent.
- Fabric—when choosing a fabric consider water-repellency/waterproofing, weight, resistance to wear, breathability and wind resistance.
- Size—many backpacking tents are small and lightweight. However, these types of packs do not provide any living space. Consider your need and expected use of a tent and select an option that will meet your needs.
- Poles—tents come with all types of pole configurations. Very small backpacking tents can be pole-free domed tents with

only enough space to lay down. Some tents have a single pole and other tents may have many poles. The more poles a tent has, the more difficult the set up and the heavier the load. Consider a tent that will be easy for you to manage alone and that will meet your personal needs.

- Price—tents are available in a wide range of prices. Choose an option that meets your needs and suits your budget.

It is possible to build a shelter from items found in the field whether manmade or natural. However, you will be much more comfortable and find it much easier to secure a shelter from the contents of your Ready Pack. In the event your tarp fails you or blows away, other items in your pack can be used to build an improvised shelter—clothing, rain gear, etc.

Personal SAR Equipment—Water and Hydration Systems

The SAR Resource Minimum 24 Hour Personal Equipment List requires every Field Responder to carry a hydration system, a 1 liter canteen or bottle and a water purification method. Water is vital to your safety and physical well-being in the field. The requirement to carry multiple water source options will protect you in the event of a ripped hydration bladder, lost canteen or a situation in which the water you carried was not enough. Water is the heaviest item in your ready pack, it should be carried in containers that are light, durable and strong.

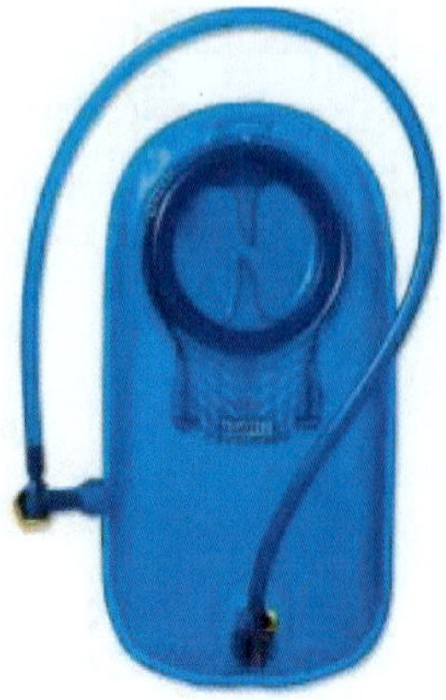

Water containers need to withstand SAR conditions whether it's heavy-duty field work or weather extremes. The most common types of water hydrations systems are Camelback® and Platypus®. Many field responders commonly refer to this type of hydration system by these brand names, but there are other brands available. These systems are often integrated with backpacks or hiking vests making them very convenient to carry. They consist of a plastic bag, or bladder, that holds water and is comfortably carried on the back. A hose leads from the bladder, out the backpack and over the shoulder. The hose is secured on the front of the shoulder of the field responder, making it convenient to grab the hose, bite on the valve, suck the water through and take a drink. Bladders come in many sizes. Choose an option that allows you to carry at least 2 liters of water. Integrated bladder hydration systems are the most convenient way to carry water, but it is possible to encounter technical difficulties with a bladder hydration system, so a second method of carrying water is required. The hose, bladder and bite valve of these hydration systems can fail and can freeze in very cold conditions. You may want to consider investing in an extra hose and valve to maintain as part of your Base Camp Ready Pack.

Water bottles and canteens are the second most convenient way to carry water. The water bottle type that you choose is a personal choice, but look for types that are durable, light and have a wide mouth. The most common type of water bottle is Nalgene®. Nalgene® is a brand of plastic products developed originally for laboratory use, including such items as jars, bottles, test tubes, graduated cylinders, and Petri dishes, that were shatterproof and lighter than glass. The properties of plastic products make them suitable for work with many substances in various temperature ranges. Nalgene® is a brand name of bottles and also a common name for polyethylene plastic. Water bottles can be worn on your person with the use of loops and hooks on your pack, loops on your belt, carrying holsters or carried inside your pack. However you choose to pack your water, it should be convenient for you to access and drink.

The third type of water system required in the 24 Hour Ready Pack is some sort of water purification system. In the event of a long mission or a very hot day, you can easily deplete the full contents of your water source. Water purification systems can be in the form

Courtesy of REI, Inc.

of tablets, solutions, water bottles, or "pens." Tablets and solutions are very easy and convenient to carry, but they can result in a metallic or bad taste. Many tablets and solutions are iodine-based. Ensure you do not have an allergy to iodine before choosing this method. Water purification bottles are convenient, but may contain many components and parts. Water purification bottles require hand-pumping and commonly used a carbon filtration systems. Other water purification bottle systems may include a purification pen or they may use another method of purification. Purification pens use Ultraviolet (UV-C) light rays to safely sterilize clear water by destroying 99.99% of protozoa (including Giardia and Cryptosporidia), bacteria and even viruses. SteriPEN® is a brand name of purification pens designed to protect you from risks that cause botulism, cholera, dysentery and typhoid, just to name a few. They can be purchased separately or as a part of a water bottle purification system As always, choose the type that best meet your needs and situation keeping weight, durability and price in mind.

Personal SAR Equipment—Fire and Cooking Gear

The SAR Resource Minimum 24 Hour Personal Equipment List includes a device/stove that will allow you to heat water. You will also need to carry food that will replenish your body's needs over a 24 Hour period. A small stove can be used for warmth, cooking or to boil water. A larger stove should be considered for use at Base Camp. Many types of stoves and fuels are available, and as with other equipment, choose the type of stove that is best suited to your needs and environment. Factors to consider when choosing a stove include:

- Weight—another 3 pounds added to your pack may feel like 10 on your back on a long walk on a hot day. Consider the weight of the stove and the fuel.
- Size—stoves are available in a wide range of sizes. A stove used in the field will be much smaller than one chosen for base camp.
- Fuel—stoves are available in a range of fuel types. Choose the fuel type that is best suited to your environment and your needs.
- Repair and Maintenance—all stoves require repair and maintenance. Consider the extra supplies that your will need to maintain and repair your stove. Some options may require more tools and fuel than others.
- Environment—consider the environments you are expected to typically search in and choose a stove that is suited to your environment. If you are deployed on many missions in the plains, especially on windy days, you may want to consider a stove that includes a wind screen. If you are deployed in very cold environments, you may want to consider the effect of cold on the different types of fuel before choosing a stove.
- Price—as with all SAR equipment, stoves are available in range of prices from very budget-friendly to very expensive. Choose a stove that meets your needs and balances your budget.

Chemical fire stoves are common and can be practical for infrequent use in the field. These types of stoves use Sterno, Canned "heat" (i.e. canned gel), or heat tabs to produce heat. Some of these fuels are heavy and short-lived. They would not be suited to cooking a full meal. Newer heat tablets are available that burn clean, generate intense heat and provide a longer burn time than older methods.

Courtesy of REI, Inc.

Other stoves use liquid fuels. Alcohol stoves are lightweight and easy to start but have low heat output. Some stoves burn white gasoline, kerosene or a combination of both. These types of stoves can be lightweight, have a controllable heat output but require priming and special handling. Gasoline is extremely volatile especially in an enclosed space, such as a tent. Kerosene is less volatile than other liquid fuels. However, kerosene requires separate priming, usually with alcohol, and can have a dirty, sooty residue and bothersome odor. Several companies manufacture their own brand of camp fuel that is less volatile and tends to burn cleaner than kerosene or white gasoline. Camp fuels are widely available and easier to obtain than white gasoline.Gas cartridge stoves use liquefied gas, such as propane or butane, under pressure in sealed containers. When pressure is released, liquefied gas boils, turning to a flammable gas. The canisters in which liquefied gases are stored must be strong to withstand the pressure of the gas which also means a heavy canister. However, gas cartridge stoves are convenient, easy to use and do not require priming. Gas cartridge stoves provide the best weight to heat ratio, but also the most expensive fuel.

When choosing a stove for use at Base Camp, you have the same options as those discussed for stoves for use in your Ready Pack. Depending on the environment, you may also choose a wood-burning stove. If wood is readily available, it provides you with a convenient, inexpensive and reliable heat source. Stoves chosen for Base Camp are not required to be carried in your 24 Hour Ready Pack; and therefore, they can be heavier, have a larger cooking area and have the desired type of fuel, regardless of weight.Whether choosing a stove for a Ready Pack or Base Camp, consider that the main danger is overheating the fuel. Familiarize yourself with any stove prior to its use. Read the manufacturer's recommendations and safety instructions. Ensure you know the proper priming, lighting and operation of any stove prior to its use. Additionally, provide a safety briefing to anyone who will be using your stove prior to leaving them to

Courtesy of REI, Inc.

manage it. Be prepared in the event of an accident with a stove or fire and have a plan of action to mitigate an accident.

If you find yourself having to build a shelter in the field, you may also need to build a fire. The 24 Hour Ready Pack requires each field responder to carry fire-starting material, matches, a candle, and a lighter. It is entirely possible that all of these methods of lighting a fire could fail in extreme weather conditions, therefore, additional starting materials such as a fire-starting flint and some tinder materials is also recommended.

Personal SAR Equipment—Head Lamps and Flashlights

The SAR Minimum 24 Hour Personal Equipment List requires every field responder to carry a headlamp and a flashlight. Having a light source available is paramount to safety at night, but is also convenient for daytime use when searching dark areas, deep vegetation and looking into tunnels and under bridges.

With today's LED lighting systems, we have reliability not seen in the past. Versatile headlamps offer spot and area lighting, and frequently include colored lighting to help preserve night vision. But these are "mechanical" devices that can fail. It is strongly recommended that you carry a second source of lighting. That second source should be a handheld flashlight which will give you flexibility in lighting clues such as when using tracking tactics.

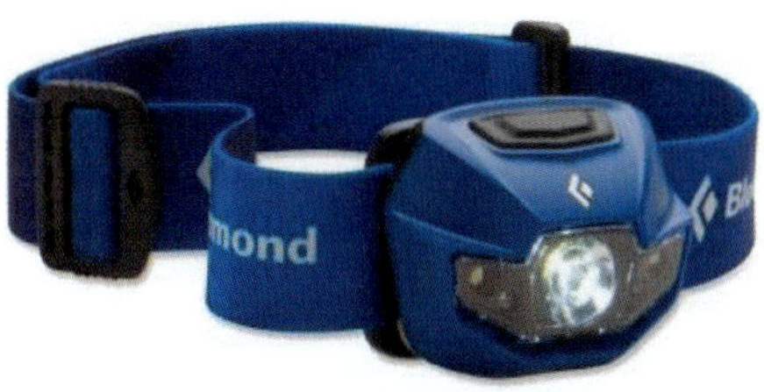

Courtesy of Black Diamond

An additional lighting source that has proven valuable to field responders is the lighting stick. These chemical devices provide substantial light, without batteries, for up to 12 hours. They can be used to identify teammates, clue locations and personal gear in addition to being a reliable, inexpensive light source.

Personal SAR Equipment—Rope Systems

In Chapter 12, we will discuss rope and rescue systems in great detail. When evaluating this category of items for inclusion in your pack, consider all the techniques reviewed in that chapter. Additionally, rope and associated gear can be very helpful in improvisation. Examples include shelter construction and pack repairs.

Personal SAR Equipment—Comfort and Hygiene Items

Whether you are in the field for four hours or four days, there are some items, you will learn, just shouldn't be left behind. Consider toilet tissue. If you find you need to relieve yourself of bodily waste, you will regret not bringing some when clean up time arrives! Many field responders will also pack a plastic hand trowel. This item can be very useful in proper disposal of human waste. And remember, expulsion of bodily waste should occur at least 60 meters (approximately 200 feet) from any water source and at least 30 meters (100 feet) away from a trail. Moist towelettes are a comfort item that is lightweight and small. Yet, when you need to wipe the sweat from your face and body, they provide great relief.

Food and snacks are in this category, but are also considered necessities. SAR field work requires substantial calories to maintain energy levels. You should consider two types of nutritional support for carry in your pack. First, healthy snacks that can be consumed on the go. Trail mix, granola bars, etc., can be consumed without thought allowing you to continue focusing on your search technique while eating. There is no excuse for getting light-headed from hunger when you can prevent this by carrying snacks.

The second form of nutrition comes in the form of easily prepared or pre-prepared foods. This includes items that can be prepared with only boiling water (such as: oatmeal, ramen, tea/coffee, dehydrated trail food, etc.) and fully cooked meals like MREs and survival food which frequently contain their own heat source. Having a substantial food type is especially comforting when working in cold and wet conditions. Since you will be likely to take some extended breaks

on longer or strenuous tactics, you can easily heat water or use the included heat source to prepare these heartier food choices.

Sunscreen is also very important to your comfort and personal safety. Sunscreen (also commonly known as sun screen, sunblock, suntan lotion, sunburn cream, sun cream or block out) is a lotion, spray, gel or other topical product that absorbs or reflects some of the sun's ultraviolet (UV) radiation on the skin exposed to sunlight and thus helps protect against sunburn. The sun may not be bright, there may be clouds in the sky, or it may not feel hot outside, but you can still get a sunburn. You can save yourself from much discomfort by protecting yourself from the sun. Additionally, exposure to the sun increases your risk of skin cancer, wrinkles and sagging skin and other skin conditions. For the best protection, a broad-spectrum (UVA/UVB) sunscreen is recommend. Broad-spectrum sunscreens block UVA radiation which can increase the rate of melanoma and photodermatitis. For maximum protection look for a sunscreen with an SPF of at least 30. Many medical professionals state that higher SPF is a waste of money as it offers little additional protection. Consult your physician for recommendations on sunscreen type and SPF. And remember…choose a sunscreen free of fragrances for maximum protecting from insects.

Insect repellent is essential for comfort and safety. Insects can crawl through your clothing, bite through your hat and fall into your shirt. Take every precaution possible to protect yourself from unwanted pests. There are non-chemical approaches to repelling insects, but if you have ever been in the woods in prairie or high plains, you know that none of this will protect you from millions of ticks with attitude. Ticks, fleas, chiggers, mosquitos and many other insects are prevalent and persistent in urban and wilderness environments. Many insects can spread disease, cause allergic reactions or create bothersome wounds, so protecting yourself from all of them is very important. Insect repellents containing DEET have been found to be most effective in combating insects. A repellant with the highest percentage of DEET (minimally 28% to 35%) tolerable to the individual responder is recommended, but remember that DEET is neuro-toxic. Only use a strength high enough to prevent bites/stings over longer periods of time. If you experience any type of skin reaction, cease using the product immediately and look for an alternative that does not contain DEET. One such alternative would be topical applications that contain Picaridin®. Picaridin® has shown to be effective in many cases.

Repellents applied to the skin are just the first step in protecting yourself from insects. You may also want to consider spraying your clothes, hat, boots, gaiters and pack with a product containing Permethrin®. Permethrin® is a common synthetic chemical, widely used as an insecticide, acaricide, and insect repellent. This chemical is found in common household insect sprays, but is not intended for use on the skin. Be very careful not to spray your skin with Permethrin®. By spraying all of your clothes and exposed gear with Permethrin®, and letting it dry before donning, you will greatly limit the ability of insects to crawl through your clothing or into your pack and bite you, or worse, go home with you.

Personal SAR Equipment—Navigation Equipment

Navigation is discussed in both *SARAware*™ and Chapter 8 of this text. Please refer to those sources for details on the navigation items you will need. As a word of caution, navigation is a primary skill to save your subject (or yourself!). The items you pack/carry are paramount to your ability to properly navigate. Be sure to secure them to your pack or person so as to not lose them. Additionally, even compasses will eventually fail (develop air bubbles, magnetic pointers will jam, etc.). Having a second compass, even a less expensive model can be "cheap insurance."

Personal SAR Equipment—General and Emergency Use Items

It can be very handy to have some repair items in your pack. Examples would include duct tape and wire ties. In keeping with the multiple use concept, these items can also be used to construct a shelter or improvised litter.

Courtesy of Leatherman

Another item that has improved dramatically in recent years is the knife or multi-tool. Experience has shown us there is no pressing need to carry a large sheath type knife for search & rescue purposes. Yet a small, simple folding knife would require us to carry additional tools such as screw drivers, pliers, scissors, saw, etc. An entire industry has developed with manufacturers trying to outdo each other on how many options they can include on a multi-tool and still have it fit in your pocket or belt case. It is an amazing story that began over 70 years ago with the Victorinox "Swiss Army knife." Today it is possible to acquire a quality multi-tool with 21 (twenty-one) different components for less money than dinner at a casual dining restaurant! We are hard pressed to recommend anything else when it comes to a SAR tool with multiple functions.

Summary

As stated in the title of this chapter, your ready pack is the "House on Your Back." It is essential that this "house" have all the items you and/or your subject might require. Yet it must be light and comfortable enough so as not to interfere with your functioning in the field. It must also contain enough comfort items to keep your morale up while working in some of the most debilitating conditions possible. To achieve this state, developing your personal ready pack will never stop. It is likely you will change packs, modify contents, add or delete items or entire groups, throughout your SAR career. Don't worry, though your pack will never reach perfection, it will get more comfortable while providing readiness for any eventuality, as you continue to refine it.

Reference

Camping & Wilderness Survival, The Ultimate Outdoors Book (1999)
Paul Tawrell, *Paul Tawrell*, Shelburne, VT/Green Valley, ON Canada

Wikipedia—The Free Encyclopedia, Various Discussions and Information (2015)
Wikimedia Foundation Inc., San Francisco, CA

www.rei.com – Numerous Articles (2014)
Recreational Equipment, Inc., Sumner, WA

www.sierratradingpost.com – The Buying Guides (2015)
Sierra Trading Post, Cheyenne, WY

Functioning in Diverse SAR Environments

6

Objectives

Courtesy of National Geographic

- Understand the importance of environmentally differentiating field responder functional and travel techniques
- Describe considerations of functioning in the Urban SAR environment
- Discuss general considerations of travel in the Wilderness SAR environment
- Identify travel skills in varying categories of Wilderness Environment topography including:
    - Trails
    - Brush
    - Grassy and Loose rock (Talus & Scree) Slopes
    - Hydrology
    - Desert
- Describe considerations and techniques of travel in snow
- Discuss the necessity of specialty training for functioning in certain environments

Working in diverse SAR environments

Many, if not most search & rescue resources are called to work in different environments. At times the tasking may include more than one. For instance, wooded/thick vegetation combined with medium to high density population areas. How we travel and the techniques we use to search will vary based on these environments. Regardless of which environment you routinely search in, it will help you to function better when you understand these different environments.

Search in the urban environment

If you are the typical reader of this text, you are concerned with learning the skills necessary to function in the wilderness setting or have focused your training to-date on preparing to search in the wilderness. Studies show, however, that the most frequent search we are called to perform is for the dementia (e.g. Alzheimer's) subject. As you might surmise, many of these incidents, in fact most of these incidents, occur in high density (urban and suburban) population environments. Unless you live in a truly rural/wilderness area, far from a town or population center, it is likely you will be called upon to participate in a search involving manmade structures and interacting with large numbers of people.

After having spent your life walking in towns and population centers, we won't spend time discussing "how to walk." But as always, our number one priority is safety. That is no different in the urban environment. The difference lies in the types of hazards and consideration of how to avoid them or mitigate the risks.

Courtesy of g1nab1na.blogspot.com

Imagine trying to perform search tactics in an area like the image above. We rarely can "close down" search segments in a population center. Will you be able to see holes in the pavement in time to avoid them? How will your search canine perform with vehicles and pedestrians congesting the area? Are you able to search in high crime areas, safely? Are you prepared to search for subjects who have an easy time becoming (intentionally or unintentionally) concealed? Let's look at some of those considerations to functioning in this environment:

- *Land Navigation*—You may be surprised to learn that searching in the urban environment still makes heavy use of GPS, so responders must be proficient in the use of GPS. Additionally, the urban searcher must be proficient in the use of city street maps, transit maps and other maps available for the metropolitan area.
- *Tracking*—Remembering that tracking is the finding of signs of human passage, it might be difficult to imagine how this is accomplished in the urban environment. Through awareness of the differences in sign from wilderness to urban areas, the searcher can become proficient in locating and following clues (in the form of sign) in densely populated metropolises. There are still "natural" track traps in the urban environment so the searcher must still be observant of opportunities to discover prints left from the subject, while still seeking evidence of "sign" the subject traveled in this segment.
- *Clue Consciousness*—This concept remains global in nature. In the urban environment (as in all environments) the searcher's task is to locate clues that will allow Search Management to conduct efficient operations leading to finding the subject. Clues that can be attributed to the subject will be included among all the clutter and debris found in population centers. Searchers in the urban environment must be especially observant and conscious of evidence/crime scene protection to determine a clue without disturbing the surrounding area.
- *Search Techniques*—Urban search tactics will be considerably different from wilderness. The search resource may be tasked with "clearing" a search segment to a high degree of certainty. This task varies distinctly from wilderness operations where

resource taskings rarely result in "clearing" a segment. Clearing a segment is likely to include checking pipes. culverts, dumpsters, crawl spaces, vacant/abandoned buildings and many other hazardous locations. A plan for searching every possible risk location must be implemented and trained for.

- *Terrain Travel Skills*—Knowledge of proper travel techniques in the metropolitan area is a required skill. There is still the implied need for a suitable level of physical fitness, both to successfully complete the assigned task and to maintain the required level of personal safety. Repeatedly climbing and descending building stairs can be as tiring as traveling in the wilderness. Agility is another requirement for search tactics in a metropolitan area. Getting in and out of tight places is likely to be necessary during urban tactics.
- *Personal Survival Skills*—With the availability of shelter, water and sustenance, survivability becomes more a study of safety. In the urban environment the searcher encounters manmade hazards combined with dangerous human interaction. The need for situational awareness is equally important to that of the wilderness environment. Additional preparations for searcher safety must be made. Dealing with the implications of human refuse in the metropolitan area certainly requires the use of personal protection equipment. Should the searcher be tasked with looking through trash, unoccupied structures, culverts and sewage routes, or other hazardous areas protocols for safety must include the use of gloves, eye and even whole body protection.
- *Lost Person Behavior*—The majority of subjects we seek in the urban environment are not "lost" in the classic sense. The many dementia and young children subjects, which are the largest percentage of urban incidents, likely have no sense of being lost. All our subjects will still be reacting and responding to their "situation" or facing criminal malfeasance (abduction, assault, etc.) in the urban environment.
  The study of lost person behavior gives insight to those

Courtesy of ssheltonimages.com

common (by category) reactions/responses encountered in the urban environment. In the urban environment, we must also be aware of "human behavior" as it applies to the persons we encounter and/or interview during the urban search. Training and practice in interview techniques and handling (possibly) hostile property owners is essential.

More on urban searcher safety

Frequently the SAR resource will be tasked to search areas that are considered "high crime risk" areas. Since SAR responders are usually in "uniform" they could be perceived as being law enforcement. Besides making the gathering of information more difficult, this misperception could potentially place the SAR responder in a dangerous situation.

You will remember from SARAware™, that basic safety protocols require having a minimum of 3 humans on every search resource deployed. This is equally imperative in the urban environment. Situational awareness in densely populated areas becomes both more critical and more difficult to accomplish. Additionally, never hesitate to request law enforcement escort when venturing into areas where your safety is a concern. In fact, should you be assigned to search in a high crime area, you should request/demand law enforcement escort. Search at night, in high crime areas, without law enforcement presence with the search team is unacceptable.

Searching in the Wilderness Environment

Regardless of the terrain and the climatic environment or season, it is reasonable to assume that the basic skill set for all responders would require knowledge and proficiency in, at least, the following areas:

- *Land Navigation*—Wilderness responders must be proficient in the use of map and compass, as well as GPS. Expertise in navigation is likely the most important field skill in wilderness SAR. Searchers who cannot confirm location of clues or worse—get lost themselves, are of no use to the subject.
- *Tracking*—Wilderness responders must be proficient in basic mantracking techniques, including knowledge and awareness of sign, as well as "step by step" tracking (of footprints). Man tracking is a highly evolved technical skill, but in the wilderness environment, all searchers must have a fundamental understanding and skill level to conduct tracking tactics until higher level trained trackers can be deployed.
- *Clue Consciousness*—Understanding the premise that proper Search Management does not focus on searching for the subject, but rather the large number of clues and evidence that will lead us to the subject, wilderness responders must have a trained awareness of clue seeking. Clues in this environment may be extremely hard to detect. The searcher must be diligent in seeking clues as the absence of clues is also very meaningful to the incident management team.
- *Search Techniques*—Searching in the wilderness environment requires the ability to safely travel through difficult terrain and weather conditions, while meeting navigational and communication demands, and still employ proper individual search tactics to enhance success in clue detection.
- *Terrain Travel Skills*—Traveling in dense vegetation and frequently changing elevation requires knowledge and training for movement in the environment. There is also the implied need for

Courtesy of wilernessrescue.org

a suitable level of physical fitness, to both successfully complete the assigned task and maintain the required level of personal safety. Those responders planning to be tasked in more hazardous terrain and conditions such as steep elevation changes; snow and ice; caves, mines or pits; require significantly higher levels of training and certification, as well as additional complex equipment.

- *Personal Survival Skills*—Whether participating in a search operation or participating in an outdoor recreational activity, it is essential the responder understands, and is prepared with knowledge and gear for, staying alive in extreme conditions. No one knows when they will be thrust into a survival situation. While it's unlikely it will happen during an incident, to searchers, we must be aware of the challenges to our subject.
- *Lost Person Behavior*—The science of human reaction to being lost continues to evolve rapidly. Researchers have developed categories of subjects, in each type of environment, with certain commonalities in their behavior when finding themselves out of their comfort zone or known surroundings. The wilderness responder must have a basic understanding of the subject's reactions and responses to his/her plight in order to determine tactics likely to find clues or locate the subject.

Suburban and Rural Environments

The challenge of operating in suburban and rural environments becomes one of flexibility. Most often resources will encounter elements of both urban and wilderness environments while conducting search tactics in suburban and rural areas. It is likely (though Search Management attempts to segment a search area to minimize multi-environment assignments) that a resource will need to transition from skills and techniques of the urban environment to the wilderness environment and back again, while completing a single operational task! In these environments, completing a structure search immediately followed by searching in densely wooded areas is common.

An additional safety consideration in the suburban and rural (as well as the wilderness) environments may be limited availability of law enforcement support during incident operations. As the local law enforcement agency may not have the number of personnel or specialized operations available in the urban environment, it can be difficult to have officers specifically assigned to assist on the incident. Limited law enforcement can also lead to challenges in a legal matter discussed in *SARAware*™ and reviewed below, namely trespassing.

Trespassing

In review, SAR team members cannot search private property without permission from the owner. Trespassing laws vary from state to state. SAR members need to understand and comply with those laws to prevent being prosecuted for trespassing. When in doubt, the resource should request a law enforcement officer to accompany them.

There are specific exceptions or exemptions from trespass laws. The term most commonly used is *exigent circumstances*. This is defined as when a circumstance exists that requires immediate action on your part to preserve "life or limb." An example would be hearing a voice call for help or a discovering a blood trail. Again, be familiar with the trespass laws in your state.

Additionally, use extreme caution when searching on or near private property. Some property owners will resort to physical or even deadly force to protect their privacy and their property. This is especially troublesome if the searcher inadvertently encounters illegal activity (drug labs, etc.).

Traveling in hazardous conditions in the wilderness environment

For those tasked with searching in the wilderness, knowing how to walk is not only a safety issue, but assists in enhancing endurance. Using proper travel technique will also allow you to focus more on seeking clues rather than walking.

- *Trails*—When hiking vs. walking the first thing to realize is that you will be slower. A natural trail requires more care in where you step—you will not be able to racewalk it. A well planned tactical assignment will allow you enough time to complete your search while carefully observing rather than hurrying to the extraction destination.

  Going uphill will work out your muscles. Like a bike shifting to a new gear to go uphill, shorten your steps. It is natural to lean into the hill a bit. Try to keep that lean to a minimum, keep your torso over your hips. If you lean too much you put yourself off balance. Do not lean backwards, that will unbalance you. Leaning too far forward or back can strain your lower back. You shouldn't be lifting your knees higher than 6 inches, if you are then you need to shorten your step even more. Hills will raise your heart rate, breathing, and exertion level as more muscles are used to carry you both up and along. Keep your exertion at an intensity where you can still speak in sentences rather than just gasping out single words.

  Walking downhill may seem to be a breeze, but it actually puts more strain on your knees and ankles as you hit the ground harder. Your stride will naturally elongate going downhill. This over-striding is bad on level ground, but going downhill it helps to brake you a bit while gravity keeps you moving faster than usual. If you find yourself going too fast, shorten and/or slow down your steps and keep it natural. You will find yourself leaning back. Leaning back will put you off balance, instead stay upright over your hips and knees. On very steep slopes or those with a loose surface, take a serpentine path and angle for a few steps left, then a few steps right. This switchbacking is a common trail design to reduce steepness either uphill or downhill. A hiking/tracking stick or even a pair of hiking poles can give you an extra stability. Traveling uphill or downhill on scree/talus is especially hazardous.

Scree is bits of broken rock piled up at the base of a cliff. In the mountains, daily heating and freezing of moisture on the solid rock causes it to slowly break the rock apart and tumble down. A scree slope will pile up to its steepest possible angle. Depending on the size and shape of the rock chunks, that angle may be shallow or steep.

Any additional rock that falls on the slope will roll down until it finds a resting place or hits the bottom. The same is true for your foot! When you step onto a slope of loose rock, just like sand, it will give way under the weight until the material under it settles with the new weight. This may be 1/32 of an inch or it may be a few inches. In some cases, you may be sliding down the slope along with a couple tons of rock, all looking for stable places to rest!

Talus is really what *scree* is. People just tend to call smaller bits of rock Scree and bigger stuff Talus. Really big Talus is called Boulders. It's all the stuff that has broken off of mountains and piled up. Depending on the composition of the original rock, the pieces of talus will be tiny, huge, or somewhere in between.

- *Crossing water*—At some point is it likely you may have to cross where there are no bridges. Rocks and debris in the river may seem like stepping stones but in fact be slippery hazards. It can be wiser to move down to where the stream has fanned out and is shallow and just accept wet feet rather than crossing at the narrow point where it is rushing and can sweep you off your feet.

First assess the situation. Scout the river (ideally from an elevated perspective) or look both up and downstream for alternatives. Be conservative and assume the worst. Invariably, streams are faster and deeper than they appear. The preferred crossing will be a point where the water is straight, wide and shallow. That's what you're looking for when identifying a place to cross. Look for braided channels. The crossing may be wider where a river breaks into separate channels. But the current's intensity will be dissipated and there may also be small islands or gravel bars where you can take a break and plot your next steps.

Watch out for debris. If the river is carrying a lot of debris, such as branches and small logs, it's not a good idea to cross here. The debris is an indication that stream flows are high. And objects flowing downstream can create a serious hazard if they strike you as you're crossing. If there's no debris floating downstream, toss a branch and watch how swiftly it moves downstream. That will give you a better sense of the direction of the main current and how fast it's moving.

Don't cross where flows are above your knees. Even comparatively shallow water can knock you off balance and carry you downstream if it's flowing rapidly enough. The only time to wade through deeper water is if you locate a flat pool with little or no current.

Loosen your pack before crossing. Undo your waist belt and let out the shoulder straps so that it's easier to remove. If you fall in and your pack gets soaked, it can drag you down or get snagged. You might lose your pack but consider the alternative.

Look for low and open exit points on the opposite bank. Once you reach the other side, you'll want to be able to get out of the stream as quickly as possible. A scramble up a steep bank could lead to a slip that puts you right back into the stream.

When crossing the stream, face upstream and shuffle sideways. Slide your feet along the bottom while facing the river. Cross at an angle diagonally to the flow and move in a slightly downstream direction toward the opposite bank. Always maintain two points of contact with the bottom. Use your poles to steady yourself as you shift your feet. The more contact you have with the bottom, the more stable you'll be. Remember, there's strength in numbers. Crossing with a partner or with your team creates additional stability. Link arms and coordinate your movements.

- *Traveling in desert conditions*—Searching in the desert presents all of the types of terrain and conditions we have discussed. You will encounter steeps, scree, slippery vegetation, loose sand, even water crossings! All with the added burden of working in the hostile, dry heat of the desert. So prepare to employ all the travel techniques you've learned with one additional caveat. Whenever possible, limit travel in the desert to nighttime. Unless there is compelling evidence requiring foot travel searches, daylight hours should be left to alternative methods (vehicle, airborne, etc.) of travel.

COURTESY OF ISRAEL—TOURGUIDE.INFO

- *Searching in snow*—First, let's restate our objective in presenting this information. This chapter seeks to make the responder aware of differing techniques required by operating in diverse environments. It is not our intent to offer any form of technical specialty training. Our discussion of searching in snow specifically excludes the alpine environment, which requires extensive technical specialty training.

Searching in snow can be slow going. You will cover much less terrain than in a typical search assignment. Your feet may be soaked. Occasionally you will *posthole* (i.e. the process by which a responder sinks lower than shin depth while walking on soft snow) up to your waist. Look at it as a challenge. Be patient, remember your duty and retain your sense of humor.

A couple of general hints: Whenever possible, avoid routes that take you above or along the base of cliffs or bluffs. If you are working in a group and you have no choice but to traverse such potentially hazardous areas, always do so one at a time. Be patient and walk softly. When crossing snowfields in the spring avoid going too close to rocks, where the snow will be softer due to warmer temperatures heating the rocks. If searching in an area where you will be forced into traversing steep slopes, seek an alternative route. Steep slopes covered in snow and ice are best left to the experts. Use of trekking poles may also assist with balance and minimize the chances of slipping. They can also be used to probe snow depth and solidity.

There are a few suggested techniques for travelling uphill and downhill in snow: When ascending a snow slope keep your steps short, decrease the gradient by zig-zagging and if the snow is soft enough, kick steps with the toes of your shoes. If the snow is too hard for kicking steps and you are not trained or have traction devices such as crampons, instep crampons or microspikes available, the alternative is to seek another route. When descending a snow slope, assuming that the snow is not frozen solid, the ideal method is the *plunge step*. Landing heel first, let the weight of your body drive your foot into the snow. Keep your knees slightly bent to maximize balance and avoid a hyperextension injury.

Summary

Today's SAR field responder will likely be called upon to search in varying terrain. As we noted, you might even encounter diverse environments or conditions on a single tasking. Some of the environments/conditions might normally be assigned to a technical SAR resource, but can arise unforeseen. You must be aware of the hazards, the immediate contingencies to overcome them, and continue the mission. So plan well, overcome unexpected obstacles, but if you prefer to participate in operations in more extreme environments, seek out the technical specialty training to prepare you for those operations.

References

Urban Search – Managing Missing Person Searches in the Urban Environment (2007)
Christopher S. Young & John Wehbring, *dbS Productions*, Charlottesville, VA

Managing Land Search Operations (2006)
Robert C. (Skip) Stoffel, *Emergency Response International*, Cashmere, WA

SARAware—Awareness Level Search & Rescue for the Responder (2013)
Dion Petaros, James Keck & Wes Podboy, *AERIE Publications*, Lake Dallas, TX

www.hikingdude.com, - Numerous concepts and discussions used herein (2014)

National Outdoor Leadership School – Winter Camping (2005)
Buck Tilton & John Gookin, *NOLS*, Lander, WY

Chronology of a SAR Incident—The Field Operator's Perspective

7

Objectives

COURTESY OF FREEDIGITALPHOTOS.NET

- Understand the importance of having a personal and Team/Resource Preplan
- Describe some components of a personal preplan
- Describe some components of a Team/Resource preplan
- Identify information requirements for Field Responder Initial Notification/Call Out
- Discuss the importance of the Incident Check-in requirement
- Describe the use of pertinent Field Responder ICS forms
- Identify some of the major Incident Base Facilities including:
  - Command Post
  - Staging Area
  - Base
- Differentiate between General Briefings and Tactical Briefings, including information provided
- Discuss the necessity of Tactical Debriefings and the information required
- Discuss the need for rehab between tactical assignments
- Describe the importance of the Check-out procedure including follow up after arrival home
- Discuss the post Incident process including immediate gear rehab and preplan updating

The unfolding of a SAR incident

Now that you have decided to become a SAR incident field responder, it's time to discuss your expectations of the response process and the expectations of the requesting agency. An extremely important point must be made... Professional responders NEVER deploy to an incident without a specific request from the agency with jurisdiction over the incident. Incidents conducted by trained management personnel develop very specific plans to control the operation. This includes plans for specific resources necessary to fulfill the plan. Anyone who "shows up" uninvited is usually sent away and "marked" as unprofessional. If you wish to be called to respond to future incidents, wait to be summoned to help.

Preplans

If we are to be successful in any endeavor, we must have a plan that will outline the steps that will lead us to the desired outcome. Then we must follow each step until it no longer produces the desired result. But having a plan means we can now implement contingent steps to get back on course. As with all plans, a SAR Preplan begins with the requirements of the highest level goals. In our case, this is the Agency having overall responsibility for the conduct of the incident. The next level necessary will be at the Resource or Team Level. Finally, we must each have our own personal plan that will guide us to be the most competent, proficient and professional responder.

The Agency Preplan

For agencies having responsibility for Search & Rescue incidents, the Agency Administrator is ultimately accountable for ensuring his/her agency has a written plan for conducting SAR Operations. This Preplan must minimally contain the following SAR specific components:

1. Purpose and Objectives
   This section must tell the user why and what the Plan is designed for.
2. Mission Priority
   This section details the incident priorities of the Agency responsible for the Plan. Where does SAR fit in should there be multiple incidents/hazards?
3. Responsibilities and Functions
   Describes how various responding agencies and resources are accountable for particular tasks and jobs.
4. Functional Organization
   This section should contain both the Agency required ICS minimum organization for basic searches and guidance on expanding for larger, more complex incidents.
5. Emergent Authorities and Responsibilities
   Describes the conditions that require changes in management structure (e.g. agency jurisdiction) or strategies (e.g. criminal act vs. lost person).
6. Knowledge of the environment
   Refers to the location of GIS (Geographic Information Systems-like mapping software) or actual maps. Particular care to safety should be included.
7. First Notice and Urgency Guidelines
   This section contains details on procedures to follow upon receipt of a call regarding a lost or missing person. It also contains guidelines for notifying initial response personnel. This section includes forms and policies to document Search Urgency, Lost Person Questionnaire and other types of initial Planning & Searching Data.
8. Collection and Analysis of Past Incidents
   This section includes references to previous SAR incidents in the jurisdiction including summary data and locations of complete incident documentation. Reference should also be made to global Lost Person Behavior statistics and the location of these resources.
9. Interviewing and Investigation

This section includes protocols for the investigation unit and all the policies and procedures for clue gathering, analysis and documentation.

10. Strategy

    Even with availability of trained Search Managers, the Preplan should include a section on considerations to determine scope of the incident and methods to determine strategies for finding the subject(s). Protocols for typical ICS components such as operational periods, Incident Action Plans, briefings/debriefings, demobilization, logistics, etc., should also be included.

11. Tactics

    While tactics vary widely from incident to incident, it is possible to summarize various options that can be employed to find and/or rescue lost or missing persons. Such options should be included in this section.

12. Resource Management

    This section presents the guidelines for resource qualifications (including education, certifications, currency and fitness levels), limitations, restrictions for use, and documentation methods for tracking resources. Policies for rarely used or specialty resources must be included.

13. Incident facilities

    Describes protocols for use of permanent and temporary facilities. Considerations beyond Command/management facilities, including shelter, food service, sanitation, medical care, storage, briefing/debriefing, interviewing, family seclusion, press room, etc., are equally important.

14. Communications

    This section includes protocols on all forms of communications. Examples include radios, computer/internet, cell phone voice and messaging, etc.

15. Briefing and Debriefing
    Presents specific requirements and protocols for general briefings and debriefings, tactical briefings and debriefings, Unified Command/Agency briefings, media briefings, etc.
16. Medical considerations
    When operating solely within jurisdictions of specific agencies it is preferable to create an ICS Medical Plan (Form 206) that will only require slight modifications on specific incident basis. The changes usually concern the on-scene triage/care for injured responders.
17. Rescue Considerations
    As this task is frequently hazardous and almost always highly technical, it is recommended you establish protocols for "when, who, and how" to conduct rescue operations. "Routine" overland evacuation/extrication of injured subjects should be addressed here.
18. Fatalities
    It is essential that policies and procedures be established to deal with a deceased subject. Scene preservation is vital from a legal/criminal perspective, as well as coroner/medical examiner considerations.
19. Incident De-escalation and Suspension
    Criteria must be developed to assist the Incident Commander in making decisions about de-escalating or suspending active response to the incident. Policies should define who is empowered to make such decisions and how (and to which agency representatives) they must be communicated.
20. Demobilization
    This is one of the most overlooked aspects of incident management. Careful consideration must be given to the demobilization of human and equipment resources to return them to ready status.

21. Incident Documentation
    Requirements for compliance with ICS documentation procedures remain with the Agency maintaining jurisdiction over the incident. Utilization and completion of mission forms, reports and paperwork must be an Agency policy. Proper long term storage of the incident documents must also be accounted for.
22. Critiques/After Action analysis
    It is highly recommended the agency sponsor a post incident analysis with participation from key members of incident management and representatives from responding agencies. This usually takes place a few weeks after the incident is terminated or suspended.
23. Special Considerations
    This section contains protocols for all actions not covered in other sections, but requiring unusual response or handling. Examples include:
    1. Downed aircraft
    2. Interaction with the subject's family
    3. Interaction with the media
    4. Safety requirements
    5. Preventative measures *(PSAR)*
24. Appendices
    1. Resource Lists
    2. Phone lists
    3. Organizational Charts
    4. Memoranda of Understanding/Agreement
    5. Hard copy forms

This Agency Preplan is a public document and should be available to your resource/team for review. It is important for your resource/team to understand the agency's operations and how to properly fit in that agency environment. No team or individual can properly perform their duties without that understanding.

An important part of the Agency Preplan is the section discussing agency requirements for any resource participating in incidents with that agency. These requirements will minimally include:

1. Resource Organizational Requirements:
   This section will contain requirements for corporate structure (Not-For-Profit, Governmental, etc.), Lists of officers, Membership requirements, Financial structure (membership dues, grants, sponsorship, etc.), Insurance requirements (Liability, Workers Comp, etc.) and other matters related to resource/team formation.
2. Education, Certification and Training Requirements:
   This is where you will find the agency's requirements for operational readiness of each of the resource members. The team and resource may have to provide written documentation of compliance for any/all responders arriving at a SAR incident. Especially important will be items such as:
   - General SAR Education and Training Courses required including team provided and national level courses.
   - Specialty Education and Training Courses required including team provided and national level courses. For example: Canine, Equine, ATV, etc. requirements.
   - General SAR Certifications including team provided but will usually have national or state level requirements. Team provided certification is typically no longer enough.
   - Specialty SAR Certifications including team provided but will usually have national or state level requirements. Team provided certification is typically no longer enough. For example: Canine, Equine, ATV, etc. requirements.
   - Ongoing Training requirements including individual, team and higher level events.
3. Response and Sustainability Requirements:
   Every agency needs to know how a resource can/will respond. Components include:

- Specialty availability—Are all the specialties the resource claims to offer available 24/7/365 or only at certain times.
- Notice to Respond—How long will it take for the resource members to assemble and travel to the Incident Check-in location.
- Self-Sustainability—This describes the ability to shelter, feed, water and resupply the members of the resource, without agency assistance, during an incident. This is especially important during SAR components of a disaster type incident.

The Resource/Team Preplan

It is essential that any resource or team have proper written documentation concerning its structure and organization. This includes written policies and procedures for its governance and protocols for members. Properly creating and operating a resource demands that the resource be treated as a corporate entity. Whether the resource is actually incorporated (strongly recommended) or not is irrelevant regarding the need for written documentation. These and other important resource/team organizational requirements were discussed in the *SARAware*™ (Awareness Level SAR for the Responder) Textbook and can be reviewed there. Our discussion here relates to the components required in the actual response to an incident.

Photo by James Keck

For a resource to be a valid response organization, it should minimally have the following components in its written preplan. Many of them are directly related to the agency requirements noted above:

1. Human Resource/Member Management—The resource should have a written plan regarding requirements for all members, especially those who will respond to incidents. This plan should include how a member applies, criminal background checks, probationary period requirements, financial (e.g. Dues or Contributions) requirements, meeting attendance requirements, etc. The plan should also include the process of keeping member records. A personnel record must be kept on each member.
2. Educational Requirements—A written plan must include the formal courses a member must take (and pass) to be an active responder. These can include FEMA courses, Law Enforcement classes, Medical classes and of course SAR classes (such as those provided by national organizations such as AERIE). The plan must include provision for currency/recurrency as required by the provider of each course.
3. Certification Requirements—The resource must have a written plan outlining the certification requirements of each member, based on their proposed participation or specialty. While the resource may have "in-house" testing requirements in addition to "outside" certifications, most agencies now require state or national level certifications. Beware of the resource that only requires in-house certification. The plan must also account for currency/recurrency as required by the provider of each certification.
4. Training Requirements—Each resource must have a Training Plan. That plan includes a Training Calendar and the requirements upon each member for participation. Such participation begins with the required attendance. Most (professional) resources have, at least, a required percentage of training a member must attend. The truly professional will delineate that attendance based on the type of training. For example, how often must the member attend "basic" SAR training, training in the member specialty, seminars, team/regional/state exercises, etc.?

5. Physical Fitness Requirements—This requirement is becoming more critical each year. As our society becomes more overweight/less fit, we are finding the same in our response community. This is unacceptable! Our citizens count on us to be able to work long hours in physically and mentally demanding roles. It is mandatory that resources implement physical fitness standards for all its field responders.
6. Logistical Requirements—If a resource is to be self-sustaining (typically for 72 hours), there must be a plan to provide for the care of its responders. The equipment and supplies necessary to safely respond to a callout must be fresh (not expired), well maintained, appropriate for the operating environment, conveniently cached and packed ready for immediate deployment. The plan must also include post-incident rehab, resupply, and replenishment.
7. Deployment Protocols—This section must explain how an agency contacts the resource. Who receives the request for deployment? What information is required to accompany the request? How is the request evaluated for acceptance? Who conducts the risk assessment analysis? How are members selected for deployment for the requested mission? What procedures are implemented to notify members for deployment? What information is required to be presented to deploying members? The time of simply calling all members to deploy to every request is past. There must be a plan that evaluates whether the resource will accept the request and who will respond if accepted.

The Personal Preplan

All responders must have a personal plan to prepare for deployment to an incident. This is especially important for the field operator. These responders will encounter hazards and deal with many issues that must be countered if they are to provide professional response in the critical need to participate in quickly and safely locating the subject(s). Let's examine some possible components of a personal preplan:

1. Human Resource/Member Management—Just as with the agency and resource levels, the responder should have a written plan regarding personal requirements for participation. This plan should include how a member budgets his/her finances for participating in SAR activities; membership, training, equipment, medical and veterinary supplies, and associated costs. Recordkeeping must also be accounted for. Plan to keep updated copies of all your education, training, certification and proficiency records. Don't rely on your team/resource.
2. Educational Requirements—Once again, as with the resource level, your written plan must include the formal courses you must take (and pass) to be an active responder. As noted above, these can include FEMA courses, Law Enforcement classes, Medical classes and of course SAR classes (such as those provided by national organizations such as AERIE). How do you plan to participate in continuing and recurring education? Many of the noted classes have expirations and must be retaken periodically.
3. Certification Requirements—Your plan must include details on becoming and maintaining appropriate national level certifications. Many of the national certifications have multiple levels. How do you plan to progress through these levels? All of the national organizations offering credible SAR certifications include expiration of the credential. What is your plan to maintain these certifications in current status? How often will you study/train? Will you retake the exams prior to expiration, if it is available locally? Or will you travel when your credential reaches expiration? All considerations must be planned for.
4. Participation Requirements—Your resource must have a Training Plan. That plan includes a Training Calendar and

the requirements upon each member for participation. Such participation begins with the required attendance. How do you plan to balance work, family and SAR activities? If you plan to participate in a specialty, it is likely you will have more burdensome participation requirements. Have you and your family discussed the amount of time away that is acceptable to them? SAR incidents occur any day of the week and any time of day. Is your employer aware of your participation and willing to give you time off to train and/or respond to an incident? It is helpful to have this agreement (from your employer) in written form (email or letter, etc.) in case there is a change in supervisor.

5. Physical and Mental Fitness Requirements—This requirement becomes more critical as we age. Do you regularly participate in a physical fitness activity? What is your current weight versus your ideal weight? Have you measured your physical fitness against a known standard? Understanding that the typical volunteer SAR responder is well beyond the age of peak physical performance (typically 18-22 years of age), there are realistic standards for all ages. Your local law enforcement and fire service agencies are likely using such a standard. Meeting the same requirements as the agency you will respond for/with will increase your credibility with these agencies. Becoming and staying fit will not only make you a better responder, it will allow you to better enjoy all aspects of your life!

   You must also plan how to consider your psychological readiness to participate. If you cannot focus on the mission you will be a safety issue to yourself and your colleagues. Analyze and plan what stressors will preclude your participation in training. What stressor will preclude your participation in a SAR incident? Some examples might include: family stressor, job stress, financial stress, etc. To be effective as a responder, you must be at your physical AND psychological best.

6. Logistical Requirements—Your plan must include acquiring and maintaining required gear, equipment and supplies. This is an expensive endeavor. A plan is required to avoid "wasting" money. You must also plan periodic replacement of gear and supplies. Scheduled inspections are necessary to monitor status of all gear. Many supplies (food, medications, batteries, etc.) have expirations or simply lose effectiveness. Shelters can wear out or develop deficiencies. Without a plan to account for all gear and equipment you will likely find yourself without a necessary item at the time it is most critically needed. Your plan should detail when and how you will rehab/resupply your gear after training or deployment. Trying to resupply when called to deploy is never an effective plan.
7. Deployment Protocols—The personal preplan must detail how you will be contacted. Consider when you are available by mobile phone or by landline. Who has the authority to activate you for deployment? What information must you have for deployment? While we all want to know about the incident we are responding to, details about the subject or nature of the incident is not required for call out. Having a plan will direct you to ask appropriate questions to prepare a proper deployment for the environment and conditions at hand. You must do a personal risk assessment analysis. Are you physically and mentally prepared to deploy? Is your gear ready and appropriate for this deployment? Are you trained *and proficient in the type of response needed for this incident, or is the requesting agency simply calling out all resources* (a very bad idea!!)? What are the travel plans required of you and can you safely comply? Just as with the resource level, you must determine if it is safe and proper for you to deploy at this time.

Initial Notice of Deployment

Now that you have prepared and implemented your "plan" let's consider the elements you must include in your initial call out phase. These elements must also be included in all levels of the Preplan, but the initial notice (call out) for deployment is the first "active" phase of a specific search & rescue incident.

In order to properly prepare yourself for deployment, it is important to have pertinent information when requested to deploy to the incident. Suggested deployment information includes:

- Incident Designation (name)
- When to respond (day, date, time)
- Where to respond (check-in location) and whom to report to (ICS Section or Unit, contact phone)
- A brief description of the situation (i.e. lost person(s) description, likely scenario)
- Type of resource(s) requested (e.g. ground, scent specific canine, technical rescue, etc.)
- Requested length of deployment
- Current and forecast weather
- Description of Search Area (urban, suburban, wilderness—mountainous, vegetation cover)
- Required gear (mandatory field gear, suggested base gear)
- Logistics provided or required from resource/responder
- Specialized equipment required from resource/responder
- Enroute contact number (of resource should "stand down" be necessary while enroute)
- Reference to terms of MOU (if applicable) or determination of liabilities and reimbursement

Providing such information will result in better prepared responders and the reduction in confusion between the requesting authority and the responding resource. If you are the contact for a requested resource (or even if you are simply responding as a member of a

Image by Claudia Amendola

resource), you should require all this information prior to accepting the deployment.

Arriving at the Incident

Among the more important information required is that of check-in. The incident management team must be keeping written record of what resources (1) have been requested, (2) have arrived on-scene and (3) have been returned home. Imagine showing up for an incident, receiving an assignment, then while performing the assignment become injured or even ("Heaven Forbid") lost! If there is no documentation of your attendance, who will know to come looking for you? Who will know if you don't make it back home safely? You must follow the required check-in requirements. Additionally, if you arrive at an incident where check-in is not required, you should insist on notifying the Incident Commander of your presence and probably consider whether or not (strongly recommended) you will participate in future incidents with this agency/management team, until they learn how to conduct an incident under the proper ICS guidelines.

ICS Forms for the Field Responder

Image by Claudia Amendola

This is an appropriate time to begin discussing ICS forms the field responder is likely to encounter. Proper and complete documentation is necessary if we are to successfully complete our duties and for the incident to have any chance at success. Some of the more likely documents the responder should expect are:

- ICS 211—This is the document you will enter your personal information on during Check-in.
- ICS 204—This is the document you will be given detailing your specific tasking (each time you are assigned to conduct a

specific search tactic). It will be used in the Tactical Briefing so no information is overlooked.

- ICS 214—This is the written log used to record all actions performed by you and your team while performing an assigned task. It should be very detailed, especially when recording clues, safety hazards and unusual/unexpected occurrences.
- ICS 204A—This is the form the Planning Section will use to debrief you/your unit to make sure no information is overlooked.
- ICS 225—You may encounter this form at the end of the incident or sometime after attending an incident. It is used to evaluate your performance during your deployment. It should not be used as a "weapon" against you or your resource, but rather a tool to help all of us improve our ability to participate.

You may also be shown/given copies of Incident Action Plans, Incident Safety Analyses, Inventory Plans, Air Operations Summary, etc. All documents given to you or used by you/your team must be approved ICS forms or be specifically approved for use by the ICS management team. It is not only improper to use your own forms/documents, but may result in legal issues should the matter of this incident come up in court. **It is best to use only NIMS approved ICS forms.** Examples of many of these ICS forms are included in the Appendix.

Incident Facilities

While we're on the subject of ICS protocols, you may remember from your *SARAware*™ training that all facilities used in an incident have specific names. This is one of the requirements of the Incident Command System. Here's a review of the facilities most frequently encountered by field responders:

A. *Command Post*: This is the location where the incident is planned, managed and directed. It is managed by the Logistics Section as requested by the Incident Commander.
B. *Incident Base*: This is the location where the logistical needs of responders are provided. It includes food, water, shelter, sanitary functions, medical care, etc. It is managed by the Logistics Section as requested by the Incident Commander.
C. *Staging Area*: This is a designated location to contain resources available for immediate deployment to the field. Resources in this location can deploy on three minutes notice. It is managed by the Operations Section.
D. *Camps*: These are "remote" locations where resources may be temporarily located to allow more efficient deployment in distant search segments. They are "managed" by the Logistics Section, but may be nothing more than a clearing in which the resource has chosen to camp.
E. *Helibase*: These are locations where helicopter aircraft are based. The services available include overnight parking, fueling, maintenance, and logistical support for personnel. Of course, the best Helibase is the local airport! Helibases are "managed" by the Logistics Section with technical expertise provided by the Air Branch or Group.

Image courtesy of DoD

F. *Helispot*: Much like camps, these are basic locations where a helicopter can land to load or unload. No services are provided. While "managed" by the Logistics Section, helispots are usually established by Operations Resources on an as needed basis.

Briefings and Debriefings

Courtesy of Flickr.com

Los Alamos (Police) briefing

One very important function of incident facilities is to provide a location to conduct briefings and debriefings. The field responder will certainly participate in *Tactical* briefings and debriefings, and may (as time and space allows) attend *General* briefings. These briefings were discussed in the *SARAware*™ textbook but let's review them. Our reasoning for this is the entire incident is likely to fall into disarray without proper general briefings and the field responder/resource is unlikely to safely and successfully perform the assigned search tactic without receiving a proper tactical briefing. If management does not immediately debrief a resource after completing a tactical assignment valuable information is lost and further search planning happens in a void!

General Briefing—This briefing is normally conducted at the beginning of each operational period. As indicated by the name it is an overview of the incident to date and the expectations for the current (about to be undertaken) operational period. Typically the General Briefing is conducted by the Planning Section Chief, with the entire incident management team participating. The foundation of this briefing is the Incident Action Plan developed by the Incident Commander, the Planning Section and the Operations Section. If the facilities allow enough space, the Incident Manager is likely to have as many responders as possible attend. Areas that should be covered in the General Briefing include:

- Situation status—*Known facts at the time*
- Strategy—*Emphasis on specific search segments & alternative strategies*
- Objectives for this Operational Period

- Overview of Tactical Assignments
- Safety Hazards and Considerations
- Media, Family, Friends—*Protocols for dealing with*
- Updated Subject Profile—*Limited by HIPAA law as this is an open forum*
- Expected terrain, vegetation & weather—*For the field responder: Visual impacts to searching*
- Examples of visual cues to look for & techniques for searching
- Debriefing instructions & what to expect after searching

There is much information presented during a General Briefing that can assist the field responder in performing the assigned search tactic.

Tactical Briefing—This briefing is conducted with members of a resource immediately prior insertion to the assigned search segment and performance of the search tactic. Very often the briefing is conducted in the Staging Area so the unit/resource can be immediately deployed. While it is still appropriate for Planning Section personnel to conduct the Tactical Briefing, it is very often conducted by Operations Section personnel for staffing reasons and because Operations is the "expert" on search tactics. During this briefing the field team/resource is given a copy of the ICS 204, a "fresh"/current map, a current satellite photo and other documents pertinent to the assignment. An incident where field resources are not specifically and individually briefed, as well as provided with these documents, is considered poorly managed. Once again, there is a list of topics that should minimally be included in the Tactical Briefing:

- *Incident Data*—Details concerning the incident name, operational period, etc.
- *Task Timing*—It is essential the unit is briefed on the expected time of insertion and time of extraction. The entire time in the search segment should not exceed 6 hours.
- *Insertion Location*—A highly trained and certified resource should be allowed to develop their own plan to achieve the

desired tactic results. In the case of lesser trained resources it will be necessary to designate the insertion point and perhaps predetermine the entire search route.

- *Extraction Location*—Again, this will be necessary when employing lesser trained (lower certified) resources.
- *Expected Results*—This is typically expressed in terms of coverage, but may be in terms of POD for lessor trained resources.
- *Safety Considerations*—Specifically what hazards/risks should the resource beware of this particular search segment.
- *Weather Update*—To prepare the resource in terms of protective gear and clothing required.
- *Updated Subject Details*—This will include information subject to HIPAA rules and material/evidence the field search resource will use for clue consciousness.
- *Communications Data*—The field resource should be provided with appropriate incident communication devices (e.g. radios) and the frequencies for the communications protocols. Lost comm instructions should also be given in the briefing. This data should include information on the scheduled "status checks" contact during the assignment and the requirements for reporting clues or subject acquisition. Since ICS requires the use of plain language (English) communication, there should be no 10-code or other codes used with the possible exception of subject status.
- *Clue/Evidence Handling*—The resource should be provided instructions on how incident management wants clues managed in the event the resource does not have communications with the Command Post. Remember all clues must be considered as evidence unless law enforcement stipulates it is not. "Chain of custody" and evidence handling rules apply in all cases.
- *Debriefing Information*—The resource should be given details on expected debriefings. This should include details on items to be collected during debriefing (e.g. cameras/phone cameras, GPS units, notes, forms, etc.). Additionally, the

resource should be told when and where the debriefing will be conducted.

- *Additional Information as required*

Tactical Debriefing—The Tactical Debriefing is equally important to the briefing. During the tactical debriefing the resource will be asked to recount their activities from the moment of insertion to the moment of extraction. Though there may have been extensive communication with the Command Post during the assignment, it is imperative to discuss all details regardless of how insignificant they may seem. The information acquired during the debriefing will be used for planning subsequent taskings (including safety concerns) and strategic planning for subsequent operational periods. Just as with briefings, an incident where debriefings are not conducted is considered poorly managed. To insure that no pertinent information is overlooked, the debriefer will use an ICS 204A form as a guide and to document the debriefing. Personnel conducting the debriefing will also collect notes, photos, documents, recovered (when requested to be recovered by incident management or law enforcement) evidence, GPS units (to download the track followed) and other team records from the assignment. Information requested during the debriefing should minimally include:

Photo courtesy of DoD

- *Detailed Recounting of All Activities*—This should be discussed in chronological order including time marks and GPS coordinates as appropriate.
- *Estimated Coverage*—If coverage cannot be ascertained, estimate POD with consideration of responsive and unresponsive subjects.

- *Detailed Information of Clues/Evidence Found*—This must include current disposition as well as time marks and GPS coordinates.
- *Gaps in Coverage*—It is essential that areas of the segment not covered by this assignment be discussed. There is no retribution involved. Incident Management does not realistically believe a resource will actively cover every "square foot" of the search segment assigned. Only then can a decision be made whether to research this segment and if a different type of resource should be used.
- *Detailed Information on Hazards Encountered*—Safety remains the number one priority of every incident. Advising incident management of hazards will allow informed risk assessments and decisions on deploying resources into this segment.
- *Suggestions, Ideas & Recommendations*—Professional incident managers (whether paid or volunteer) recognize the expertise in formally trained and certified resources. They appreciate your input and ideas on the segment you just searched and its place in the incident.

There can be no substitutes for proper and timely briefings and debriefings. Trained incident managers would never conduct an incident without including them as routine. Sharing of information with field responders enables them to better accomplish their tasks. Trained and certified field responders should also expect to be debriefed after every assignment. This enables incident management to better plan the search to give a better statistical chance of success.

Rehab

Photo courtesy of cnn.com

While we're not sure of the rules for the rest requirements of wildlife, be assured that field responders definitely require "R & R" (rest and rehabilitation) between tactical assignments. There are a few basic guidelines that are taught in Incident Management classes (including SAR incidents), you should be aware of:

- Field responder assignments should not be longer than 6 hours in any one 12 hour operational period.
- Field responders should not be tasked in sequential operational periods. For example, if a responder/resource is tasked during the "day" operational period they should not be assigned in the subsequent "night" operational period. If it is absolutely necessary to use resources in consecutive operational periods, the Incident Commander (or designee) must ensure the resource has had a minimum of 8 hours rest between ending the first assignment and beginning the second.
- Whenever possible incident management should refrain from allowing responders to return (travel) home from an incident within 8 hours of completing an assignment. This is especially important at night when the responder's biological clock is programmed for sleep. **More incident responders are killed or injured when returning home than while performing assigned tasks during the incident!**

The field responder will be encountering physical, psychological and emotional stress on each assignment. There must be time for each person to recover and reduce these stress levels as much as possible. Additionally, the responder tires from expending large amounts of energy and remaining mentally focused while performing search duties. Each of us has differing levels of tolerance and endurance, but by taking the time to eat, rehydrate and rest your body and mind, you will avoid or lessen the negative effects of being a field responder. You will also be able to perform your best, mentally and physically, on each subsequent tasking.

One more consideration for rehabbing during the incident. That is the need to rehab equipment and supplies. In Chapter 5 we discussed the SAR Ready Pack. As the name implies we must have gear and materials "ready" for many different occurrences. Any supplies used on an assignment must be replaced. Any equipment used must be inspected and repaired. Don't assume you won't need those items on the next assignment. Make your ready pack ready!

Heading Home

Once you've been released from duty and told to return home, it's time to implement your personal demobilization plan. To make sure you don't overlook any steps it is very helpful to develop a checklist for this purpose. Let's discuss a few steps you should include:

1. **Rest/Rehab:** Do not even begin the demobilization process until you have rested, rehydrated and eaten. Even if you must remain at the base, or local to the incident, overnight, that is your best option. Having to reschedule any appointments you may have is much better than never getting to those appointments.
2. **Organize:** From your personal preplan and your preparation following the Notice for Call Out, you should have lists of equipment, gear and supplies that you brought with you. Taking into consideration the expendables used, you can now organize your belongings for repacking and loading.

3. **Check-out:** Every incident **must** have a formal process to sign you out of the incident. In fact if you participate with an agency that doesn't do this, you should seriously consider how professional they are and whether it is safe for you to work with them. Personnel accountability is a cornerstone of incident safety. Follow the incident check-out process to ensure accountability that you have left the incident.
4. **Travel:** Remember that you are still tired and still distracted by your thoughts of the incident. That's a dangerous combination. Force yourself to focus on the drive! Additionally, we strongly recommend that you return straight

home. There is always the temptation to "stop" enroute, whether to run an errand for the family, or to "catch-up" with friends at a restaurant or pub. This is not a good choice. And remember that your "coverage" (workers comp, liability, etc.) likely ceases when you make that stop (unrelated to the incident) before going home. Stopping for gas or food for the travel is considered "related."

5. **Confirmation of Safe Return:** You must contact the incident management team, via the method they prescribed, to inform them you have arrived safely at your house or other stop that is unrelated to the incident. If they don't hear from you within the expected arrival (home) window, they will commence communications efforts to locate you. Should those efforts fail, they will commence a new incident—**with you as the subject!**

Image courtesy of www.thescenisdead.com

As with all incident management you must have a plan. Going home is not what is what is actually occurring during this phase. It is a demobilization process no less critical than that of preparing to deploy. If you don't have a plan, you are planning to fail.

Post Incident Actions

Now that you've made it safely home, there's a few more tasks to accomplish. Some are immediate and others can be completed in the next week or two.

- *Gear, Equipment and Supply Rehab*—This activity needs to be completed as soon as you feel rested. Since we don't have the luxury of "scheduling" our incidents, we must be ready to immediately deploy again. Make sure your ready pack is complete, per the SARResponder™ 2 list with additions required by situation or your resource policies, except for perishables. It is recommended you create a list of perishables (e.g. snacks, batteries, medications, etc.) that you will put in your pack when an actual deployment occurs.

- *Logging Your Participation*—It is essential that our participation in actual incidents is recorded. Besides demonstrating proficiency in required skills to our client agencies, this is a good way for you to evaluate your own performance with an eye towards training needs. These documents should be kept as a part of your personal "personnel" file. Try to make these entries within 24-72 hours of returning home. This way the details will still be fresh in your mind.
- *Updating the Preplan*—It would be a shame to waste the knowledge we gained through experience by participating in actual incidents. The best way to use this knowledge is to update our personal preplans with it. Was there some action you took that was not as effective as designed? Did an unexpected safety concern arise? Did a piece of equipment fail during use? These questions present an opportunity to revise your preplan so you can be "better, safer and more effective" next time. Make sure to update (in writing!) your preplan every time you participate in an incident.

Summary

Now you have an understanding of the basic timeline of all SAR incidents. On smaller, less complex incidents, they may be compressed or even combined since the time the incident is operational will be short. But regardless of the size or intensity of the incident, they will always incorporate these phases.

References

National Fire Protection Association - Publication 1620: Recommended Practice for Pre-Incident Planning (1998 Edition)

The Handbook for Managing Land Search Operations (2001)
Robert "Skip" Stoffel, *ERI Publications & Training*, Cashmere, WA

Urban Search (2007)
Christopher S. Young and John Wehbring, *dbS Productions*, Charlottesville, VA

Search is An Emergency (1987)
Patrick "Rick" LaValla and Robert "Skip" Stoffel, *ERI Publications & Training*, Cashmere, WA

SARAware—Awareness Level Search & Rescue for the Responder (2013)
Dion Petaros, James Keck and Wes Podboy, *AERIE Publications*, Lake Dallas, TX

Field Navigation Techniques for the Responder

8

Objectives

Courtesy of visualphotos.com

- Demonstrate the process of orienting a map to magnetic north
- Demonstrate the process of orienting a map using terrain or manmade features
- Describe the process of taking a bearing to a known location
- Describe the process of navigating to a location using a known bearing
- Demonstrate the ability to transfer a field bearing to a map
- Demonstrate the ability to measure walking distance using the Tally Stride method
- Describe the process to convert map distance to Tally stride
- Discuss different techniques for field navigating while actively searching

Navigation Concepts for Field Responders

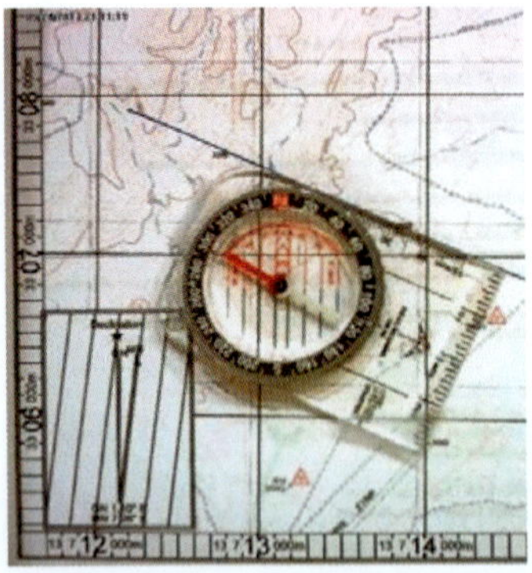

This chapter will introduce the field responder to navigation techniques using compass and manual methods. GPS will be discussed in a later chapter. If you're using this textbook in a classroom setting, your Instructor will be working with you on performing GPS navigation. But first, you must make sure that you are extremely comfortable using maps and compass (on the map). It is essential that you are very capable of using the USNG or UTM coordinate system to ascertain locations, quickly calculate straight line and road (map) distances in the metric system, determine declination adjusted bearings between two points on a map, adjust bearings reported from the field and plot them on a map to perform a resection determination of location. If you're not adept at performing these tasks, or perhaps need current practice to gain proficiency, it is strongly recommended you refer to the *SAR-Aware*™ textbook chapter on Map & Compass. A field responder will routinely be required to perform these map functions on missing and lost person incidents. When you're ready, we'll proceed to learning the additional techniques, complementing map skills that the field responder will also routinely utilize while participating on incidents.

To be successful in achieving our assigned search coverage requirement we must be able to accurately navigate through our search segment. We must not only know how to do this, but must maintain proficiency at all times. Navigation is not a difficult skill, but it is perishable. Once you learn how, you must practice on a regular basis!

Orienting Maps

When using a map in the field, it may be necessary to orient it to magnetic north. This is dependent on the type of compass you wish to use (baseplate, orienteering, or lensatic) in the sense that to use a lensatic compass on map problems *requires* the map to be oriented to True North. You might think that you only need to position the map

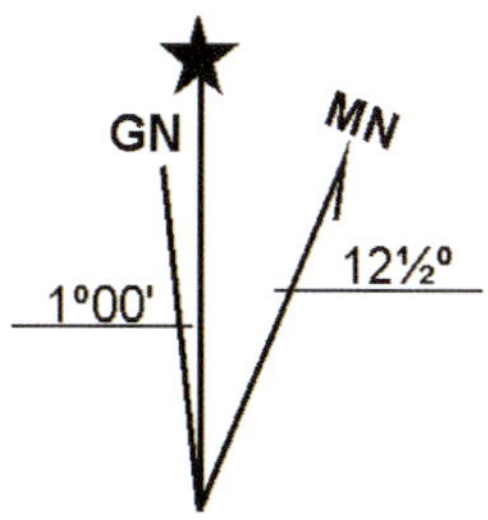

with the "top" towards north, but that can leave you inaccurate by at least a few degrees. As we discussed in the *SARAware*™ textbook, many maps are printed with the "top" slanted towards Grid North. Since lensatic compass use on maps is possible only when the map is oriented to Magnetic North it is especially important you learn how to orient a map if you choose a lensatic compass. Proper orientation of a map can also facilitate identification of terrain features or landmarks. Interestingly, you can actually orient the map using those same terrain features and landmarks! Let's discuss the two methods—Orienting by Compass and Orienting by Terrain Features:

Orienting by Compass—To orient your map to Magnetic North is a reasonably simple process when using a compass.

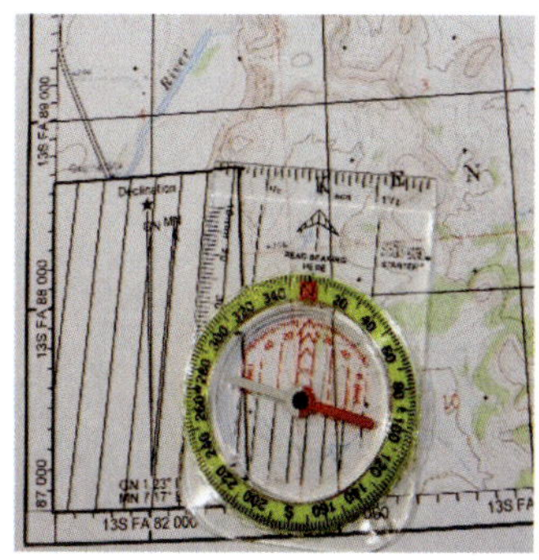

Compass on Magnetic North Line

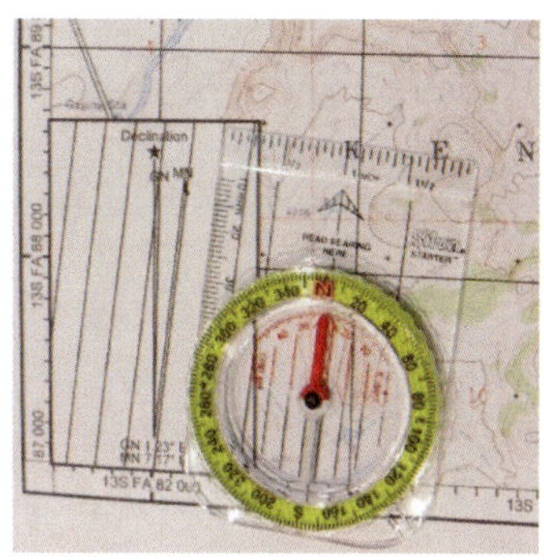

Compass on Magnetic North Line —Map Oriented

1. Place your map on the ground away from any metal or electrical objects. Locate the declination diagram on your map and identify the magnetic north indicating line. This is usually identified with the letters "MN."
2. Rotate your compass bezel so the orienting arrow indicates 360° (sometimes shown by an "N" on the compass) to the direction of travel arrow/line.
3. Place the compass straight edge on the map declination diagram *magnetic north line.*
4. Rotate the map and compass, together, being careful to keep the compass straight edge on the declination diagram magnetic north line, until the magnetic pointer/arrow indicates 360°. On a baseplate or orienteering compass this is known as "putting Red Fred in the Shed."

Orienting by Terrain Features—As the name implies, we are going to line up our map visually using natural or manmade features. The challenge is to accurately identify at least 2 (preferably 3) or more features on the map that can be confirmed in the real world. You must be proficient with reading topographic maps to accomplish this. This process is similar to the "triangulation/resection" method of determining your location by using the bearings to geographic or manmade features that you can identify on the topographic map.

1. Identify the first map feature, then locate it in the real world.

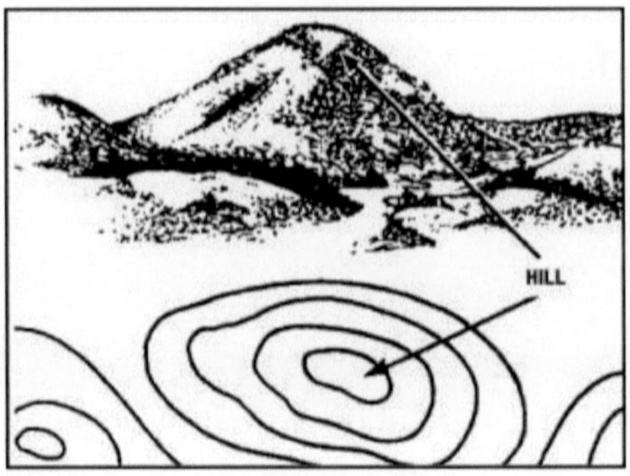

2. Identify the second map feature, then locate it in the real world.
3. Now holding map steady, rotate your body so both features in the real world line up with those on the map.

Image courtesy of National Wildfire Coordinating Group

Compass Bearings in the Field

In the *SARAware*™ textbook we learned how to plot bearings/azimuths on a map. Now it's time to learn how to travel on a bearing in the field and to determine the azimuth to/from a target. Just a point of clarification... the terms *bearing* and *azimuth* can be used interchangeably. Let's begin.

As we are already familiar with the different types of compasses used in field navigation, let's consider some guidelines common to all:

- Inspection—Before using your compass you should inspect it for condition and operation. This inspection should ensure that the fluid filled bezel (or crystal) is not cracked and does not contain any air bubbles, all numbers and lines are readable, the bezel is secure yet turns as required and the magnetic needle moves freely. If you discover any issues, do not use this compass.
- Limitations near metal or electrical sources—metal and electricity in proximity to a compass will cause it to function erratically and cannot be relied upon for accuracy. Even metal zippers and eyeglass frames have been known to interfere with compass operation. Cell phones should be positioned so the body shields the compass from the phone's emissions. The following separation distances are recommended:

    - High-tension power lines.............................. 55 meters.
    - Vehicles and metal buildings........................ 18 meters.
    - Telephone wires and barbed wire .... 10 meters.
    - Metal tables.. 2 meters.
    - Metal zippers and eyeglasses...................... 1/3 meter.

- Accuracy—Compasses should be periodically tested/checked against known/surveyed azimuths (declination station). If your resource has not set up a declination station, you should verify your compass against a number of others using a fixed location and designated target.

- Protection—When not in use, a compass should be kept closed (if foldable), covered and away from magnetized sources.

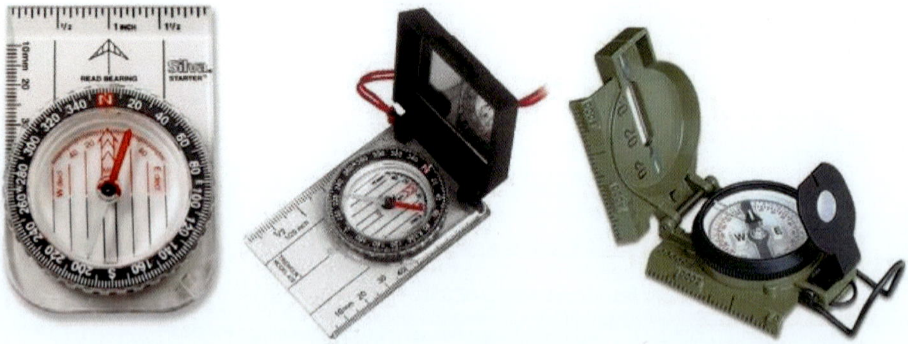

Baseplate, Orienteering and Lensatic Compasses

Now let's look at how to properly hold a compass. If you have a baseplate compass, or plan to use your orienteering or lensatic compass in a *centerhold* technique do the following:

- Finger/Hand position—The most widely used (due to stability and accuracy) has the thumbs crossed at the rear of the compass and the index fingers extended on either side of the baseplate. As an alternate method you can position your thumbs extended on either side of the compass, as the above method uses the index fingers. See the images below:

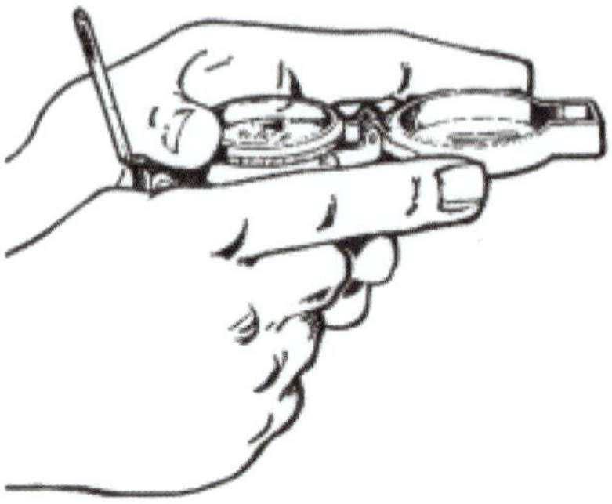

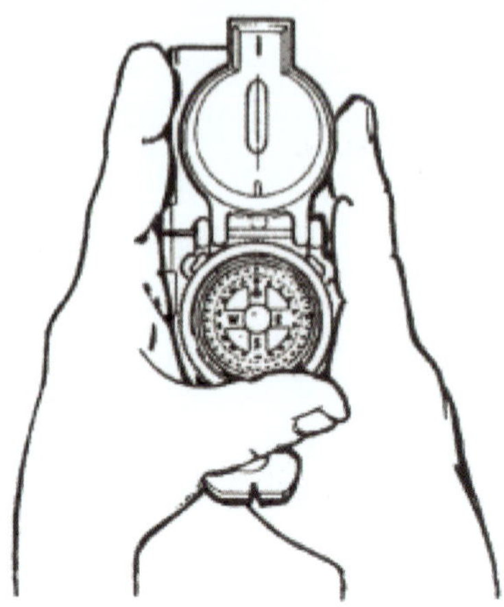

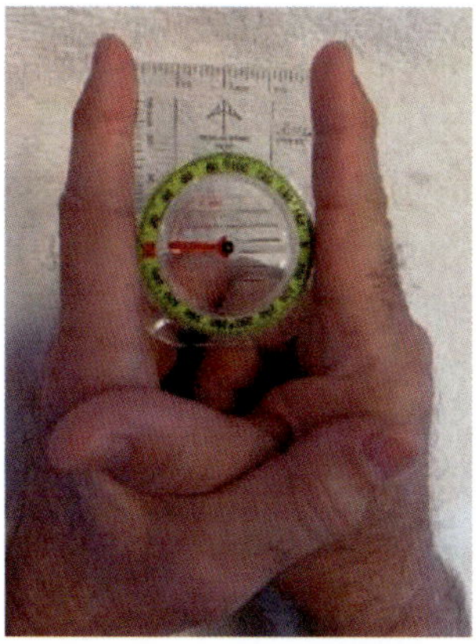

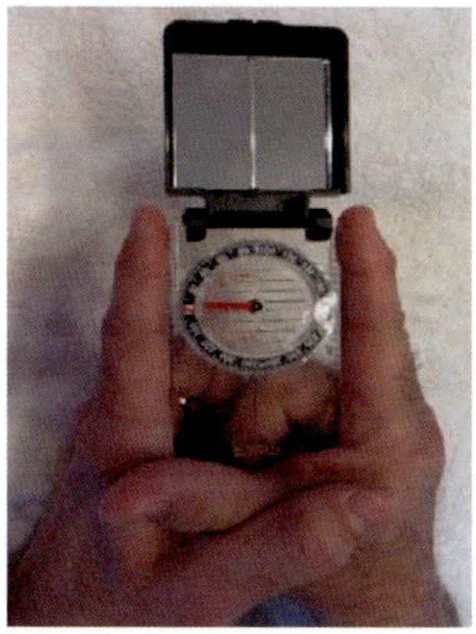

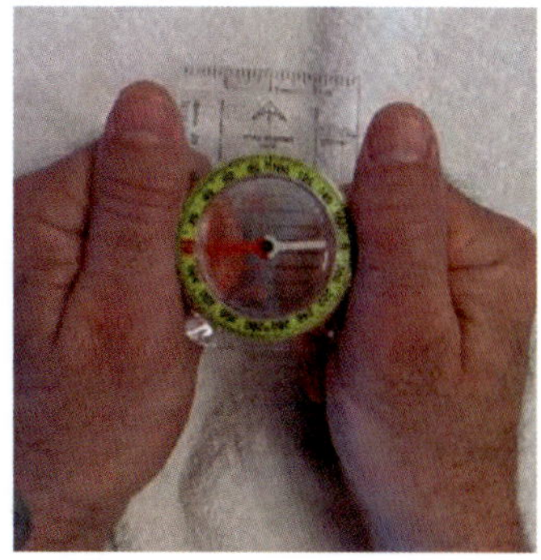

- Lock your elbows—Keeping your elbows against your side will place the compass between your chest and waist and provide a stable platform. Very importantly, it also limits your ability to move the compass side-to-side without turning your body.
- Level the compass—It is very important to keep the compass level. If the compass is tilted up or down the magnetic needle will touch the top or bottom of the bezel and will not float freely.
- Turn with your body—It is also extremely important that you *do not drive or steer* the compass by turning it with your wrist. When trying to align the magnetic needle with the orienting lines ("putting Red Fred in the shed") in the bezel (or 360° in the case of a lensatic compass) you must learn to turn your entire body. Do not pivot on your feet or twist your body. You must rotate your entire body, including shuffling your feet, to achieve the desired direction. More on this technique should be covered by your Instructor when you receive your practical training.
- Head position—When using the centerhold method you must position your head directly above the compass. This positions your head to rotate exactly 90° forward up and down to look at the compass and then the target while maintaining your head straight. Also, if your head and eyes are not directly over the compass you will not position the magnetic needle directly in the orienting lines to accurately determine azimuth.

If you are using an orienteering compass the recommended holding technique is the *pistol sighting* method. Holding the baseplate with index finger crooked under the baseplate and thumb on top, clench remaining fingers as if holding a pistol. Position the compass in front of the dominant eye with the sights above the mirror at a height that allows you to see through the sight to your target and also into the mirror only by moving your eye. It is very important the compass remains stationary. Should the compass be moved it can change your sight picture enough that you will choose the wrong target for the desired azimuth. See the image below:

If you are using a lensatic compass the usual method of holding the compass is known as the *compass-to-cheek technique*. In this method the grip is much like the pistol sight grip noted above. This grip is somewhat easier on the typical lensatic compass as there is usually a lanyard ring that is held between the index finger and the base of the thumb, or by placing the thumb through the lanyard ring. The compass is then positioned against the cheek. Tilt your head so you are sighting a target through the sight on top of the magnifier with the sighting wire in the compass cover centered. The wire must be centered in the cover slot and magnifier sight, and on the target simultaneously. Just as with the orienteering compass head position should be such that you should only need to move your eye up to sight your target and down to read the azimuth through the magnifier. If your compass is positioned correctly, your head will not move at all. Otherwise, your determined bearing or navigation track will be inaccurate. See the images below for this method:

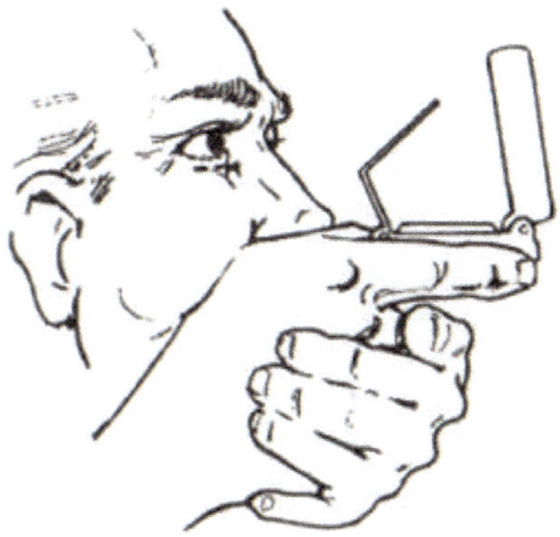

Now that we know how to hold our compasses and how to look at/through them, let's consider using them to navigate to a target. There are two scenarios we need to learn. The first scenario will cover navigating to a target with a known azimuth. This is the typical setting when we have used our map to determine a direction (magnetic bearing) of travel from one location to another. The second scenario will cover determining the bearing to a known target. As an adjunct to this we will learn how *reverse azimuth* may apply in this case. This setting is the most frequently encountered when using triangulation/resection to determine our current location. We will learn both these scenarios exclusive of distance measuring which will be covered later in this chapter.

Navigating to a target via a bearing—Let's assume you have been given a search segment assignment. You've correctly performed your map work and have determined the bearing (adjusted for magnetic declination) for each leg. Now it's time to start your travel. Let's start with using a baseplate or orienteering compass. Put the compass lanyard over your neck and:

1. Set the bezel—When a known azimuth is to be followed, we need to set that bearing in our compass. This is accomplished

by twisting the bezel until the desired azimuth is placed directly under the fixed index line in the bearing wheel or against the index mark against the bezel wheel, depending on the model of compass you are using. As with all compass techniques, it is essential you be very precise. **For each degree you are inaccurate, you will be 18 meters (left or right) of the target after only traveling 1000 meters!**

2. Select an intermediate target—It is rare that we can navigate to the ultimate target in one segment. So we will need to select intermediate targets on our bearing line. Holding your compass as described above, carefully rotate (shuffle) your entire body until the red magnetic pointer is exactly centered between the bezel orienting lines at the N(orth) indicator. This is the famous "putting red Fred dead in the shed" we have discussed. Once again, this centering must be precise. **Do not move the compass twisting your wrist or waist! You must center the magnetic pointer by moving your entire body, including your feet.** If using a baseplate compass, lift your head directly (do not turn or twist your head at all) to find a fixed object that lies centered on the azimuth in your compass. If you are using an orienteering compass you should raise your eye up to look through the sight on top of the mirror to locate a fixed object centered in the sight. See the textbox hint to avoid some pitfalls.

> HINT
>
> Many new navigators make two mistakes in selecting their "intermediate targets." 1. Choose a distinct object that will be identifiable as you approach it—Be careful of trees as they start looking alike as you get close! 2. Your chosen object must lie exactly on your azimuth. Even slightly off course will cause an error that will grow/compound as you travel further! Be precise!

3. Travel to the intermediate target—Once you have identified the object you will use as an intermediate target, let your compass dangle from its lanyard or put it back in its case. Do not attempt to "steer" to your target using the compass.

If you've chosen a proper target you can simply walk to the target, or perform your search technique between your current location and the target.

4. Repeat Steps 1, 2 and 3—Now you must continue these actions until you complete the leg and reach your ultimate target.

If you are using a lensatic compass you will still follow the same four steps noted above. The difference lies in setting the desired azimuth with the bezel. To do so:

a. Hold the compass level in the palm of the hand.
b. Rotate it until the desired azimuth falls under the fixed black index line (for example, 320°), maintaining the azimuth as prescribed.
c. Turn the bezel ring until the luminous line is aligned with the north-seeking arrow. Once the alignment is obtained, the compass is preset.

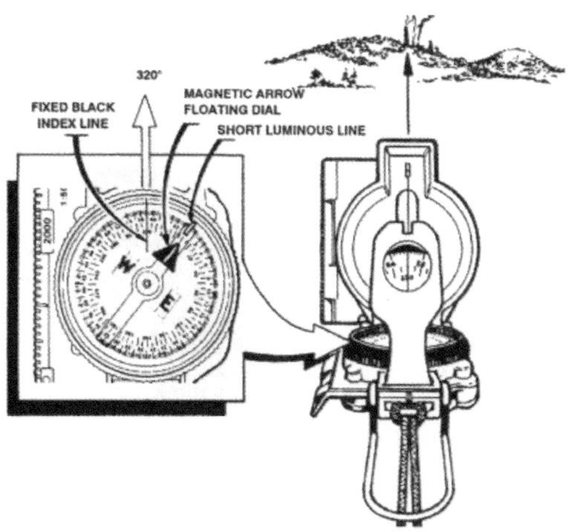

Determining a bearing to and from an object/target—Now that we've learned how to sight a known azimuth to a target, let's discuss how to determine a bearing to a known target. This is especially important in defining our current position accurately. As before we'll start with baseplate and orienteering compasses. The steps to do so are as follows:

1. Sight your target—Using the sighting techniques we previously described, line up your direction of travel arrow or your mirror sight directly on your target.
2. Rotate your bezel—While maintaining your target centered in your compass sight (or with the direction of travel arrow), rotate the bezel until the 360° (N) mark is centered on the red magnetic pointer. This is the classic "put red Fred dead in the shed" technique we previously described.
3. Read the bearing—Now read the azimuth at the index line in the bezel (or at the index mark adjacent to the bezel if your compass does not have a transparent bezel). This is the bearing *to* the target.

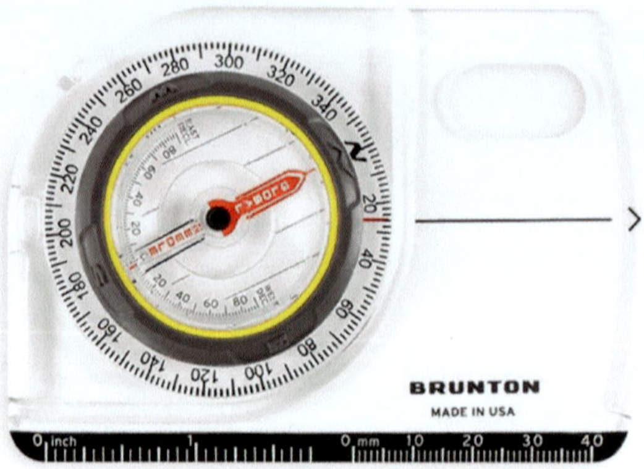

Compass showing a bearing of 26°

Determining the bearing to an object with a lensatic compass is even easier. Hold the compass against your cheek, as previously discussed. Center your target using the guide wire in the cover slot and the sight on the magnifier. While maintaining the target centered, move your eye to look through the magnifier. Read the bearing on the azimuth dial that is under the fixed index line. This is the bearing *to* the target.

Reverse Azimuth—When trying to determine our unknown position using known features or landmarks, we will need to know the bearing *from* each of these points. There are also times when we navigate in teams or "buddies." The responder in the lead will need to verify the track by shooting a bearing *back* to the primary navigator. These *back* (or "from") bearings are known as *reverse azimuths.*

Mathematically we can easily calculate the reverse azimuth. First, remember that a circle, in this case the compass rose, consists of 360°. To calculate a reverse azimuth, we will add or subtract 180 to/from the bearing to the object. If the bearing to the object is less than 180°, simply add 180. For example, if the bearing to our landmark is 120°, add 180 for a reverse azimuth of 300°. The second example has a bearing to the landmark of 200°. Since this is greater than 180, we will subtract the 180 for a reverse azimuth of 20°.

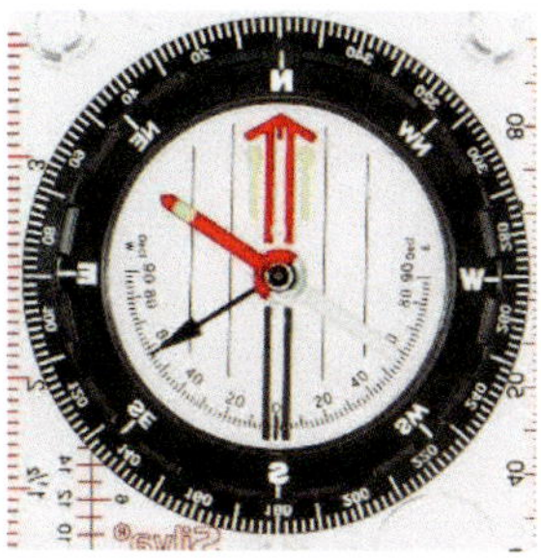

Plotting Field Bearings on a Map

We have learned to use a compass to navigate on a known bearing, determine an unknown bearing to a target and calculate a reverse azimuth. Frequently, we must plot these bearings on a map. In order to do this, we must apply the concept of magnetic declination we learned in SARAware™. Remember to use map bearings in the field we add or subtract the local magnetic declination to/from that bearing based on its orientation West or East. This same concept applies in converting field bearings to map bearings, only in reverse. Use the table below in applying magnetic declination:

Declination Orientation	Apply Map to Field	Apply Field to Map
East	Subtract the Declination	Add the Declination
West	Add the Declination	Subtract the Declination

Practice this map and field skill diligently. During the field skills portion of this course your Instructor will be giving you assignments that presume your proficiency.

Whatever environment (wilderness, urban, etc.) we find ourselves searching, it will be necessary to measure distance. Unless we're fortunate enough to be searching a road with distance markers, we must have a method of determining how far we have traveled (on foot) or when we have traveled far enough to have reached our destination. One way to measure ground distance is the pace count.

A pace is equal to one natural stride. A stride consists of two natural length steps. An easy way to think of this is to count every time a particular foot hits the ground. For example, if you take your first step with your right foot, then your left foot is your "anchor foot." A stride will be counted each time the anchor foot (in this example your left foot) is placed on the ground.

To accurately use the pace count method, you must know how many paces it takes you to walk 100 meters. To determine this, you must walk an accurately measured course and count the number of strides you take. A pace course can be as short as 100 meters or as long as 600 meters, but is typically based on the 100 meter distance. The pace course, regardless of length, must be on similar terrain to that you will be walking over. It does no good to walk a course on flat terrain and then try to use that pace count on hilly terrain. The same concept applies to vegetation or obstacles. The measured pace course must reflect these factors as well.

To determine your pace count on a 100-meter course, count the paces it takes you to walk the 100 meters. It is strongly recommended you walk back on the same 100 meter course counting your strides on this return trip. Taking the average of the two pace counts will be more accurate than just a single pass. Now divide 100 by the (average) paces. The answer will give you the average length of your stride. This is also known as the *stride factor* or just *factor*. You will need to know this to calculate distance walked when you don't know the distance to your target. Let's say that it takes you 66 paces to walk 100 meters in the tested terrain. Doing the math results in an average length stride or factor of 1.52 meters. Once we know this, we can now calculate how far we have walked.

Let's assume we have walked 30 strides. Simply multiply the paces (30) times the factor (1.52 meters) to determine the distance traveled. In this case 30 x 1.52 = 45.6 meters. Now let's consider the situation when we need to travel a known distance. By applying the same mathematical principles (simple algebra) we can adapt the formula to calculate the paces required to cover that distance. For example, our map work tells us we need to travel 90 meters to reach a target where we will change course (bearing). We need to divide the distance (90 meters) by stride factor (1.52). In this case, 90/1.52 = 59.2 strides. Decimals or fractions of a stride are distances too short to worry over. It is recommended that you round according to mathematical principles. If the decimal is less than .5 round down. If the decimal is .5 or higher, round up. In our example (59.2 strides) we would choose to walk 59 strides. This is essential knowledge to the responder. It is important that you remember the formulas in the table below:

DESIRED RESULT	FORMULA
Factor	Factor = Distance Walked/Number of Paces
Distance	Distance = Number of Paces X Factor
Paces	Paces = Distance/Factor

It is imperative that each person who navigates knows his pace count in the specific environment. It is also very important to not lose track of our pace count or we will be forced to go back and start that leg over again! Let's discuss two devices and one "natural way" to keep track of our paces:

1. The "natural" method involves picking up a stick or pebble. For example, choose a multiple of paces to pick up a pebble. Perhaps we pick up a pebble every 20 strides. When we have 5 pebbles in our pocket we know we have traveled 100 strides. The same can be done with sticks. You can also put knots in a string or marks in a notebook. The trick is to keep it simple so you don't get distracted from your assigned task.

2. Using the tried and true military method is also an option. This involves the use of "Ranger Beads." Notice in this image there are two sizes of beads. There are 10 of the smaller ones on the cord. If we move a small bead every 10 strides we will have traveled 100 strides when we have moved all 10 small beads. Now move one of the large beads and replace the small beads to start again. Once you have moved all the large beads you can begin the entire process over again.

3. Another popular device is a commercial inventory counter, also known as a "clicker" for the sound it makes. Use of this device is very simple. You can choose a multiple of strides or even activate the clicker with each stride. It is perhaps the easiest method to keep track of our pace count. This method can be performed mostly subconsciously. Especially if we "click" the device each time our anchor foot hits the ground.

Earlier, we noted that certain conditions will affect your pace count in the field. You must allow for them by making adjustments. The best method is to use a 100 meter course that closely resembles the environment you will be navigating. But knowledge of these effects can help you if conditions change:

1. Slopes—Your pace lengthens on a downslope and shortens on an upgrade. Keeping this in mind, if it normally takes you 70 strides to walk 100 meters, your pace count may increase to 75 or more when walking up a slope.
2. Winds—A head wind shortens the pace and a tail wind increases it.
3. Loose Surfaces—Sand, gravel, mud, snow, and similar surface materials tend to shorten the pace.
4. Weather Elements—Falling snow, rain, or ice cause the pace to be reduced in length.

5. Clothing—Excess clothing and boots with poor traction affect the pace length.
6. Visibility—Poor visibility, such as in fog, rain, or darkness, will shorten your pace.

Searching While Navigating

For those of us in Search & Rescue it is not enough to navigate. We must conduct search tactics while performing the required navigation. The tactics necessary to be successful will vary based on whether you are working in the urban or rural/wilderness environments. As most of our compass use will occur in the wilderness setting, let's discuss two methods of staying on "track" while searching in this environment.

Solo navigation—We'll never really search a segment on our own. We'll always be part of a team/unit. But it is possible that one person on the team will be designated the navigator. That person is responsible for keeping the entire unit headed in the correct direction while searching. If it is daylight conditions, this technique works well:

1. Set your compass for the desired bearing and select an appropriate target in line with that bearing.
2. Walk towards your target, counting your paces.
3. If you are unable to reach your target without straying from your bearing, go as far as you can walk straight and plant your tracking stick. If you can continue all the way, straight, to your target fasten flagging tape on the target. Note your pace count and calculate the distance traveled.
4. Now, advise your team to conduct their search tactic from the point you started to a line equal to your current position.
5. When they reach the virtual line equal to your position, repeat the process until the search segment is covered appropriately.

Buddy navigation—This is an effective method to use in very thick vegetation or at night when it's difficult to select a distinctive target.

While similar to solo navigation, it requires two people to work as a navigation team:

1. Set your compass and sight a general direction based on the desired bearing.
2. Have your "buddy" begin walking along the track of your bearing. They may need to be waving their tracking stick (with flagging tape attached) or be wearing a visible light source to keep track of them. The buddy must be performing a pace count technique and calculate distance traveled.
3. Have your buddy stop (some form of communication must be available or they must be within shouting range) at the edge of your visual range.
4. Now instruct your buddy to move to his/her left or right until they are centered on the correct azimuth.
5. Your buddy should now take a bearing on you to ensure that you are centered on the reverse azimuth.
6. Now inform your team to conduct their search tactic from the starting point to a line equal to your buddy's position. You will be able to assist in the search effort as your navigation duties are temporarily fulfilled.
7. Once the unit reaches the distance traveled by your buddy, repeat the process.

In the urban and suburban environments it is likely we will search segments bordered by streets or other fixed and visible boundaries. So while we have spent our time focused on navigating with compass make sure your map knowledge and technique is current and proficient to function well in these environments.

Circumnavigating an Obstacle

If we lived in an ideal world, we would be able to conduct all our navigation on a straight line with no obstructions in the way. Since that is not the case let's consider how we can get around obstacles and back on our original track required by our search assignment. The most accurate way is to employ right angles, also known as blocking.

Blocking—As noted above, using right angles to move around an obstacle is the preferred method. Let's use the example where you are tracking a 090° azimuth when you encounter a body of water too deep to cross directly:

1. Proceed on your 090° bearing to a point close to the obstacle but still allowing space to turn "around" the obstacle. Choose the direction that will provide the shortest distance to clear the obstacle.
2. Set your compass to a bearing that is 90° towards the direction you have chosen. Let's choose to turn right as it is the shortest distance to the edge of our obstacle. The gives us a new azimuth of 180°.
3. Navigate on this new (180°) bearing until you have cleared the obstacle, measuring the distance traveled from the point where you turned onto this heading. In our example it is 150 meters.
4. Set your compass back to the original azimuth of 090°. Then proceed to navigate on this bearing until clear of the other side of the obstacle. You must record this distance and add it to your original distance traveled, on the 090° heading, until you encountered the obstruction.
5. Now set your compass to the reverse azimuth of your original deviation. In our example the reverse azimuth of 180° is 360°. Set your compass to 360° and navigate the same distance as your original deviation. In our case that was 150 meters.
6. After navigating this 150 meters, change your bearing to 090°and you are back on your original azimuth line. Resume your navigation on this heading.

Two important points to remember: First, whenever navigating on your original heading, continue to add your distance. This keeps your cumulative distance to the ultimate target accurate. Second, always use 90° offsets/deviations. When you do so, and remain accurate with your offset distances, you will return on your precise, original bearing track. See our example in the image below:

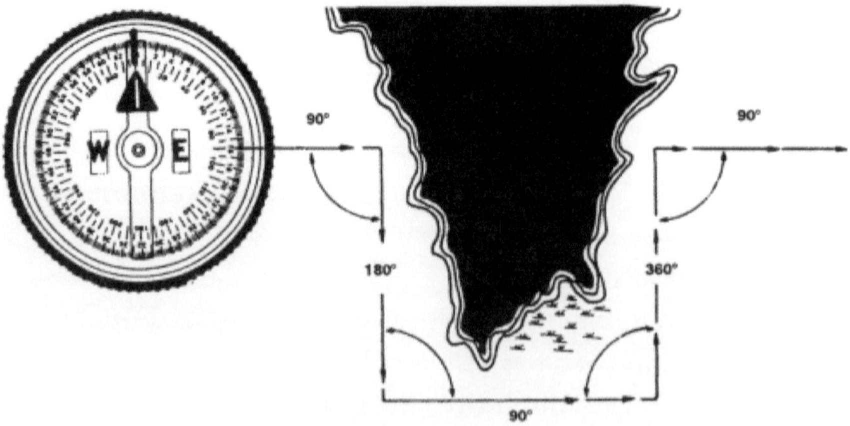

Summary

We hope you have learned much about navigating, in the field, using a compass. When you combine this skill with the map & compass techniques taught in *SARAware*™ you have the foundation to develop competence in navigation. What remains for you is to join a qualified Instructor to review and practice these skills. Once you become proficient, remember that these skills are perishable. You must continue to practice on a regular basis to be ready to serve your fellow man whenever the call comes.

Reference

The Essential Wilderness Navigator: How to Find Your Way in the Great Outdoors, 2nd ed. (2001) Seidman D. & Cleveland P., *Ragged Mountain Press*, Camden Me

Wilderness Navigation: Finding Your Way Using Map, Compass, Altimeter & GPS 2nd ed. (2004) Burns B. & Burns M., *The Mountaineer Books*, Seattle WA

Be Expert with Map and Compass, Rev ed., (2010) Kjellstrom-Elgin C (prev ed. & Kjellstrom B), *John Wiley & Sons*, Inc., Hoboken NJ

Field Manual No. 3-25-26 Map Reading and Land Navigation, (2001) Headquarters, *Department of the Army*, Washington DC

SARAware-Awareness Level Search & Rescue for the Responder, (2013) Petaros D, Keck J & Podboy W, *AERIE Publications*, Lake Dallas TX

9

Using GPS in SAR

Objectives

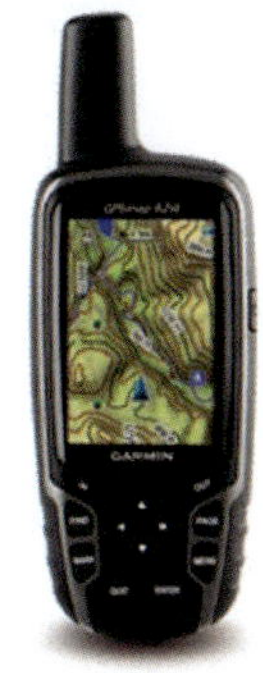

Courtesy of Garmin

- Describe the GPS satellite constellation, including the international components
- Discuss how GPS technology utilizes range to determine location
- List some limitations to accurate GPS functioning or use including:
  - Obstructions to Line of Sight
  - Limited accuracy to altimetry
  - Human input errors
  - Misreading screen display
  - Battery failure
  - Moisture
  - Satellite outage
- Describe GPS components accessible or utilized by the user
- Discuss GPS setup/customization including units, datum and position format.
- Define datum and why correct datum selection is important.
- Describe the concept of waypoints and their uses in SAR.
- Explain the concept of routes/tracks
- Discuss transferring of GPS data from field unit to Command Post computer

In ancient times, when man's understanding of the earth's magnetic poles and magnetic compasses were thousands of years from being invented, man looked into the night skies for a means of navigating across the lands and the seas. Many centuries later, man is still, in a sense, looking towards the sky for a means to navigate the lands, seas and skies of our planet. With the advent of technologies like radio, space travel and digital processing we have been able to achieve incredible accuracy of not only knowing which direction to head towards, but also more importantly to know exactly where we are standing on earth to a precision of less than an inch.

History of Radio Navigation

Photo courtesy of Google

Early military radio site

Courtesy of Wikipedia

Sextant

In the early days of radio, scientists where trying to understand how a man made signal is transmitted. Additionally, scientists wanted to understand how a radio signal propagates or travels through the atmosphere and what affects the path of that signal. When World War II started, the British and American Navies were searching for a means to improve navigation for its massive shipments of war relief supplies to England and later on U.S. military personnel, supplies and equipment needed to support the war effort in both the European and Pacific theaters.

The need for improvement in navigation was not so much as how to navigate to a specific location, but more importantly of where that ship/convoy was located at any given moment. The North Atlantic Ocean can be a very inhospitable place because of its frequent storms and its abrupt changes in currents. The skies might cloud over for many days and nights making navigation with a sextant or star maps impossible.

If a ship was attacked by an enemy submarine, a call for help would only be met by delays in attempting to locate the vessel's last known position. A better way had to be found and it was discovered in a radio system known as LORAN. LORAN is an acronym for LOng RAnge Navigation.

Photo courtesy of Wikipedia

LORAN Radio Equipment

The LORAN equipment was big and bulky and utilized vacuum tubes that required a significant amount of power to operate. The equipment was not portable and had to be mounted in ships and aircraft.

LORAN was an incredible leap in knowledge and technology for its time. Many scientific break throughs were the result of LORAN development.

Scientists were able to determine the speed at which radio waves traveled and therefore they could determine the distance or range from the transmitter in a given time period of where the ship or aircraft was located. However, a single transmitter could not provide very accurate locations.

The scientists began experimenting with two transmitters, each transmitting simultaneously on a given frequency. Each transmitter provided a timing pulse contained in its signal. By determining the arrival time of each pulse, a mathematical calculation could measure the distance from each transmitter. A line could then be drawn on a map plotting the intersection of both transmitters' signals at their respective distances and a ship's location could be determined.

The accuracy was initially tens of miles. With the addition of more transmitters, the accuracy could be improved to within a few thousand feet. This was the beginning of Radio Location/Navigation.

Looking to the stars

In 1957, with the Cold War in full swing, the (former) Soviet Union launched the first manmade satellite, known as Sputnik, into orbit around the earth. This single event created an arms race between the United States of America and the former Soviet Union.

While Sputnik was orbiting the earth, U.S. Scientists were monitoring the radio signals from Sputnik. They were able to determine through calculation based upon certain changes in the satellite's radio signals, its location at any point in its orbit. What the scientists discovered was the Doppler Effect. Doppler Effect or Doppler shift is a change in the received frequency produced by a moving object. This is very similar to the sound of a train whistle that changes as a train passes by the listener. Even though the whistle does not change its transmitted frequency, speed distorts the sound to the listener, or to the receiver in the case of the satellite.

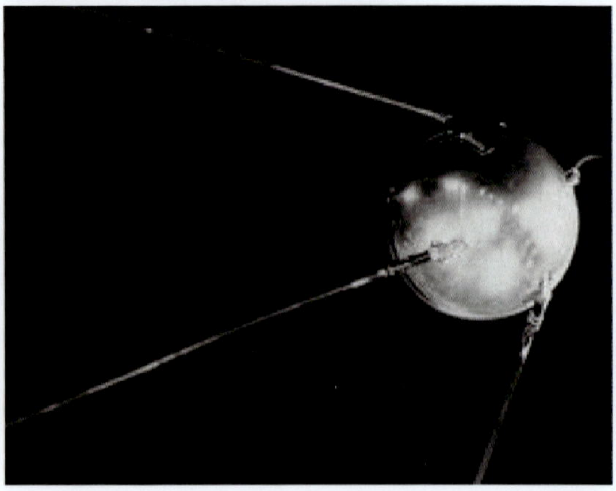

Photo Courtesy of NASA JPL

Sputnik.

This discovery of the ability of predictable locations launched the Department of Defense investigation into satellite based navigation systems, which allowed the Navy to increase the accuracy of its submarine based ballistic missiles. The US military developed several satellite based systems in the early 60s and 70s for military use. These systems were based upon multiple satellites orbiting the earth.

The systems, or more appropriately called constellations, utilized satellites with very precise atomic clocks on board. The satellites sent a timing pulse embedded in their signal. The receivers on the ground had a very accurate clock (these were not atomic clocks). These receivers were able to determine the delay between the satellite's transmitted signal and the

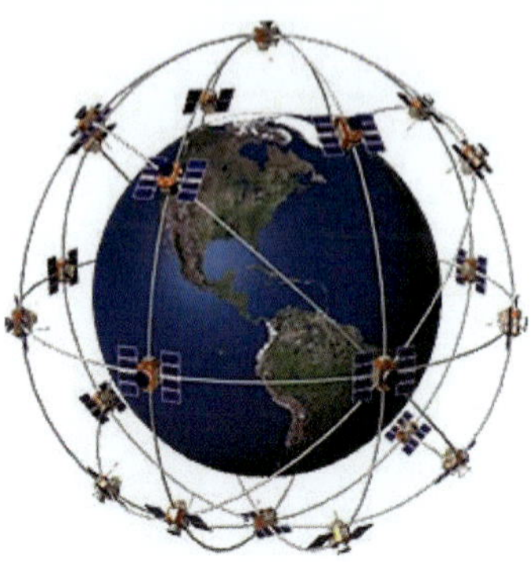

Courtesy of Google

GPS constellation

receiver's internal clock and compare them with an internal database of the satellite's orbital parameters.

By comparing the clock pulses from more than one satellite, a location could be calculated with increased accuracy and even the altitude of the receiver could be determined. Ideally, 4 or more satellites were needed for reasonable accuracy as well as altitude and velocity information.

In 1983, then President Ronald Reagan issued a directive making GPS (Global Positioning Satellite) system available for the common good. The first of the current GPS constellations was launched just prior to 1990.

The current system supports both military and civilian users. However, initially, the civilian portion of the system had intentional errors introduced into the data stream that was transmitted. This was called Selective Availability. These intentional errors caused decreased accuracy of civilian GPS receivers for location and altitudes of more than 100 meters. This was purposely done to prevent terrorists and anarchists from utilizing the GPS for very accurate delivery or detonation of explosive devices.

During President Bill Clinton's administration, he issued a directive to turn off the Selective Availability, for civilians, in May of 2000. This change in operational function improved civilian GPS accuracy to within 20 meters. Since that time, many improvements have been made to the system of which additional satellites and new technologies have been employed to improve accuracy to less than 20 meters for the common GPS receiver.

While the United States has made GPS available for everyone world wide, other governments including Russia, China, Japan and several European countries are developing their own constellations. These constellations will also introduce new technologies as well.

Personal Locator Beacons

Courtesy of Pains Wessex

Maritime EPIRB

One expanding use of the GPS technology is the Emergency Personal Locator Beacon. There are several types of these beacons. Some systems are government owned and others are private.

The Emergency Position Indicator Radio Beacon (EPIRB) was originally designed for maritime use. When activated, it transmits an emergency digital message containing the vessel's name and registered owner on frequency 406 MHZ to the COSPAS-SAR satellite system. Using the Doppler Effect, the satellite command center determines the location of the beacon in a geographically small area. Rescuers then utilize another frequency to home in on the beacon. By using this method, there is no need for a constellation of satellites, thereby reducing costs.

Some of the EPIRB beacons can utilize a separate GPS receiver and encode more specific location information in the transmitted digital message sent to the satellite.

Courtesy of ACR Aertex

Personal Locator Beacon

PLBs or Personal Locator Beacons are used by individuals. These are beacons that operate very similar to the EPIRBs. These units are required by law to be registered with the appropriate governmental agencies in the participating countries. The registration information is placed into a database that also contains the EPIRB and PLB's Electronic Serial Number (ESN) so quick identification can be made with responsible parties. The service is free of charge.

There are also several private companies that provide a pay for service for PLBs. These units receive GPS location information and then when activated send the information to a commercial satellite. The satellite then relays the ESN and location information to the companies' respective control centers. This is a subscription service and the companies are under no obligation to process emergency requests for units belonging to non-subscription customers.

ELT or Emergency Locator Transmitter

Courtesy of National Library of Australia

ELT

For decades, commercial aircraft have been required to have locating beacons installed in the aircraft that would be activated manually or upon impact. These beacons operate on 121.5 and 406 MHz. Ground and Air Search units can radio direction find or "home in" to the distinct signal. The process was not terribly accurate and required a great deal time for searching large areas of land and sea.

One of the features of most of the EPIRBs and PLBs is that they will still generate a signal on 121.5 MHz in combination of the 406 MHz data uplink. This allows EPIRB and PLBs that do not have a GPS data option to still provide a means for locating the beacon after a generalized area has been determined.

Limitations of GPS

While there are many advantages to using a GPS in SAR, there are some noted issues and concerns. The user must consider these if we are to make accurate and proper use of these tools.

A. GPS requires line of sight between the GPS receiver and the GPS constellations. Being in heavy vegetation or deep narrow canyons may preclude the receiver from seeing any of the current 32 satellites in orbit.

B. Accuracy is a function of the GPS receiver. Most current GPS receivers have 12 or more parallel channel receivers built into the unit. The more satellites that can be viewed by the receiver at any one given time, the more accurate the information displayed will be.

C. When it comes to errors, the human factor is the most significant concern. Incorrect data entered into the GPS unit will obviously produce errors and undesirable results. For example, entering the wrong Datum. In addition to bad input data by the user, incorrect reading or interpolations of the screen display will cause unwarranted errors.

D. The GPS receiver is an electronic device and as such requires electrical power to operate. In the case of units in the field, they require batteries and the potential for equipment failure exists unless the user maintains a supply of fresh batteries.

E. As with any other electronic equipment, moisture or water damage may render the GPS unit inoperable. However, most modern GPS units are water proof or at least water resistant, thereby reducing that concern to the operator.

F. An additional problem is the possibility of Satellite outages. Typically when there is an issue with a Satellite, it will send an "unhealthy" indicator in its transmissions so that receivers can therefore ignore that particular satellite.

G. Other reasons for satellite outages include high sunspot activity and radio signal interference. These issues can and will produce failure of the GPS receiver or will at least produce significant errors in its accuracy.

Using GPS for SAR

One of the most important aspects regarding GPS and SAR is the selection of a GPS receiver. Having the correct features and options are very important to the SAR member.

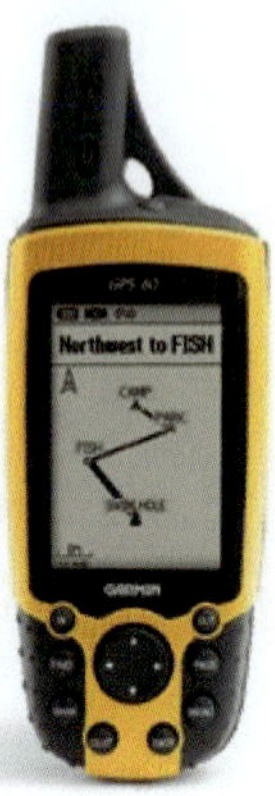

Courtesy of Garmin

Handheld GPS Unit

Size and weight: A small handheld GPS is now very commonplace. The unit weighs ounces, not pounds, and can fit into a shirt pocket. These units are typically powered by 2 or 3 AA batteries and provide 12-20 hours of operational time. Standard off the shelf batteries become a significant convenience for the operator. Rechargeable batteries are not recommended for field operations.

Waypoint: Waypoints are navigational locations that can be manually added to the memory of the GPS for later recall. These locations could be evidence that has been found, tracks, starting points of search areas, hazards or even helispots for later extractions of patients or ground crews. In short, waypoints can be anything that is worth noting.

Tracks: Tracks are an automatically generated series of waypoints based upon measured time and distance. They are then loaded into the memory of the GPS unit. These tracks are sometimes referred to as "bread crumb trails" or routes. The tracks are ideal for later recall of exactly which search areas have been covered and how much of the assigned area was effectively covered.

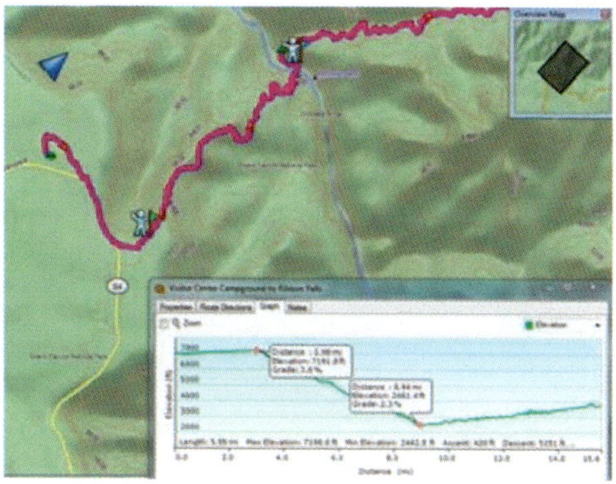

Courtesy of DeLorme

GPS Track

Maps, Datums and Grid Systems: Most of the newer GPS units have the ability to download topographical maps into the units so the user has the ability to view maps in detail without the necessity of carrying multiple maps. This also allows the SAR personnel to view the bigger picture of the environment which they are searching in.

Datums are mathematical references developed from a known and surveyed location on the earth. All maps utilize a datum of one form or another. A problem is created when a different datum is input in the GPS than is used on the applicable map. The actual field locations could be hundreds, if not thousands, of meters different than noted on the map.

This issue of datums must be resolved before search teams are deployed. All teams must utilize the same datum. Examples of common datums are NAD27 (North America Datum 1927) or the more commonly used WGS84 (World Geodetic Survey 1984). Most topographical maps will indicate what datum the map was surveyed with. The second part of the map datum issue is that SAR personnel must know what type of map grid system is going to be used: UTM

(Universal Transverse Mercator), Longitude Latitude (and its variations), Township Range, etc.

Most importantly, everyone needs to be on the "same page" with GPS configurations or critical errors in locations will be introduced into search operations. The Datum and grid format should be a part of every briefing given to teams before deployment.

Courtesy of Garmin

Typical SAR GPS

Data Export: One of the greatest advantages of modern GPS receivers is the ability to export the data from the searchers' GPS to the Command Post's computers. Waypoints and tracks can be overlaid onto the search maps and an accurate map can be created. This presents incident management a detailed graphic of which areas have and have not been searched. This information becomes critical for planning search areas during the next operational period. Another good idea is to have searchers bring the data cable for their GPS with them to the command post. There are many different GPS units available and each requires a different data cable to download tracks and waypoints.

Typical Search Configuration

While providing exact setup procedures for each and every GPS unit would be nearly impossible, a generic sequence can be provided.

1. Ensure that your batteries are fresh or if the unit has rechargeable batteries make sure they are fully charged.
2. Clear all existing waypoints: There is no need to down load old data on to a search map. In some cases, you may be working a search area that is the scene of several searches each year. No need to clutter the search map with old and incorrect data that may confuse the operations and planning teams.
3. Clear all existing routes or tracks: Remember one of the benefits of modern GPS units for SAR is that they can record a track or route of a search team in their assigned area.

Again, old data will only will only clutter and confuse the search map and provide inaccurate information.

4. Set the map datum: Make sure that you are using the correct map datum or inaccuracies in locations will be generated.
5. Set the correct map format: i.e. UTM, Longitude Latitude (dd. mm.ss etc). Everyone must be using the correct format or errors will occur.
6. Load critical map locations: It is very common for search managers to provide specific location references. These include search team insertion and extraction points, subject last seen locations, helicopter landing zone or extract, areas etc.
7. Load waypoints for your search area: Define your search area with coordinates (4 or more corners, etc.). This will help you determine if you have covered your assigned area thoroughly and increase your POD.
8. If possible, make sure someone else on the team has a GPS and has configured it correctly. Now, in the event of equipment failure, you have backup data.

The GPS is a wonderful tool for SAR, but as mentioned previously, it must be configured and operated correctly or faulty data will be introduced into the operation. Good graphical information that shows waypoints indicating tracks or evidence can greatly help planners visualize patterns. These patterns are helpful in determining victim behavior or tendencies and hopefully lead to an expedient and successful outcome.

The GPS has become a staple in the lives of most Americans. It is almost a standard feature in our vehicles. Airlines and small aircraft use it to navigate the skies. Fishermen use it to locate their favorite fishing spots. And Search & Rescue uses GPS to save lives.

The GPS is a powerful tool that each SAR member needs to master. This includes knowing its advantages and disadvantages. However, the GPS is not a replacement for the map and compass. A compass does not need batteries nor does it become dependent upon a constellation of satellites. There are times in SAR that you will revert to the basics like map and compass to get the job done. Remember to not forsake one skill for the other and to keep all of your skills up to date.

References

Wikipedia, The Free Encyclopedia 2013, Loran—Pictures and information
http://en.wikipedia.org/wiki/LORAN

Wikipedia, The Free Encyclopedia 2013, EPIRB, PLB's—General information
http://en.wikipedia.org/wiki/Distress_radiobeacon

Federal Communications commission, Personal Locator Beacon Technical Information
http://www.fcc.gov/encyclopedia/personal-locator-beacons-plbs

Clue Orientation—the Key to the Mystery

10

Objectives

COURTESY OF WWW.COMPUTERCLIPART.COM

- Describe the concept clue detection and its importance in search
- Discuss the four categories of clues:
  - Physical
  - Documentary
  - Testimonial
  - Analytical
- Explain the roles of:
  - The Sensor
  - The Search Object
  - The Environment
- Describe at least 5 principles of clue orientation
- Discuss the Searcher Cube and the benefits it provides to clue acquisition and situational awareness
- Review Search Data and where it originates
- Describe POD, Coverage, and factors that affect them
- Differentiate the concepts of sign and track
- List the basic equipment required of field responders to conduct tracking tactics
- Explain how to identify, measure and label tracks
- Describe the processes of sign cutting
  - Step by step

    - Jump tracking
    - Bracketing
- Discuss how to properly communicate clue information from field to the Command Post

Search—the classic mystery

In our *SARAware*™ training, we learned that while searchers are always conscious of directly seeking out the subject, their main focus is on finding clues/evidence. Why you might ask? First there are many more clues left by the subject(s) than the number of subjects themselves. Search Management will assemble those clues found to modify current operations and update plans for continued search, hopefully leading to the acquisition of more clues. Finally, without clues we cannot plan how to conduct our search to maximize efficient use of our (always) limited resources.

If all participants perform their jobs appropriately, we will assemble enough clues to come to reasonable conclusion(s). Unlike the traditional mystery novel, we don't always find our subject. But by finding enough clues, and analyzing the clues and the circumstances around them, we can develop reasonably accurate theories. These theories will include: How the subject came to be missing. What has happened to the subject while missing. Where has the subject traveled while missing. And (perhaps) even where the subject is now—whether that location is precise enough to acquire or not.

Types of Clues

In developing the strategies to resolve the incident at hand, we must evaluate tactics that will reveal clues about the past and current situation. To do so we group clues into four categories: Physical, Documentation, Testimonial and Analytical.

- Physical Clues—This category is much as the name describes. These are physical items or sign, typically generated by the subject. They are frequently referred to as "hard evidence."

This category can include anything from footprints to discarded items, to vehicles to broken branches.

- Documentation—Generally considered as "written" evidence. Trail registers, credit card receipts, letters and computer records are all examples of this type of clue.
- Testimonial—This type of evidence is typically acquired through our investigatory interviewing techniques. It is the direct word of the subject's friends, peers, relatives, etc. It also includes the statements of any alleged "eye witnesses" to occurrences in the incident. This type of information is always questionable as to reliability and accuracy. It involves issues of misinterpretation and incompleteness. The interpreter must also look to eliminate "hearsay" and seek out first-hand information.
- Analytical Evidence—This category is also known as "statistical evidence." The most prevalent forms are databases. These include local databases reflecting information on previous cases that may bear some similarities and also national/international databases like ISRID (International Search and Rescue Incident Database). ISRID serves as the foundation for the most updated information on Lost & Missing Person Behavior.

  Another form of analytical evidence occurs through deduction (if "A" happened, then "B" must result) and consensus. Consensus happens when alternatives are presented to a group of knowledgeable individuals. When the group agrees on some likely alternatives, possibly with the assistance of other types of clues, we have consensus.

Factors affecting clue seeking

To continue our discussion of clue seeking, there are three major components that must be understood to enhance positive and counter negative effects. These are the concepts of The Sensor, The Search Object and The Environment.

Sensor—This is our field searcher. Our primary search sense is our vision. There are, of course, several limitations to the human sense of sight. But with technological aids in the form of binoculars, infrared, night vision and thermal sensing, we can improve the basic sense of sight. When we add the abilities of our other senses to our search efforts, we greatly enhance the likelihood of finding/acquiring physical evidence. As we are the sensor, this is the component we have the most control over. Search management must ensure that the searcher (sensor) has the most opportunity to detect the search object (clue). Management's primary efforts must be to come up with a strategy that will place searchers in segments where clues are likely to exist.

Next, management must ensure that the search resources are "clue aware" through extensive training and practice. Searchers must also be limited in their activities to prevent fatigue and boredom. U.S. Coast Guard and Air Force experiments demonstrated that the first four hours represented peak search effectiveness. It declines sharply after four hours, reaching least effectiveness by eight hours.

Searchers must be trained in the theory of *vision* and *recognition*. It is estimated that our subjects leave as many as 2000 pieces of evidence for every mile they travel. Searchers must be trained to both see those clues **and** to recognize them as clues. Searcher expectation plays a large role in both detection and recognition.

Searchers who don't believe the subject to have been in their assigned segment are much less likely to detect even obvious clues. Additionally, the likelihood of detecting clues when the same segment is "re-searched" by the same resource is dramatically lower than when using a different resource. Searcher attitude is the key to detection in both these examples. But there is one more searcher "expectation" that is vision/recognition oriented.

When we consider how we recognize an object we see, that object is more readily recognized when viewed in an "accepted" perspective. Consider this example: Draw a teacup. It doesn't matter how artistic you are, just draw a teacup the way you think of it. During research studies, most people drew something like this:

Why? Why didn't the research subjects draw the cup from above, like this?

It has to do with the concept of *canonical perspective.* Our brains are programmed to think of an object in this accepted perspective. When we see an object in the accepted view it is almost immediately recognizable. But when seen in a perspective that differs from the accepted view, the object, while seen, is not recognized and is not "detected." So some clues will not be detected because they are in a state that does not agree with the expected view. We'll discuss how searchers can improve their detection capabilities later in this chapter.

- Search Object—While we can't influence the features and appearances of the objects being sought, understanding the effect of those characteristics is essential to successful clue detection. Included in the list, among other things, is:
    - Size
    - Color
    - Contrast with the background
    - Amount of movement
    - Noisemaking ability

- Expectations of Searcher (Does the object appear in the expected view?)

The more information a searcher knows about the subject and possible search objects, the better the chance for detection. Briefing this information is among the more important functions of search management.

- Environment—A rather extensive list of environmental factors affect the ability of the sensor to detect the search object. They include:
  - Lighting and Shadows
  - Time of Day
  - Precipitation
  - Terrain footing
  - Vegetation
  - Obstacles
  - Distractions (in the Urban environment for example)

While we cannot avoid these conditions, we can practice our skills in a variety of circumstances. In doing so, we will better perform regardless of the environmental surroundings we may encounter.

Principles of clue orientation

As we've discussed clue detection is the foremost task of the field responder. In order to become truly aware, we must understand eight principles of clue orientation. Let's review these principles:

- Clue Seeking is a never-ending process. It begins with preplanning, continues through the active search operations and circles around with the after-action critique and updating of the preplan.

- Detection of clues is a learned skill. It is also perishable. Therefore clue seeking must be practiced on a continuing basis. It is best if you can incorporate this practice in everyday activities, as well as during your SAR exercise.
- Speculation on the nature of clues is allowed. But don't form concrete opinions unless you have all the clues and information. Of course, you'll never know when you have it all.
- Don't presuppose or form an opinion of the presence or value of clues. If you believe no clues are present in your segment you will not find the ones that are there. And, the next find or piece of information can change it all.
- Gather information from as many sources as possible. No single source can provide enough information to identify all possible clues.
- The more complete the subject profile you assemble the greater number of clues will be available. Your efforts to identify the clues as pertaining to the subject will also be more accurate.
- Conduct complete briefings of all personnel, especially field responders, to include reviews and information on "personal expectations," "canonical perspective," "snapshot" vs. scanning and the different categories of evidence. For example, individuals encountered in the search segment should be interviewed.
- Clues are often fragile, transitory or short lived. So document, photograph and preserve them as quickly as possible.

Search Data

During our study in SARAware™, we learned of information and clues garnered from the investigation process. While investigation never ends, we must act upon information gathered, once there is enough to formulate some hypotheses. Planning data gives us the information to determine the initial search area and the initial planning point. This part of planning will now allow us to begin deploying field resources. Some of these field resources may be used to

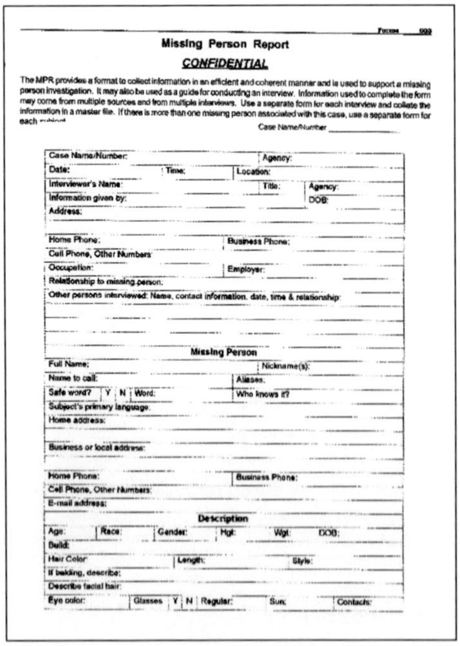

Missing Person Report

CONFIDENTIAL

The MPR provides a format to collect information in an efficient and coherent manner and is used to support a missing person investigation. It may also be used as a guide for conducting an interview. Information used to complete the form may come from multiple sources and from multiple interviews. Use a separate form for each interview and collate the information in a master file. If there is more than one missing person associated with this case, use a separate form for each subject.

Case Name/Number

Case Name/Number: | Agency:
Date: | Time: | Location:
Interviewer's Name: | Title: | Agency:
Information given by: | DOB:
Address:
Home Phone: | Business Phone:
Cell Phone, Other Numbers:
Occupation: | Employer:
Relationship to missing person:
Other persons interviewed: Name, contact information, date, time & relationship:

Missing Person

Full Name: | Nickname(s):
Name to call: | Aliases:
Safe word? | Y | N | Word: | Who knows it?
Subject's primary language:
Home address:
Business or local address:
Home Phone: | Business Phone:
Cell Phone, Other Numbers:
E-mail address:

Description

Age: | Race: | Gender: | Hgt: | Wgt: | DOB:
Build:
Hair Color: | Length: | Style:
If balding, describe:
Describe facial hair:
Eye color: | Glasses | Y | N | Regular: | Sun: | Contacts:

confine the search area in the hope of keeping the subject within our area of operations. Others may be used in hasty searches (also discussed in SARAware™) to seek out a direction of travel or other clues indicating the past or current presence of the subject.

Once we have assembled enough planning data to develop strategies, we can deploy as field resources in a more logical and methodical form to acquire more clues. How do we identify potential evidence as pertaining to the subject, rather than a distraction? That is the purpose of search data. Our investigation informs us of the clues to seek that, while perhaps not unique in nature, are known to pertain to our subject. Examples of potential clues that investigation reveals as search data includes:

- Name of the subject—This may sound basic to the point of unnecessary. But there have been many SAR incidents where field responders have been deployed without knowledge of even the subject's name!! Should they be lucky enough to happen across the subject, how would they know? What other clues would be ignored because the searchers have no idea who or what they're looking for? It is also very useful to call out the subject's name in those cases where the subject wants to be found.
- Physical description—Much like knowing the name of the subject, if we are to locate the "ultimate clue" (the subject) our searchers must know what the subject looks like.
- Footwear—While we typically think of subjects leaving tracks in the wilderness environment, there are many "track traps" in urban and suburban environments that can retain evidence of

passage including footprints. Knowing the brand and model of the subject's footwear can help determine a tread pattern that may be detectable in most of our operating environments.

- Clothing worn—This knowledge can alert searchers to colors and patterns that may draw attention to look in spots that might otherwise be overlooked. Additionally, it is not unusual for subjects to lose pieces of clothing or actually shed entire garments. Knowing what the subject is/was wearing (types, brand, colors, layers, etc.) can assist in discriminating cloth/clothing clues from distractions.
- Equipment—Knowing the type of equipment that might assist in the subject's survival or self-rescue can provide information to searchers for subject location and clue detection. In the case of weapons (firearms, knives, etc.) this can alert searchers to safety considerations. This is especially applicable when the subject is a despondent or potentially hostile to responders.
- Miscellaneous items—This includes a whole host of objects the subject might have on their person and could possibly discard. Items include such things (type, brand, etc.) as cigarettes, gum, snack foods, soft drinks, water, etc.

Detection techniques

We have talked about factors that affect our ability to find and recognize clues. Our considerations included management and searcher limitations, subject information and the operating environment. Now let's look at actual methods and procedures to enhance our efforts to detect clues.

One technique that has proven especially helpful is for the searchers to perceive themselves inside a three dimensional box or cube. This *searcher cube* assists the field responder in seeking evidence in all directions. Clues can be found above, beside and behind us, just

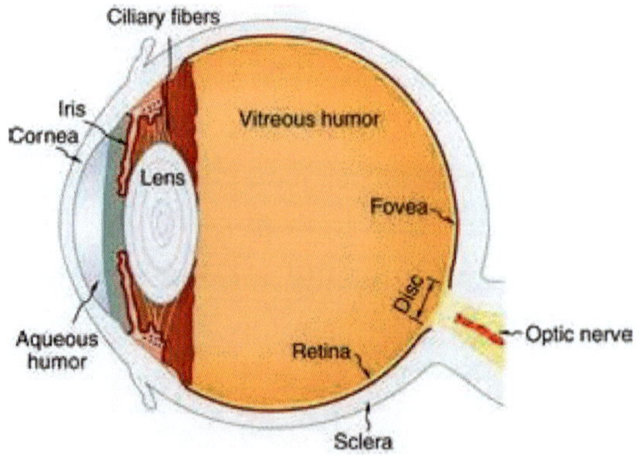

as well as in front of us. Having a mental picture of being inside this cube reminds us to look in all directions, not just in front.

Next is the question of *scanning* versus *"taking a visual snapshot."* If we analyze the process of vision we encounter the concept of "foveal vision." Studies have shown that sharply defined visual images to the brain occur in a small 1–2 degree conical area. Once an image is outside of a 10° cone around the fovea your brain only processes 10% of the image. This very small field of view means that an image transmitted to the back of the eye that falls outside of the fovea may not be recognized. Images that fall outside the fovea tend to be blurred. Continued movement of the head and eye does not allow time for the image to print on the fovea. The searcher must take momentary "snapshots" of the environment and refrain from "scanning."

Another technique field responders should consider is how they walk/travel while on a search tasking. If you remember the discussion on canonical perspective you recall that the human brain has an expectation as to how an object appears/looks. If you approach a clue from numerous, different angles, chances of recognition are greatly improved. So we use a technique known as *purposeful wandering*.

Rather than walk in a straight line we travel in "S" shaped and semi-circular patterns. This results in two benefits. The first benefit helps reduce the negative effect of canonical perspective. When using purposeful wandering, we often get multiple "snapshots" of the same item, only from different perspectives. The chances of recognizing an object as being a possible clue are increased as viewing the object from more than one angle can give our brain enough additional information about the item to enable identification.

The second benefit of purposeful wandering is the viewing of more of our search lane than traveling a straight line would afford. This additional coverage gives a higher likelihood (probability) that we will see a clue or the subject. As we expand our discussion to include search theory, and in later chapters on applying that theory to tactics, you will see the advantage in statistical terms that assist in resolving the overall incident.

Search Theory and Clue Orientation

For most of the history of Search & Rescue, management focused on direct actions to look for the subject. There was no real science behind how and what we did. There was no understanding of a logical sequence of planning and tactics to gather information and clues about the incident, leading to a solution of what actually occurred. Unfortunately, too many jurisdictions in this country (and throughout the world) still attempt to conduct their SAR operations without applying modern scientific methods.

$$f_1(x,t) = \frac{8\epsilon^2(k_2^2 e^{2\eta_1} + k_1^2 e^{2\eta_2})}{\tau^2}$$

$$f_2(x,t) = \frac{8(k_2^2 e^{-2\eta_1} + k_1^2 e^{-2\eta_2})}{\tau^2}$$

$$f_3(x,t) = \frac{16(k_2 - k_1)^2}{\tau^2}$$

In the last half of the 20th century a culture shift occurred in Search & Rescue. Scientific studies were undertaken to understand the similarities in missing and lost subject incidents. These studies found there was a statistical basis that allowed planning of our actions, measurement of the effectiveness of our tactical efforts and the predictions of overall success. In the last few decades, we have combined this mathematical basis with analysis of lost person behavior and crime databases to revolutionize our approach to Search & Rescue management. This mathematical foundation is predicated on the statistical concept of *probability* or the likelihood that something will occur. The formula that provides the basis for this theory of management is:

POS = POA x POD

POS—The *Probability of Success* is the ultimate goal of our mathematical calculations. Given certain information (see POA and POD below) we can calculate the likelihood or chance of our success—In this case of finding the subject or a clue in our search segment (or the search area). This value is normally expressed as a decimal (e.g. .20) in the formula and as a percentage (e.g. 20%) when spoken.

POA—This component is the *Probability of Area*. It represents the likelihood that the subject or a clue is in the search segment (or the entire search area). No matter how strong our containment or accurate our information, we can rarely (never?) be (100%) certain that the subject will be in our search area. The same possibility applies to the likelihood that a clue is present in the search segment or area.

POD—This represents the *Probability of Detection*. Given that a clue (or clues) or the subject is in a given search segment or area, Probability of Detection represents the likelihood that our efforts would result in finding the clue or subject. This component is the one most directly related to field search tactics. Or even easier...If there were 10 clues in your segment, how many would you have found? Example—If you find 3 out of 10 you have a 30% POD.

In a properly managed search incident, the field search resources will be given objectives in their tasking that will include expected or predictive PODs. The search management planning function relies heavily on the use of statistical probabilities. Part of this function is to calculate the required POD from a search tasking to meet the overall requirements of the search plan. This required POD is then briefed to the search resource and made a part of their objectives. The search team will then conduct their search in a manner that will return the required POD. The methods used by the search resource to modify their search tactic to achieve the requested POD will be discussed in the next chapter.

Another form of determining effectiveness of our search efforts is that of *Coverage*. Search planners most often use Coverage as a means of more accurately calculating the POD reported by the field search asset. One note, while Coverage is an abstract number that is not representative of any particular unit, the user should be consistent in units of measurement. If you select meters, then always use meters. The same would apply to yards, etc.

To calculate coverage we must first know the *Effective Sweep Width* used by the search resource. Unfortunately, there is no definitive way to determine sweep width accurately without conducting lengthy experiments in your region. So in the absence of experiments conducted in your area, think of Sweep Width in this way. Imagine a lane with a known number of clues inside the lane and outside of the lane. The Effective Sweep Width would be wide enough that a searcher would have an equal chance of missing clues inside the lane as seeing/detecting clues outside the lane. For example, let's assume we know there are 30 clues in our search lane. If the searcher missed 10 clues inside the lane, but detected an additional 10 clues outside the lane, the distance from side to side (width) of the lane is our Effective Sweep Width. Then, Total Sweep Width is determined by the width of each team member's individual search lane added together.

Next we need to know the actual distance walked by the search team during the active search process. This distance is known as *Track Line Length*. It can be determined accurately by GPS tracking, or by estimating the speed traveled times the time spent searching, or by pace count. So, if you searched at an estimated one thousand meters per hour, for three hours, your Track Line Length would be three thousand meters.

Now we can calculate the *Area Effectively Swept*, by multiplying the (total) Sweep Width by the Track Line Length. For example, if our Total Sweep Width is 50 meters and our Track Line Length is 3000 meters, we would multiply 50 x 3000 which equals 150,000 square meters.

One final calculation is necessary to determine coverage. We need to take our Area Effectively Swept and divide it by the *Area of Search Segment*. The Area of Search Segment represents the total size of the segment in which the resource was assigned. For our example, we'll assume the Area of Search Segment is 300,000 square meters. The formula would appear as:

$$\frac{\text{Area Effectively Swept}}{\text{Area of Search Segment}} = \text{Coverage}$$

150,000/300,000 = 0.5

This example results in a Coverage of 0.5. In order to determine the corresponding POD, we need to apply this Coverage (0.5) on a %POD vs. Coverage graph, also known as the Exponential Detection Graph shown below.

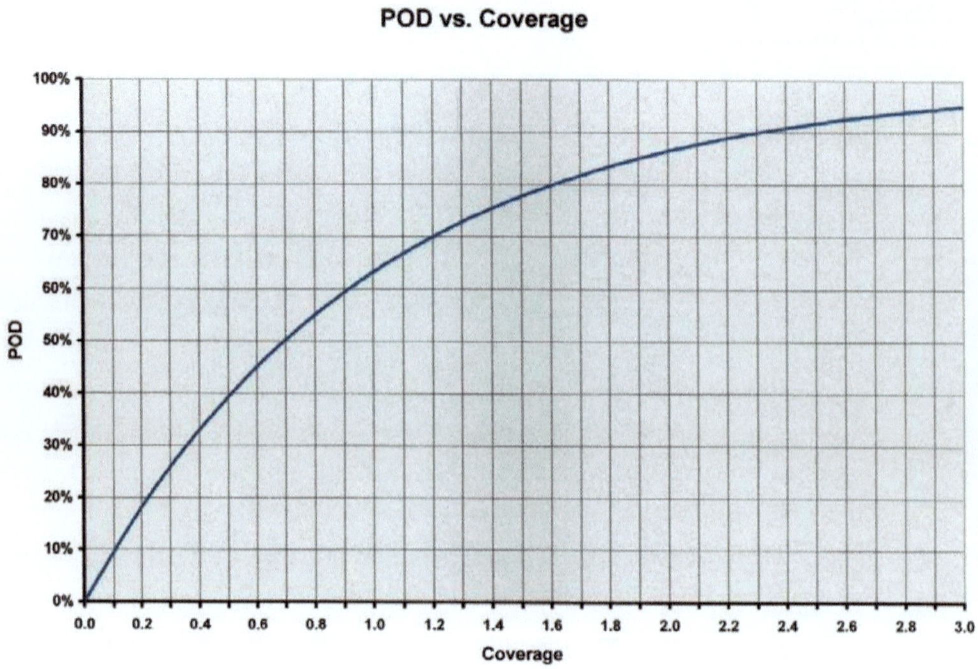

If we plot the Coverage (0.5) on the curve, then move to the POD axis, we derive a POD of approximately 39%. As you can see on the graph, even if the resource passed over every square meter of the search segment, presenting a Coverage of 1.0, the resulting POD would be approximately 63%. If the original Sweep Width and Track Line Length can be accurately determined, this method of calculating POD will be more accurate than other methods using visual and spacing field techniques described in the next chapter.

Tracking

Image courtesy of http://plj.myqnapcloud.com

While discussing the concept of clue orientation, we should take the opportunity to discuss what some perceive as the pinnacle of clue awareness. Once again, you must understand our goal is not to make you an expert tracker. We only seek to provide you awareness of an additional tool to make you a better field searcher. Expertise can only come through knowledge (training) and practical application (practice) leading to a depth of experience you cannot gain from a text book. If mantracking/sign-cutting is interesting to you, you should seek out nationally recognized schools/Instructors for more extensive training.

The simple definition of tracking is "following signs, of travel or presence, left by someone or something." Of course, nothing is ever simple. While we can visualize scenes of astute mantrackers examining (foot) prints, there is much more to tracking a subject. Skilled trackers don't limit their efforts to finding prints. They seek a varied group of *sign* that includes footprints, but involves many different indications of human passage.

A wise search manager will have numerous tracker trained resources on the resource list in the preplan. Tracking resources should be among the first deployed, even before the search area is established. Getting trackers involved early, when sign/clues are least contaminated by bystanders, searchers and Law Enforcement, can benefit the search to:

- provide clues like: direction of travel, timelines, shoe description
- aim the search such as: reduce the search area by skewing the circle produced around the IPP into a pie slice radiating out from the track sign

- preserve evidence that may be time, weather or environment sensitive

The procedure a tracker uses to establish a starting point is called *sign-cutting*. So sign-cutting is used to locate the first sign or print, from which subsequent sign or track can be followed. Sign-cutting is different from tracking in that tracking follows the "path" traveled by the subject, while sign-cutting is performed perpendicular to that path. The sign-cutter is seeking sign that intersects with a prospective route of travel by the subject. We will discuss sign specifics later in this chapter, but there are 5 characteristics of sign a sign-cutter seeks:

1. Flattening—leveling of rocks, twigs and dirt (e.g. caused by weight and pressure of footfall)
2. Regularity—lines, circles or geometric shapes pressed into ground by shoe/foot pressure
3. Color change—color change in soil, vegetation, or twigs, rocks etc. caused by foot pressure (e.g. snapped twig, turned leaf, soil difference from scuffing, etc.)
4. Disturbance—dislodging of stones, twigs, vegetation
5. Transfer—materials moved by sole of shoe impact

Once the tracker has succeeded in the first phase (sign-cutting) it is time to move to the second phase, *tracking*. In this phase it is not only important to know what to look for, but how to look. The tracker must learn to differentiate between the urban environment where colors and contrast are much more stark and bold than in wilderness setting. A skilled tracker will looks for signals or visual cues rather than specific tracks or prints. If the tracker has a preconceived notion of what should be seen, much of what can help locate evidence will be disregarded. So the tracker seeks these visual cues that attract attention, for a more thorough investigation. These visual clues tend to fall into five categories:

1. Outline—boundary or perimeter around an area that delineates it from its surroundings. This can be a small line to a complete perimeter around a track.
2. Shape—large enough to have been caused by human passage. Typically involves flattening that is unusual for the environment.
3. Contrast—a difference in color, texture or shape from its surroundings. The greater the difference, the more compelling the cue.
4. Color—in nature, usually milder tones, but differences can be detected. More important in urban (manmade) environments than natural ones.
5. Texture—rough or smooth. Contrast in the consistency of a surface.

Now that we are in phase two, there are three techniques that you may encounter. They are *Jump Tracking, Step-by-Step Tracking* and *Bracketing*:

- Jump tracking is a form of tracking that involves finding a large and obvious footprint, then proceeding along the presumed direction of travel until another, obvious, track is found. This form of tracking involves guesswork, luck and little skill. It is a poor, and possibly negligent, choice when the subject's well-being depends on skillful tracking. This type of tracking also greatly increases the risk that clues will be erased or destroyed. Since this is not a recommended skill, it will not be discussed further.
- Step-by-step tracking is a disciplined teaching system where a tracker sees each step in sequence and proceeds no further than the last visible track. Then stride length is employed to determine the location of the next sign. This system ensures that searchers become clue conscious and track aware. It serves as the standard to which an experienced tracker will strive. While it is not always possible to detect every clue left by the subject, it is still the goal of the tracker. Some small gaps are thus acceptable.

- Bracketing is an acceptable method of interpolating between tracks when the Step-by-Step technique does not reveal the next clue/sign. This is meant as an expedient measure and uses the predetermined stride length to "skip" the step that cannot be located and proceed to the next track. Then the tracker works "backwards" to the missed sign. This does not create a license to perform Jump Tracking. It should only be used infrequently to maintain continuity on important track.

Now let's consider some requirements to perform tracking. As with any skill, there are certain human characteristics that will, at least, aid the person in being a better tracker. Some of these qualities include: Patience, Inquisitiveness, Determination, Endurance and Open-mindedness. These traits will be necessary beginning with training and continuing through practice and into the actual conduct of a mission.

As with much of search & rescue, there is also some equipment required. The good news is there is not very much required and you likely already have everything you need at home! Let's review the basics.

1. Appropriate Clothing—Tracking is performed in all weather and terrain conditions. Regardless of the environment, when you are performing step-by-step tracking, you are also going to be on the ground for most of your assignment. You will need to wear the correct clothing for the temperature, vegetation and/or personal protection requirements. And don't forget a hat with a brim. This will help protect your eyes and also provide "shading" of the sign or track while the sun is high in the sky.

2. Tracking or Sign-cutting Stick—A lightweight pole (that can also double as a walking stick) that is at least 40 inches (100 centimeters) long. It is recommended that the stick have some type of measurements or "O" rings/colored rubber bands to assist in recording lengths, especially stride.

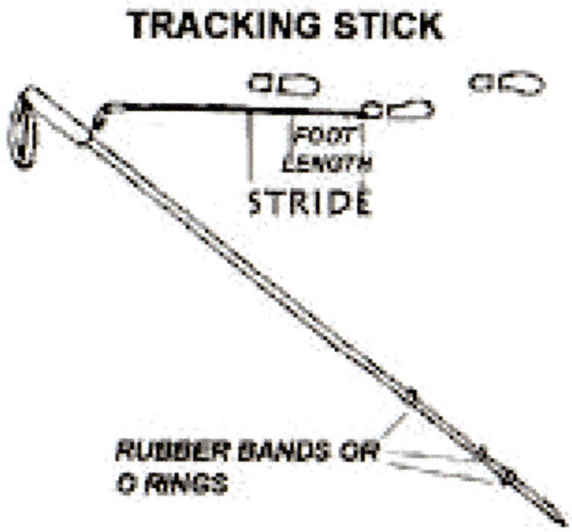

Courtesy of www.ceceliatravis.com

3. Measuring Device—A separate, from the tracking stick, measuring device that is especially valuable in precisely measuring print. Using a tape measure, carpenter tool, etc. will provide greater accuracy than a measuring device on the tracking stick.
4. Notepad and Pencil—You will need to record measurements and fill out a tracking report. So notepad and pencil are essential. It will also be very helpful to have a copy of a "blank" print. This will assist in documenting all the required measurements and sole pattern instead of relying on the memory or the novice tracker.

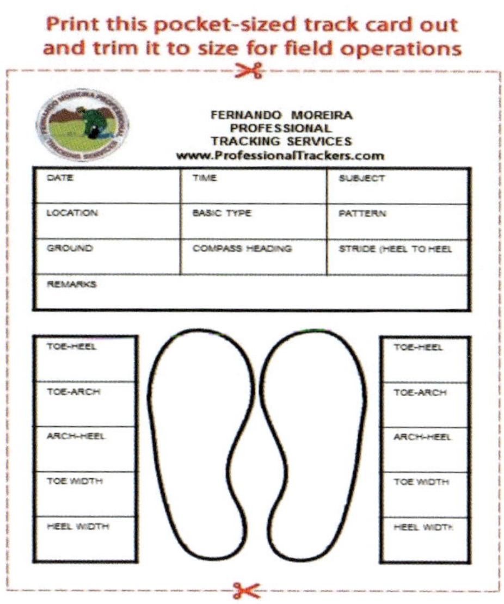

Courtesy of www.professionaltrackers.com

5. Marking or Flagging Tape—It will be necessary to mark and cordon off evidence to prevent it from destruction. Surveyor tape works well, but will have to be removed after the incident is terminated or suspended. Biodegradable tape is available, but make sure the environmental conditions will not cause premature degradation (before the incident concludes evaluating the evidence).
6. Flashlight—Tracking is performed in daylight, low light and night conditions. Since shadows are so important in tracking, you may need an artificial light source to correctly reveal clues. Along the same line, a mirror can be used to redirect natural light for use in daytime hours.
7. Your Brain & Vision—Regardless of the application of the above noted gear, your skill and perseverance combines with your (all five) senses as the primary tools used in tracking.

Step-by-Step print tracking

We have now discussed the concepts of clue detection, vision and perspective, and tracking techniques and requirements. As a final topic, let's describe how to perform step-by-step tracking of prints, including description and labeling. (While we're locating footprints, don't forget to detect other sign/clues in the area!) As a matter of convenience, we will begin with a (rare) Class 1 print (full print, very easy to identify all features).

1. First start with a general description of the print. Some examples include:
    - Is it a right track or a left?
    - Is it a flat track without a heel, or is there a heel and toe?
    - What is the shape of the track?
        - Is the toe rounded, pointed or square?
        - Is the leading edge of the heel straight or curved?
        - Is the instep high or low?
    - What is the sole pattern?
    - Does it have a border? Does it have labels, numbers, nails or stitching?

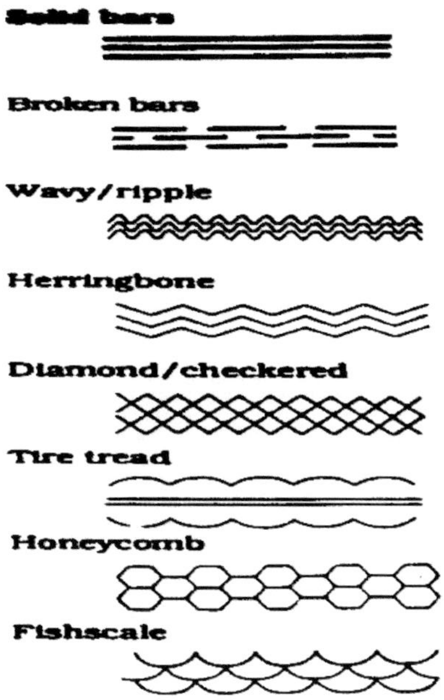

- What is the pattern type? Plain (no pattern), regular or irregular?
- Are there bars, ripples, diamond, herringbone or other shapes?
- Does the pattern have circles or semi-circles, arcs, stars, suction cup circles, bars (straight, curved, diagonal)?

2. Now let's take the pertinent measurements. There are five that we should record, though personal preference may include additional measurements:
   - Overall Length—Heel to toe
   - Heel Length—Instep edge of heel to back edge of heel
   - Ball Width—Width measured edge to edge across ball of foot
   - Heel Width—Measured edge to edge at center of heel
   - Stride Length—This measurement is best performed, initially, with your tracking stick, but should be recorded in appropriate units after using your

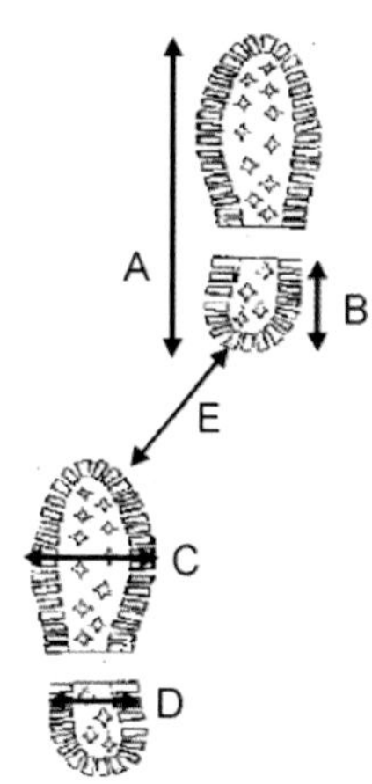

measuring device to determine length indicated on the tracking stick.

- First, find two good prints and put the tip of the stick on the center or heel of the front track.*See Note below.
- Then, put a piece of tape or colored O-ring around the stick at the back edge of the heel on the rear track.
- Next, put another piece of tape or colored O-ring around the stick at the toe of the rear track. This way, you have two marks defining the length of the print and, from there, the tip of the pole defines the length of the stride.

*NOTE

Some Instructors teach that it's better to place the tip of your tracking stick at the center of the front track rather than at the heel. Their reasoning is because when you use your stick to find the next print, you know the tip should be somewhere within that print, unless stride length has increased or decreased, possibly by changing travel speed or reacting to steepening terrain.

Other Instructors don't like this method, preferring to measure stride heel to heel, which is the traditional (and more widely used) method.

3. The next step is to use the measurements on our tracking stick to locate subsequent prints.
   - Place your stick near the ground with the two markers framing the last known print. Then move the tracking stick back and forth in an arc. The tip of your pole or stick should be passing over the next print, so study the ground ahead at that point as it moves and see if you can pick it up.
   - If the first track is a right foot, the next track is a left foot. Try moving your tracking stick slightly to that side, and

vice versa to the right for the subsequent track.

- Be careful not to touch your tracking stick to the ground. This can cause a disturbance or make even a faint impression that can confuse you when looking for obscure sign.

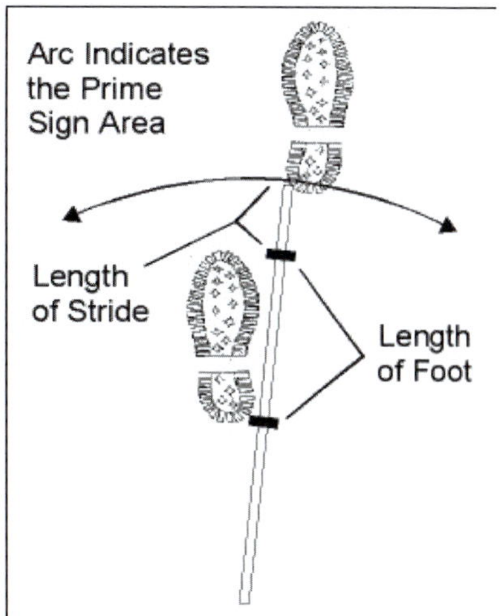

Figure 3 The Tracking Stick

4. Every print should be marked. In addition to using flagging tape in the vicinity of the print, the print itself should be labeled. The preferred technique is to carefully place a mark designating a complete or partial print and whether it is believed to be a right or left foot. For a complete track we will circle the entire print and include a hash mark towards the side correlating with whether the foot is left or right. If the print is only a partial, we will scribe a semi-circle around the base of the print and again include a hash mark indicating a left or right foot. The image below demonstrates the marking technique.

Labeling Tracks

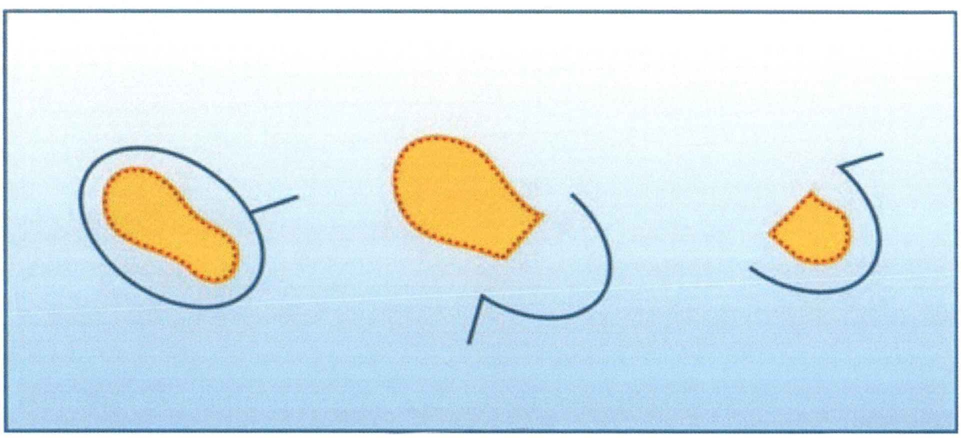

Remember to look up from the ground periodically. This may seem like a no-brainer, but it's easy to get so caught up in tracking that you get tunnel vision, focusing on the ground while forgetting the bigger picture.

It is possible to become so intent on finding the next print that you can fail to raise your eyes from the ground just a couple of feet ahead. Not doing so can cost time going print to print when a clear print may be seen without using your tracking stick. So, make it a point to look up when you're man-tracking and scan the area for what could be your subject's print (or even the subject!) in the distance or perhaps another type of clue.

If you're not sure what you're seeing, you can either mark the current print you're on and come back to it if what you find ahead proves not to have been made by your subject, or, better yet, send a teammate to check it out. By marking the last known track with flagging tape (and a GPS coordinate), you're ensuring that you'll be able to return to it if you find you've deviated and followed the wrong path. Or another team can come along and pick up the track.

Communicating clues to the Command Post

Whether you are firmly convinced you have discovered evidence related to the subject or believe it to be a possible clue, or not, you must communicate information about the clue to the Command Post. Most of the time, this will occur via radio. You should still take photos to share with Command, either electronically or upon return to Base. As the sender, you will have to provide certain details about the clue and to "paint" a picture of the evidence for the receiver. Regardless of the nature of the clue (object, documentation, print, etc.) there are certain required details you must deliver:

- Time—The precise time the clue was located.
- Location—The precise location coordinates are ALWAYS required. It is strongly recommended you not initiate contact until you have noted the coordinates from your GPS or map work.

- Description of surroundings—The area around the clue, both immediate and near term, must be described to the receiver. This is important to aiding the understanding of the subject's travel and whether the clue was actually deposited in this location or was otherwise transported here.
- Identity or nature of evidence—State the type or identity of the clue using familiar words that don't need further explanation and are not ambiguous. Be precise.
- Description of the clue—Keep it simple, again using terms that are familiar to all and that will create that mental image you are trying to communicate. Be sure to include some standard details required of all types of evidence:
    - Age—If you can estimate the age of the clue based on correlation with the environment (recent weather events, etc.), do so and explain your analysis. If not, be sure to describe the age condition of the clue (e.g. rusty, faded, deteriorated, new, current edition, etc.). When communicating (tracking) sign and prints this is especially important.
    - Manufacturer and model—If you have discovered an object, try to identify the make (brand) and model (e.g. Trident cinnamon gum wrapper, Marlboro Special Blend Gold package, etc.).
    - Color—While this may seem straightforward it is frequently forgotten.
    - Miscellaneous—Add additional details that complete the image of the find.
    - Tracking clues—Communicating sign and print should follow the outline described in the Step-by-Step method described above.
- Disposition of the clue—If you have not been given specific instructions as to what to do with the clue (e.g. Leave it in place and mark the location, retrieve it, using chain of evidence technique, and bring it to Base, leave it undisturbed, etc.), you must inform the Command Post what actions you

did or did not take with regards to the location, condition and preservation of the evidence at the current time.

Summary

Now you understand the basic concepts of becoming clue aware. But this skill is perishable. You must make your observation techniques part of everyday life. Take notice of your surroundings. What do you see? Is there evidence of human travel or presence? What are the clues you notice? This is essential to your proficiency at search. When the call comes to deploy, it is too late to practice.

References

Lost Person Behavior—A Search & Rescue Guide on Where to Look- for Land, Air and Water (2008)
Koester, Robert J; *dbS Productions*, Charlottesville, VA

Managing Land Search Operations (2006)
Robert C. (Skip) Stoffel, *Emergency Response International*, Cashmere, WA

SARAware—Awareness Level Search & Rescue for the Responder (2013)
Dion Petaros, James Keck & Wes Podboy, *AERIE Publications*, Lake Dallas, TX

Tracking – Signs of Man, Signs of Hope (2005)
David Diaz, *The Lyons Press*, Guilford, CT

Search & Rescue—Basic Tracker Training (2012)
Joel C. Hardin, *Joel Hardin Professional Tracking Services*, Clearwater, ID

Fundamentals of Mantracking—The Step-by-Step Method (1992)
Albert "Ab" Taylor and Donald C. Cooper, *ERI International*, Olympia, WA

Performing Search Tactics

11

Objectives

- Review the difference between strategy and tactics
- Differentiate between the categories of passive and active tactics
- Describe and differentiate the following search tactics:
  - Hasty Search
  - Loose Grid (Efficient or Type II) Search
  - Tight Grid (Thorough or Type III) Search
  - Evidence Search
- Explain the Field Team roles of:
  - The Leader
  - The Navigator
  - The Pace Counter
  - The Communicator
  - The Recorder
- Define the following Grid Search Terms:
  - Baseline
  - Guideline
  - Guide Person
  - Search Lane

- Discuss the concepts of:
  - Critical Separation
  - Effective Sweep Width
  - AMDR vs AROD
- Differentiate between ground team "Area Search" and "Route Search"
- Describe Urban Search Tactics including:
  - "Door to Door" Canvassing
  - Building Search
    - Single Story
    - Multi-story
  - Institution Checks
  - Mantracking
  - Review basic protocols for Ground Searchers to function as Flankers in a canine unit

Performing search assignments

Having studied the preparatory concepts to being a SAR field responder, we now begin our discussions on the actual procedures you will perform during your search assignments. As a basic "ground" searcher you will be called upon to utilize different techniques based on environment, thoroughness of coverage and other considerations important to search management. Never forget that, ultimately, we work for the "subject", but to be successful, the field searcher must perform their duties in a manner that will provide the search managers the information needed to plan effective use of our limited resources.

Strategy versus Tactics

If you are new to incident response you may not understand the difference between strategy and tactics. This is an important distinction. You may want to return to your *SARAware*™ textbook to review this concept in greater detail. *Strategies* are set by the Incident

Commander and (typical to SAR) expanded upon by the Planning Section. They will include broad mission goals and the *objectives* that are required in order to achieve the goals. Once the objectives have been determined, the Operations Section will develop the *tactics* to be performed, necessary to meeting the objectives.

This model of strategy, objectives and tactics applies to all incident response, not just search & rescue. Regardless of the "hazard" we are responding to, the Incident Command System requires us to utilize this method of planning and operations. Unfortunately, you will encounter significant numbers of "incident managers" who do not understand this and will give out operational (tactical) assignments with no prior thought or planning for more global strategies and objectives. When asked what the objectives are for this operational period the untrained search manager will usually reply "find the subject" and have no other (more) specific objectives in mind. In this case, finding the subject becomes more a matter of luck than of skill.

Categories of Tactics

In SARAware™, we discussed the differences between *passive* and *active* tactics. As a field responder, you will be called upon to participate in both types. Though you may pursue advanced training and certifications, even into various specialty disciplines, you may still be assigned to duties in such tactics as containment/confinement. Remember, this is not about you. Your assignments are determined by the needs of the *Incident Action Plan*. In a well-managed incident, this plan will have been briefed at the beginning of the operational period (see the chapter on "Chronology of a SAR Incident") and is available for review by all responders. If the incident managers have determined it is more important to contain the subject in the search area (generally one of the most important strategies/objectives), then it may be necessary for trained field responders to participate in this tactic. As a review, let's discuss passive and active tactics:

- Passive Tactics: Passive tactics are considered to be those activities that do not involve the physical act of searching for clues (in the field) or the subject. These actions are normally directed at finding chronological clues (credit card usage, documents, lost person data, etc.) and attracting or confining the subject. The *SARAware*™ text describes these tactics in detail, but some examples are:
    - Investigation
    - Signs/Flyers
    - Confinement/Containment
    - Attraction Signals
- Active Tactics: These tactics involve the physical act of going into the field to locate the subject and/or clues. With rare exception, these actions are performed by trained and certified field responders only. Examples include:
    - Hasty Search
    - Loose Space (Efficient) Grid Search
    - Close Space (Thorough) Grid Search
    - Evidence Search

As our goal is to prepare you with the concepts to become a field "searcher", let's expand on these active tactics:

Hasty Search—This tactic is usually reserved for assignment to the highest level (Level 1) of trained and certified field searchers. Most often, a Hasty Team is comprised of three of these expert searchers. Hasty teams typically move rapidly along travel routes rather than "bushwhacking" through swaths of wilderness or urban terrain. These travel routes may have a local history of missing subjects being lost (or found). If there are structures or terrain features where the subject may be hidden, the Hasty Team may perform a quick search of the structure or feature, or notify the Command Post to include these objects in later taskings.

Hasty Teams travel fast and light and do cursory searches looking for clues. However, hasty teams are mainly intended to look for the subject in obvious places or locate easily seen clues and not venture too far from the routes that the subject may have travelled.

Loose Space Grid Search—This tactic is frequently referred to as an *efficient* search because it seeks to balance speed and thoroughness. In this case, the search planners are willing to accept a lower level of detection (of clues) in order to cover a search segment. This makes efficient use of our (limited) resources. Assignments of this type are typically reserved for intermediate level (Level 2) or higher certified resources. The resources we apply to these "efficient" techniques will focus their efforts on locating clues and evidence. Of course if the Efficient Team happens to come upon the subject, that's the best clue out there!

These efficient resources are well trained and practiced in clue detection. They will travel at moderate speeds while looking for objects that our investigation revealed the subject might have with them. Since our *Search Objectives* always have a desired measurement of success, these teams are trained in performing their task in a manner to deliver a specific level of coverage in a specific amount of time. Based on environmental factors, the Operations Section will determine which type of efficient resource is best suited to accomplish the tactic in accordance with the Planning Section's desired results.

Close Space Grid Search—This tactic is normally assigned to our least trained and certified resources (Level 3). As the search incident continues without success in locating the subject, the incident management team may elect to utilize "thorough" techniques to discover clues. This decision is never taken lightly because the expenditure of resources in terms of personnel and time is incredibly large in thorough tactics. These tactics involve resources moving very slowly, while spaced very closely together looking for any small clue or sign that the subject may have been here.

Often times, untrained ("spontaneous") volunteer responders are used to perform these tactics. A word of caution applies when using untrained responders. As noted by the word *untrained*, these individuals are not "clue conscious." They will likely overlook as much evidence as they find. Because they aren't aware of the clue, they will often, inadvertently, destroy the evidence and the surrounding area, rendering it useless for future examination or analysis. There is also a large liability issue in using these individuals in the field. Should they become ill or injured, cause injury to others, or damage to property, the agency with jurisdiction for the incident may find itself involved in extensive litigation.

One final note about thorough search tactics: They are never utilized until all other efforts have been unsuccessful. Using thorough tactics as initial or early efforts indicate an untrained or inexperienced management team. Unless this incident/search is a true law enforcement evidence search for a crime where the suspect has been apprehended, do not use this technique until all else fails.

Evidence Search—As noted above, this tactic is used to gather as much (preferrably all) evidence that can be found in a small search segment. Focus is on extreme thoroughness as much of the evidence may be very small in size. The technique is the same as a close space grid search, but with the searchers operating "side by side", almost touching each other. While Law Enforcement may utilize untrained volunteers, the same caveats discussed above apply here with an additional concern... We are always aware of preserving *chain of custody* of clues as any search can become a Law Enforcement matter. In the case of an evidence search, that has already been determined. Clues found will need to be handled in a manner consistent with evidence that will be presented in court. The typical "spontaneous responder" will not have this knowledge. Careful instructions should be given to not approach or touch any clues/evidence, but to summon a Law Enforcement Officer to handle the evidence.

> Field Searchers are required to know how to preserve and handle evidence. Most jurisdictions require they have formal training in evidence handling. Many of these courses are available online.

Search Team Positions

Throughout this text we have made reference to the "search team." You may have heard this unit referred to as a "search crew" or even a "search (SAR) resource." Regardless of the characterization applied, this team, as with any other organized unit, has functional positions that must be filled. In the case of a search team, there are five functions that must be fulfilled. These positions are officially recognized and required by the Incident Command System. Each of these roles can be combined and assigned to one individual, but when possible it is more effective to have one person assigned to each position.

- Leader—The defintion of a leader generally comes in two ways:
    1. One that leads or guides.
    2. One who is in charge or in command of others.

But what responsibilities does a search crew leader have? Let's assume that our leader is a "good" leader and wants to perform their duties well!

- Safety—This is always the primary responsibility of every team member, but especially so for the leader. The leader must be constantly aware of every member of the team and of any hazard that could affect the team or any of its members. This includes setting an appropriate pace and commanding sufficient rest periods.
- Navigation—Regardless of having delegated this duty, the leader remains responsible for knowing where the team is and how to return to a suitable extraction point in the event of an emergency.

- Evidence/Clues—the leader is ultimately responsible for ensuring that clues are processed correctly and that evidence is properly maintained according to chain of custody requirements.
- Assignment Progress—Situations will arise that prevent the team from completing its assignment within the time parameters set by incident management. The leader must maintain awareness of the progress of the team and determine if it is satisfactory or needs to be revised.
- Briefing/Debriefing—In many incidents logistical constraints allow only the leader to attend General and Tactical briefings/debriefings. The leader then becomes

responsible to conduct briefings/debriefings of the team to maintain appropriate two way communication of information with incident management.

    - Member Proficiency—Though the team leader may not be in a permanent position as the leader, they must ensure that all the members of the team are not only trained and certified, but proficient and currently capable of performing the required tasks of the search assignment. This should be accomplished prior to commencing the assignment.

- Navigator—As implied by the name, this team member will have the primary responsibility to plan, verify, and maintain the team on course for this assignment. The navigator must also know the boundaries of the assigned search segment, as well as the current position of the team, at all times. This position requires proficiency with map & compass and GPS.
- Pace Counter—This position has primary responsibility for planning, verifying and recording distance traveled. Generally, this is done on a "leg by leg" basis. In the wilderness environment that will necessarily be shortened to a "target by target" basis. At the conclusion of the assignment, the pace counter must be able to report the total distance ("track length") traveled as this will be used in calculating search coverage of the segment.
- Communicator—Routine contact with incident command is required. The command post will expect periodic check-in as briefed. If the team misses two scheduled check-ins, a search mission, to locate the team, will be initiated. This takes resources away from searching for the subject and can not be tolerated. The communicator must be familiar with proper radio technique and be able to accurately submit information to the Command Post. As described in SARAware™, no codes ("10 code" or otherwise) are to be used on an ICS incident. All communication is performed in standard English.
- Recorder—The recorder is tasked with keeping all the notes, photographs, documents, retrieved clues, etc., acquired

during an assignment. This position will also be required to complete the ICS 214 (Unit Log) form by the end of the search assignment. As "keeper of the clues", the recorder must be familiar with "chain of custody" procedures to ensure proper submission of all items, photos and documents that may be used as evidence.

Grid Search Terminology

Hasty searches and Loose Space Grid searches are the most prevalent types of active tactics assigned to ground searchers involved in a SAR incident, with Loose Space searches being the most frequent. In keeping with a major tenet of ICS (refer to the Incident Command System chapter in *SARAware*™ for more details) requiring common terminology, modern search management employs standard terms to describe components of these efficient type searches. Some of these terms are:

- Control Line—This is an imaginary line used to stage the search team members perpendicular to the planned direction of travel, much like a starting line at a race. This line is sometimes referred to as the *Base Line* when it is used at the beginning of the grid search. As necessary, the team leader may call the team to reform on a control line, during the search effort, to reorganize the group, as necessary.
- Guide—This is the method of navigational control used to orient the team and keep it on course during the search effort. Choices include a compass bearing, a manmade or natural route (such as a trail, creek, fenceline, etc.) or fabricated course (such as a string line, established for use in the incident).
- Guide Person—This is the team member who will be responsible for maintaining navigational control of the team. There are three physical locations, within the control line, the Guide Person can occupy. The Guide Person can assume their position on the extreme left or right ends of the line, or be

located in the center of the control line. The choice is usually based on the type of Guide in use. For a route or fabricated system, the Guide person will frequently be positioned on the end of the Control Line closest to the route being followed. When using a compass bearing, the Guide person is usually positioned in the center of the Control Line to provide better control in keeping the team on course.

- Search Lane—This term describes a defined area that resembles a bowling alley. Each searcher is assigned a search lane with the width of that lane determined by the probability of detection desired from the effort. (More on how to "calculate" that width later.)

Grid Search Nomenclature

In the 1980s, Explorer Scouts (now called *Venturing)* in the Pacific Northwest were very active in participating with researchers conducting studies in various aspects of search & rescue. While engaged in these studies, the Scouts frequently performed Loose Space and Close Space grid searches. In order to quickly describe the details of these grid searches, they developed a naming system that remains in use today. The system utilizes a sequence of numbers and words to anotate how the search was performed. Hyphens (dashes) are used to separate each component in the (naming) system. Read from left to right:

- Number—this first number indicates how many searchers are positioned on the Control Line. Note that it only includes searchers on the line. If the team leader is incorporated on the line then they will be included in the count. Should the team leader be directing the effort from behind the line, then they will not be included in the count.
- Word—We have two choices for this position in the nomenclature: Guide or Compass. If we are employing a compass bearing, the word "Compass" will be used. In some cases, the actual heading/bearing will follow the word

"Compass." If this technique (indicating the actual compass bearing) is used, the bearing should be included with the word compass and some form of punctuation, such as quotation marks (e.g. "Compass 030").

If the search is performed using a Guide, then the word "guide" will be inserted here. When using a guide (and the word "guide" is inserted), it is customary to indicate the position of the Guide Person. This is done by including the term "left", "right" or "center" along with the word "guide." Once again, using punctuation to combine the words will reduce confusion. An example using quotation marks would be "guide left."

- Number—This number refers to the average distance between searchers. Another way to look at this would be to use the *Sweep Width*, which is the distance from the center of one search lane to the center of the adjacent search lane, as determined at the start of the search effort. Since ICS utilizes the metric system we will use meters in our examples and calculations. But the system works equally well using the English system and describing the distance in feet. Just be sure to stipulate what units you are describing.

Let's consider two examples. In our first example we have seven searchers using a lake on the right side as a guide and their spacing is fifteen meters apart. The resulting "name" would be: 7—"Guide Right"—15. Example two has a team of five searchers using a compass bearing of 045° with a sweep width of twenty meters. The result is: 5—"Compass 045"—20.

Effectiveness of Search Effort

In a previous topic we discussed the idea of effectiveness. We discovered that in a properly managed SAR incident, search assignments are given with an expectation of effectiveness. In the chapter on clue orientation, we discovered the concept of POD (Probability of Detection). This is one of the most important pillars of search management. For the field search resource, it represents whether we have been successful in performing our assigned task.

During the tactical briefing on our upcoming assignment, we will be given a "requested" POD to achieve. This requested POD is based on a calculated value that is required to meet an objective for the search segment for that operational period. The search manager is attempting to "clear" a segment by achieving a high level of POD. To do so usually requires multiple searches of the segment over multiple operational periods and frequently involves differing resource types (e.g. ground, canine, aviation, etc.). Though many factors can preclude our achieving the requested POD, it is the goal of the resource to attain the requested POD unless physically unable or where doing so would encounter risks that endanger the team.

The next question is how can a search team determine they are performing their duties to attain the requested POD? If we have practiced our clue awareness techniques, we have become good sensors of clues. The current weather and terrain conditions are a factor, but can be included in our planning determinations. That leaves a question of how far from a (reasonably sized) clue can you be and still detect the clue? We call the distance where you have zero chance of detecting the clue your *Visual Horizon.*

Now picture yourself in the center of a lane that is as wide as the distance to your visual horizon on one side to your visual horizon on the other side. If you were to walk straight down the middle of the (search) lane, you would miss the clues that are near the borders. But by wandering (side to side, making "S" turns, etc.) within the limits of the lane (looking up, down, behind and forward), you significantly increase both the amount of lane you have covered and the Probability of Detection for all clues. That is the concept of *Purposeful Wandering*. But we still have to determine a method of describing our efforts numerically. That is... in terms of POD.

What would be the effect of narrowing our search lane on POD? Theoretically, you would be able to see (and detect) more clues because they would be within your visual horizon. That would increase the POD. So search lane width has an inverse affect on POD.

Increasing the width of the search lane decreases the POD and vice versa.

Critical Separation—In the late 1980s, Dave Perkins and Pete Roberts of the Northumberland (U.K.) search organization, were looking for a way to maximize efficient use of limited resources. They determined that spacing searchers' lanes far enough apart, so there would be no overlap of the searchers' visual horizon, would be the most efficient way. They called this spacing distance *Critical Separation.* The measurement is said to be elastic because it will vary with "purposeful wandering" and the difficulty of the terrain as the searchers pass through the segment.

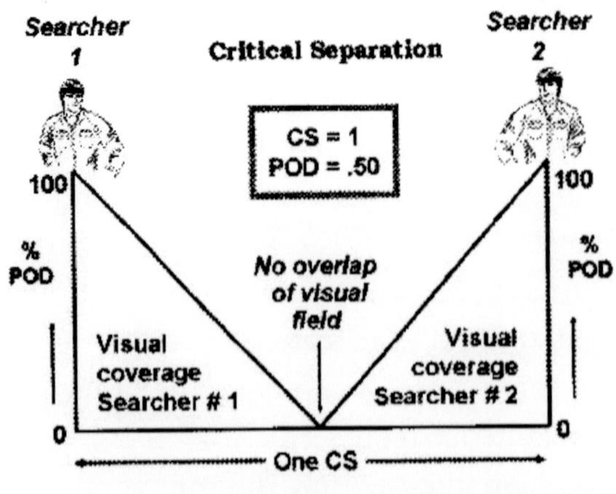

When Perkins and Roberts began evaluating the results of this technique they also found impressive results in increased finds (POD). Critical Spacing seemed to combine increased efficiency and a way to estimate POD. So each team became responsible for determining the critical separation at the start of their search assignment. The technique used became known as the "Northumberland Rain Dance."

After reviewing maps and looking at the segment they are to search, the team chooses an "average" location for vegetation cover and other environmental considerations. Should the conditions change once the search tactic has begun, the team performs the rain dance again to modify the spacing for the new conditions.

In the past decade, there has been a lot of speculation about just how this procedure is conducted. An object is placed on the ground that is similar in size and color to the object being sought. For many purposes a rucksack is a suitable, easily available object. This could be anything from a cigarette pack to a bag the size of a body or an actual person.

Searchers (preferably 8—10, but at least 4) are stationed around the object or person at a distance beyond where they can see the object or person being sought. Each searcher then walks slowly in a circle around the object for a few meters all going in the same direction. They then turn 90 degrees and walk toward the object until they can clearly see it. This procedure was designed to simulate that the searchers really didn't know where the object was.

At the point where the object is visible, each of the searchers then paces off the distance from "detection" to the object. All of the distances are then averaged. This is known as the *Average Range of Detection* or *AROD.* Twice the average distance is what is called Critical Separation. Commonly the configuration of the circle will be ellipsoidal and the developers of the tactic (Perkins and Roberts—1989) advocate that the differences between the maximum and minimum distances will be an indication of the amount of purposeful wandering that will be needed in a particular segment.

When searchers are spaced at a distance equal to Critical Separation (CS=1) the theoretical POD (Probability of Detection) was supposed to be right around 50%. However, during field trials of the procedure when trained teams are "purposefully wandering" through an area, PODs have proven to be consistently closer to 80%. Because of this, it has been postulated that a trained group, searching with spacing equal to Critical Separation, can be a very efficient use of search manpower.

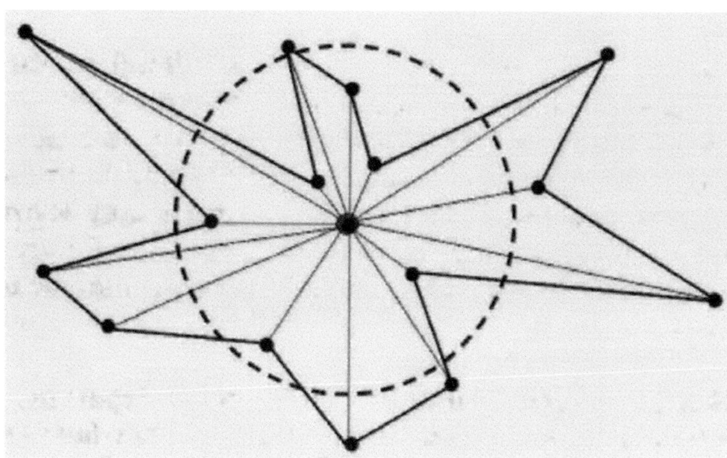

Average distances from object in rain dance to determine Critical Separation

Average Maximum Detection Range (AMDR)—The concept of Average Maximum Detection Range expands upon that of critical separation. When the procedure is carefully performed to enhance accuracy, it can provide more precise spacing and, in fact, can produce a rough (conservative) estimate of *Sweep Width*.

The process to determine AMDR is considerably more time consuming than Critical Spacing, so it is important to properly select a location "average" to the conditions of your search segment so you can reduce the possibility of having to perform the procedure again, for widely changing topography. The technique can be performed by one searcher or by eight, but requires that eight distances be used in the calculation of the average. For our description, we will use the example of one searcher performing the procedure.

For each clue type (size, color, etc.) to be searched for, place an example at a location judged to be representative of the conditions in the search area as a whole, usually at the beginning of the search track. Beginning at the object, walk away from the object until it is no longer visible. Keep track of the number of paces of known length (sometimes called a tally) and use these to estimate the distance. Record the distance to this point. Continue away from the object for another 50 to 100 meters. Travel clockwise around the object about 45 degrees and move toward the object until it is sighted. Record the distance from this point to the object by counting the paces to the object from the point of sighting while returning to it along a straight line. Then move away from the object at 90 degrees to the right of the initial departure, which should be about forty-five degrees from the direction of approach just used. Again measure the distance to the point at which the object disappears. Repeat these sequences until eight detection distances and eight extinguish distances are established, as shown in the figure below.

Eight of the distances will have been measured while moving away from the object (*Extinguish*) and eight measured while moving toward the object (*Detection*). These distances can be easily estimated by having calibrated the length of one's pace and knowing the number of paces traveled. The average of all those (two) values

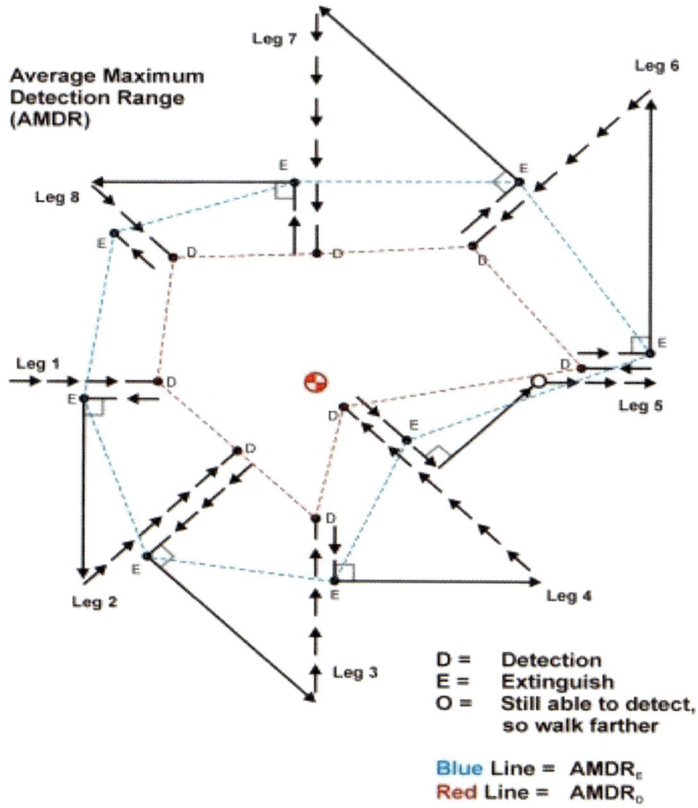

(Detection and Extinguishment) will be the AMDR for that object in that environment.

The calculation of AMDR requires that the person estimating the value make a reasoned judgment about the effects terrain and vegetation have on the resulting distance. For example, when moving away from the object, the searcher may descend into a small hollow that obscures the line of sight to the object. However, if the object was still clearly visible just before this descent and the searcher believes it will still be quite detectable when ascending the far side of the hollow, the searcher should continue away from the object. If the searcher is able to see the object after coming up out of the hollow, then the searcher should continue away from the object until it can no longer be seen. On the other hand, if the searcher is reasonably sure there is little to no chance of re-acquiring the object visually at a greater distance, there is no need to proceed further.

Sweep Width—Or more importantly, *Effective Sweep Width* is a measure of detectability. Factors that influence sweep width include: characteristics of the search object, the sensor (searcher) and the environmental conditions surrounding the search object. Determination of accurate sweep width values can only be achieved through rigorous scientific experiments. Due to the wide variation of the factors noted above, it is highly unlikely we will ever see a comprehensive (global) set of land SAR sweep width tables, as exists for maritime search. However, the methodology for conducting experiments to establish such sweep width tables, within a prescribed geographical area, has been published (*Sweep Width Estimation for Ground Search and Rescue*, R. Koester, D.C. Cooper, J.R. Frost and R.Q. Robe, 2004). It is strongly recommended that teams within the same geographical area develop their own sweep width tables using the experiments described in that publication.

Knowledge of precise sweep width values will allow the search resource to employ that spacing. Then, following completion of the search tactic, the calculations can be performed to determine the *Area Effectively Swept* and ultimately *Coverage*. The POD vs Coverage graph can then be used to accurately determine the POD rendered by this search effort.

Area Search versus Route Search in the Wilderness Environment

Let's continue our examination of Loose Space searches, as they are the most frequently performed, assuming the incident continues beyond the Reflex Tasking stage (refer to *SARAware*™ for more details on this). As we've seen in our discussion of grid searching, there are two main methods of navigation when performing a search: Compass bearing and landmark or route following. We'll discuss some effective techniques that can be used for each type of navigation method.

Area Search—A ground team conducting a search tactic using a compass bearing is performing an *area search*. Prior to beginning the search, the leader must decide if the navigator is to be a searcher on the line or a guide for the other team members to refer to. In either case, the team Leader must brief the team on how clue detection will be handled. This includes whether the entire team will stop and wait until the clue is processed, or whether the remaining searchers will continue searching until reaching a predetermined distance. Let's look at both navigator scenarios.

- Navigator as a searcher. This is easier in daylight hours if the Navigator is also the Pace Counter and located in the center of the search line.
  1. The team is assembled on the base line and spaced according to the determination of Critical Spacing, AMDR or Effective Sweep Width believed to produce the required POD or Coverage. Using flagging tape to mark the edges of each search lane assists with visualization.
  2. The navigator will "shoot" the bearing and acquire a target as discussed in the chapter on field navigation. The remaining team members may want to also shoot this bearing for an idea of the direction they will search, keeping in mind the navigator's bearing is the controlling one.
  3. The navigator will walk towards the target counting tally strides to measure and record distance. If the navigator reaches the target, flagging tape can be used to mark it. If the distance is greater than 50 meters the navigator might consider establishing an interim target by "planting" his/her tracking stick on the bearing line.
  4. The navigator then returns to their position on the base line and the entire team begins the search, performing purposeful wandering in their respective search lanes, up to a subsequent base/control line at the indicated target.
  5. The sequence is repeated until the segment is searched in accordance with the briefing, or until the assignment requires a switch to a route type search.

6. If this type of search is conducted in darkness, a (bright) light stick (also known as Cyalume®) can be attached to the target, or the navigation process can be performed using the "buddy" technique described in the chapter on field navigation. In that case, the "buddy" will be the Pace Counter and return to the search line after establishing/marking the navigation target, to join the search in their respective lane.

- Navigator as a guide. Once again this task is easier performed if the navigator also functions as the Pace Counter. It is essential for the navigator to be located in the center of the search line, though they will not be part of that line. If spacing is wide or vegetation thick, the task may require additional navigators for the searchers to guide on.
  1. The team is assembled on the base line and spaced according to the determination of Critical Spacing, AMDR or Effective Sweep Width believed to produce the required POD or Coverage. Using flagging tape to mark the edges of each search lane assists with visualization.
  2. The navigator will "shoot" the bearing and acquire a target as discussed in the chapter on field navigation. The remaining team members may want to also shoot this bearing for an idea of the direction they will search, keeping in mind the navigator's bearing is the controlling one.
  3. The navigator will slowly walk towards the target counting tally strides to measure and record distance.
  4. At the same as the navigator is walking towards the navigation target, the searchers begin their purposeful wandering to search their lane(s). The navigator must be walking slowly enough that the searchers do not pass the navigator (in distance) while searching.
  5. The navigator will command the team to stop and reform upon reaching the navigation target, once all searchers have completed searching their lane up to that distance.

The figure below presents an example of an area search conducted with the navigator serving as a guide only. Due to the number of searchers and sweep width (spacing) in this example, there is more than one navigator/guide.

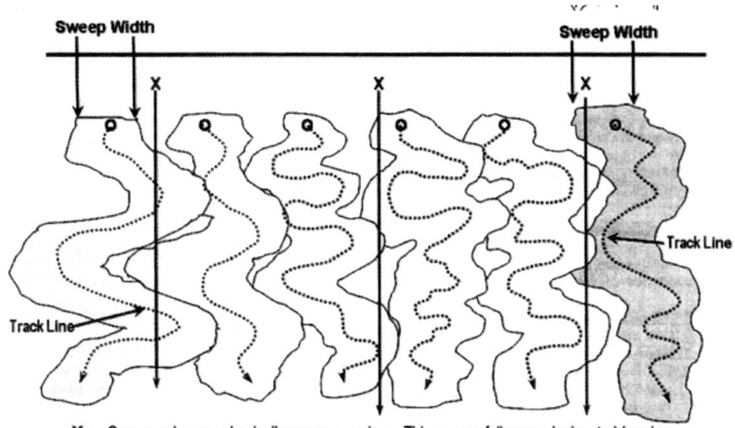

X = Compass bearer - basically a non searcher. This person follows a designated bearing.
O = Searchers - free to wander, checking likely spots, continually "guiding" on the compass bearer.
Notice that each team member has a definite scan range each side of the track line. This sweep width diagram indicates the reality of missing small areas of terrain inside the area being searched.

Route Search—This type of search is very much a combination of both types of area search. In this case the navigator will be a searcher, but the team will move along with the navigator (at the same time), using the navigator as a guide. The navigator may require a narrower search lane as they must remain in visual contact with the landmark they are using as a reference to navigation. For a route search, the navigator will normally be located on either end of the base line, unless the team is required to search on both sides of the route/landmark, in which case the navigator will be positioned in the center of the base line.

1. The team is assembled on the base line and spaced according to the determination of Critical Spacing, AMDR or Effective Sweep Width believed to produce the required POD or Coverage. Using flagging tape to mark the edges of each search lane assists with visualization.
2. The navigator paces off along the landmark route to record a set distance. Upon reaching the desired distance a marker is set and the navigator returns to the base line.

3. The entire team (including the navigator) begins its purposeful wandering search of the respective search lane(s), with the navigator keeping the landmark route in sight, and the team guiding on the navigator.
4. The navigator gives commands/information based on the upcoming contours of the route. The intent is to allow the team to move together and maintain spacing. In the case of hard (angular) turns, the end of the line nearest the turn, will slow (and move very little) while the end away from the turn will travel a great deal (possibly quickly) to keep the line formed. This resembles military marching and column turning.
5. Should a clue be detected, the recommended practice is to stop the entire line in order to maintain line integrity and sweep width, until the clue is processed. Then the command will be given for the line to begin searching again.
6. Upon reaching the distance marker, the line is stopped and reformed to ensure proper sweep width/spacing.
7. The sequence is repeated until the final distance is attained or the tactic requires modification as in changing to an area search.

The figure below represents an example of a route search along a lake shore. Note the black line, representing the purposeful wandering of the navigator, is much narrower so the navigator can maintain visual contact with the landmark route (in this case, the lake shore).

Search Tactics in the Urban Environment

As you might imagine, there are differences in the tactics you will employ in a population center as opposed to the wilderness. But you must remember that in today's western civilization, you may be confronted with conducting operations in an environment that presents both types of surroundings. Be prepared to add or include techniques used in environs other than the one in which you began your search, should the need arise. For example, you may encounter a home in the wilderness requiring you to employ your "canvassing" technique, or a building requiring a search as if it were in the urban environment. There are also many dense population areas with significant "greenbelts", requiring application of your wilderness search tactics. For now let's consider some urban tactics including, house-to-house canvassing, building searches and institution checks.

- House-to-House Canvassing—This includes checking around the area of the missing person's last known location and/or their (if known) destination. Frequently it will include interviews of people in these areas to determine any information important to the incident. Often searchers will go door to door conducting these interviews. Before beginning this tactic, searchers must be given a thorough briefing. The briefing includes questions to be asked during the interview. It is recommended the searcher who will be asking the questions (only one person should "do the talking" and the other team members—this team is a minimum of two, preferably three members—should be taking notes) should practice the questions prior to deployment. This will let the conversation seem "natural" and not like an interrogation. There are three levels of interviewing/residence searching:
    1. Level 1—Household Interview with a property and yard search by Search & Rescue responders, with a request the residents conduct an interior search of the domicile.

- This level implies there is reason to believe the subject may be on the property and could be inside one of the structures.
- This activity can take 20 minutes or longer per property.

2. Level 2—Household Interview with a request the residents conduct an interior search of the domicile and a search of the property to include any outside structures.
   - This level implies there is little reason to believe the subject is in any of the property structures and would likely be visible if on the property grounds.
   - This activity can take 10-15 minutes per property.
3. Level 3—No residents are home or on the property. Place a flyer on the door with a description and picture of the missing person along with a request the residents search their dwelling and property.
   - Should be followed up
   - Be aware of laws and incident policy concerning private property if there is strong possibility the subject may be on/in the absent homeowner's property.
   - This activity should take 5 minutes or less per property.

TYPICAL CANVASSING INTERVIEW QUESTIONS

- Do you know this person? (use photo)
- Have you seen this Person? (use photo)
- How long have you been here?
- Would you have seen him if he were in the area?
- Would someone else have seen him?
- Did you hear or see anything unusual?
- Did you notice anyone or anything in the area?

As previously noted, there are significant safety issues in any search tactic, especially in the urban environment. Certain protocols should be followed when searchers are conducting urban tactics, especially when not accompanied by a Law Enforcement Officer:

- Unaccompanied urban tactics should be limited to daytime hours. No night assignments should be given unless the team is to be accompanied by an LEO.
- Never have a searcher approach a dwelling alone. Team integrity must be maintained with at least two members at all times.
- Be alert. Let your senses warn you if something is out of the ordinary when approaching a property.
- Have an Escape Plan! There might be a hostile animal (dog?) on the property, some criminal activity being conducted on the property, or just hostile owners.
- Listen before knocking on the door.
- Knock loudly on the door, while standing to the side. Do not use the doorbell.
- Stand far enough away from the door (when the resident answers) to encourage the resident to step outside the door.
- Never enter a dwelling, even if invited, unless approved and accompanied by an LEO.
- Be especially suspicious of persons who seem overly eager to help or provide information.
- If they seem to have good information, get contact information for later follow-up.
- After the interview, make notes on what seemed normal and what did not.
- Be alert to "unknowing witnesses."
- Always be polite and thank people for their time.

Building Searches

Prior to conducting a building search (whether single or multi-story), the exterior must be contained. If you have enough resources, station a responder at every exit. At the minimum, position one member at opposite (diagonal) corners. Each one will have a view of two sides of the building. There's no point letting the subject leave the premises you are about to search!

Courtesy of www.bluprintchicago.com

Every locked area must be opened and checked, then secured against entry and exit. You have no way of knowing if the door was locked or open prior your arrival. It is essential to have a building employee, with a master key, accompany you.

If enough resources are available, they should be assigned to conduct the building searches. Do not enlist the building staff or occupants to search the building, the search should be performed by the incident's responders.

- Single Story Building—Once convinced the building is contained and the subject could not have gotten past the confinement:
    1. Start at one end and search systematically, room by room, toward the other.
    2. Move the containment to hallway intersections as the teams search through so the subject cannot slip through while you are searching.
    3. Upon completing the search, secure the building against entry and exit, or you must leave external containment in place.
- Multi-story Building—The techniques we employ in a multi-story building were adapted from years of police, fire and military experience. To inhibit internal movement by the subject, containment should include one person at each elevator in the building.
    1. Moving containment will include one searcher at the top (initially) of each stairwell.
    2. Starting on the roof, search all mechanical and utility accesses. Check all doors, ledges, alcoves, storage areas. When complete

3. Move to the top floor. If there is an attic, search the attic area. Then continue the search on the top floor, room by room, securing them as you complete each one. Don't forget to include cabinets, large boxes, furniture, etc. You will be astonished at places subjects can crawl into. Once this floor is completed, descend to the next floor.
4. Containment should now descend one level so the subject cannot ascend to a floor that has already been searched.
5. Search this next lower floor, room by room, completely as you did the top floor. Secure all rooms as you finish searching them. When you complete searching this floor, descend to the next floor.
6. Moving containment follows your descent with their own, again preventing the subject from moving to the upper floors already searched.
7. The sequence is repeated until you have searched the entire building, including the basement and parking garage (vehicle searches are required) if there is one.

The key to successful building search is to always conduct these searches very systematically. Don't exclude any door, space, locker, ceiling space, utility space, etc. Your best option is to get a set of building plans so you can check off each space and floor as they are searched. You should also use non-permanent methods (flagging tape, dry erase marker, colored chalk, masking tape, etc.) to mark each space that has been searched. Masking tape has the additional benefit of "sealing" the space. The tape would show signs of tamper if someone attempted to enter the space after you seal it with the tape. You can also write the name of the person who searched the space, including date and time, on the tape.

Institution Checks

This is an important procedure. Hospitals, jails, substance abuse detox centers, homeless shelters, and domestic violence centers are examples of facilities to check. It is possible that a person who appears disoriented, could be assumed to need care in such institutions.

The first checks will likely be made via telephone. If you physically visit any of these facilities, be sure to leave subject information, including a photograph, at the admissions or registration center. Should there be a need to search such a facility, you will need to be accompanied by an official of the institution who has authority and access to enter any location in the entire facility.

Mantracking in the urban environment

It may seem strange to think about mantracking in the city. After all, streets and concrete sidewalks don't lend themselves well to retaining foot prints. But remember, skilled mantrackers are detail oriented. They seek all sorts of sign, not just footprints.

Begin by immediately deploying the mantracking team to the IPP (LKP/PLS), before the area is greatly disturbed by Law Enforcement, searchers, bystanders, etc. The trackers will look for all disturbances, like dust on floors, countertops, and doors for sign left by the subject. The biggest problem for the tracker in an urban environment is discriminating the sign left by the subject (or their abductor!) and the multitudes of other people who may have passed through the same area. This is another example where a detailed missing/lost person questionnaire can assist in identifying clues belonging to the subject.

Assisting a canine unit on a search assignment

There may be occasion when a canine unit arrives at the incident without any team members other than the handler and canine partner. From SARAware™, you remember that any field team requires a minimum of three (3) human members to be deployed. In such a situation, the operations section may assign ground searchers to the canine unit as *flankers*. This is different from operating as a task force. The flankers are member of the canine team and have duties relevant to how such a team operates.

- Team Leader Considerations—While some of my canine handler colleagues will become hostile over this point, the handler is NEVER the team leader. A professional handler understands that his/her focus must be totally involved with the canine. This leaves the handler no ability to assume the (whole) team leadership role in Safety, Navigation and Communication. So the Team Leader must be one of the flankers.
    - Safety—the team leader is always responsible for team safety. Working with a canine-handler pair increases the workload. The handler will subject themselves to extreme risk to protect their canine partner. The team leader must anticipate as many of these hazards as possible, before and during the assignment, to prevent subjecting the canine and handler to the danger.
    - Navigation—As with any search tactic, the team leader must know where the team has been, where it is and where it needs to go. While handlers are trained and tested on navigating when working their canine, the best results of both canine search and navigation functions are achieved when the tasks are delegated separately.
    - Communication—On a typical ground team, communication centers on that within the team and between the team and the Command Post. Now there are two additional channels: Communication between the handler and the canine (which should be monitored by the Team Leader) and communication between the handler and the team (including the leader). The team leader must facilitate these additional channels and ensure accurate bi-directional communication in all cases.

- Handler Strategies—In SARAware™, we were introduced to the broad categories of canine SAR. In each subspecialty, the handler will determine the strategies that best suit the dog's abilities, the terrain, the environment and the subject considerations. Prior to deploying on the assignment, the handler will brief the team on the anticipated maneuvers from the canine's perspective.
  - Air Scenting/Area Search—This canine seeks and orients on airborne human scent. Since this canine is (usually) not "scent specific", or tracking a specific human's scent, the search segment should have been cleared of humans for at least a few hours prior to inserting the canine resource. The handler will plan the tactic based on scent theory. This will give the canine the best opportunity to acquire any scent and follow it to the source. This canine is free ranging (off leash) and will require the team to be downwind of the canine.
  - Tracking/Trailing—These canines may or may not be scent specific, but work in similar fashion. The typical mode is on-leash (though it may be a long lead!) with the canine first seeking the scent and then following it as if on a trail. Rather than following scent cells in the air, these canines use scent left on "ground." Examples are vegetation and tracks.

  - Human Remains Detection (HRD)—This specialty utilizes the canine to locate cadaver scent. A well trained canine can find cadaver scent that is extremely old and/or contaminated (combined) with other strong scent, as in a burnt structure. They can also locate scent from body parts that are very small and buried or underwater! These canines normally work off leash, so much of the flanker preparation and tactical considerations will be similar to a search with an area search canine.

- Expanded concepts—Let's look at a few specific concerns when working as flankers to a canine resource.
    - Safety—Canines are used very effectively in difficult terrain and ground cover, and hazardous structures. Still, they can be injured. Anticipating danger zones and notifying the handler is a responsibility of all flankers. Be aware, the handler will blindly follow their canine into a hazardous situation if they believe the dog to be in danger! The handler should know the best methods to rescue the canine from danger, but the flankers may be called upon to extract the handler.
    - Navigation—As noted above, handlers are trained in navigation, but the responsibility for this task lies with the flankers. Flankers need to "track" where they have traveled, know their precise current location and especially keep the team within the borders of the search segment. It is essential to have briefed these borders, including action plans (with consent from Command) in the event the scent leads the canine out of the assigned segment.
    - Flanker Search—While flankers have the additional responsibility to assist and serve the handler-canine pair, they are still responsible for searching. Each flanker is expected to be clue conscious and detect evidence that may relate to the subject or incident, regardless of the canine's activity on the assignment.

Summary

This chapter has presented a brief overview of some of the tasks a basic ground searcher will be called upon to perform. As with all your search & rescue field skills, you will need to expand upon this knowledge with field training and constant practice. If you are a member of a SAR organization, review their training opportunities and take advantage of their experience. When qualified and proficient you will be able to bring assistance to those in need.

References

Urban Search (2007)
Christopher S. Young and John Wehbring, *dbS Productions*, Charlottesville, VA

SARAware—Awareness Level Search & Rescue for the Responder (2013)
Dion Petaros, James Keck and Wes Podboy, *AERIE Publications*, Lake Dallas, TX

Lost Person Behavior—A Search & Rescue Guide on Where to Look- for Land, Air and Water (2008)
Koester, Robert J; *dbS Productions*, Charlottesville, VA

Managing Land Search Operations (2006)
Robert C. (Skip) Stoffel, *Emergency Response International*, Cashmere, WA

A Method for Determining Effective Sweep Widths for Land Searches (2002)
R. Quincy Robe and J. R. Frost, *Potomac Management Group, Inc.*, Alexandria, VA

Sweep Width Estimation for Ground Search and Rescue (2004)
R. Koester, D.C. Cooper, J.R. Frost and R.Q. Robe, *Potomac Management Group, Inc.*, Alexandria, VA

Basic Rope Techniques & Awareness Level Wilderness Rescue Gear

12

Objectives

Courtesy of www.ropesthatrescue.com

- Describe and differentiate between natural and manmade materials used to manufacture rope
- Define the following characteristics of rope construction:
  - Laid rope
  - Braided rope
  - Kernmantle rope
  - Dynamic rope
  - Static rope
  - Safety Factor
- Describe and differentiate between construction types of webbing
- Discuss rules of rope etiquette and rope care
- Define the following knot terms:
  - Bight
  - Bend
  - Hitch
  - Standing End
  - Running End
  - Tail

- Explain how the following (rope) knots are used in the field:
  - Square knot
  - Figure 8 on a bight
  - Figure 8 bend
  - Figure 8 follow through
  - Clove hitch
  - Munter hitch
  - Double fisherman's bend (Grapevine)
  - Prusik's wrap
- Describe how the following (webbing) knots or systems are used in the field:
  - Overhand bend/Water knot
  - Improvised harness
- Differentiate the materials used in manufacturing carabiners
- Discuss the types of carabiner construction and proper usage including:
  - Oval
  - "D" shape
  - Pear shape
  - Locking vs. non-locking
  - Loading and care
- Explain the construction and use of a hazardous terrain crossing system
- Explain the construction and application of improvised field litters

DISCLAIMER

The information presented in this module is in no way intended to train the student to be a rope or rescue technician. Those specialties require highly technical training courses, taught under the safe and strict supervision of certified Instructors.

Additionally, training in tying the knots described here, as well as the rigging of the rope and webbing systems discussed, must also be conducted by a qualified Instructor.

SEEK OUT THE PROPER TRAINING!

COURTESY OF WIKIPEDIA

Piece of 16th century rope,

As you may have concluded from the above disclaimer, the use of rope systems and rescue gear has evolved into a highly specialized and technical discipline. Our goal is to present you with the knowledge of the application of very basic concepts to employ rope, webbing, and systems that may assist you during your SAR taskings. Other texts will instruct you on the actual techniques of tying knots and constructing rope/webbing systems. We believe that instruction is best left for the classroom environment. That being said, included in the Appendices are documents describing the tying of knots.

Rope

The use of ropes for hunting, pulling, fastening, attaching, carrying, lifting, and climbing dates back to prehistoric times. It is likely that the earliest "ropes" were naturally occurring lengths of plant fiber, such as vines, followed soon by the first attempts at twisting and braiding these strands together to form the first proper ropes in the modern sense of the word. In the Middle Ages rope-making became more sophisticated and became a trade. As society entered the Renaissance, the rope-making trade evolved into an industry. This allowed for rope construction of great lengths, especially necessary for the burgeoning maritime industry of sailing ships.

Refinements in construction continued in the ensuing centuries, but the creation (some may say discovery) of nylon in the 20th century led to rapid scientific development of new rope construction, application and safety. While we continue to see some rope made of natural fibers, synthetic fiber construction is the most common type of rope encountered today. Regardless of the fibers used, there are three main construction techniques used in modern rope-making: Laid Rope, Braided Rope and Kernmantle Rope.

Laid Rope—Laid rope, also called twisted rope, is historically the prevalent form of rope, at least in modern western history. Common twisted rope generally consists of three strands and is normally right-laid, or given a final right-handed twist, but can be found with a left twist.

Twisted ropes are built up in three steps. First, fibers are gathered and spun into yarns. A number of these yarns are then formed into strands by twisting. The strands are then twisted together with additional strands to "*lay*" the rope. The twist of the yarn is opposite to that of the strand, and that in turn is opposite to that of the rope. It is this counter-twist, introduced with each successive operation, which holds the final rope together as a stable, unified object.

Courtesy of www.k9-search-and-rescue.com

One limitation or negative property of laid rope is partial untwisting when used. This can cause spinning of suspended loads, or stretching and kinking of the rope itself. An additional drawback of twisted construction is that every fiber is exposed to abrasion numerous times along the length of the rope. This means that the rope can degrade to numerous inch-long fiber fragments, which is not easily detected visually. Another limitation of laid rope is how you coil them. Twisted ropes have a preferred direction for coiling. Normal right-laid rope should be coiled clockwise, to prevent kinking. Coiling this way imparts a twist to the rope. Rope of this type must be bound at its ends by some means to prevent untwisting.

Braided Rope—While a rope may be made from a simple flat braid of three, five or greater odd number of strands, a modern braided rope will usually consist of a braided (tubular) jacket over strands of fiber (these may also be braided). Some forms of braided rope with untwisted cores have a particular advantage; they do not impart an additional twisting force when they are stressed. The lack of added twisting forces is an advantage when a load is freely suspended, as when a rope is used for rappelling or to suspend an arborist. Other specialized cores reduce the shock from arresting a fall when used as a part of a personal or group safety system.

Braided ropes are generally made from nylon, polyester, polypropylene or high performance fibers such as high modulus polyethylene (HMPE) and aramid. Nylon is chosen for its strength and elastic stretch properties. However, nylon absorbs water and is 10-15% weaker when wet. Polyester is about 90% as strong as nylon but stretches less under load and is not affected by water. It has somewhat better UV resistance, and is more abrasion resistant. Polypropylene is preferred for low cost and light weight (it floats on water) but it has limited resistance to ultraviolet light, is susceptible to friction and has a poor heat resistance.

Braided ropes, as well as objects like garden hoses, fiber optic or coaxial cables, etc., that have no *lay*, or inherent twist, will uncoil better if coiled into *figure-8* coils, where the twist reverses regularly and essentially cancels out. This is the preferred method of coiling if no cylinder can be used to roll the rope on.

Braided rope can be found in three typical forms:

Single braid consists of an even number of strands, eight or twelve being usual, braided into a circular pattern with half of the strands going clockwise and the other half going counterclockwise. The central void may be large or small; in the former case the term **hollow braid** is sometimes preferred.

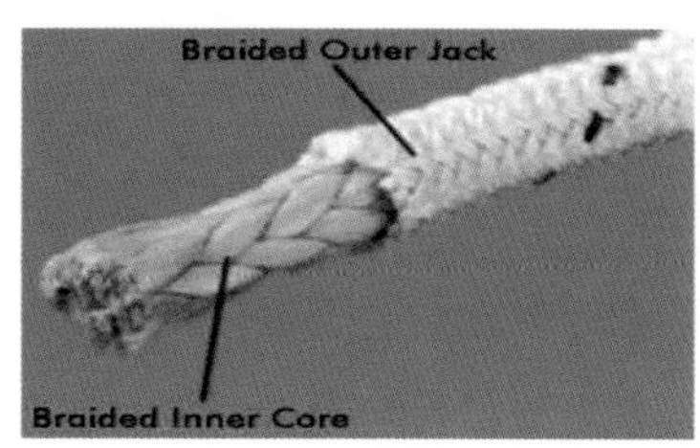

Double braid, also called **braid on braid**, consists of an inner braid filling the central void of an outer braid that may be of the same or different material. Often the inner braid fiber is chosen for strength while the outer braid fiber is chosen for abrasion resistance. This example of mixing rope construction materials demonstrates how we can strengthen and reduce negative characteristics of our rope.

Solid Braid consists of the strands all traveling the same direction, clockwise or counterclockwise, and alternating between forming the outside of the rope and the interior of the rope. This construction is popular for general purpose utility rope but rare in specialized high performance line. Its solid density, when constructed with nylon fiber, makes this braid rope extremely strong with good elasticity and memory under heavy loads. It's a good choice when strength, resistance to the elements, and continuous wear is important. The solid braid gives it a smooth, even surface which knots well. It cannot be unraveled, even when cut.

Kernmantle Rope—Kernmantle rope has braided outer sheath or mantle of woven fibers. This mantle provides about 30% of the rope's strength, but more importantly provides protection for the rope's core (kern). The kern provides 70% of the rope's strength and will be constructed based on the rope's desired function. The core can consist of twisted fibers, untwisted fibers or even a solid tube-like material. The mantle is the chief determinant of the handling properties of the rope while the core determines the flexibility and "stretch ability" of the rope. When discussing the stretching capability of Kernmantle rope we speak in terms of "*dynamic*" or "*static*" rope.

1. Dynamic—A dynamic rope is a specially constructed, somewhat elastic rope used primarily in rock climbing, ice climbing and mountaineering. This "stretch" is what makes it "dynamic." Greater stretch allows a dynamic rope to absorb the energy of a sudden load, such as from a fall, more slowly, which reduces the peak force and therefore

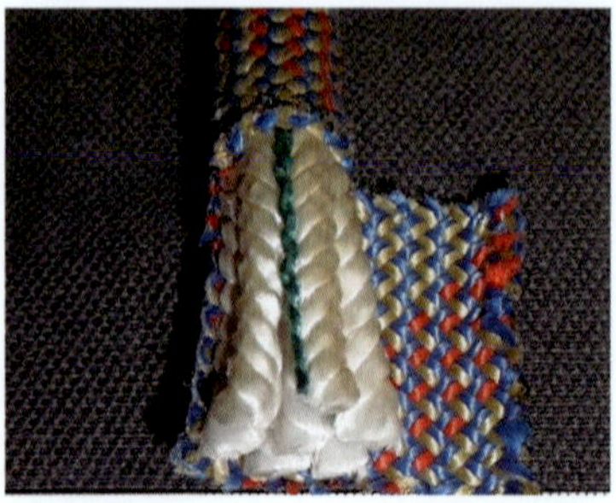

the chance of catastrophic failure of the rope. Dynamic Kernmantle rope will usually have a twisted fiber core and a looser braid mantle. To make the rope even more stretchy, manufacturers will use chopped (shorter length) twisted cores.

2. Static—A static rope is a rope that is designed to not stretch when placed under load. Static ropes have a wide variety of uses, for instance in fire and rescue operations, as well as caving. Static Kernmantle ropes are made with untwisted core fibers and tighter braid, which causes them to be stiffer in addition to limiting the stretch. The modern static Kernmantle rope frequently has a solid polymer core making the rope even less able to elongate.

Webbing

Cordage, such as rope, is extremely adaptable to many (if not all) lifting, hauling and traversing applications. Some, however, are better served with a flatter construction. For these applications, we use woven nylon in a strap-like construction called webbing.

Webbing is a strong fabric woven as a flat strip or tube of varying width and fibers often used in place of rope. The name webbing comes from the meshed material frequently used in its construction, which resembles a web. It is a versatile component used in climbing, slacklining, load securing and many other outdoor and rescue applications.

Originally made of cotton or flax, most modern webbing is made of synthetic fibers such as nylon, polypropylene or polyester. Webbing is also made from exceptionally high-strength material, such as Dyneema and even Kevlar. Webbing is both light and strong, with breaking strengths readily available in excess of 10,000 lbs (44.4 kN)!

There are two basic constructions of webbing. Flat webbing is a solid weave, with seatbelts and backpack straps being common examples. Tubular webbing consists of a flattened tube, and is the preferred type used in climbing and rescue applications.

Tubular Webbing

Flat Webbing

The most popular rescue webbing is one inch tubular but it is available in two and three inch widths which in earlier days were often used in lieu of climbing harnesses. Wrapped around the waist several times, they were less bulky and more comfortable than the old school method of tying the rope around the waist. Modern configurations include leg loops, which are essential to hold a climber who has fallen or otherwise found themselves dangling. If left supported only by rope or webbing wrapped around the waist, the diaphragm could be constricted and many climbers died as a result of asphyxiation.

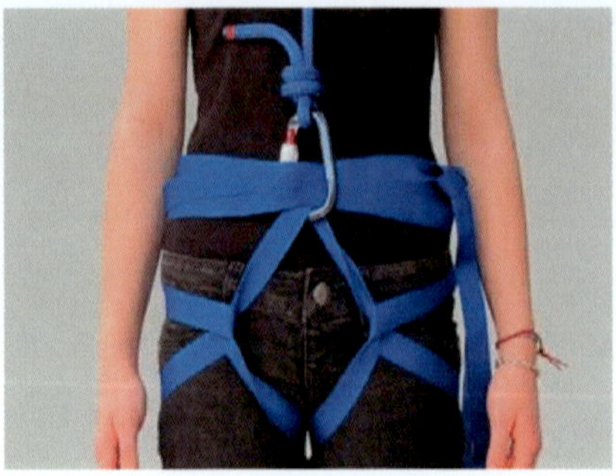

Safety Factors

In the United States, the National Fire Protection Association (NFPA) is the organization most widely accepted for setting standards for rope, webbing and rescue gear. Typically, they update the standards every five years. The standard that applies to rescue gear, including rope, is NFPA 1983. The most recent version of this standard is 2012 with updates expected in the fall of 2017.

There is a difference between the tensile strength of a rope and its safe working load. Tensile strength is the force required to break it, which can be determined by testing. However, in the real world of outdoors and rescue applications there are factors that impact or reduce the strength of any rope. These include; tying a knot in the rope, its age, environmental deterioration (hot and cold), abrasion and rubbing on objects, harmful substances, water and sand/grit, and the rope's previous use and care. If a person is on the end of a lifeline we obviously don't want the rope to break. To factor in the above variables we use an arbitrary number to reduce the actual load that is placed on the rope. This number is called the "*safe working load.*" This is the maximum (safe) weight we can suspend on the rope. The ratio between the working load and the rope's tensile strength is termed the safety margin. If a rope is rated at 5000 lbs tensile and we wanted to maintain a 15:1 safety margin, the maximum working load would be 333 lbs.

Throughout various professional associations there remains controversy about what standard should be adopted for safe working load of rope. Generally, cavers, mountaineers, and other outdoor activity groups accept a safety factor of 10:1, but the National Fire Protection Association (NFPA) previously recommended a 15:1 safety factor. The 2012 standards dictate a breaking strength of not less than 40 kN for lifelines. One kN equals approximately 225 lbs (102 kilograms) in terms of safe working load. This means the tensile strength of a lifeline should (minimally) be 9000 lbs or a safe working load of 600 lbs. Based on the 15:1 standard a "5000 lb. rope" would have a maximum safe working load of 333 lbs. If you wanted a rope to hold a 200 lb. rescuer, plus a 150 lb. victim, the total of 350 lbs would exceed the safe working load of 333 lbs by 17 lbs. Would the rope actually break in this instance? We don't know, but safety standards dictate that we must either lighten the load or use a rope with a stronger tensile strength, and therefore a higher safe working load. In search & rescue operations, we recommend you follow NFPA standards.

REMEMBER THE OLD ADAGE: "*BETTER SAFE THAN SORRY*"!

Rope Etiquette and Care

Even using your rope only to cross hazardous terrain requires you understand proper care and treatment of this equipment. There are certain guidelines to follow to ensure your gear is in proper condition and to extend the useful "life" of the rope and webbing.

The "Do" List:

- Uncoiling a new rope: Hold it as if on a spool and have a partner pull the rope from the "spool," stacking it in a random pile.
- Coiling: Use a "backpack" or "butterfly" coil to avoid twists. To do so, stack the rope in the palm of your hand or behind your neck. Rather than looping it over your neck, go back and forth, putting a bight of rope on the one side, then the next. Cinch the rope in the standard way.
- Twisted or knotted rope: Let it hang free and encourage the twist to unwind with your hand.
- Rope bag: Between outings, store your rope in a rope bag to protect it.
- Rope tarp: Use a tarp or ground cloth to keep the rope clean while out in the field.
- Logbook: Record all rope use in a logbook (one book for each rope), especially note sharp jolts like falls.

The "Don't" List

- Nylon on nylon: This contact burns rope and webbing. You should especially avoid running 2 ropes through the same top-rope carabiners, and never run a top rope directly through slings.
- Dirt: Minimize contact with dirt. Dirt works into the fibers and the sharp crystals can cut rope fibers, weakening the rope.
- Stepping on the rope: Stepping on a rope can damage the mantle. At the least, this works dirt into the rope.

- UV rays: Sunshine from day-to-day use is not likely to damage your rope. Too much sun, however, such as leaving the rope out all day for a fixed line or webbing at a belay station, can considerably weaken your rope. If your rope or webbing is becoming faded from the sun, consider replacing it.
- Chemicals: Most chemicals will weaken or destroy nylon and derivatives. Strong acids, such as battery acid, or alkali are extremely hazardous to your rope. Avoid having chemicals come in contact with your rope at all costs.
- Poor usage technique: Fast or jerky loading of a rope can cause damage due to burning the sheath, as well as loss of control. Learn to be smooth with steady increases of weight loading.
- Marking the middle: UIAA tests of a few years ago showed that marking ropes with liquids such as those in felt-tipped pens can damage the rope; this even includes those markers sold specifically for marking ropes. Therefore, the UIAA Safety Commission warns against marking a rope with any substance unless it has been specifically approved by the manufacturer of that rope. A bicolor rope where the pattern of the woven sheath changes is a better way to identify the middle of the rope.

Cleaning, Storage and Replacing

- Inspect: Inspect your rope often. Look at and feel every inch for cuts, nicks and abrasions in the sheath and for sections of mushy, ballooning or flattened core.
- Washing and drying: Wash ropes by hand in your bathtub or top-loading machine using warm water and mild soap. Avoid letting your rope kink. Hang to dry, uncoiled, away from direct sunlight.
- Storage: Store in a cool, dry area away from chemicals. Use a rope bag, hang it from a sling girth hitched around whole rope or hook the whole rope over a smooth dowel.

- Replacing: Ropes must be replaced when damaged or old. General guidelines:

  - Heavy sport climbing or rescue use, with repeated stress: 3-6 months
  - Heavy climbing or rescue with little or no stress: 1-2 years
  - Frequent weekend use with little or no stress: 2-3 years
  - Occasional use with no stress: 4-5 years
  - Large jerks or falls, or other noted damage: immediately!

Rope Terminology

Now that we have discussed the basic construction, care and safety considerations of rope and webbing, it's time to prepare ourselves with knowledge of how to use this equipment. To enable our understanding and provide for easier learning, let's first review some common terminology:

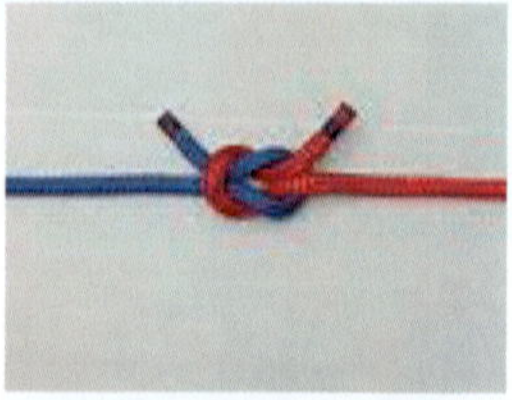

- Bend: A bend is a knot used to join two lengths of rope.

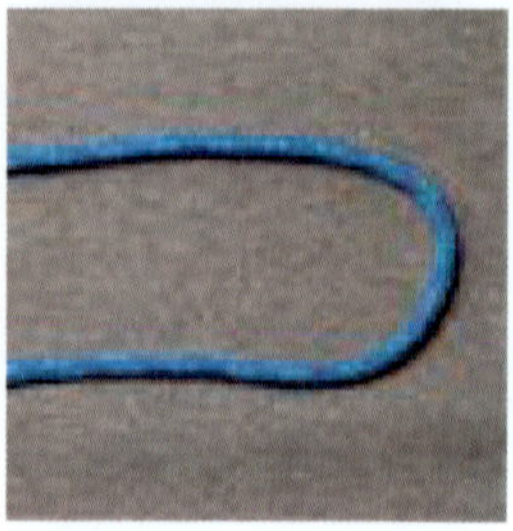

- Bight: A bight has two meanings in knotting. It can mean either any central part of a rope (between the standing end and the working end) or an arc in a rope that is at least as wide as a semicircle. In either case, a bight is a length of rope that does not cross itself.
- Dressing: Knot dressing is the process of arranging a knot in such a way as to improve its performance. Crossing or uncrossing the rope in a specific way, depending on the knot, can increase the knot's strength as well as reduce its jamming potential. While dressing a knot may "improve" its

appearance, the real purpose is to improve the knot's structure/ function.

- Hitch: A hitch is a knot that attaches a rope to some object, often a ring, rail, spar, post or rope.

Rolling or Friction Hitch

- Loop: A loop is one of the fundamental structures used to tie knots. It is a full circle formed by passing the working end of a rope over itself. When the legs of a closed loop are crossed to form a loop, the rope has *taken a turn*.

- Standing end: The standing end (or standing part) of a rope is the part not active in knot tying. It is the part opposite of the working end.
- Tail: This is the rope that is left over after tying a knot in rope or webbing. In many cases it will be used to tie the safety knot to prevent the main knot from slipping or coming untied. Excessive tail presents a danger of entanglement or jamming and should be secured or tucked away (as in a pocket).

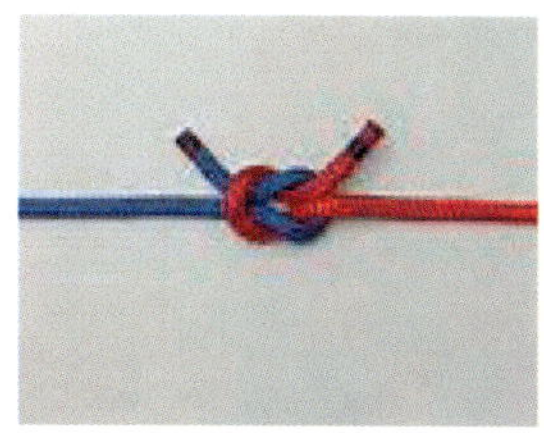

Tails from ends of square knot

- Whipping: A whipping is a binding knot tied around the end of a rope to prevent the rope from unraveling.

- Working end: The working end (or working part) of a rope is the part active in knot tying. It is the part opposite of the standing end. This end of the rope is also known as the *Running End* which demonstrates this is the end of the rope that is actually (moving) tying the knot.

Now that we are properly prepared, let's review some knots frequently used in search & rescue applications. You should note that knot tying is a matter of *muscle memory*. Rather than try to learn too many knots, learn a few that you can tie well, quickly. As you gain proficiency with those knots, you can always add to your "repertoire"! Fortunately, there aren't too many knots to remember, for search & rescue, out of the hundreds (perhaps thousands) of possible knots.

- Overhand knot: The overhand knot is one of the most fundamental knots and forms the basis of many others. In its standalone form, it is most frequently used as a safety knot to better secure and strengthen other (more complex) knots. As a safety knot the overhand knot is very secure, to the point of jamming. As a basis of other knots you will most often use it to tie a Fisherman's knot in rope or a Water Knot in webbing.

- Square knot: The square knot is a simple knot that is best used for applications involving low strain. Examples would be securing the ends of an improvised (webbing) harness, securing a rope around an object when no load is to be placed on the rope, creating jewelry etc.

- Figure 8 on a bight: The Figure-8-on-a-Bight knot is an excellent and easy-to-tie knot, tied on a loop or bight of rope. It is widely used for tying a rescuer on a lifeline into an anchor because it

is both very strong and also easy to untie after being tightened. You will also see this knot used to secure into a carabiner that is attached to a harness.

- Figure 8 bend: The figure-eight bend knot is used to "splice" two ropes, not necessarily of equal diameter, together. If tied, dressed and stressed properly, the figure-eight bend is fairly secure but susceptible to jamming in systems. For additional security, "stopper" or "safety" knots (i.e. Overhand) should be added to the tails.

- Figure 8 follow through: The figure-eight follow-through, also often referred to as the figure-eight retrace and the rewoven figure-eight, is one of the hardest working knots in climbing and rescue applications. It is likely you will use this knot often to tie a loop to a ring, a carabiner, a post or your own harness. While the resulting knot looks exactly like a Figure 8 on a bight, the process of tying this knot is entirely different. It is tied using the running end of the rope, as opposed to using a bight in the rope.

- Clove hitch: This is a fairly simple knot that can be useful for securing ropes to trees, posts, or other things that stand upright. With this knot, it's fairly easy to adjust the length of the rope if you need to. It can be used in lashing rope work as a temporary means to hold things together. A frequent use of this knot, in SAR, is to fashion an improvised litter from limbs or tracking sticks.

- Munter hitch: The Munter hitch, also known as the Italian hitch or the Crossing Hitch, is a simple knot, commonly used by climbers, cavers, and rescuers as part of a life-lining or belay system. This hitch is simply a set of wraps, using a rope or cord, around an object. Typically the object will be round like a pipe, pole or more commonly, a carabiner. Its main use is as a friction device for controlling the rate of descent or travel in belay systems. In search & rescue applications this hitch is frequently part of a system to allow safe crossing of hazardous terrain by a responder, who will then secure the lifeline to an anchor on the other end of the terrain just crossed.

- Double fisherman's bend (Grapevine): The double fisherman's knot or grapevine knot is a bend, or a knot used to join two lengths of rope or two ends of rope to form a loop. This knot is used most often in climbing, arboriculture, and search & rescue. The knot is formed by tying a double overhand knot, with each end around the opposite line's standing part. In SAR this knot is usually tied with 6-8mm Prusik's cord to create a Prusik's loop. The loop is used as part of a system to secure a responder's harness (carabiner) to a lifeline. When tied correctly the knots will slide apart on the standing ends of the rope(s). A safety knot is recommended for each tail.

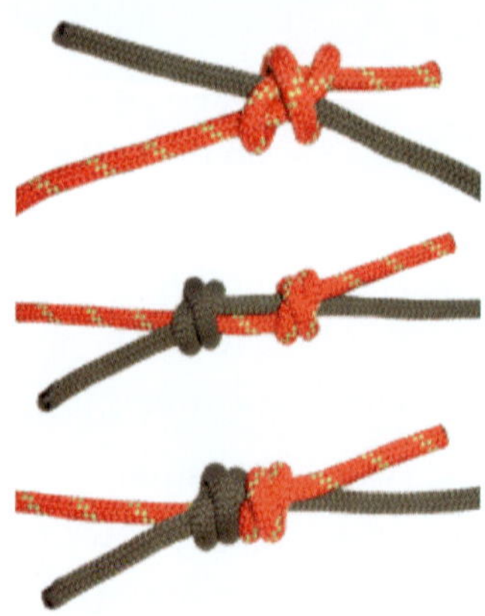

- Prusik's wrap (loop): A Prusik's wrap is a friction hitch or knot used to put a loop of cord (usually of smaller diameter) around a rope. As with many of our knots it is used in climbing, caving, and search & rescue. A Prusik's wrap made from cord does little or no damage to the lifeline it is attached to. In an emergency, it can be used in place of a mechanical ascender or as a self-belay system for travel in hazardous terrain. The knot is typically left loose over the lifeline unless the traveler falls, in which case it tightens and stops further movement along the lifeline via friction.

Webbing Knots and Systems

Some of the knots we learned in our rope discussion can also be used on webbing. But as you might imagine there are some knots that work especially well on/with webbing:

- Overhand bend/Water knot: The water knot, also known as an overhand bend or follow-through, is a knot frequently used in climbing and search & rescue for joining two ends of webbing together. For example, when making a sling or an improvised harness. It is recommended the tail(s) be secured with a safety knot consisting of a single overhand knot.

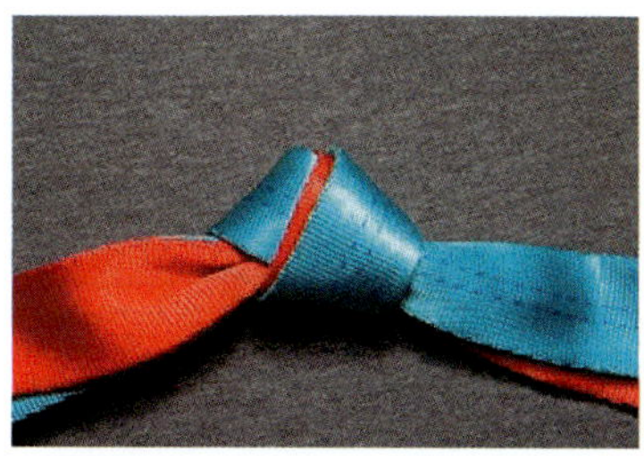

- Improvised harness: Consider the frequency with which we need to use a harness in search & rescue. It soon becomes apparent that there is no routine need to devote the weight and space to carry this highly specialized (single function) piece of gear. Remember, from the chapter on your SAR ready pack, the goal of carrying multi-function equipment.

Unless there is an absolute need for a piece of single purpose gear, we should strive to find alternative uses for gear we're already carrying. Webbing (and rope for that matter) can be used for a number of functions. When the need, infrequent though it may be, arises for a harness, one can be quickly fashioned using your webbing. There are a number of varieties of improvised harnesses you can construct. One of the more popular is known as the *Swiss Seat*. Properly tied, this harness is safe and effective.

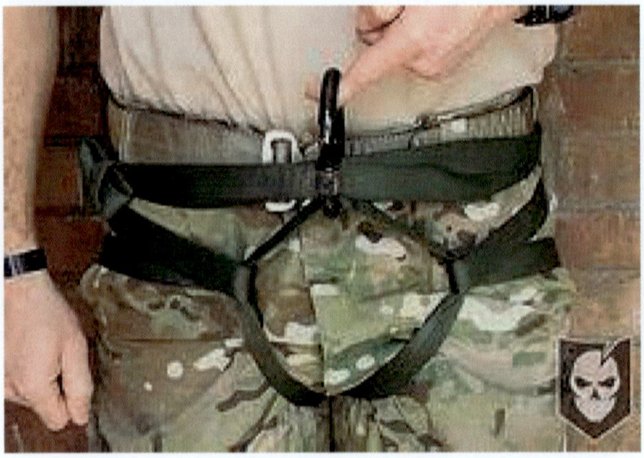

Carabiners

You may have noticed that much of our rope and webbing work is designed to attach to a carabiner. This metal piece of hardware is an integral part of almost every rope or webbing system. Safe functioning of those systems depends not only on good rope or webbing but on the quality of the carabiner employed.

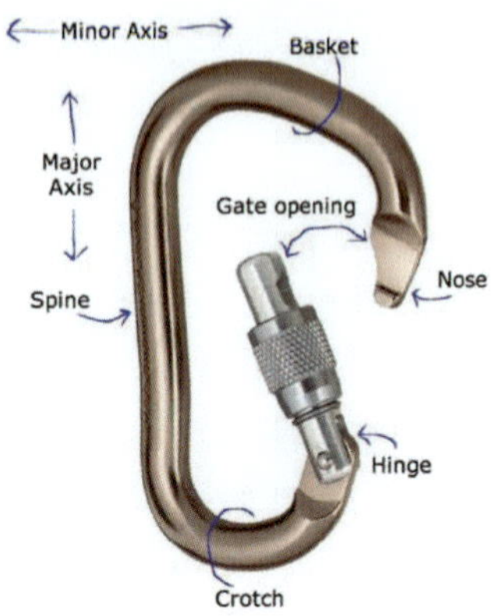

Simply stated, a carabiner is a metal loop with a spring-loaded gate used to quickly and reversibly connect components, most notably in safety-critical systems. Carabiners are widely used in rope-intensive activities such as climbing, arboriculture, caving, sailing, rope rescue, construction, industrial rope work, window cleaning, whitewater rescue and acrobatics. They are predominantly made from both steel and/or aluminum. Those used in sports tend to be of aluminum which is lighter weight than steel carabiners used in commercial applications and rope rescue.

If your use of carabiners is infrequent and the load requirements light, you might choose the lighter weight aluminum models. Beware of dropping these as they will suffer damage from rough handling. Conversely, if you expect high utilization of your carabiners, or anticipate high loads and stress on them, you might prefer to use the steel models for their extra strength and durability. Regardless of the construction material, rescue carabiners are subject to breaking strength tests much like those for rope and webbing.

Minimum breaking strength requirements and calculations for rescue carabiners are set out in National Fire Protection Association standard 1983 *Fire Service Life Safety Rope and Equipment*. The standard defines two classes of rescue carabiners. Light use rescue carabiners are required to have minimum breaking strengths of 27 kN gate closed, 7 kN gate open and 7 kN minor axis. General use rescue carabiners are required to have minimum breaking strengths of 40 kN gate closed, 11 kN gate open and 11 kN minor axis.

Carabiners are available with two types of spring-loaded gates—*locking* and *non-locking*. For search & rescue use, only locking gate carabiners are acceptable. If you choose to purchase some non-locking gate carabiners to hang equipment off your ready pack, feel free to do so. But any carabiner that will be used to lift or secure a load, be it equipment or human, must have a locking gate.

Locking carabiners have the same general shapes as non-locking carabiners but have an additional mechanism securing the gate. These mechanisms may be either threaded sleeves ("screw-lock"), spring-loaded sleeves ("twist-lock") or magnetic levers ("Magnetron").

- Screw-lock: Have a threaded sleeve over the gate which must be engaged and disengaged manually. They have fewer moving parts than spring-loaded mechanisms, are less prone to malfunctioning due to contamination or component fatigue and

Screw-Lock Carabiner

are easier to employ one-handed. However, they require more total effort and are more time-consuming than twist-lock.

- Twist-lock: Have a security sleeve which must be manually rotated to disengage, but which springs closed automatically upon release. They offer the advantage of re-engaging without additional user input, but being spring-loaded are prone to both spring fatigue and their more complex mechanisms becoming balky from dirt, ice, or other contamination. They are also difficult to engage one-handed and with gloves on.

Twist-Lock Carabiner

- Magnetic: Have two small levers with embedded magnets on either side of the locking gate which must be pushed or pinched simultaneously to disengage. Upon release the levers pull shut and into the locked position against a small steel insert in the carabiner nose. With the gate open the magnets in the two levers repel each other so they do not lock or stick together, which might prevent the gate from closing properly. Advantages are very easy one-handed operation, re-engaging without additional user input and few mechanical parts that can fail.

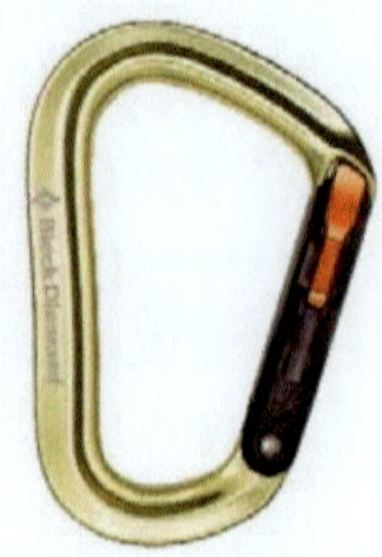

Magnetic-Lock Carabiner

There is also a variety of shapes to choose from. While you may think this is unnecessary fashion, choosing the correct size and shape to fit your specific application is important. Choosing the wrong size or shape for the system you are currently constructing could result in line jams or other malfunctions that stop you from completing the task. Shape also affects load sharing on the carabiner itself. Heavy loads require a carabiner shaped to place the bulk of the load on the spine (strongest axis) of the carabiner. Carabiners come in four characteristic shapes, with numerous subsets. Descriptions and examples are shown below:

1. Oval: Symmetric. Most basic and utilitarian. Smooth regular curves are gentle on equipment and allow easy repositioning of loads. Their greatest disadvantage is that a load is shared equally on both the strong solid spine and the weaker gated axis.
2. D: Asymmetric shape transfers the majority of their load onto the spine, the carabiner's strongest axis.
3. Offset-D: Variant of a D with a greater asymmetry, allowing for a wider gate opening.
4. Pear/HMS: Specialized oversized offset-D's used in belaying. These are usually the heaviest carabiners.

Oval Shaped Carabiner

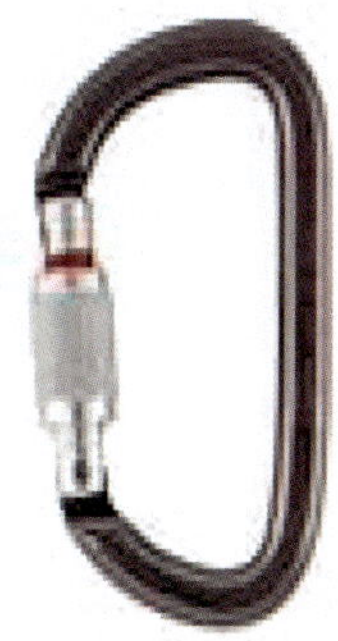

D Shaped Carabiner

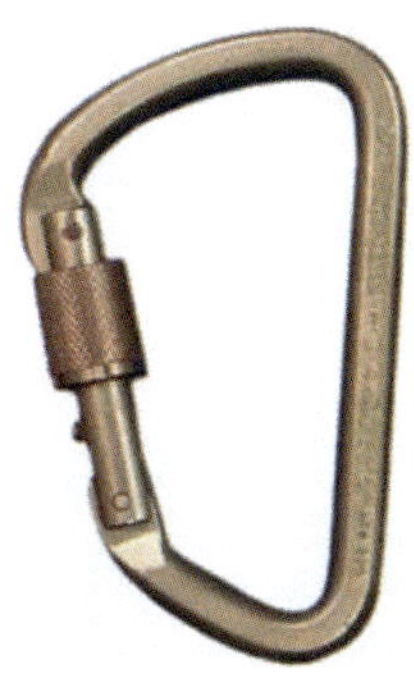

Offset D Shaped Carabiner

Pear Shaped Carabiner

One final consideration for using carabiners. While minimum breaking strength across the gate is mandated by NFPA 1983, never load a carabiner across the gate. At the very least, you will overstress the gate and need to take the carabiner out of service (replace it).

At worst, the gate will fail, possibly endangering the load. See the images below:

Correct Carabiner Loading

Incorrect (WRONG) Carabiner Loading

Hazardous Terrain Crossing

We have been discussing rope, webbing and carabiners with an eye towards use by a Level 2 and Level 1 field responder, who is not trained and certified as a Rope or Rescue Technician. One such use is rigging a system using these components in your SAR ready pack to cross terrain too hazardous to traverse without such an aid. If you participate in wilderness SAR, especially in hilly or mountainous terrain, this system can be very helpful in crossing icy trails, road embankments or low angle terrain. We will discuss the procedure to rig this system, but as previously noted, you should arrange a class with a qualified Instructor to learn the precise techniques to accomplish this.

1. Using one of your lengths of webbing, tie an improvised harness and attach a carabiner through the waist wrappings and the top of the crotch loop. Have each member of your team/resource do the same with one of their own lengths of webbing.
2. Using the other length of webbing, rig a "bomb-proof", tensionless anchor by fashioning a web sling around the natural anchor (e.g. tree, boulder, etc.) capable of supporting the force or load it will be subject to. Clip your other carabiner into the web sling.

3. Now rig a Munter Hitch with your lifeline through the carabiner on the web sling anchor.
4. Once the Munter Hitch is complete, instruct a teammate how to belay you as you cross the hazardous terrain, in case you fall.

5. Tie a figure 8 on a bight on the other end of your lifeline and clip it into the carabiner on your web harness.
6. Proceed to carefully cross the hazardous terrain, with your teammate on belay to stop/minimize any falls, until you safely reach safe ground on the other side of the hazardous terrain.
7. Untie your harness and use the webbing to rig a "bomb-proof", tensionless anchor by fashioning a web sling around a natural anchor (e.g. tree, boulder, etc.) capable of supporting the force or load it will be subject to. Clip your carabiner into the web sling and clip your end of the lifeline.
8. Clip your end (using the figure eight on a bight) of the lifeline into the carabiner you just secured to the anchor.
9. The belayer should now untie the Munter Hitch and tie a figure 8 on a bight on the lifeline and clip it into the carabiner on the originating web anchor. The figure eight on a bight should be tied at a length on the lifeline that results in a tight and secure lifeline between the two anchors.

10. All your teammates, except the belayer, should rig a Prusik's Loop by tying a Double Grapevine/ Fisherman's knot in one of their Prusik's cords.

11. Now, each of your teammates (one at a time) should tie a Prusik's Wrap/Knot around the lifeline with their Prusik's Loop and carefully cross the hazardous terrain (one at a time). Should they fall, removing/releasing their hand from the Prusik's Wrap will cause the knot to act as a friction stop and prevent further responder movement.

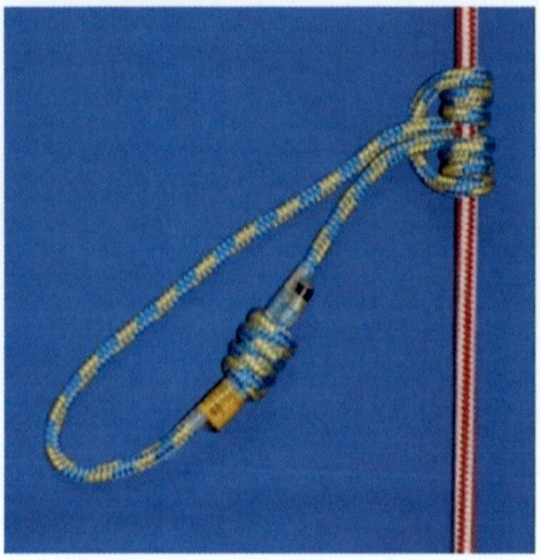

12. When the last teammate is ready to cross, he/she should untie the originating anchor and store that webbing and carabiner in his/her ready pack.
13. At the same time you should untie the lifeline terminating end figure 8 on a bight and rig a Munter Hitch on the terminating web anchor carabiner.
14. After clipping the originating lifeline end figure 8 on a bight onto his/her harness carabiner, this last teammate should carefully cross the hazardous terrain with you belaying him/ her in case of a fall.
15. After the entire team has crossed the hazardous terrain, untie all knots and return the software and hardware to their respective storage points.

As you can see this can be a complex operation. Prior to beginning your search assignment, maps and satellite photos of the search segment should be reviewed. If the review indicates the possibility of having to perform hazardous terrain crossing, your resource, in cooperation with the Operations Section, should explore alternatives or assign this segment to a resource trained and certified in using rope systems.

Litters and Field Extrication

While you may never use your rope, webbing or carabiners in a hazardous lifting or travel situation, it is very likely that you will have to assist with a litter evacuation. This is especially so if you participate in wilderness search & rescue. In some cases, you may not have quick access to ready-made litters. For example, when a teammate is injured while searching. So we'll explore three categories of litters: Full size pre-constructed, Field portable and Improvised.

Full Sized Litters—This category includes venerable litters that have been used for decades:

- Military Style—This is the famous cloth/canvas suspended between two metal or wooden poles stretcher. Newer styles are collapsible and even foldable for convenient carry. The more modern versions also have built on patient package devices such as web straps and covers.

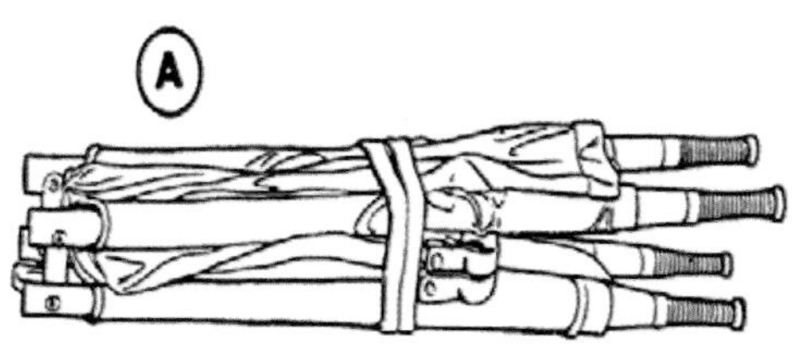

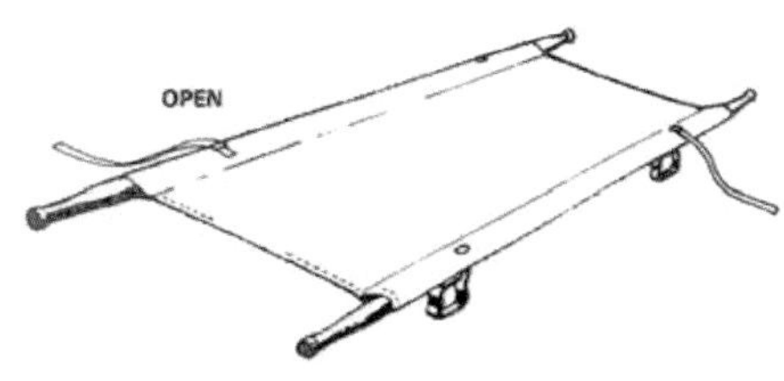

- Basket Style—This group includes the Stokes Basket and other metal frame litters you are probably familiar with. While metal is still the prevalent construction material, this style litter is also available in lighter weight plastic polymers. Since they are not very portable, responders will not typically plan to bring these litters on a search. Due to their ability to stabilize a victim/patient, they are among the best options to extract subjects from a predicament where standard Emergency Medical Personnel equipment (e.g. collapsible wheeled stretchers) is not practical. Newer models are available with numerous modifications. Especially helpful is a wheeled version mounted on a tire and suspension system, similar to a mountain bike. This makes it much easier to extract a subject with a limited number of personnel. Some models are now foldable for increase portability.

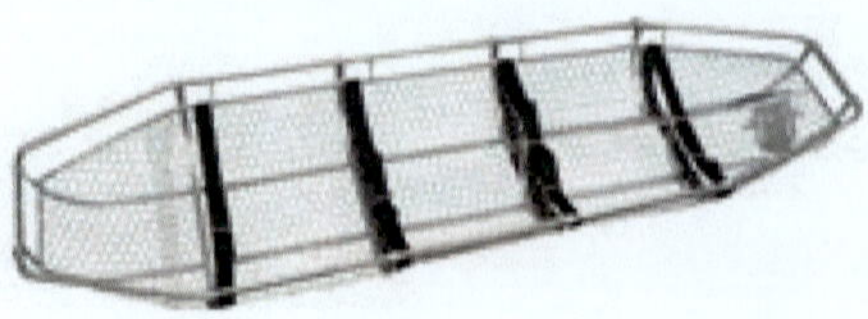

Metal Stokes Type Litter

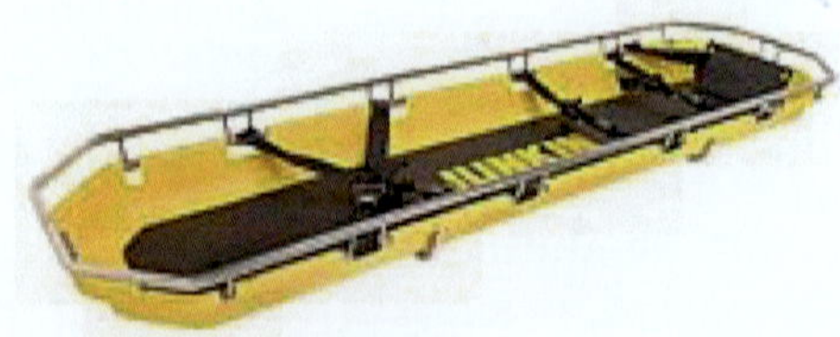

Plastic Rigid Basket Litter

Wheeled Basket Litter

Non-Rigid Litters—This category includes many lightweight, portable stretchers. Most roll up and store in a back/pack that is wearable as a backpack. While search teams might not plan to carry these units into the field, their portability allows for quicker delivery into operational areas than a traditional, rigid stretcher. They provide an excellent means for responders to extricate victims from rugged terrain and confined spaces. The biggest challenge with this type of litter is that it usually requires additional patient packaging to ensure neck and spine immobilization. While there are many options and models to choose from, some examples are shown below:

Examples of Flexible Litters

Improvised Litters—It is always better to wait for professional medical assistance before attempting to move an injured subject. But due to safety, location or time constraints, there may be occasions when you must use materials on hand to construct a stretcher to evacuate the victim. If you have your ready pack, with the suggested contents, you will be able to build a satisfactory litter. If neck or spinal injury is suspected use a method that will provide the support necessary to protect the victim from further injury.

- Tarp Litter—Using the plastic tarp in your pack, along with two limbs or extended tracking poles, you can build a serviceable litter.
    1. Place the tarp down on the ground.
    2. Place one pole approx. 1 foot from the middle of the tarp.
    3. Fold the short end of the tarp over the first pole.
    4. Place the second pole approx. 18 inches or 2 feet from the first (this distance may vary with victim or tarp size).
    5. Fold both halves of the tarp over the second pole.
    6. After placing the victim on the litter, it should remain assembled.
    7. You can now carry the subject as if using a traditional military style stretcher.
- Pole and Rope Litter—This litter is more time consuming to construct but is more rigid due to the additional poles in the litter. Using typical 44 in. tracking sticks or poles will result in a strong litter for the victim to sit on, but too short for the

victim to lie down. If you need to keep your victim's body straight (and you can't wait for professional medical help with proper equipment), you will need to use longer poles or lash additional tracking sticks to the two center poles of the litter. If you need stability, this is a better option than the tarp litter. The materials necessary to build this litter are: 50 ft. Paracord or small diameter rope, 4 extendable tracking sticks (or other suitable length poles) capable of bearing the weight of the victim, and a tarp, poncho or ground cloth.

1. Place the 4 poles on the ground, parallel to each other, approximately 12 in. apart.
2. Find the center of the 50 ft. cord and tie a clove hitch around one of the outside poles, approximately 6 in. from the center of the pole.
3. Now move approximately 12 in. along the Paracord towards the long end and tie another clove hitch approximately 6 in. on the other side of center on the same pole. This will give you two hitches approximately 12 in. apart (6 in. each side of center).
4. Proceed with each end of the Paracord to tie two clove hitches approximately 12 in. apart (6 in. each side of center) of the next (inside) pole. These knots should be parallel to the knots on the first (outside) pole.
5. Maintaining all poles 12 in. apart, continue the procedure by tying two clove hitches on the next (inside) pole in the same manner—approximately 12 in. apart (6 in. each side of center).
6. Continue with both ends of the Paracord to the (final) outside pole and again tie two clove hitches 12 in. apart (6 in. each side of center) so all knots on all poles are parallel.
7. Move down each end of the Paracord 12 in. and tie two more clove hitches on the same outside pole 6 in. towards the end of the poles from the previous two hitches. They should be 24 in. apart (12 in. each side of center) from each other and at least 6 in. from the ends of the poles.
8. Follow the process on each subsequent pole until you have tied similar spaced clove hitches all the way back to the

Evacuation & Litter Carry—Extracting a victim is always a delicate matter. Whether you need to carry the subject 10 meters or 1 kilometer, there are some techniques that will assist you in moving the victim safely, with less jostling and with less effort. Let's start with some general rules for litter carry:

- This is tiring work. When possible, at least two teams of 4-6 bearers should be employed. This allows one team to be "resting" (actually traveling, but not having to carry the patient), while the other is carrying the patient.
- If your patient is conscious, keep him informed of what you are doing. Communication will help reduce the patient's stress.
- When referring to your subject, use his name. Don't refer to him, in his presence, as "the victim."
- As much as possible, don't step over the patient in the litter. You may shower him with dirt or catch on the litter rigging.
- Remember that patient packaging is not only for your assistance, but for patient comfort and safety. Use materials that will be comfortable and secure. For example, web straps are more comfortable than rope in securing the patient.
- Keep the patient comfortable. If the sun is shining, you will need to cover the patient to prevent sunburn. Don't forget to protect the patient's eyes, from both sun and your headlamp! Watch out for falling debris and swiping limbs.
- In moving a patient, the litter bearers must make every movement deliberately and as gently as possible. The command "STEADY" should be used to prevent undue haste.
- The rear bearers should watch the movements of the front bearers and time their movements accordingly to ensure a smooth and steady action.
- The litter must be kept as level as possible at all times, particularly when crossing obstacles, such as ditches. When traveling uphill, the rear bearers will need to lift their end of the litter high, with the front bearers doing the same when traveling downhill.

- Normally, the patient should be carried on the litter feet first, except when going uphill or upstairs, in which case his head should then be forward. If the patient has a fracture of a lower extremity, he should be carried uphill or upstairs feet first and downhill or downstairs head first to prevent the weight of the body from pressing upon the injured part.

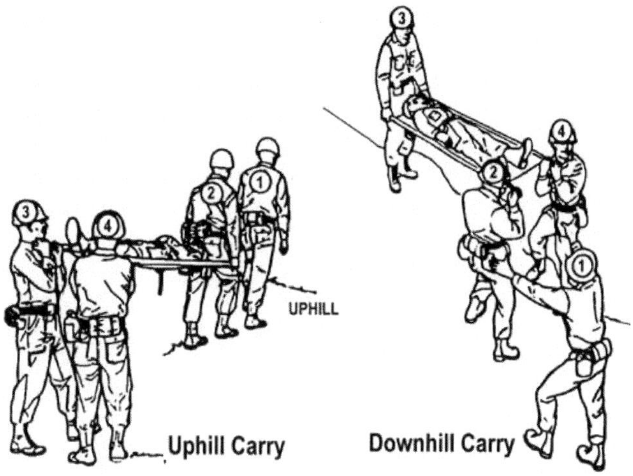

- When the patient is loaded on a litter, his individual equipment is carried by two of the bearers or placed on the litter.

Evacuating a patient, by litter, in rough terrain is a challenging task. When conditions cause footing to be too unstable or you have to pass under a low obstacle, you may have to resort to a technique known as a Lap Pass. It's a simple method that you can quickly move into.

- Upon approaching the obstacle or terrain, lower the litter to the ground at the edge of the obstacle.
- The litter bearers should now form seated lines with legs stretched out in front, ahead of the litter. The bearers on each side should be facing each other but not directly opposite. Legs should be stretched out next to the adjacent bearer with just enough space between the lines of bearers to fit the litter.
- Now begin passing/sliding the litter across the line of bearer laps. As the litter passes a bearer, that bearer gets up and

moves to the front of the line, ready to continue passing the litter. Continue this action until the litter has cleared the obstacle or terrain, then resume normal lifted carry.

On occasion the Lap Pass may not be suitable, such as a short, low-angle traverse. In this case, you may elect to rig Tag Lines on the litter to (carefully) drag it across the steep terrain.

- Make sure the patient is secured in the litter and does not slide in the litter when it is held at an angle.
- Tie webbing or rope at the head and foot of the litter.
- As many bearers as necessary to pull the load of the litter should move to the top of the angle, or remain at the top if it will be a descent instead of ascent.
- If ascending with the litter, the bearers at the top of the angle pull the tag line at the head while the bearer(s) at the foot use that tag line to stabilize and control the path of the litter.
- If descending the same technique is applied, only the bearers at the head will use the tag line to slowly lower the litter as the bearer(s) on the foot tag line guide the litter down.
- Once clear, resume normal lifted carry.

Summary

Now that you've had your conceptual introduction to ropes and rescue, it's time to find an Instructor to help you learn the actual skills and practice them properly. Until then, you're really not prepared to apply the concepts we discussed. If this topic is very interesting to you, you should seek out a rope rescue class. These classes will train you in the operational and technical level skills needed and prepare you to challenge a certification exam at the appropriate level.

References

Wikimedia Foundation/Wikipedia – The Free Encyclopedia (2012)
Various Discussions, Images and Information Used in this Book/ Publication

National Fire Protection Association – NFPA 1983 (2012)
1 Batterymarch Park, Quincy, MA

On Rope—North American Vertical Rope Techniques, 2nd Edition (1997)
Bruce Smith & Alan Padgett, *National Speleological Society*, 6001 Pulaski Pike, Huntsville, AL

Sterling Rope Company Booklet – Guide to Rope Engineering, Design, and Use (Vol. 1);
Sterling Rope Company, Inc., 31 Washington Avenue, Scarborough, ME

REI—Climbing Rope Care (2014)
Michael Silitch, *Learn at REI*, *www.rei.com*, Sumner WA

Medical Evacuation in a Theater of Operations—U.S. Army FM 8-10-6 (2000)
Headquarters, *Department of the Army*, Washington DC

Evacuation in the Field
US Army Medical Department Center and School, Fort Sam Houston, TX

Helicopter Operations for SAR

13

Objectives

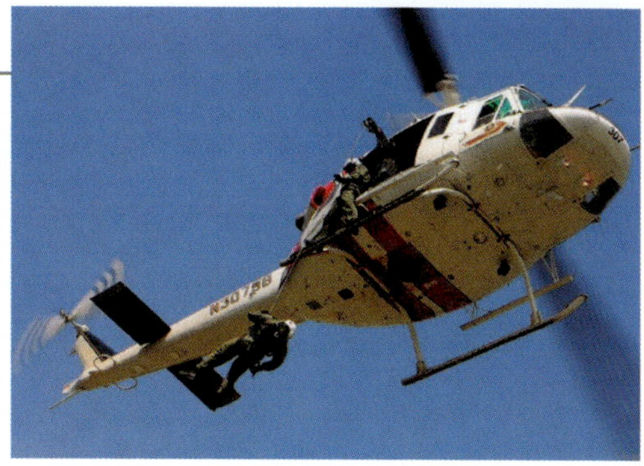

- Describe the typical applications of helicopter operations in a SAR Incident, including limitations
  - Search—Passive and Active, FLIR
  - Reconnaissance—Real time video
  - Transport—Insertion and Extraction
- Discuss safety guidelines and rule for helicopter operations including:
  - General guidelines
  - Safe approach areas
- Describe the requirements for establishing a helispot
  - Approach and Departure Area clearances
  - Appropriate size for helicopter in use, night vs. day
  - Grade limitations for operations on slope terrain
  - Obstacle and FOD clearance
  - Landing zone markings
  - Marshalling signals
  - Proper lighting methods for night operations
- List some common types of helicopters used in SAR Incidents including differences in operational requirements

When most people think of Search and Rescue, they see the iconic image of a helicopter hoisting an injured person to safety. It is dramatic, it is inspiring, and it is true. The helicopter has arguably saved an incredible number of lives since its inception and it continues to do so every day.

The first known helicopter rescue was in 1944 during the China Burma campaign of WWII by the US Army Air Corp. Lieutenant Carter Harman. He flew the mission in a Sikorsky YR-4B 180 horse powered helicopter to rescue a fixed wing pilot and his 3 British passengers. The YR-4B only had the capacity for 1 passenger so Lt. Harman had to make multiple trips to effect the rescue.

Photo Courtesy of Wikipedia

Lt Harman and his support crew

Helicopters and their operations have changed greatly since 1944 and they are now commonplace in our everyday lives. Helicopters give us traffic reports with live video and follow high speed vehicle pursuits. Law enforcement helicopters can follow wanted criminals with an array of high tech equipment. Critically ill patients are transported via helicopters to trauma centers and other hospitals for a higher level of care.

Helicopters are used for agriculture duties such as spraying fields and logging. The rotary wing aircraft are used by electrical providers to check and make repairs to thousands of miles of high voltage lines and towers. From construction to herding cattle to aerial photography and frost control, the private sector has utilized the helicopter for a multitude of needs.

The military cannot fully function without helicopter support. The helicopter saved many lives during the Korean and Vietnam conflicts by transporting the wounded to nearby MASH (Mobile Army Surgical Hospitals) units. Here surgical intervention could be accomplished within the Golden Hour after the injury occurred, therefore giving the wounded soldiers the greatest chance of survival.

The military also uses the helicopter for transport of its soldiers to and from the battlefield as well as for logistical support. The list of jobs and services for helicopters is nearly endless.

Helicopter Operations

There are many types of helicopters and each has its own operating characteristics. How high it can fly, how many people it can carry, and how fast it can go are just a few of the important factors. Understanding how a helicopter is able to fly and its limitations are important to helicopter operations.

The following terms are provided to allow you to understand some of the more critical aspects of flight and operations that affect the helicopter or rotary aircraft.

Terms

Main Rotor: These are the blades on top of the helicopter. They provide lift and there are typically 2-6 of these rotor blades. (Note: these are not propellers, they are actually wings!)

Tail Rotor: sometimes referred to as the anti-torque device. The purpose is to provide directional control and to keep the body of the aircraft from spinning opposite of the main rotor rotation. (Note: while most helicopters have tail rotors, some do not.)

Courtesy of W. Podboy

In Ground effect Hover

Hover: The ability of the helicopter to remain in a stable position above the ground.

Courtesy of Ev Wittig

Out of ground effect Hover

Out of Ground Effect: also known as OGE. The name pretty much explains what it is. The airflow or rotor wash is sent downward but no disruption or reflection of the flow is created and as such the aircraft does not benefit from this occurrence. The aircraft will require more power to remain at that altitude than if it was closer to the ground as in IGE. Typically OGE is when the aircraft is beyond an altitude of one half of the main rotor diameter above the ground.

In Ground Effect: also known as IGE. This is the distance between the aircraft and the ground where a high-pressure flow of air exists. This flow or rotor wash is disturbed as it comes in contact with the ground. The flow then spreads out across the surface of the ground. This flow allows the aircraft to use less power to effect a hover. Typically IGE occurs when the aircraft is within one half of its main rotor diameter of the ground.

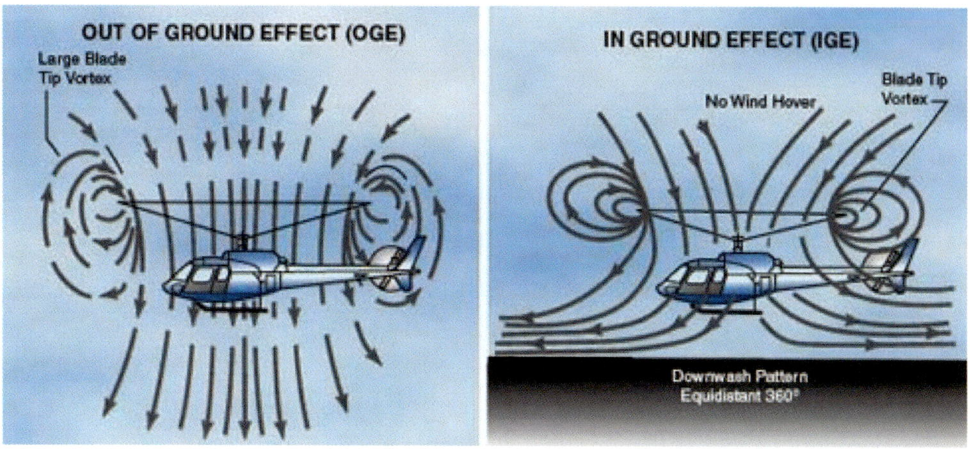

Density Altitude: The "official definition" is: *Density altitude is the pressure altitude corrected for non-standard temperature variations.* A simpler definition is: Density altitude is the altitude the aircraft thinks it is flying at.

As the temperature increases, the density of the air decreases. Therefore the aircraft has to work harder to provide the same performance as if the air was cooler or the altitude was lower. As an example, the helicopter is departing a sea level helipad on a 60-degree day. Plenty of power is available for takeoff and landing. However as the helicopter flies farther from the sea, the air temperature increases. The airport that the helicopter will be landing at has a higher altitude of 1,425 feet and the temperature is now 75 degrees. If we calculate the density altitude for the new landing location, we will find that the density altitude is 2,838 feet or an effective altitude increase of 1,413 feet at the landing airport. Therefore the performance of the helicopter is decreased, requiring more power being applied from the engine.

While this may not seem like a big change for a low level airport, the effect of density altitude is much more apparent at higher elevations. If we fly to a higher elevation to make a rescue, at 7,200 feet, for example, and the temperature remains the same, the density altitude becomes 9,873 ft. and the performance of the helicopter will be greatly diminished.

As the altitude and temperature increase, so does the density altitude. During hot weather and high altitude operations, the pilot must refer to the performance charts for the aircraft to determine if it is within safe parameters to land or hover at the chosen altitude. It is possible to exceed the performance/power capabilities of the aircraft!

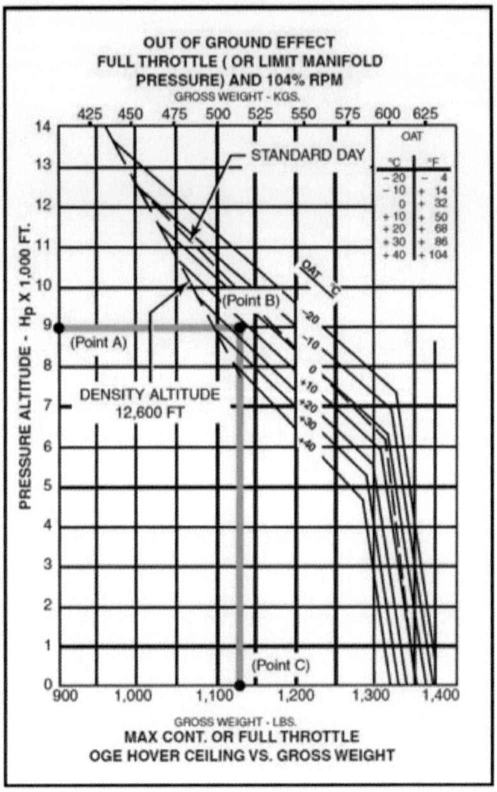

OGE Performance and Weight Chart

The helicopter may be able to land or even hover in ground effect, but an out of ground effect hover might be impossible. Sometimes reducing weight of the aircraft by decreasing the amount of equipment, passengers or even fuel is required to allow the aircraft to operate at the chosen altitude.

LZ or Landing Zone: A designated location, generally without improvements such as pavement or lights. Fuel is typically supplied from a fuel truck or even barrels on occasion. This is a temporary location in support of short-term operations.

Helispot: Temporary landing area. Used solely for the purpose of loading or off-loading passengers or supplies. No support services. Unimproved surfaces.

Types of Helispots: Other than open flat areas, are listed below from favorable to least favorable.

- *Pinnacle*: A high or lofty peak. It allows approaches and departures in any direction.
- *Ridge*: A long narrow elevation of land. Allows for multiple approaches and departures but not as good as a pinnacle.
- *Saddle*: A ridgeline connecting two higher elevations with a depression in the middle. Limited approach and departure angles with higher terrain on the sides.
- *Confined or Bowl*: A depression bottom of a semi round area or an open area surrounded by tall trees or high brush. A single approach in and departure out at steep angles. Requires higher aircraft performance.

Helipad: Recognized permanent landing area. Usually a hard surface or pavement with appropriate FAA designation marking it as a helipad, such as on hospital rooftops.

Courtesy of Ev Wittig

Hospital Helipad Bisbee Az.

FLIR

When conditions such as wind, terrain, and weather permit, the technology of thermal imaging (FLIR: Forward Looking Infra-Red) can be used at night. This technology allows the body heat of an individual to be viewed. Typically, the heat signature or shape of the individual can be seen to some extent even through the foliage and brush. In the right conditions, even the footprints may be visualized if they are not too old.

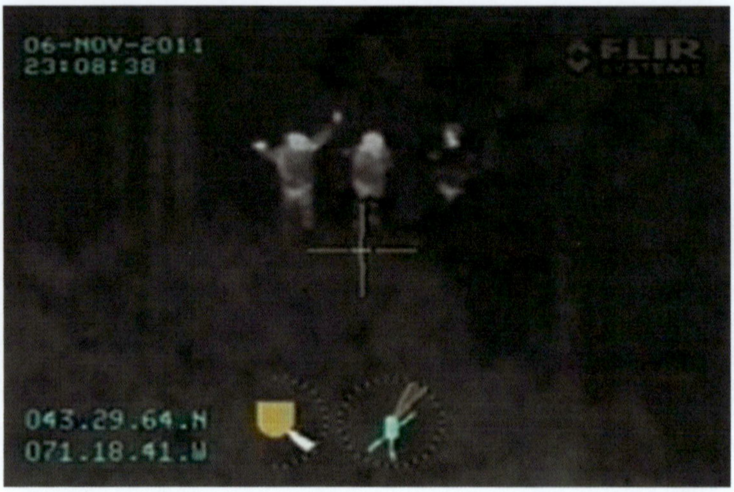

COURTESY OF FLIR SYSTEMS

3 subjects viewed by infrared (FLIR)

Real Time Video

Another technology that can be coupled with the FLIR systems, or even with stabilized cameras on the aircraft, is Real Time Video. Real time video is live video transmission from the aircraft back to a central location where, for example, search managers and search planners can watch the video "live" without any delays. If something of interest is spotted, they can advise the aircrew to concentrate on that particular area.

Real time video is also useful during natural or manmade disasters. Managers and planners can see exactly what resources are needed to deal with the situation at hand. The more information available to management, notably visual information, can provide a original outside pole. All knots across the four poles should be parallel.

9. Now tie overhand safety knots on the last two hitches. You should still have cord leftover that can be used to secure the victim to the litter.
10. Lay the tarp or ground cloth on the litter to help keep the victim from pushing through the space between cords. If you have a pad or sleeping bag place that in the litter to increase the subject's comfort.

There are some concerns you should remember when lifting this type of litter:

- Hand placement matters—The load bearing strength of this litter is in the sections of Paracord and not from the poles. Minding the balance of the victim, hands should be placed on the poles where the clove hitches are tied.
- Test the litter—Always remember this is an *improvised* litter. Test it before putting your victim in it! Use multiple packs or even a teammate (don't lift them too far off the ground) to simulate a heavier load than your victim. Don't exacerbate your subject's injuries by having the litter fail with them onboard.
- Secure your victim—Once you deem the litter safe, ensure that the victim is secured in the litter. Even though this litter will naturally "wrap" around the subject, use webbing or another length of Paracord to safely keep the victim onboard.

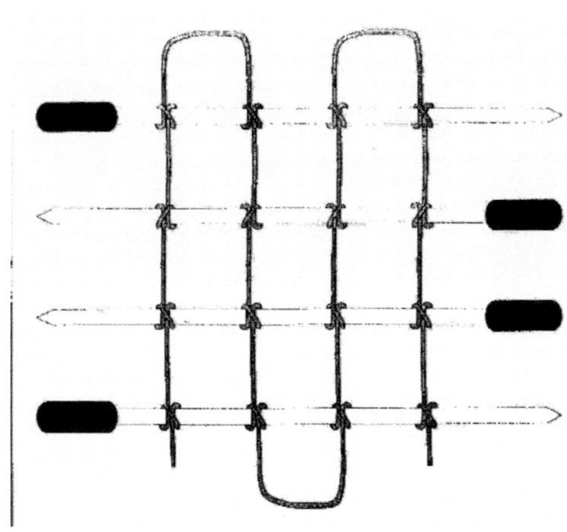

clearer representation of the situation and needed resources, thereby lessening confusion and false interpretation.

Night Vision

Night vision is another technology commonly used onboard aircraft. Whereas FLIR uses thermal means to produce an image, Night Vision Goggles (NVG) utilize ambient light which is amplified hundreds and thousands of times to produce a visible image in the user's view finder.

There are some limitations to the use of NVG imaging. The image is flat with only shading of green color and there is almost no depth of field perception. Nonetheless, a well-trained NVG flight crew learns to use various visual clues that enable them to work near rising terrain and even land in very tight Helispots for example.

Courtesy of AINONLINE.Com

Helicopter Crew with NVG Goggles

Helicopter Transport

The helicopter really comes into its own when people and materials need to be transported to isolated locations. Depending on the aircraft used, materials and equipment can be transported inside the aircraft or externally on a cable. All-Terrain Vehicles, water, food supplies, ropes, and stretchers can all be carried external to the aircraft if needed.

Courtesy of angelfire.com

Military Aircraft with External Load

The pilot and the performance capability of the aircraft determine the amount of people and gear that can be transported. Fuel and crew weights as well as weather and altitude become part of the decision process of the pilot. The pilot must be certain that the aircraft can be safely operated and not endanger the passengers or crew.

Courtesy of KVAL.com

US Coast Guard Helicopter Crash

Disclaimer:

Each agency or operators of aircraft, have their own standards and procedures for aircraft operations. Some agencies require specific training and equipment in order to operate near or even be transported in their respective aircraft. For example, helmets and fire resistant clothing, are required on certain federal and state aircraft. When requesting aircraft resources, make certain you understand their operating requirements and that your organization can function within those operational requirements. It would be considered prudent to have annual training with the specific agencies or operators that your organization routinely works with.

This text should only be considered as a general guide in helicopter operations and is not all encompassing of information and procedures.

Creating a Helispot

Establishing a Landing Zone must be done with attention to details. It is necessary to appoint someone with helicopter experience to become the LZ manager.

It is generally accepted that the LZ should be at least 100 feet x 100 feet (31 meters x 31 meters) in size.This size allows most helicopters in the public safety or civilian domain to operate. If your operation is utilizing military aircraft, confirm what type of aircraft is being utilized and what their LZ requirements are. Some military aircraft have rotor diameters nearing 100 feet and a standard LZ will not work for them.

Courtesy of Fourums.jetphoto.net

Military "Chinook Helicopter" evacuating soldiers

The approach to the LZ by the aircraft should be free from obstructions such as power lines, poles, tall trees, towers and antennas to name a few. Wires and antennas are generally not visible to the pilot due to ground clutter.

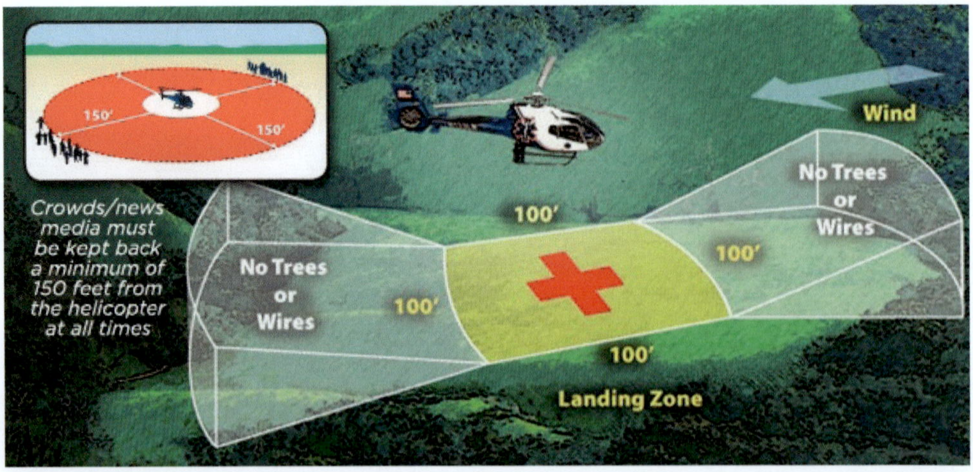

COURTESY OF MERCY AIR

Landing Zone configuration

The expected approach to the LZ should be into the wind. This provides additional lift and allows the helicopter to utilize less power. Be prepared to advise the pilot, by radio, of the wind direction and approximate wind speed. Some form of windsock can be made utilizing a pole with several 5 foot strands of surveyors tape. The pole can be located 90 degrees to the landing direction of the aircraft and at the perimeter of the LZ.

The ground itself should be, if at all possible, flat (no greater than 10 degrees of slope) with grass or brush no higher than one's knee. Tall brush can hide ground hazards such as rocks and stumps. Additionally, tall brush can reduce IGE capability of the aircraft. Conversely, freshly bulldozed areas can create a brown out situation

COURTESY OF WPAFB.AP.MIL

Brown Out at LZ

when the rotor downwash blows the dust into the air and obscures the pilot's vision. (Note: This also applies to fresh dry snow and causes a similar condition known as a white out). The brown out condition can be mitigated by using the local fire department to wet down the LZ area with copious amounts of water.

Prior to the arrival of the aircraft, a FOD Walk (Foreign Object Damage) is required to locate and remove any objects that can pose a hazard to the aircraft. Trash, tarps, branches and other objects can be blown up and into the rotor system or the engine intake and produce catastrophic results. The best way to accomplish a FOD Walk is by utilizing a shoulder-to-shoulder grid search line. Any and all objects need to be collected and removed before helicopter operations can begin.

Staging Area—Loading the Aircraft

People and equipment to be transported by the helicopter, should be staged 90 degrees to the touchdown point at least 50 feet (15 meters) outside of the LZ perimeter. All personnel must be wearing helmets and goggles prior to moving towards the aircraft.

The LZ manager is responsible for the movement of people in and around the aircraft. The LZ manager or a member of the flight crew should provide a passenger safety briefing to include the following information:

1. Follow all aircraft crewmembers' instructions
2. Keep seatbelts or restraint straps on at all times
3. No smoking in or around the aircraft
4. Do not open or close aircraft doors unless specifically instructed to do so
5. Do not exit the aircraft until instructed to do so
6. Never exit and move uphill from the aircraft during off site landings

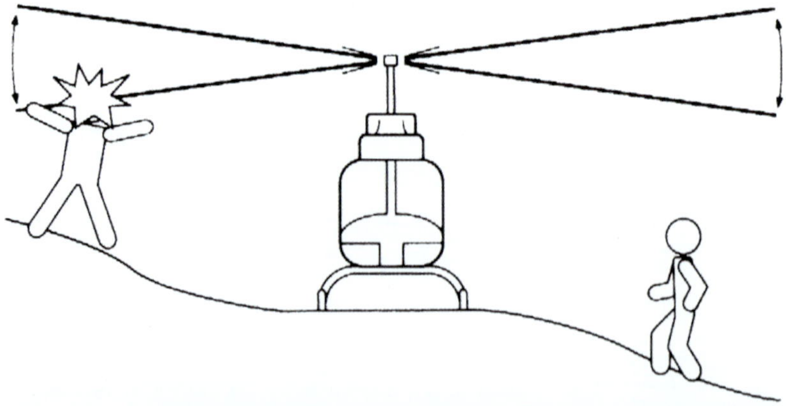

When, and only when, the aircrew signals to approach the aircraft may the LZ Manager escort passengers, wearing their helmets and eye protection, towards the helicopter. Packs should be carried against the chest in front of the boarding personnel. Tools and equipment like poles, shovels and such need to be carried horizontally to prevent possible contact with the rotor system.

SAR personnel should let the aircraft crew or LZ manager load and secure equipment into the aircraft, thus reducing possible damage to the aircraft and ensuring safe storage of the gear. When indicated, passengers may board the aircraft. Each passenger should have a means to secure themselves to the aircraft such as a seat belt or strap.

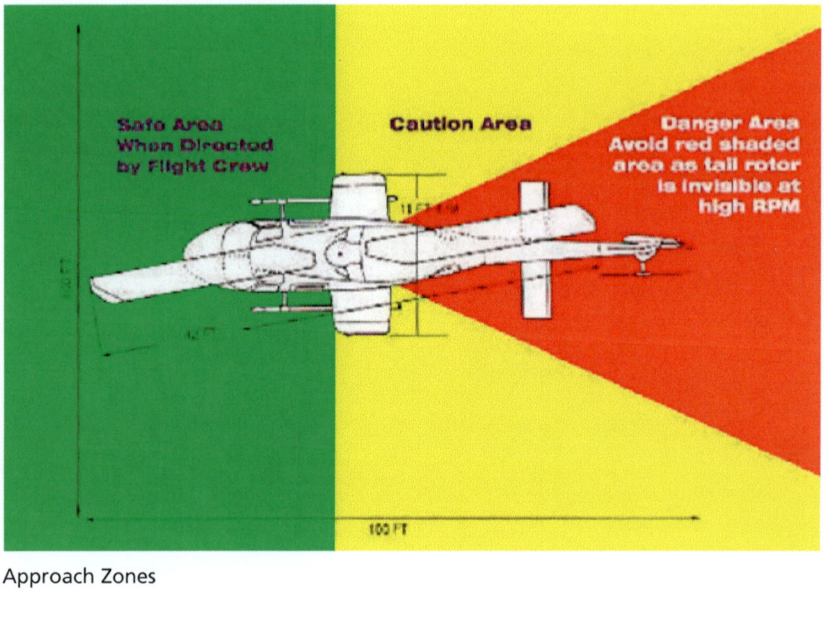

Courtesy of Mercy Air

Approach Zones

In the event of a delay in loading, passengers should stand either next to the aircraft or in an area outside of the rotor disk. Passengers should not move any further towards the tail of the aircraft than the last door to avoid possible contact with the tail rotor.

While inflight, remain seated and be prepared to follow additional instructions prior to and after landing. Remember to exit downhill and or away from the aircraft if possible. In the event that movement away from the aircraft is not possible, crouch down next to the aircraft but avoid the skids and wait until the aircraft departs and is well clear before any movement. Keep poles and tools horizontal until the aircraft has departed the area.

Night Operations

Depending on whether the aircraft provider's operational policies permit night operations, you may need to prepare for such a contingency. The LZ's perimeter will need to be identified by some low level light source. The four corners at a minimum should have some sort of light that shines directly up or produces a defused light bright enough to be seen on the helicopter's approach.

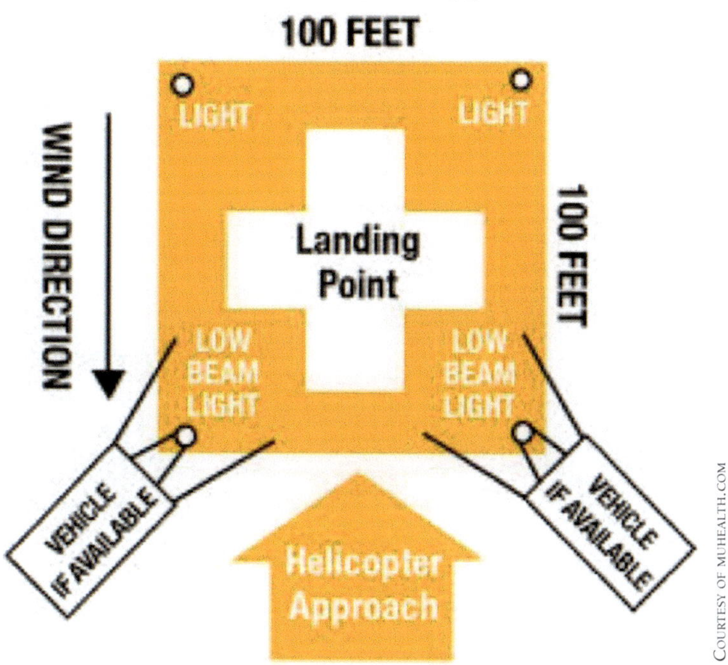

Night LZ Configuration

Depending on the pilot, you may be asked to provide "offset lighting" by using vehicle lights. Placing vehicles at 45 degrees to the LZ from the approach end can provide sufficient light to allow the pilot to land. Do not allow anyone to shine flashlights directly towards the aircraft as it may blind the pilot.

Note: The use of road flares are not recommended due to fire hazards.

If the pilot is operating on Night Vision Goggles, you may be requested to utilize the "Shake and Break" light sticks (Cyalume® lights) and mark the perimeter of the LZ.

Use of Hand Signals

As noted earlier in this chapter, each aircraft operator has their own procedures for aircraft operations. The use of hand signals may not be utilized or desired by the pilot of the aircraft.

Hand Signals vary with each aircraft operator. Again, prior training with the aircraft provider is paramount to proper hand signal communications as well as confidence between the pilot and the person giving the hand signals.

A single person should provide hand signals to the aircraft. Multiple people will only create confusion for the pilot. Ideally, the person providing the hand signals should be standing well upwind from the aircraft or touch down point (remember the aircraft will land into the wind) and be well outside of the rotor diameter of the aircraft for safety.

The person providing the hand signals should ideally wear bright or distinctive colored clothing or a vest so as to capture the pilot's attention. Additionally, the person giving the hand signals should also be wearing goggles, helmet and hearing protection.

Hand signals should be large and exaggerated so the pilot can see the communication from a distance. Small gestures cannot be clearly seen at a distance so whole arm movement is best.

The following graphic presents the hand signals recommended by the State of California. They are the minimum any LZ Manager or aircraft marshaller should be familiar with.

HELICOPTER HAND SIGNALS

Special Helicopter Operations

The versatility of the helicopter allows special operations such as Hoist Rescues, Long Line and "Helirappel." This enhances capabilities for moving SAR members and victims into and out of areas where helicopters cannot land.

Hoist operations require skilled and trained crewmembers, a high performance aircraft and exceptional communications among the aircrew. Typical hoist operations require the use of a "Crew Chief" or "Hoist operator."

The crew chief will stand either inside the aircraft or outside on the skid of the aircraft, depending on the type of hoist used. The crew chief is secured to the aircraft by safety straps and is connected to the intercom system on the aircraft.

The pilot will determine if the aircraft has sufficient power and capability to effect the rescue or extract. The pilot will determine if the mission is possible and can be done safely by considering and calculating such factors as wind, weight, and altitude.

The aircraft will enter a hover near the extract point. As the pilot approaches an overhead position to the selected point, the pilot is unable to see what is directly beneath the aircraft. The crew chief then becomes the eyes for the pilot by providing directions. In addition, tail rotor and main rotor clearances must be given to the pilot to ensure that no blade strikes occur which could result in a crash of the aircraft.

A constant verbal dialog is maintained between the crew chief and the pilot throughout the whole rescue process. The crew chief skillfully operates the hoist, placing the hook or pendant into the hands of the rescuer. Skill and judgment become the factors for a successful hoist evolution.

Keeping the cable directly overhead is essential to limiting a pendulum movement of the individual who is being hoisted. Again, constant direction by the crew chief to the pilot will ensure appropriate positioning of the aircraft and minimize the pendulum swing.

Courtesy of W. Podboy

Hoist Operation

Long Line operations are typical of aircraft that cannot support a fixed hoist, usually due to the physical size or performance capability of the aircraft.

A long rope or cable is attached to the aircraft that allows a person or litter to be suspended below the aircraft. The pilot, usually accompanied by a crew chief, will fly the long line into position and physically lower the aircraft so the ground personnel can attach the litter to the long line.

Again, communication with the pilot is critical due to the limited visual perspective of the pilot directly below the aircraft. Once the litter is attached and the operational criteria are met, the pilot will increase altitude until the litter is clear of any obstructions. The pilot will then fly to a location where the litter can be lowered to awaiting support personnel.

Courtesy of Ev Wittig

Arizona DPS Long Line Operation

Another means to insert SAR personnel is by Helirappel, which is similar in configuration to the Long Line. Helirappel allows for specifically trained SAR personnel to rappel from the aircraft into a specific location otherwise inaccessible by other means when a hoist is not available.

The use of a crew chief is required for the same reasons as in a hoist or long line operation. The crew chief is responsible for attaching the SAR member to the rope and ensuring that the aircraft is hovering over the correct location before the SAR personnel begin the rappel from the aircraft.

Special Operations will require special training of the aircraft crew. Practice and communications are the key components of a safe and successful operation.

Courtesy of Ev Wittig

Arizona DPS Helirappel Deployment

Summary

Helicopter operations are inherently dangerous. Knowing the limitations of the aircraft and the operational procedures of the aircraft provider can reduce the risk of accidents.

Train with your aircraft providers at least annually. Follow the instructions of the aircrew and always be aware of the danger of the rotor blades.

Every day of every year, helicopters help save lives. SAR teams are transported to remote areas. Accident victims are transported to trauma centers for life saving procedures. Human transplant organs are transported to hospitals to save lives that otherwise would have perished without the helicopter's involvement.

If a Medal of Honor for life saving could be awarded to a tool, this author believes the medal should be given to the helicopter!

References

The First Helicopter Rescue

Wikipedia, The online encyclopedia, http://en.wikipedia.org/wiki/Sikorsky_R-4.

Helitac Operations and Landing Zone Selection document

Corporal Mike Ells, San Bernardino County Sheriff's Aviation Division

Helicopter Hand Signals

State of California

The Next Steps—Where Do You Go From Here?

14

Overview

Notice the question mark at the end of the title of this chapter? You are now confronted with making a decision to become involved in an activity that will demand expenditure of large amounts of time, energy and money. We do not seek to discourage you, but wish to honestly inform you of the dedication and perseverance required to participate in search & rescue.

The authors of this text have endeavored to present you with the didactic knowledge and skills information to prepare you to become a basic "ground" searcher. *Regardless of any future specialty or discipline you may participate in, you must develop proficiency and gain generic SAR experience by serving in this field searcher capacity first.* Just as a physician learns the basics of medicine and gains clinical experience before entering a specialty training program, you too must start at this level of "practice."

Many readers will have already chosen a specialty/discipline, or perhaps have become involved in search & rescue specifically to participate in that specialty. We caution you that your value in any incident will be limited if you don't have the ability to serve as a "plain vanilla" ground searcher. When conditions do not allow deployment of the specialty resource you will not be called to the incident and certainly not be deployed if already called out. Your lack of understanding of the entire incident will eventually tarnish your reputation.

You must ask yourself what is your purpose in joining the SAR community? Is it to expand upon a hobby you already enjoy or are you truly looking to aid your fellow citizens? If you are dedicated to working for the benefit of others, your goal must be to provide expert service in *any* capacity, not just one that you prefer.

Skills Training

There is no way a book can provide the level of skills training offered in a classroom or field setting, with a qualified Instructor. To become truly skilled in your craft you will need to participate in the physical training necessary to become proficient.

Where can you find those training opportunities? If you're not yet a member of a SAR organization (or even if you are), you can attend a formal class providing the field training required. There are a number of national organizations that provide such courses. Of course, we hope you'll join us in an AERIE SARResponder™ course that is designed to train you in the field skills necessary to serve as a ground searcher. This course will also prepare you to challenge the SARResponder™ 2 certification exam to demonstrate your commitment and expertise in search & rescue.

If you already participate with a professional SAR organization, it is likely they have an annual training calendar in place. These regularly scheduled training sessions present an excellent opportunity to get hands on practice of these field skills and benefit from knowledge of those members with greater experience. If your team doesn't have mandatory training events, you may be able to prompt them to bring in "outside" instructors to present training and classes of interest. Such classes are necessary to develop expertise and maintain proficiency. Failing that, you might consider seeking a more serious and professional organization to serve.

While it is true that you will need to gain competence and proficiency in SAR specific skills, some of the skills we have presented are, in fact, outdoor *fieldcraft*. These skills can be fun to learn and experience. If you're fortunate to have a local retailer that specializes in outdoor recreation (such as REI, Cabelas, Gander Mountain, etc.), you will find they offer events to learn and practice these field skills. These events are always fun and informative. You may even meet some folks with whom you can share some recreation activities, or entice to join your SAR team!

Another excellent opportunity comes in the form of multi-day SAR exercises conducted by state and regional search and rescue associations. These "conferences" usually offer classroom and field training sessions that will benefit you in learning and expanding your skill set. These exercises frequently offer the chance to apply your current or newly gained knowledge by conducting SAR incident simulations. These simulations are normally conducted as "full-blown" ICS incidents with management overhead and field resources. They will typically include "real" subjects to provide realistic training. Such simulations are fun and very beneficial in enhancing your knowledge and abilities. Creating and conducting realistic SAR exercises may be of interest to a group (this is a big undertaking not recommended for a single team to attempt) of SAR resources in your area. If there is enough interest, your group may be able to receive assistance from local, county and/or state agencies.

Certifications

Regardless of your "career" goals in search & rescue, you will likely need a national level certification as a ground searcher. Note that we said "national" level. There are SAR "teams" who only require internal approval to be "mission ready." Remember, while we serve the subject in need, we work for the government agency or public safety department with jurisdiction for the incident. The employees of these agencies and departments have had to successfully complete "outside" education and certification. If you wish to be considered a "professional" (albeit unpaid in most cases), you will need to demonstrate that professionalism by seeking and attaining recognition beyond the in-house ones offered through your team. Many of these agencies now require national level certifications be held by the responders they call upon.

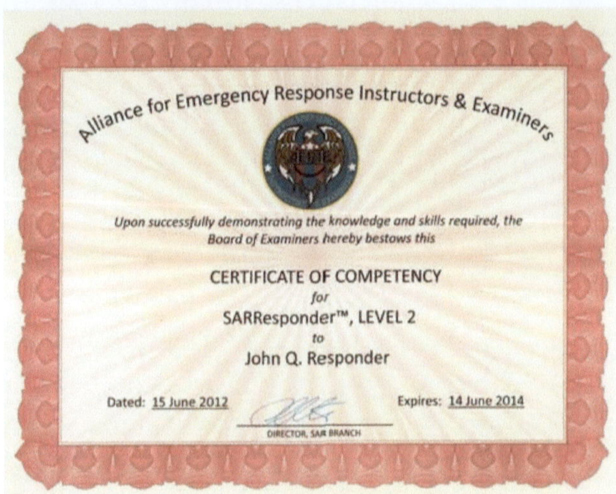
Alliance for Emergency Response Instructors & Examiners

Upon successfully demonstrating the knowledge and skills required, the Board of Examiners hereby bestows this

CERTIFICATE OF COMPETENCY

for

SARResponder™, LEVEL 2

to

John Q. Responder

Dated: 15 June 2012 Expires: 14 June 2014

DIRECTOR, SAR BRANCH

Some states also have certification programs for search & rescue field responders. These are excellent programs usually modeled on the national certifications. In many cases, the state will accept a national level certification in lieu of completing the state process. In this case, the responder benefits from being qualified to respond in the state and having a credential respected in virtually any other jurisdiction, in state or out. The AERIE SARResponder™ 2 is one such national level SAR field responder certification.

Before discussing the various specialties available to SAR responders, we offer two other considerations. The first is the role of leadership. Once you have refined and enhanced your response skills and gained significant experience participating in real world (and varied) incidents, you may wish to share that expertise by assuming a leadership role. There are numerous opportunities to participate in classes and training to provide you with the knowledge required to be an effective leader. Such courses are offered by local/state/federal Public Safety agencies (and may be free to your team), training companies, and perhaps your employer. Gaining this knowledge and applying it to (initially) small unit leadership, such as a field SAR team leader, is a needed contribution.

The second role is that of incident overhead. While it may take years of training and experience to fulfill a leadership role in incident management, incident support personnel are in great demand. Assisting in the Planning, Operations and Logistics sections will bring you great satisfaction and keep you "in the thick" of the incident. Another advantage of this type of participation is it is less affected by physical impairment. We all get sick or injured occasionally. Depending on your incident overhead function, it may be possible to participate even when you're not 100% physically fit. Of course, this also provides an opportunity for continued participation as we age and can no longer sustain the physical rigors required for field searching. Interested in communications? Have a background in medicine (EMT/Paramedic, Nurse, Physician, etc.)? Trained in use of Information Technology? All these are needed in the Incident Management community. To get started, go to the FEMA website and begin taking the "distance learning" online courses relevant to the Incident Command System. This will not only prepare you to assist in SAR incidents but will give you knowledge relevant to all incident management. Then consult with the agencies responsible for incident response in your community. We're sure they will welcome your help gratefully. The AERIE Leadership: Emergency Response™ course can assist you in developing your leadership skills.

Now let's touch upon some specialties that may interest you. Understanding that there are too many SAR specialties, with a great many sub-specialties, to have an in-depth discussion, we'll attempt to give you some ideas. This list is not intended to be all-inclusive.

- Canine SAR—When it comes to perception of search & rescue responders, this is one of the more prevalent images in the public's mind. The expense and training time commitments for this discipline are high. Do your research thoroughly before embarking into the canine community.
  - Area Search—Wide ranging non-scent specific, these teams are tasked with locating any human scent.
  - Human Remains Detection—These teams are trained to locate human scent that emanates from decomposing tissue. They can be called upon to function on land or water (two different specialties) when it is suspected the subject is deceased.

  - Tracking/Trailing—Scent-specific canine teams that invoke an image of a bloodhound tracking down the subject. Today's tracking dogs include numerous breeds, but you get the idea.
  - Disaster—These teams are specifically trained to search in disaster environments. This may involve confined space and collapsed structure. Much of this specialty is controlled by FEMA as the nation's leading disaster response agency.
  - Avalanche—Canine units specifically trained to find human subjects as victims of avalanches. This specialty may also require specialty search training (alpine, etc.) of the handler as well.

- Mounted SAR—This rapidly developing specialty can be extremely helpful in a range of incident types including SAR. Note that this specialty does require SAR specific training. It is not enough to "ride around" looking for the subject. There is even a recent sub-specialty involving "scenting" by horse. Turns out that our equine partners can be trained to be scent-specific in tracking our subject(s) much like our tracking/trailing canines. As with the canine specialties, be prepared for a large financial and training time commitment for participation in this specialty.

- Vehicle SAR—We're grouping a number of specialties here. They include (but are not necessarily limited to): ATV, "Jeep", Mountain Bike and others. This is a relatively recent class of SAR specialties and the formal training courses may be in development. If any of these are of interest to you, continue your ground SAR training and get some safety classes completed for your vehicle type. Then "search" for SAR training applicable to your vehicle choice.
- Aviation—No you don't have to be a pilot (but we welcome them too!). In fact, aviation SAR requires trained Observers and Scanners so the pilot can focus on safely flying the aircraft. Some Public Safety agencies offer observer specific training, but in the volunteer community, the Civil Air Patrol remains pre-eminent in training observers and training. Contact your local CAP squadron for more information.

Courtesy of Civil Air Patrol

- Public Safety Diving—This specialty is still predominantly handled by the Fire Service in most communities. As such, they may require you to first be a firefighter, then train to become a Public Safety Diver. But there may be opportunities for you to train and participate as a volunteer, especially in those jurisdictions with volunteer fire departments. PADI (Professional Associations of Dive Instructors) now offers Public Safety Diver training for those affiliated with an agency providing such services.

And the opportunities for your participation continue to expand. Research in search & rescue continues to present new and innovative techniques that will continue to challenge us to develop new skills. As Public Safety agencies are now recognizing volunteer SAR as a professional endeavor, the demand for trained responders is increasing. You are joining us during very exciting times and we welcome you!

THANK YOU FOR CHOOSING TO LEARN WITH US, BUT EVEN MORE IMPORTANTLY, THANK YOU FOR YOUR SERVICE!

Appendices

New Cooper Age and Gender Base Standards for Law Enforcement

*Vertical Jump (Measured in Inches) Males

20 - 29	30 - 39	40 - 49	50 - 59	**59+	%	Category
30.3	28.4	25.1	22		99	Superior
26.5	25	22	21		95	
25	24	20.3	19.5		90	Excellent
25	23	19.5	18		85	
24	22	19	17		80	
23	21	18	16.5		75	Good
22.5	21	18	16		70	
22	20	17	15.5		65	
21.5	20	17	15		60	
21	20	16.5	14.5		55	Fair
20.5	19.5	16	14		50	
20	19	16	14		45	
20	18.6	15.5	13.5		40	
19	18.5	15	13.5		35	Poor
18	18	14.5	13		30	
18	17	14	12.2		25	
17.5	16.5	14	11.9		20	
17	16	13	11		15	Very Poor
16	15.5	12.1	10		10	
13.6	14.5	11	9.3		5	
10.3	12.1	6.9	6.5		1	

*These norms are based on a small sample of police officers (n=500) and should be used cautiously.

**No data gathered.

Resources: The Cooper Institute of Dallas, Texas

Form generated by: Sgt. Sheldon Riches (August 6, 2007)

When looking for a shelter site, keep in mind the type of shelter (protection) you need. However, you must also consider--

- How much time and effort you need to build the shelter.
- If the shelter will adequately protect you from the elements (sun, wind, rain, snow, etc.).
- If you have the tools to build it. If not, can you make improvised tools?
- If you have the type and amount of materials needed to build it.

To answer these questions, you need to know how to make various types of shelters and what materials you need to make them.

One-Man Shelter

A one-man shelter you can easily make using a tarp requires a tree and three poles. One pole should be about 4.5 meters long and the other two about 3 meters long.

To make this shelter (Figure 5-7)--

- Secure the 4.5-meter pole to the tree at about waist height.
- Lay the two 3-meter poles on the ground on either side of and in the same direction as the 4.5-meter pole.
- Lay the folded tarp over the 4.5 meter pole so that about the same amount of material hangs on both sides.
- Tuck the excess material under the 3-meter poles, and spread it on the ground inside to serve as a floor.
- Stake down or put a spreader between the two 3-meter poles at the shelter's entrance so they will not slide inward.
- Use any excess material to cover the entrance.

The tarp makes this shelter wind resistant, and the shelter is small enough that it is easily warmed. A candle, used carefully, can

Figure 5-7. One-man shelter.

keep the inside temperature comfortable. This shelter is unsatisfactory, however, when heavy snow is falling as it will cave it in.

Field-Expedient Lean-To

If you are in a wooded area and have enough natural materials, you can make a field-expedient lean-to (Figure 5-9) without the aid of tools or with only a knife. It takes longer to make this type of shelter

Figure 5-9. Field-expedient lean-to and fire reflector.

than it does to make other types, but it will protect you from the elements.

You will need two trees (or upright poles) about 2 meters apart; one pole about 2 meters long and 2.5 centimeters in diameter; five to eight poles about 3 meters long and 2.5 centimeters in diameter for beams; cord or vines for securing the horizontal support to the trees; and other poles, saplings, or vines to crisscross the beams.

To make this lean-to--

- Tie the 2-meter pole to the two trees at waist to chest height. This is the horizontal support. If a standing tree is not available, construct a biped using Y-shaped sticks or two tripods.
- Place one end of the beams (3-meter poles) on one side of the horizontal support. As with all lean-to type shelters, be sure to place the lean-to's backside into the wind.
- Crisscross saplings or vines on the beams.
- Cover the framework with brush, leaves, pine needles, or grass, starting at the bottom and working your way up like shingling.
- Place straw, leaves, pine needles, or grass inside the shelter for bedding.

In cold weather, add to your lean-to's comfort by building a fire reflector wall (Figure 5-9). Drive four 1.5-meter-long stakes into the ground to support the wall. Stack green logs on top of one another between the support stakes. Form two rows of stacked logs to create an inner space within the wall that you can fill with dirt. This action not only strengthens the wall but makes it more heat reflective. Bind the top of the support stakes so that the green logs and dirt will stay in place.

With just a little more effort you can have a drying rack. Cut a few 2-centimeter-diameter poles (length depends on the distance between the lean-to's horizontal support and the top of the fire reflector wall). Lay one end of the poles on the lean-to support and the other end on top of the reflector wall. Place and tie into place smaller sticks across these poles. You now have a place to dry clothes, meat, or fish.

Swamp Bed

In a marsh or swamp, or any area with standing water or continually wet ground, the swamp bed (Figure 5-10) keeps you out of the water. When selecting such a site, consider the weather, wind, tides, and available materials.

Figure 5-10. Swamp bed.

To make a swamp bed--

- Look for four trees clustered in a rectangle, or cut four poles (bamboo is ideal) and drive them firmly into the ground so they form a rectangle. They should be far enough apart and strong enough to support your height and weight, to include equipment.
- Cut two poles that span the width of the rectangle. They, too, must be strong enough to support your weight.
- Secure these two poles to the trees (or poles). Be sure they are high enough above the ground or water to allow for tides and high water.
- Cut additional poles that span the rectangle's length. Lay them across the two side poles, and secure them.

- Cover the top of the bed frame with broad leaves or grass to form a soft sleeping surface.
- Build a fire pad by laying clay, silt, or mud on one comer of the swamp bed and allow it to dry.

Another shelter designed to get you above and out of the water or wet ground uses the same rectangular configuration as the swamp bed. You very simply lay sticks and branches lengthwise on the inside of the trees (or poles) until there is enough material to raise the sleeping surface above the water level.

Natural Shelters

Do not overlook natural formations that provide shelter. Examples are caves, rocky crevices, clumps of bushes, small depressions, large rocks on leeward sides of hills, large trees with low-hanging limbs, and fallen trees with thick branches. However, when selecting a natural formation--

- Stay away from low ground such as ravines, narrow valleys, or creek beds. Low areas collect the heavy cold air at night and are therefore colder than the surrounding high ground. Thick, brushy, low ground also harbors more insects.
- Check for poisonous snakes, ticks, mites, scorpions, and stinging ants.
- Look for loose rocks, dead limbs, coconuts, or other natural growth than could fall on your shelter.

Tree-Pit Snow Shelter

If you are in a cold, snow-covered area where evergreen trees grow and you have a digging tool, you can make a tree-pit shelter (Figure 5-12).

To make this shelter--

- Find a tree with bushy branches that provides overhead cover.
- Dig out the snow around the tree trunk until you reach the depth and diameter you desire, or until you reach the ground.
- Pack the snow around the top and the inside of the hole to provide support.

Figure 5-12. Tree-pit snow shelter.

- Find and cut other evergreen boughs. Place them over the top of the pit to give you additional overhead cover. Place evergreen boughs in the bottom of the pit for insulation.

Beach Shade Shelter

This shelter protects you from the sun, wind, rain, and heat. It is easy to make using natural materials.

To make this shelter (Figure 5-13)--

- Find and collect driftwood or other natural material to use as support beams and as a digging tool.
- Select a site that is above the high water mark.
- Scrape or dig out a trench running north to south so that it receives the least amount of sunlight. Make the trench long and wide enough for you to lie down comfortably.
- Mound soil on three sides of the trench. The higher the mound, the more space inside the shelter.
- Lay support beams (driftwood or other natural material) that span the trench on top of the mound to form the framework for a roof.

Figure 5-13. Beach shade shelter.

- Enlarge the shelter's entrance by digging out more sand in front of it.
- Use natural materials such as grass or leaves to form a bed inside the shelter.

Desert Shelters

In an arid environment, consider the time, effort, and material needed to make a shelter. If you have material such as a poncho, canvas, or a parachute, use it along with such terrain features as rock outcropping, mounds of sand, or a depression between dunes or rocks to make your shelter.

Using rock outcroppings--

- Anchor one end of your poncho (canvas, parachute, or other material) on the edge of the outcrop using rocks or other weights.
- Extend and anchor the other end of the poncho so it provides the best possible shade.

In a sandy area--

- Build a mound of sand or use the side of a sand dune for one side of the shelter.
- Anchor one end of the material on top of the mound using sand or other weights.

- Extend and anchor the other end of the material so it provides the best possible shade.

Note: If you have enough material, fold it in half and form a 30-centimeter to 45-centimeter airspace between the two halves. This airspace will reduce the temperature under the shelter.

A belowground shelter (Figure 5-14) can reduce the midday heat as much as 16 to 22 degrees C (30 to 40 degrees F). Building it, however, requires more time and effort than for other shelters. Since your physical effort will make you sweat more and increase dehydrtion, construct it before the heat of the day.

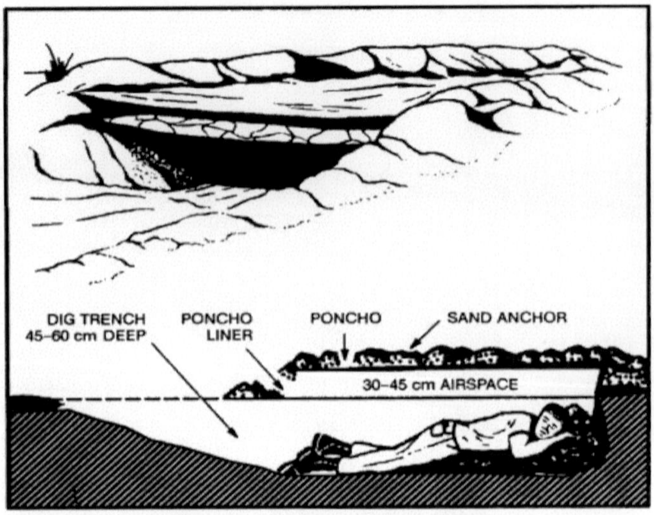

Figure 5-14. Belowground desert shelter.

To make this shelter--

- Find a low spot or depression between dunes or rocks. If necessary, dig a trench 45 to 60 centimeters deep and long and wide enough for you to lie in comfortably.
- Pile the sand you take from the trench to form a mound around three sides.
- On the open end of the trench, dig out more sand so you can get in and out of your shelter easily.
- Cover the trench with your material.
- Secure the material in place using sand, rocks, or other weights.

If you have extra material, you can further decrease the midday temperature in the trench by securing the material 30 to 45 centimeters above the other cover. This layering of the material will reduce the inside temperature 11 to 22 degrees C (20 to 40 degrees F).

Desert Tarp

This "double roofed" shelter dates back centuries among desert cultures, particularly in northern Africa and the Middle East, but it finally found widespread fame through the last century's military survival training. To get started with this shelter, you'll need two tarps and several dozen feet of rope. Find or dig your own low spot in the ground. Lay one of your tarps out over the low spot and drive each of your stakes at one corner of the tarp. Tie your tarp tightly to the stakes, and then tie the other tarp into place—so that it leaves one foot of air space between the two tarps. You can also fold over a larger tarp to create the two layers. Tie the tops of the four stakes to your four anchors, which can be stakes, rocks, logs or any other strong anchoring object.

Leaf Hut

The leaf hut is a two-sided, wedge-shaped lean-to with much better weatherproofing and insulating qualities. To build one, select a long, sturdy pole 9 to12 feet long. Prop it up in the fork of a tree; or set it on a rock, stump, or two forked prop sticks. Then, cover the sides of the pole with tree branches to act as ribs. These are placed at an angle along both sides of the ridge pole. Place the ribs close together so that your hut covering won't fall through. Next, heap vegetation over the framework (this can be anything that traps air, including grass, ferns, moss, pine needles, brush, or pine boughs). Two to 3 feet of vegetation covering all sides of the shelter is enough to keep you dry inside. Finally, fill the inside of the hut with a thick pile of vegetation for your bedding.

Ramada

Sunny, hot environments require a shelter that offers shade. The ramada's flat roof doesn't give you leak-proof rain protection, but it does block all of the sun from beating down on you. Many ramada variations exist, but most are based on four posts, some lightweight beams and a suitable covering. Tarps, mats, or even brush will do well enough on the ramada's roof as a sun block. Add some removable walls to cut the evening breeze if temps cool down, and you have a very versatile desert shelter.

Wedge Tarp

This tarp shelter is best suited for windy conditions with a constant prevailing wind direction. The wedge provides an aerodynamic shape which should resist the most biting wind and driving rain. With a minimum of 5 tie down points, the wedge is more secure than most tarps, and it even provides two corners that act as rain catches. To build the wedge tarp shelter, stake down two corners of the tarp into the wind (not opposing corners). Then tie up a line to the center of the opposite side of the tarp. Tie the remaining two corners down toward the ground. Use more cord and a less steep angle for open wings and better ventilation. Tie the last corners down sharply for the best weatherproofing. Place a few rocks or log chunks under

the tarp by the first tie downs to create deeper basins to catch water. This shelter is a dwelling and a water harvester in one.

Tarp Tipi

A bit of rope, some poles and a tarp can give you all you need to build one of the most versatile and mobile shelters that Native Americans have ever employed—the tipi. Traditional tipis were once covered with large hides, then later with canvas. For our purposes, any large fabric will work, from parachute material, to sails, or a tarp. There

are many traditions with tipi building, but for a quick field shelter, just call it like you see it. Use rope to bundle a few straight pole together or hook a few forked poles to lock in the first three or four poles. Then place other poles in a circle around the main supports. Pull the tarp or other covering into place, and tie down well. Try to size the framework so that you tarp covers it completely.

A-Frame Tarp Shelter

The A-frame is a tarp design that gives great coverage against rain and wind, when built close to the ground. When suspended higher, it still provides coverage from rain, but it allows more airflow underneath. A-frames go up fast. Once you pick your shelter site, you should have your tarp hung up in 10 minutes or less, leaving plenty of time in the day to accomplish other survival tasks. To get started, suspend a line of cordage between two trees or similar supports. Lay your tarp over the line and tie down all four corners of your tarp. This shelter is a great addition to a tarp hammock or strung up over a springy bough bed. You can even use a poncho as an A-frame tarp shelter.

Quinzhee

The quinzhee is a dome shaped snow shelter, similar in shape to an igloo, but much easier to construct. Snow must be just right to build an igloo, while most types of snowfall can be packed together for the quinzhee. To build one, start by piling up some moveable gear under a tarp. Backpacks are commonly used for this. Then pile snow over the tarp and gear. Pack the snow down, estimating when it is two feet thick all the way around. Next, insert 12 inch long sticks around the dome. Use 3 or 4 dozen of these guide sticks. Burrow into the side of the quinzhee, and retrieve the tarp and gear. Excavate snow inside the mound until you reach the base of every stick. This will ensure uniform thickness of the dome. Make a fist sized ventilation hole in the roof of the quinzhee.

Snow Cave

A snow cave may be the only shelter option in areas with deep snow. This is typically the most dangerous shelter to create, as the inhabitants could suffer from low oxygen or even be buried alive in a ceiling collapse. Snow selection is a critical part to the snow caves safe performance. Select a deep, solid snow bank or drift. Dig into the side of it, forming a tunnel into a low spot. This is the "cold well", which is a place where the colder air can fall and collect. Then dig up and over creating a shelf or platform to sleep on. This should be the highest part of the shelter. Dig a small hole about 6 inches in diameter somewhere in the roof for ventilation, especially if you plan on blocking the entrance with a doorway of backpack or big snow chunk.

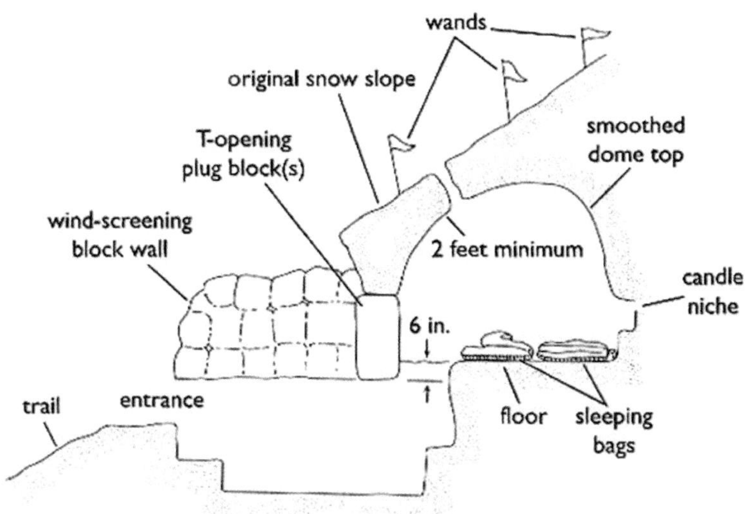

CUTAWAY SIDE VIEW

FIRECRAFT

In many survival situations, the ability to start a fire can make the difference between living and dying. Fire can fulfill many needs. It can provide warmth and comfort. It not only cooks and preserves food, it also provides warmth in the form of heated food that saves calories our body normally uses to produce body heat. You can use fire to purify water, sterilize bandages, signal for rescue, and provide protection from animals. It can be a psychological boost by providing peace of mind and companionship. You can also use fire to produce tools and weapons.

Fire can cause problems, as well. It can cause forest fires or destroy essential equipment. Fire can also cause burns carbon monoxide poisoning when used in shelters.

To build a fire, it helps to understand the basic principles of a fire. Fuel (in a nongaseous state) does not burn directly. When you apply heat to a fuel, it produces a gas. This gas, combined with oxygen in the air, burns.

Understanding the concept of the fire triangle is very important in correctly constructing and maintaining a fire. The three sides of the triangle represent *air, heat,* and *fuel*. If you remove any of these, the fire will go out. The correct ratio of these components is very important for a fire to burn at its greatest capability. The only way to learn this ratio is to practice.

SITE SELECTION AND PREPARATION

You will have to decide what site and arrangement to use. Before building a fire consider--

- The area (terrain and climate) in which you are operating.
- The materials and tools available.
- Time: how much time you have?
- Need: why you need a fire?
- Security: how close is the enemy?

Tinder	Kindling	Fuel
• Birch bark • Shredded inner bark from cedar, chestnut, red elm trees • Fine wood shavings • Dead grass, ferns, moss, fungi • Straw • Sawdust • Very fine pitchwood scrapings • Dead evergreen needles • Punk (the completely rotted portions of dead logs or trees) • Evergreen tree knots • Bird down (fine feathers) • Down seed heads (milkweed, dry cattails, bulrush, or thistle) • Fine, dried vegetable fibers • Spongy threads of dead puffball • Dead palm leaves • Skinlike membrane lining bamboo • Lint from pocket and seams • Charred cloth • Waxed paper • Outer bamboo shavings • Gunpowder • Cotton • Lint	• Small twigs • Small strips of wood • Split wood • Heavy cardboard • Pieces of wood removed from the inside of larger pieces • Wood that has been doused with highly flammable materials, such as gasoline, oil, or wax	• Dry, standing wood and dry, dead branches • Dry inside (heart) of fallen tree trunks and large branches • Green wood that is finely split • Dry grasses twisted into bunches • Peat dry enough to burn (this may be found at the top of undercut banks) • Dried animal dung • Animal fats • Coal, oil shale, or oil lying on the surface

Figure 7-4. Materials for building fires.

Look for a dry spot that--

- Is protected from the wind.
- Is suitably placed in relation to your shelter (if any).
- Will concentrate the heat in the direction you desire.
- Has a supply of wood or other fuel available. (See Figure 7-4 for types of material you can use.)

If you are in a wooded or brush-covered area, clear the brush and scrape the surface soil from the spot you have selected. Clear a circle at least 1 meter in diameter so there is little chance of the fire spreading.

If time allows, construct a fire wall using logs or rocks. This wall will help to reflector direct the heat where you want it (Figure 7-1). It will also reduce flying sparks and cut down on the amount of wind blowing into the fire. However, you will need enough wind to keep the fire burning.

If you are in a snow-covered area, use green logs to make a dry base for your fire (Figure 7-3).

> CAUTION
>
> Do not use wet or porous rocks as they may explode when heated.

Figure 7-1. Types of fire walls.

Trees with wrist-sized trunks are easily broken in extreme cold. Cut or break several green logs and lay them side by side on top of the snow. Add one or two more layers. Lay the top layer of logs opposite those below it.

Figure 7-3. Base for fire in snow-covered area.

Fire Material Selection

You need three types of materials (Figure 7-4) to build a fire--tinder, kindling, and fuel.

Tinder is dry material that ignites with little heat--a spark starts a fire. The tinder must be absolutely dry to be sure just a spark will ignite it. If you only have a device that generates sparks, charred cloth will be almost essential. It holds a spark for long periods, allowing you to put tinder on the hot area to generate a small flame. You can make charred cloth by heating cotton cloth until it turns black, but does not burn. Once it is black, you must keep it in an airtight container to keep it dry. Prepare this cloth well in advance of any survival situation. Add it to your individual survival kit.

Kindling is readily combustible material that you add to the burning tinder. Again, this material should be absolutely dry to ensure rapid burning. Kindling increases the fire's temperature so that it will ignite less combustible material.

Fuel is less combustible material that burns slowly and steadily once ignited.

How To Build A Fire

There are several methods for laying a fire, each of which has advantages. The situation you find yourself in will determine which fire to use.

TEPEE

To make this fire (Figure 7-5), arrange the tinder and a few sticks of kindling in the shape of a tepee or cone. Light the center. As the tepee burns, the outside logs will fall inward, feeding the fire. This type of fire burns well even with wet wood.

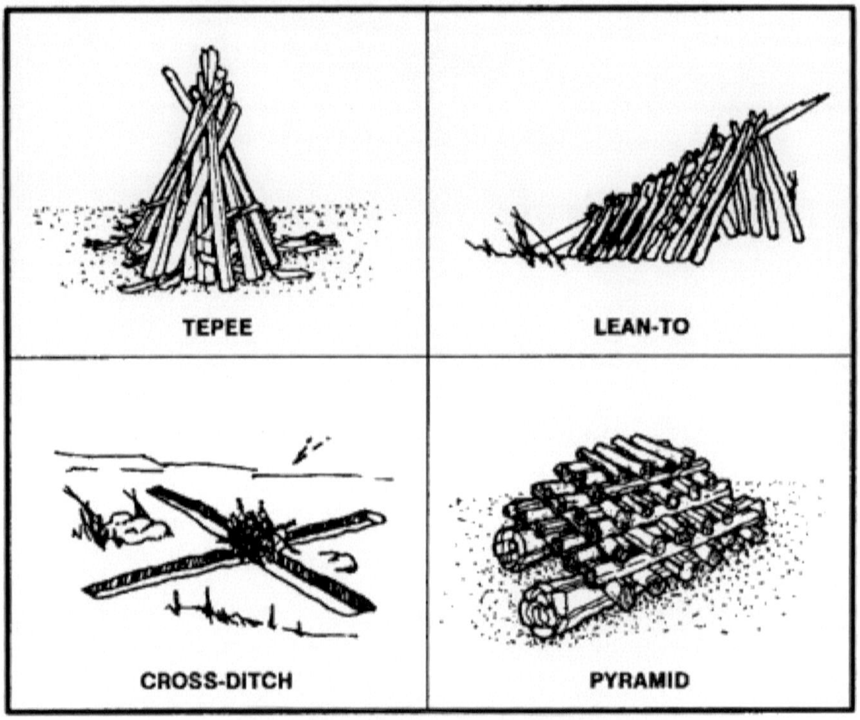

Figure 7-5. Methods for laying fires.

LEAN-TO

To lay this fire (Figure 7-5), push a green stick into the ground at a 30-degree angle. Point the end of the stick in the direction of the wind. Place some tinder deep under this lean-to stick. Lean pieces of kindling against the lean-to stick. Light the tinder. As the kindling catches fire from the tinder, add more kindling.

CROSS-DITCH

To use this method (Figure 7-5), scratch a cross about 30 centimeters in size in the ground. Dig the cross 7.5 centimeters deep. Put a large wad of tinder in the middle of the cross. Build a kindling pyramid above the tinder. The shallow ditch allows air to sweep under the tinder to provide a draft.

PYRAMID

To lay this fire (Figure 7-5), place two small logs or branches parallel on the ground. Place a solid layer of small logs across the parallel logs. Add three or four more layers of logs or branches, each layer smaller than and at a right angle to the layer below it. Make a starter fire on top of the pyramid. As the starter fire burns, it will ignite the logs below it. This gives you a fire that burns downward, requiring no attention during the night.

There are several other ways to lay a fire that are quite effective. Your situation and the material available in the area may make another method more suitable.

How To Light A Fire

Always light your fire from the upwind side. Make sure to lay your tinder, kindling, and fuel so that your fire will burn as long as you need it. Igniters provide the initial heat required to start the tinder burning. They fall into two categories: modern methods and primitive methods.

MODERN METHODS

Modem igniters use modem devices--items we normally think of to start a fire.

Matches

Make sure these matches are waterproof. Also, store them in a waterproof container along with a dependable striker pad.

Convex Lens

Use this method (Figure 7-6) only on bright, sunny days. The lens can come from binoculars, camera, telescopic sights, or magnifying glasses. Angle the lens to concentrate the sun's rays on the tinder. Hold the lens over the same spot until the tinder begins to smolder. Gently blow or fan the tinder into flame, and apply it to the fire lay.

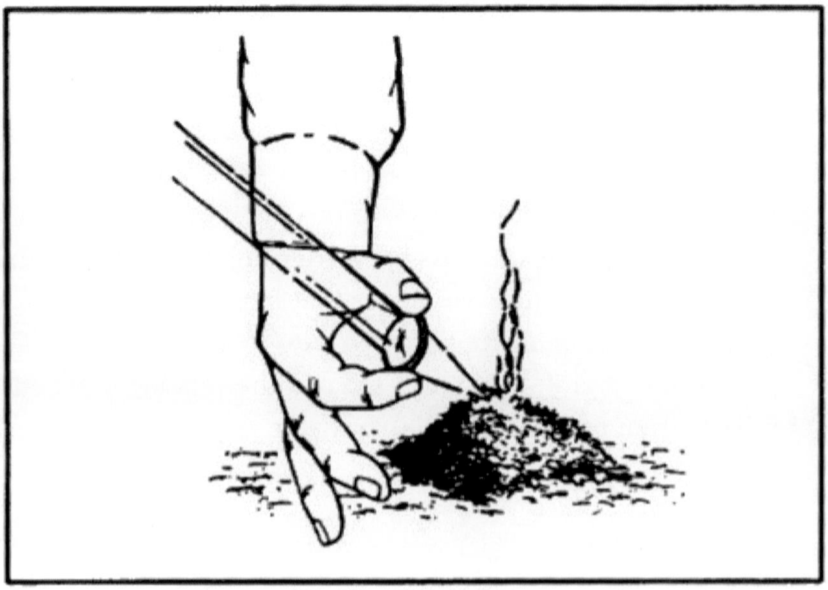

Figure 7-6. Lens method.

Metal Match

Place a flat, dry leaf under your tinder with a portion exposed. Place the tip of the metal match on the dry leaf, holding the metal match in one hand and a knife in the other. Scrape your knife against the metal match to produce sparks. The sparks will hit the tinder. When the tinder starts to smolder, proceed as above.

Battery

Use a battery to generate a spark. Use of this method depends on the type of battery available. Attach a wire to each terminal. Touch the ends of the bare wires together next to the tinder so the sparks will ignite it.

Gunpowder

If you have ammunition with your equipment, carefully extract the bullet from the shell casing, and use the gunpowder as tinder. A spark will ignite the powder. Be extremely careful when extracting the bullet from the case.

PRIMITIVE METHODS

Primitive igniters are those attributed to our early ancestors.

Flint and Steel

The direct spark method is the easiest of the primitive methods to use. The flint and steel method is the most reliable of the direct spark methods. Strike a flint or other hard, sharp-edged rock edge with a piece of carbon steel (stainless steel will not produce a good spark). This method requires a loose-jointed wrist and practice. When a spark has caught in the tinder, blow on it. The spark will spread and burst into flames.

Fire-Plow

The fire-plow (Figure 7-7) is a friction method of ignition. You rub a hardwood shaft against a softer wood base. To use this method, cut a

Figure 7-7. Fire-plow.

straight groove in the base and plow the blunt tip of the shaft up and down the groove. The plowing action of the shaft pushes out small particles of wood fibers. Then, as you apply more pressure on each stroke, the friction ignites the wood particles.

Bow and Drill

The technique of starting a fire with a bow and drill (Figure 7-8) is simple, but you must exert much effort and be persistent to produce a fire. You need the following items to use this method:

- *Socket.* The socket is an easily grasped stone or piece of hardwood or bone with a slight depression in one side. Use it to hold the drill in place and to apply downward pressure.
- *Drill.* The drill should be a straight, seasoned hardwood stick about 2 centimeters in diameter and 25 centimeters long. The top end is round and the low end blunt (to produce more friction).
- *Fire board.* Its size is up to you. A seasoned softwood board about 2.5 centimeters thick and 10 centimeters wide is

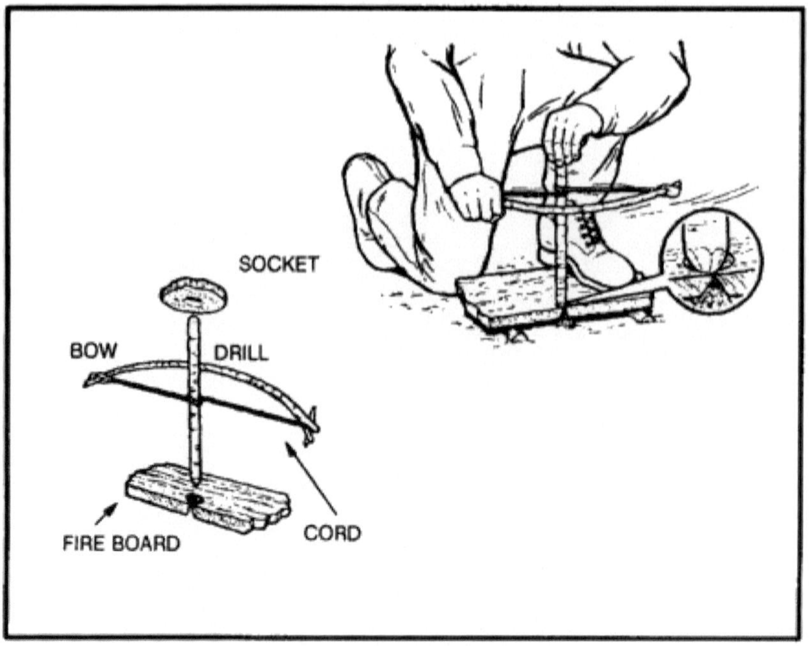

Figure 7-8. Bow and drill.

preferable. Cut a depression about 2 centimeters from the edge on one side of the board. On the underside, make a V-shaped cut from the edge of the board to the depression.

- *Bow.* The bow is a resilient, green stick about 2.5 centimeters in diameter and a string. The type of wood is not important. The bowstring can be any type of cordage. You tie the bowstring from one end of the bow to the other, without any slack.

To use the bow and drill, first prepare the fire lay. Then place a bundle of tinder under the V-shaped cut in the fire board. Place one foot on the fire board. Loop the bowstring over the drill and place the drill in the precut depression on the fire board. Place the socket, held in one hand, on the top of the drill to hold it in position. Press down on the drill and saw the bow back and forth to twirl the drill (Figure 7-8). Once you have established a smooth motion, apply more downward pressure and work the bow faster. This action will grind hot black powder into the tinder, causing a spark to catch. Blow on the tinder until it ignites.

Note: Primitive fire-building methods are exhaustive and require practice to ensure success.

HELPFUL HINTS

Use nonaromatic seasoned hardwood for fuel, if possible.

Collect large amounts of kindling and tinder (along the trail).

Add insect repellent to the tinder, but be care not to breathe fumes.

Keep the firewood dry.

Dry damp firewood near the fire.

Bank the fire to keep the coals alive overnight.

Carry lighted punk, when possible.

Be sure the fire is out before leaving camp.

Do not select wood lying on the ground. It may appear to be dry but generally doesn't provide enough friction.

SAR RESOURCE MINIMUM 24 HOUR PERSONAL EQUIPMENT LIST – Level 2

Personal First Aid

20-acetaminophen or aspirin tablets
20-antacid tablets
20-antihistamine, 25 mg Benadryl
10-antiseptic cleansing pads
1-antiseptic ointment
10-band-aids, various sizes
5-cotton swabs, non-sterile
5-sterile dressings (4x4 gauze pads)

Personal SAR Equipment

1-photo personal identification

1-pack, adequate size to carry all items
8-bags, various sizes, zip locked
2-lawn & leaf bags, 50 gal

1-bandanna, handkerchief
1-Duty Head Cover
1-clothes bag, waterproof
1-Duty Uniform
1-Outerwear, suitable for climate
1-rain suit, durable
1-underwear, extra set
1-socks, extra pair
1-shirt and pants, extra set
1-gaiters
1-helmet, ANSI Z89.1 compliant
1-Duty Boots
1-gloves, durable, even in summer
1-goggles, or safety glasses, clear
1-sunglasses, 100% UV protection
1-shelter material, 8x10 plastic or coated nylon
1-space type blanket or sleeping bag

1-whistle
1-mirror, small

1-duct tape, 5-10 ft.
8-wire ties, plastic, self-locking

1-trail snacks/food
1-sunscreen lotion
1-toilet tissue papers or baby wipes
1-lip balm, with sunscreen
1-insect repellent

1-moleskin
1-razor blade, single edge safety type
4-roller gauze bandage
4-safety pins, large
1-splinter forceps, tweezers
2-pair non-latex gloves
1-scissors, multi-purpose
Personal Medications, 72 hr. supply

1-tracking stick, minimum of 42" long
1-measuring device, 18 in. minimum
1-flagging tape, roll
1-pad and pencil
1-Photographic device, transmit capable (e.g. smart phone with camera)

1-headlamp, LED, white & colored lamps
1-flashlight, LED
1-set extra batteries, each light

1-knife, multi-purpose, "Leatherman" style
1-Sterno or stove, with fuel
1-fire starting material/aid
1-disposable lighter

SAR RESOURCE MINIMUM 24 HOUR PERSONAL EQUIPMENT LIST – Level 2 (cont'd)

1-metal cup or pot
12-matches in a waterproof container
1-candle, long-burning

1-550 Paracord, 50 feet
2-carabiners, large modified D (safety locking-screw gate)
1-webbing, 1" tubular, min 20 ft. length
2-Prussik Cords (10 ft. min) 6 – 8 mm
1-Safety Rope 75 Feet, NFPA 15/1 rated Lifeline

1-hydration system, flexible bag & tube
1-canteen or Nalgene bottle, 1 liter size
1-water purification method

1-compass, 2 degree graduation, bezel orienting lines, orienteering type
1-UTM (or USNGS) Grid Reader
1-GPS Download Compliant
1-inventory "clicker" or other counting device
1-watch or other timekeeping device

SAR RESOURCE MINIMUM PERSONAL EQUIPMENT LIST – Urban

Personal First Aid

4-acetaminophen or aspirin tablets
4-antacid tablets
2-antihistamine, 25 mg Benadryl
2-antiseptic cleansing pads
1-antiseptic ointment
6-band-aids, various sizes
2-cotton swabs, non-sterile
2-sterile dressings (4x4 gauze pads)

Personal SAR Equipment

1-Small Backpack or "Fanny-pack"
8-bags, various sizes, zip locked
1-SAR personal identification

1-bandanna, handkerchief
1-Duty Head Cover
1-Duty Uniform
1-Outerwear, suitable for climate
1-Duty Boots
1-gloves, durable, even in summer
1-rain suit, durable
1-helmet, ANSI Z89.1 compliant
1-goggles, or safety glasses, clear
1-sunglasses, 100% UV protection
1-sunscreen lotion
1-lip balm, with sunscreen
1-insect repellent
2-moist towelette

1-headlamp, LED, white & colored lamps
1-flashlight, LED
1-set extra batteries, each light

1-whistle

1-knife, multi-purpose, "Leatherman" style
1-550 Paracord, 50 feet

1-moleskin
4-roller gauze bandage
4-safety pins, large
1-splinter forceps, tweezers
2-pair non-latex gloves
1-scissors, multi-purpose
Personal Medications, 24 hr. supply

1-hydration system, flexible bag & tube
OR
1-canteen or Nalgene bottle, 1 liter size
AND
1-water purification method

1-compass, 2 degree graduation, bezel orienting lines, orienteering type
1-UTM (or USNGS) Grid Reader
1-GPS Download Compliant
1-inventory "clicker" or other counting device
1-watch or other timekeeping device

1-snacks

1-tracking stick, minimum of 42" long
1-measuring device, 18 in. minimum
1-flagging tape, roll
1-pad and pencil
1-Photographic device, transmit capable e.g. smart phone with camera)

Assignment List, ICS Form 204

1. BRANCH	2. DIVISION/GROUP	ASSIGNMENT LIST

3. INCIDENT NAME	4. OPERATIONAL PERIOD DATE ________ TIME ________

5. OPERATIONAL PERSONNEL

OPERATIONS CHIEF		DIVISION/GROUP SUPERVISOR	
BRANCH DIRECTOR		AIR TACTICAL GROUP SUPERVISOR	

6. RESOURCES ASSIGNED TO THIS PERIOD

STRIKE TEAM/TASK FORCE/ RESOURCE DESIGNATOR	EMT	LEADER	NUMBER PERSONS	TRANS. NEEDED	PICKUP PT./TIME	DROP OFF PT./TIME

7. CONTROL OPERATIONS

8. SPECIAL INSTRUCTIONS

9. DIVISION/GROUP COMMUNICATIONS SUMMARY

FUNCTION		FREQ.	SYSTEM	CHAN.	FUNCTION		FREQ.	SYSTEM	CHAN.
COMMAND	LOCAL				SUPPORT	LOCAL			
	REPEAT					REPEAT			
DIV./GROUP TACTICAL					GROUND TO AIR				

PREPARED BY (RESOURCE UNIT LEADER)	APPROVED BY (PLANNING SECT. CH.)	DATE	TIME

TEAM DEBRIEFING

TEAM DEBRIEFING	1. INCIDENT NAME	2. OPERATIONAL PERIOD	3.ASSIGNMENT NUMBER

4. RESOURCE TYPE

5. ASSIGNMENT SUMMARY

6. DESCRIBE SEARCH EFFORTS IN ASSIGNMENT

7. DESCRIBE PORTIONS YOU WERE UNABLE TO SEARCH

8. DESCRIBE ANY CLUES, TRACKS , OR SIGN LOCATED, OR ANY PERTINENT TRAIL INTERVIEWS

9. DESCRIBE ANY HAZARDS OR PROBLEMS ENCOUNTERED

10. SUGGESTIONS FOR FURTHER SEARCH EFFORTS IN OR NEAR YOUR ASSIGNMENT

11. TIME ENTERED ASSIGNMENT	12. TIME EXITED ASSIGNMENT	13. TIME SPENT SEARCHING

15. DEBRIEFER	16. DATE & TIME

14. P.O.D. SUMMARY

	H		M		L	
____%	☐	☐	☐	☐	☐	RESPONSIVE SUBJECT
____%	☐	☐	☐	☐	☐	UNRESPONSIVE SUBJECT
____%	☐	☐	☐	☐	☐	CLUES
	90%		50%		10%	

ICS 204a SAR

ATTACHMENTS

- ☐ DEBRIEFING MAP(S)
- ☐ ORIGINAL BRIEFING DOCUMENT
- ☐ SUPPLEMENTAL DEBRIEFING FORMS
- ☐ OTHER ____________________

SUMMARY

- NOTHING SIGNIFICANT LOCATED ☐
- USEFUL INFORMATION, NEEDS REVIEW ☐
- POTENTIAL CLUES, NEEDS URGENT REVIEW ☐
- ASSIGNMENT COMPLETED ☐
- ASSIGNMENT NOT COMPLETED ☐

ACTIVITY LOG (ICS 214)

1. Incident Name:	**2. Operational Period:** Date From: Date To: Time From: Time To:

3. Name:	**4. ICS Position:**	**5. Home Agency** (and Unit):

6. Resources Assigned:

Name	ICS Position	Home Agency (and Unit)

7. Activity Log:

Date/Time	Notable Activities

8. Prepared by: Name: ________________ Position/Title: ________________ Signature: ________________

ICS 214, Page 1 Date/Time: ________________

ACTIVITY LOG (ICS 214)

1. Incident Name:	**2. Operational Period:** Date From: Time From: Date To: Time To:

7. Activity Log (continuation):

Date/Time	Notable Activities

8. Prepared by: Name: ______________ Position/Title: ______________ Signature: ______________

ICS 214, Page 2 Date/Time: ______________

Purpose. The Activity Log (ICS 214) records details of notable activities at any ICS level, including single resources, equipment, Task Forces, etc. These logs provide basic incident activity documentation, and a reference for any after-action report.

Preparation. An ICS 214 can be initiated and maintained by personnel in various ICS positions as it is needed or appropriate. Personnel should document how relevant incident activities are occurring and progressing, or any notable events or communications.

Distribution. Completed ICS 214s are submitted to supervisors, who forward them to the Documentation Unit. All completed original forms must be given to the Documentation Unit, which maintains a file of all ICS 214s. It is recommended that individuals retain a copy for their own records.

Notes:

- The ICS 214 can be printed as a two-sided form.
- Use additional copies as continuation sheets as needed, and indicate pagination as used.

Block Number	Block Title	Instructions
1	**Incident Name**	Enter the name assigned to the incident.
2	**Operational Period** ▯ Date and Time From ▯ Date and Time To	Enter the start date (month/day/year) and time (using the 24-hour clock) and end date and time for the operational period to which the form applies.
3	Name	Enter the title of the organizational unit or resource designator (e.g., Facilities Unit, Safety Officer, Strike Team).

Block Number	Block Title	Instructions
4	**ICS Position**	Enter the name and ICS position of the individual in charge of the Unit.
5	**Home Agency** (and Unit)	Enter the home agency of the individual completing the ICS 214. Enter a unit designator if utilized by the jurisdiction or discipline.
6	**Resources Assigned**	Enter the following information for resources assigned:
	□ Name	Use this section to enter the resource's name. For all individuals, use at least the first initial and last name. Cell phone number for the individual can be added as an option.
	□ ICS Position	Use this section to enter the resource's ICS position (e.g., Finance Section Chief).
	□ Home Agency (and Unit)	Use this section to enter the resource's home agency and/or unit (e.g., Des Moines Public Works Department, Water Management Unit).
7	**Activity Log** □ Date/Time □ Notable Activities	□ Enter the time (24-hour clock) and briefly describe individual notable activities. Note the date as well if the operational period covers more than one day. □ Activities described may include notable occurrences or events such as task assignments, task completions, injuries, difficulties encountered, etc. □ This block can also be used to track personal work habits by adding columns such as "Action Required," "Delegated To," "Status," etc.
8	**Prepared by** □ Name □ Position/Title □ Signature □ Date/Time	Enter the name, ICS position/title, and signature of the person preparing the form. Enter date (month/day/year) and time prepared (24-hour clock).

TRACKING AIDS

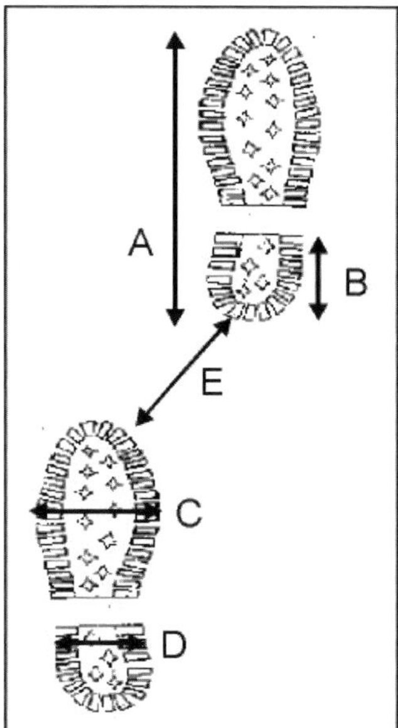

Figure 2
Measuring A Sole Print

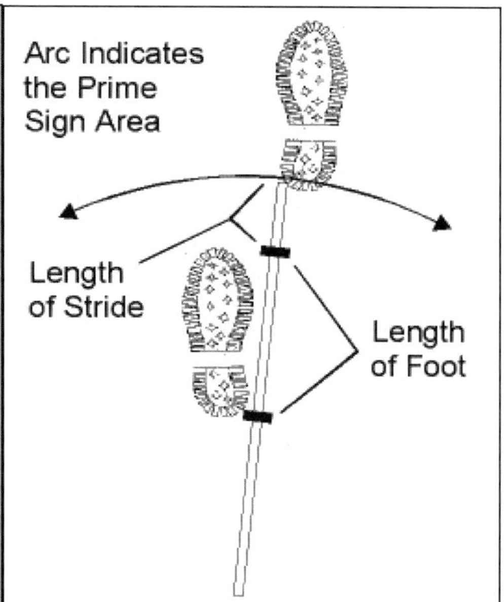

Figure 3 The Tracking Stick

TYPES OF TREAD PATTERNS

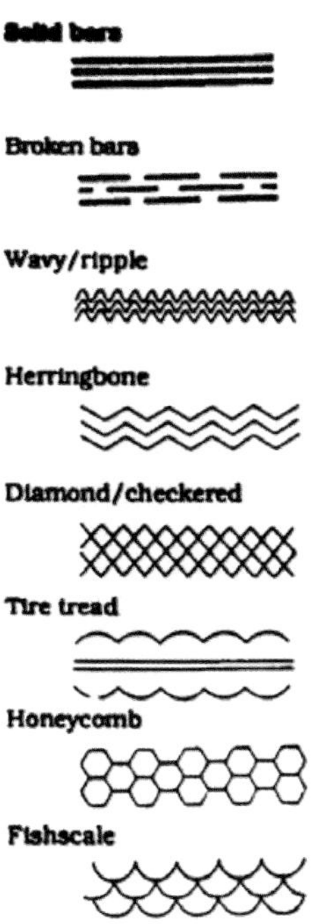

AERIE TRACKING REPORT

Search Subject:	Track found by:	Date:	Time:
UTM/USNG Coordinates:		Compass Heading:	
Type Terrain/Surroundings:	Tread/Lug Pattern:		
Comments:			

Draw Sole Pattern and Enter Measurements Below:

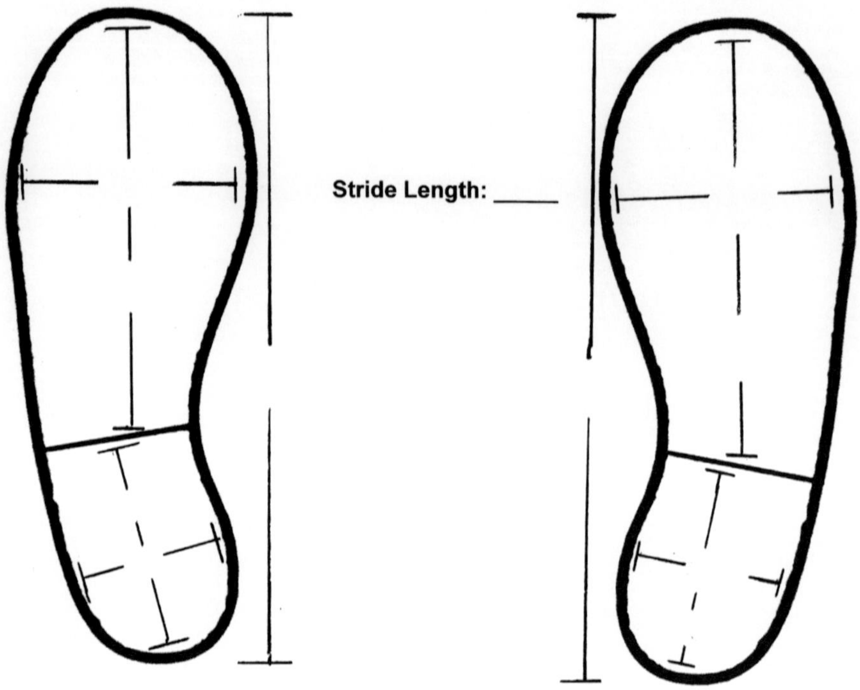

HOW TO TIE AN OVERHAND KNOT

1. Make a loop with your rope.

2. Take the running end of your rope and stick it through the loop you just made.

3. Pull both ends of the rope tight.

Images courtesy of animatedknots.com

HOW TO TIE A SQUARE (REEF) KNOT

We are using different colored cord for demonstration purposes.

1. Take each end of the rope(s) in each hand

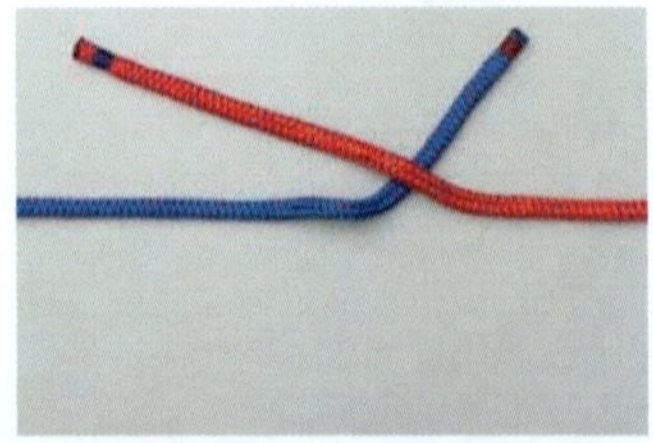

2. Place the rope in your right hand (running end) over the rope in your left hand (standing end)
3. Loop that same (running) end under the rope (standing end) you just crossed

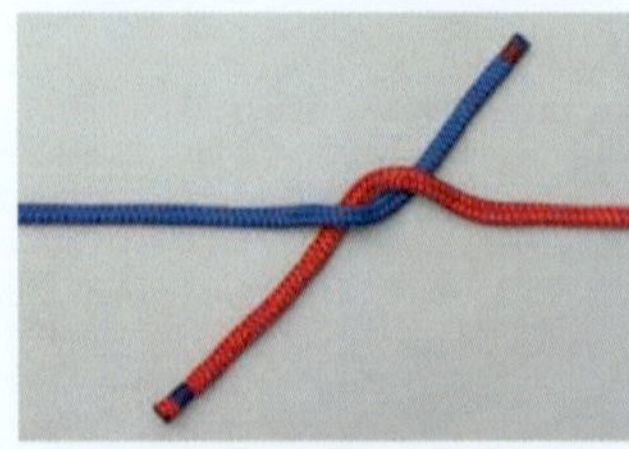

4. Using that same running end, cross over the top of the tail of the standing end

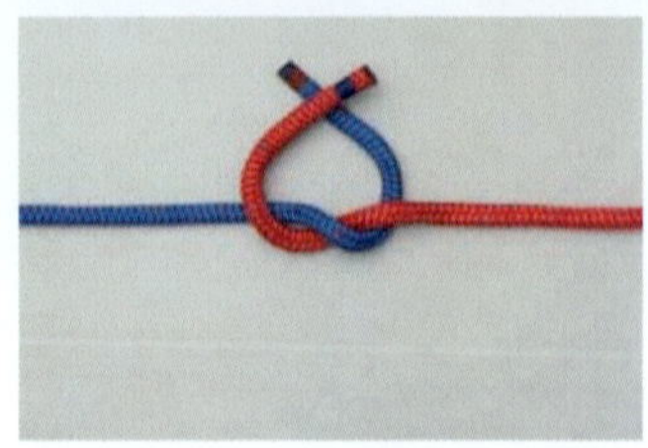

5. Now loop that running end around the standing end tail, through the loop it creates

6. Tighten the know by pulling on both the running and standing ends

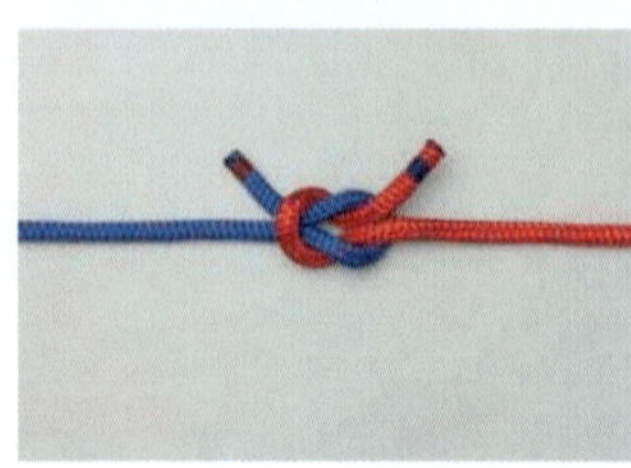

Images courtesy of animatedknots.com

HOW TO TIE THE FAMILY OF "8" KNOTS

FIGURE "8"

1. Pass the running end over the standing end, forming a loop
2. Now loop the running end back under the standing end
3. Loop that same (running) end under the rope (standing end) you just crossed
4. Pass the running end through the first loop created

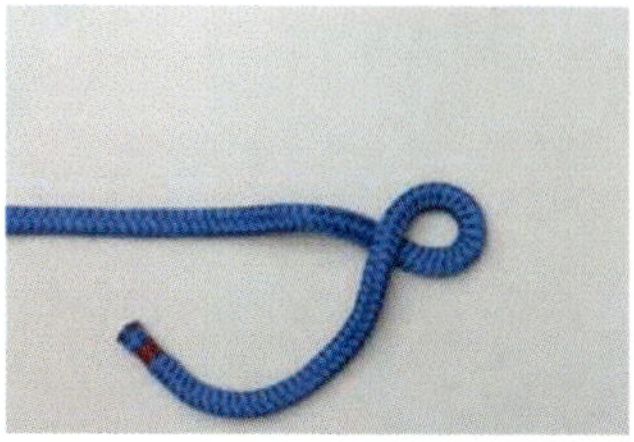

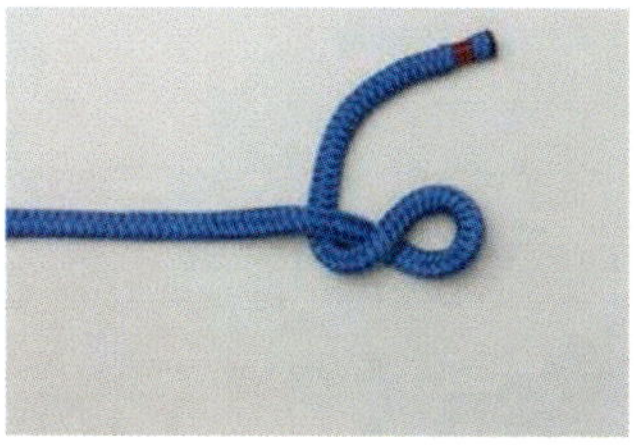

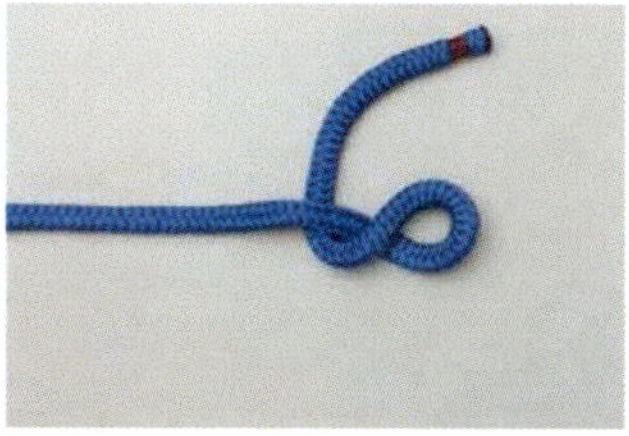

Images courtesy of animatedknots.com

FIGURE "8" ON A BIGHT

1. Form a bight on the rope

2. Pass the bight over then under the standing end

3. Now pass the bight through the first loop created when you crossed over the standing end

4. Pull the bight to tighten the knot (shown attached to a carabiner)

IMAGES COURTESY OF CHOCKSTONE.ORG

Images courtesy of animatedknots.com

FIGURE "8" BEND

1. Tie a loose Figure "8" on one (end if you're practicing with a single) rope

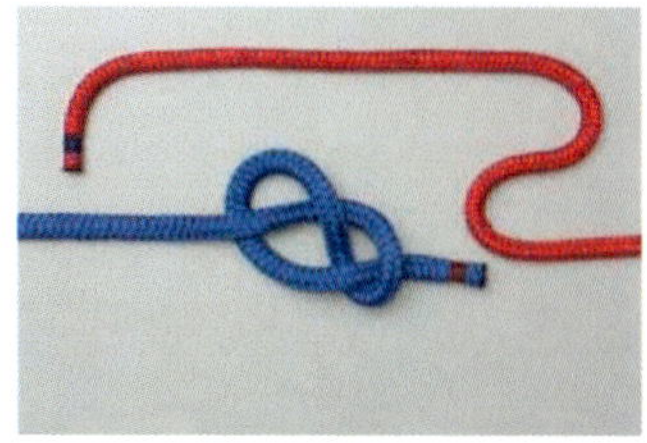

2. Now take the other rope retrace the original Figure "8" in reverse.

3. Dress the knot so the ropes do not cross each other. It is recommended you tie stopper knots on each tail

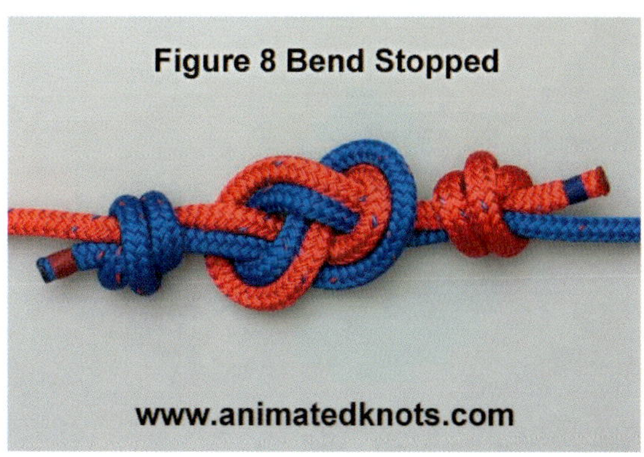

HOW TO TIE THE FAMILY OF "8" KNOTS

FIGURE "8" FOLLOW THROUGH

1.Start by tying a loose Figure "8" knot and pass the tail around the attachment point

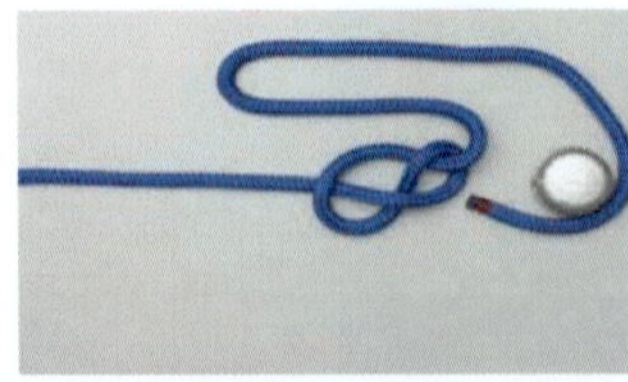

2. Now take the running end and follow through back through the original Figure "8"

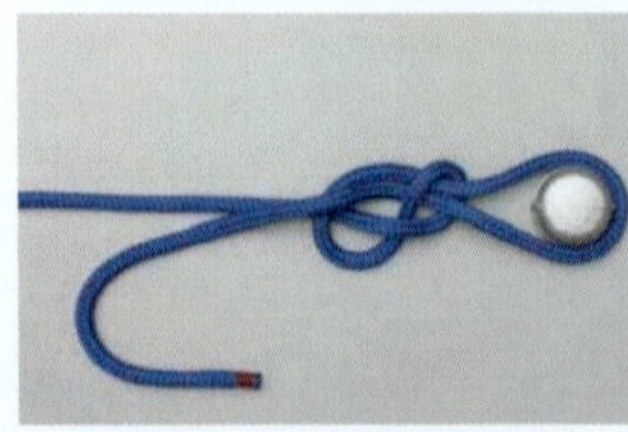

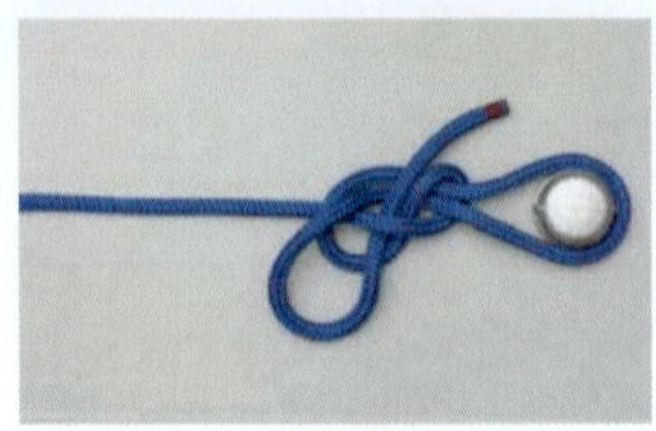

3. Dress the knot so the running end does not cross around the standing end while following through. It is recommended you tie a stopper knot with the tail

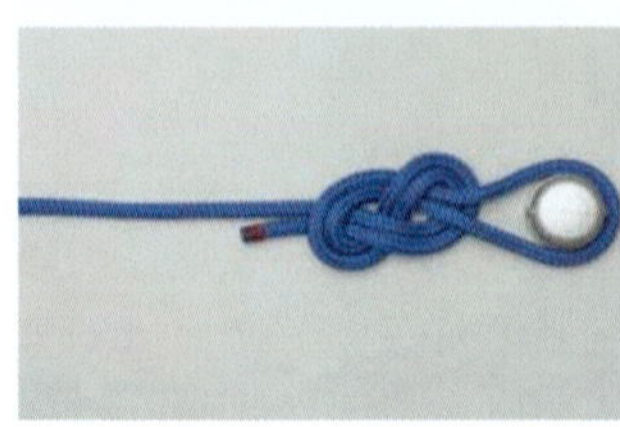

IMAGES COURTESY OF ANIMATEDKNOTS.COM

DOUBLE FISHERMAN'S BEND (GRAPEVINE KNOT) TO FORM A PRUSIK LOOP

1. With the two ends overlapped, wrap one end over the other twice

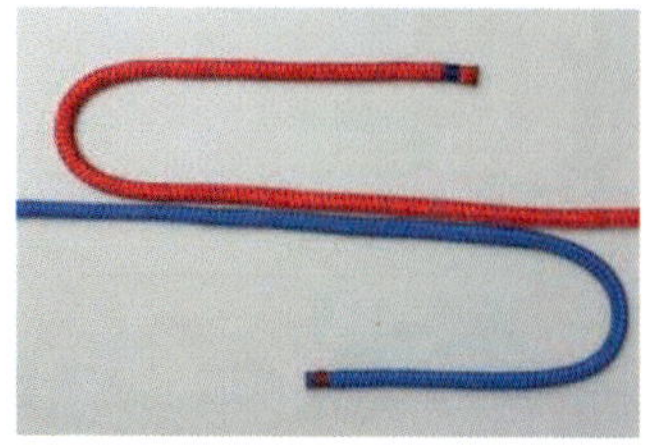

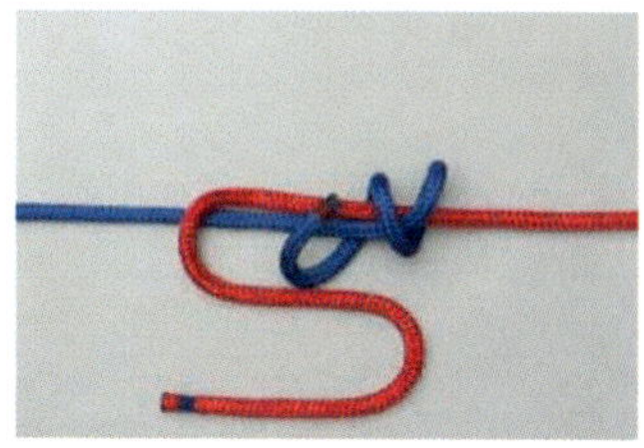

2. Now pass this running end back through the double loop just created

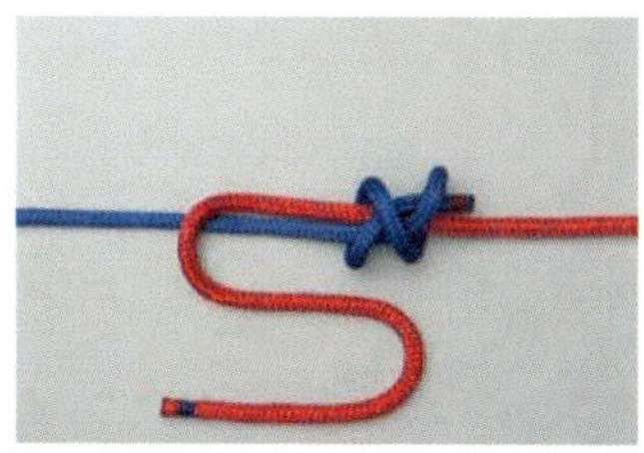

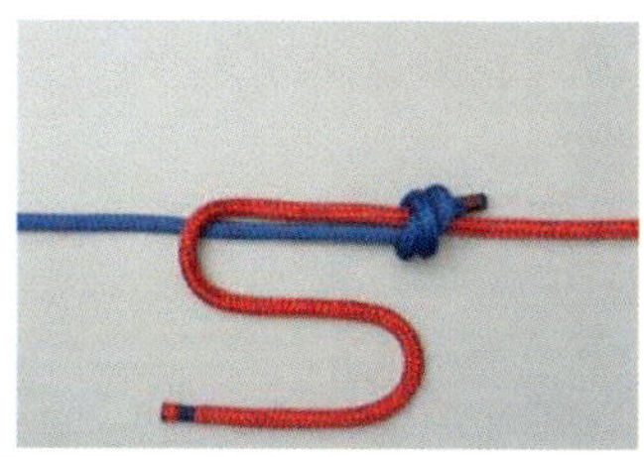

Images courtesy of animatedknots.com

3. Now pass the other end around the opposite rope twice and pass this running end back through the double loop

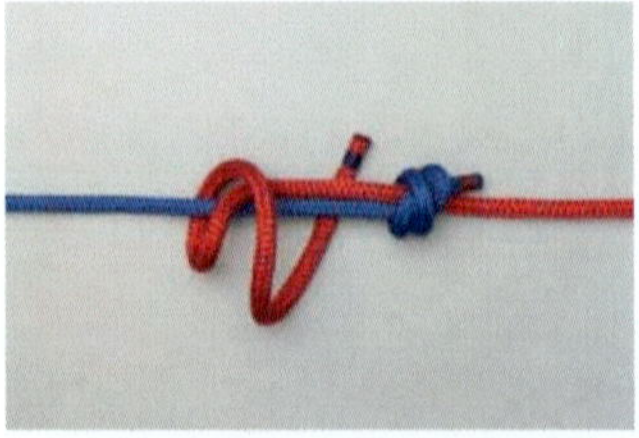

4. Pulling the two standing ends will bring the knots together tightly

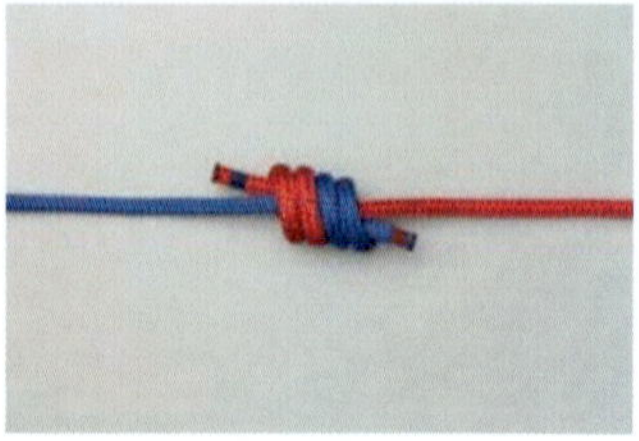

Back View

PRUSIK KNOT (TRIPLE SLIDING HITCH)

1. Using a Prusik Loop, wrap the loop around the lifeline three times, inside the Prusik Loop

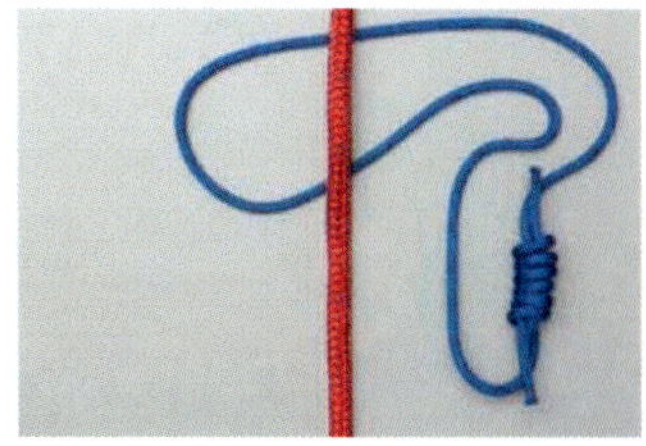

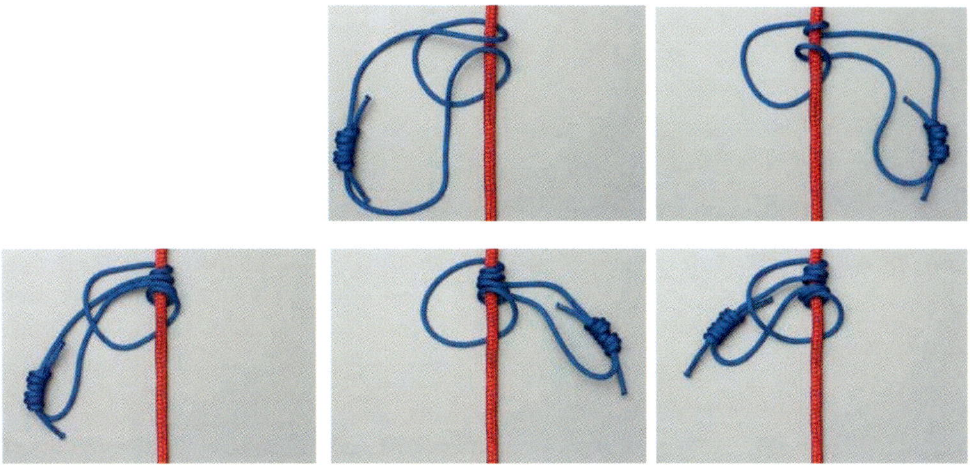

2. Pulling gently on the running end of the loop will secure the knot. It must be loose enough to slide along the lifeline until needed as a brake/friction knot to stop a fall

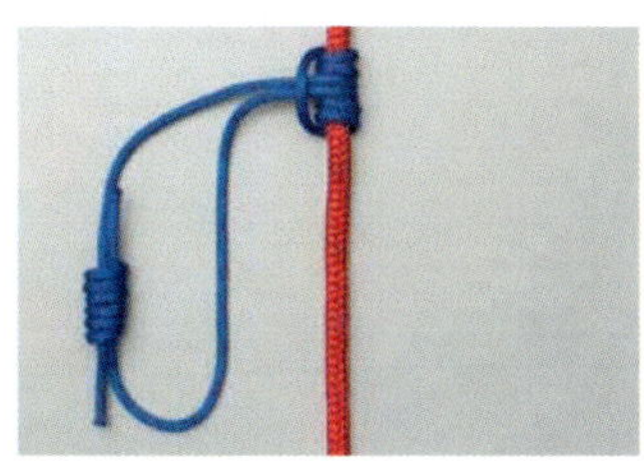

HOW TO TIE A CLOVE HITCH

1. Using the running end of the rope, wrap it halfway around the pole

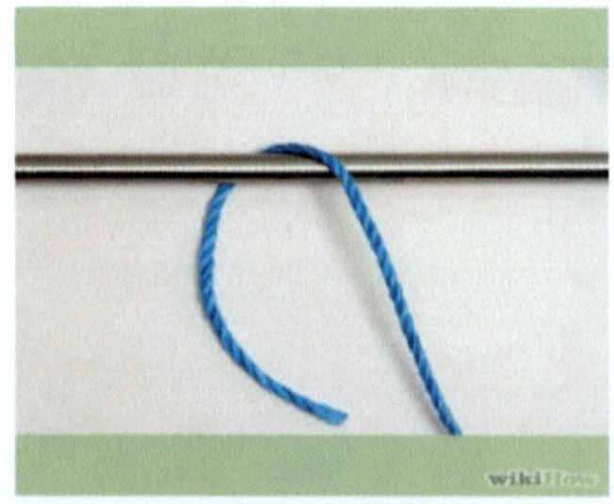

2. Cross the running end over the wrap, forming an "X", then continue back around the pole

3. Lifting the "X" pass the running end under the "X" and adjacent to the original wrap

4. Pull the knot tight

Images courtesy of wikiHow.com

HOW TO TIE A MUNTER HITCH

1. Take a bight of rope and twist it once

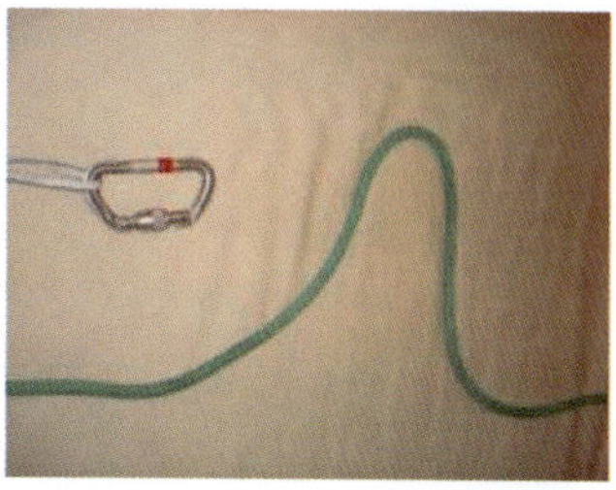

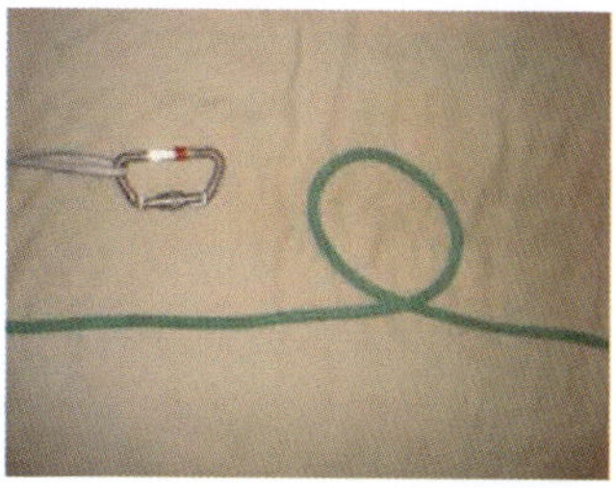

2. Pass the end that lies under the rope, over the loop creating a pretzel shape

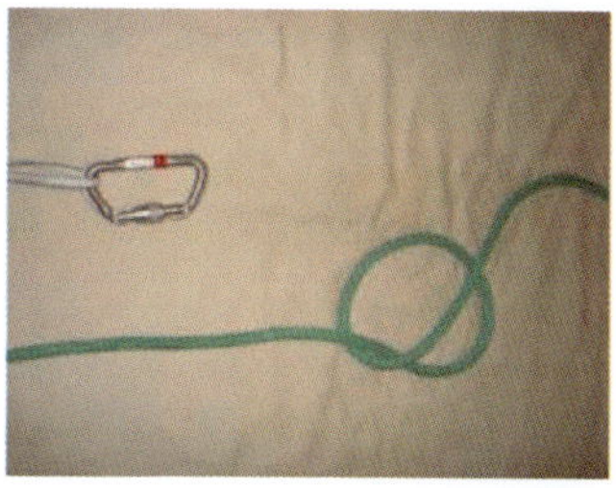

3. Clip the carabiner through the loop, including the “X” of the pretzel

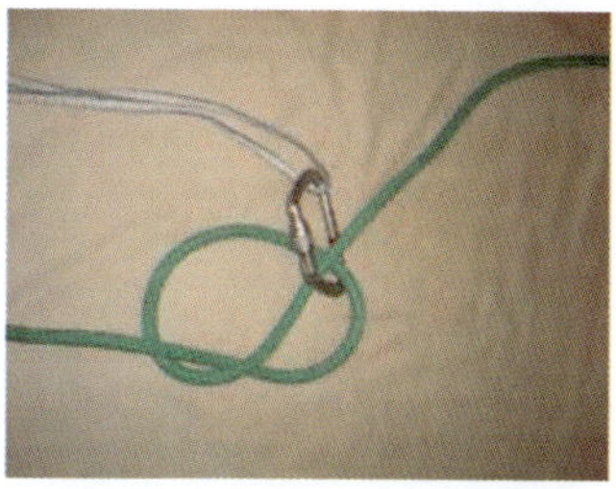

4. Tighten the hitch lightly and it’s ready to serve as a brake

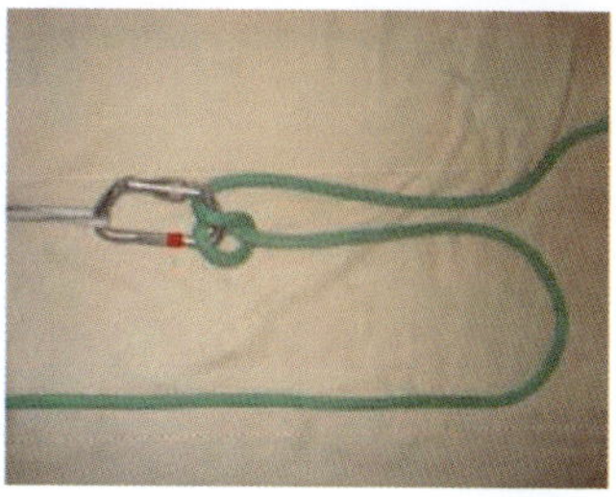

IMAGES COURTESY OF CLIMBINGTECHNIQUES.ORG

HOW TO TIE A WATER KNOT (OVERHAND BEND) IN WEBBING

1. Tie a loose overhand knot in the end (of one length, if you're splicing two pieces) of webbing

COURTESY OF WWW.FIREHOUSE.COM

2. Thread the other end of the webbing back through the original overhand knot in reverse. Be careful to follow the path exactly and don't twist the webbing

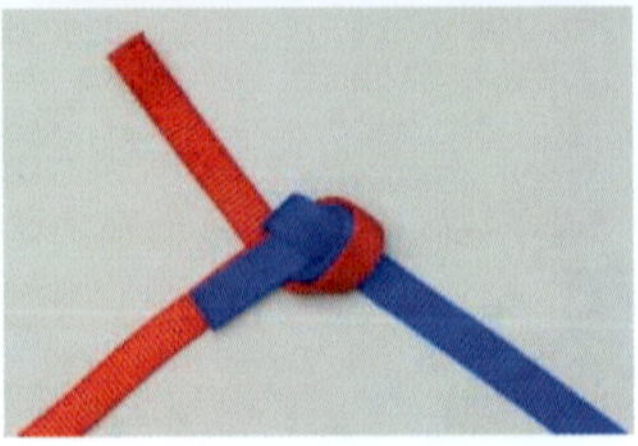

3. Pull the knot tight and use the tails to tie safety knots on both ends

HOW TO TIE AN IMPROVISED SWISS SEAT HARNESS WITH WEBBING

1. Create a bight in the webbing leaving one end approximately 1.5 to 2 ft. longer than the other. Tuck the bight in your belt or pants waistband, below your abdomen.

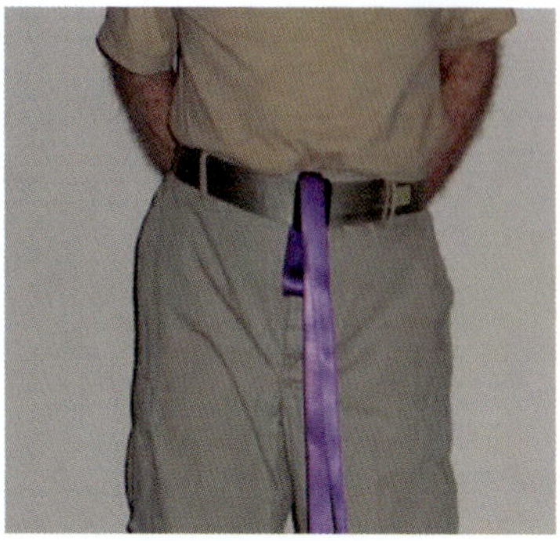

Images courtesy of animatedknots.com

2. Keeping the webbing flat against your body, pass both ends of the webbing through your legs from in front of your crotch to around your buttocks and back through the bight, pulling it out of your belt and tight. This creates triangle of webbing over your crotch area.

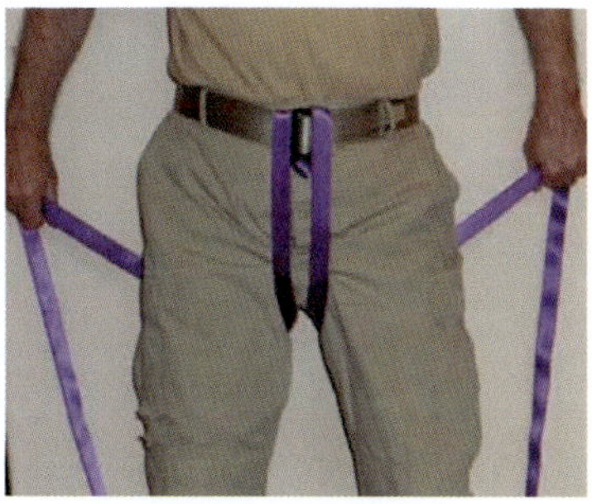

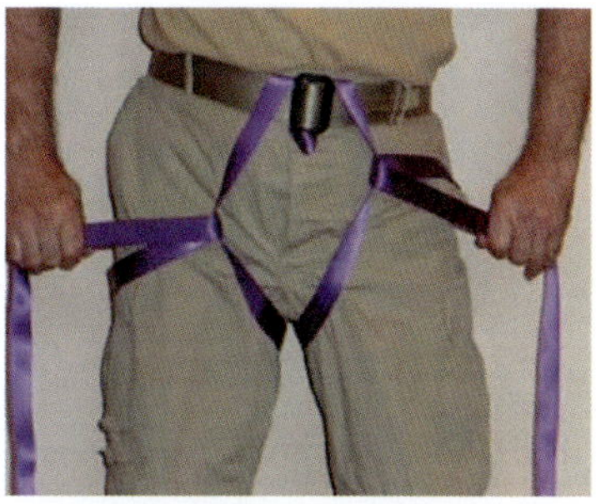

3. Now wrap the webbing tightly around your waist as many

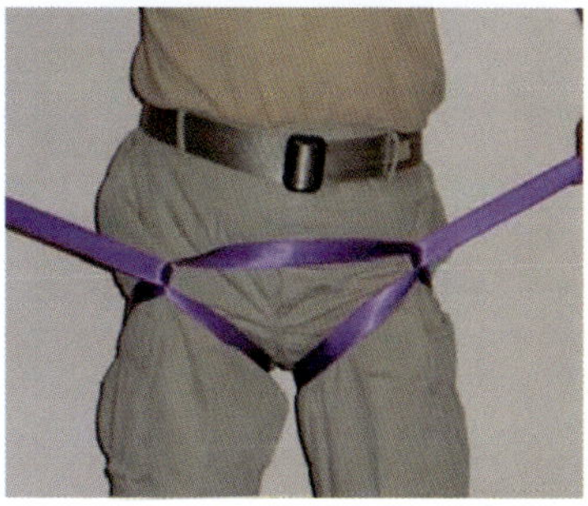

times as it takes leaving only enough webbing (on one side of your body) to tie a square knot with overhand safety knots. Tuck any excess tails into your pocket.

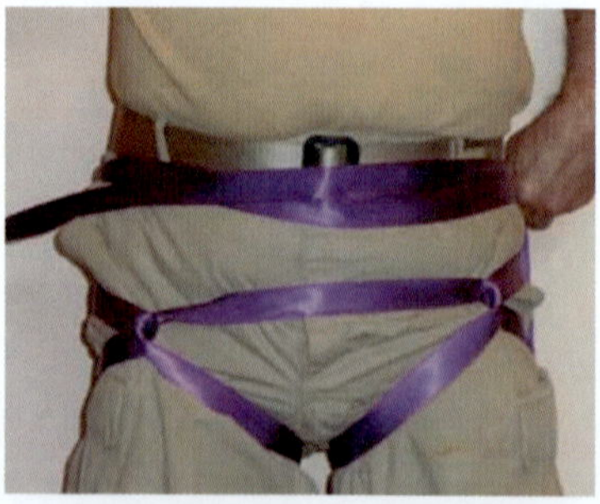

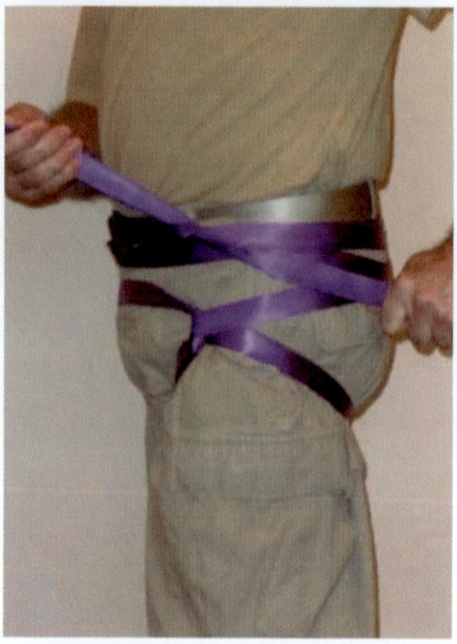

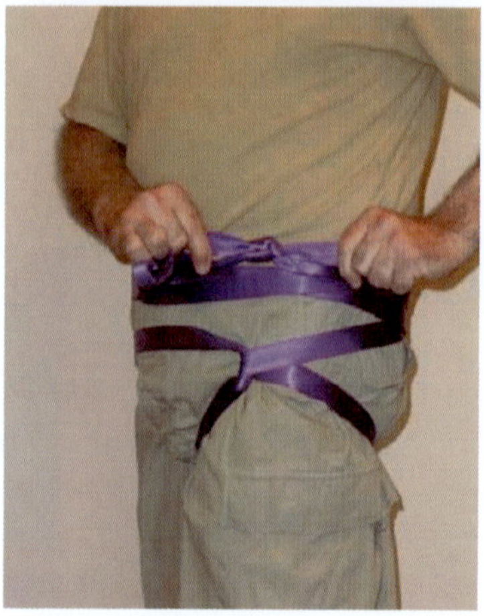

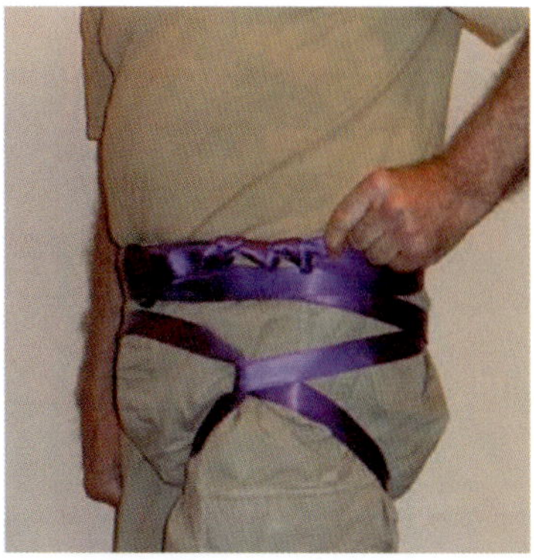

4. Clip a locking carabiner around the top of the crotch loop and all the waist wrappings

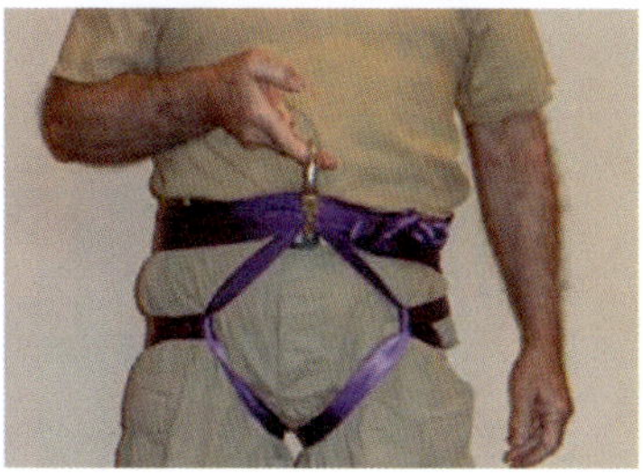

Hints: It is essential that the webbing remain flat against your body at all times. Make sure the harness is tight against your body. This will protect you from sliding out of the harness if you become inverted and better distribute your weight (load) throughout the harness.

Index

C

D

E

F

G

H

M

N

O

P

Q

R

S

Author Bios

Dion A. Petaros—Editor and Author

DION PETAROS is recognized nationally for his expertise in Emergency Response theory and practice. He is well known as a knowledgeable and enthusiastic instructor in the Emergency Response community. While Dion's responder experience includes an *all-hazard* history, his passion for Search & Rescue has led him to develop educational programs to prepare other responders for service in the SAR specialties. With more than 30 years of experience in Search & Rescue he is frequently called upon to participate in large SAR incidents, across the country, as well as to present classes to novice and advanced practitioners.

After having served on the Boards of Directors and as Education Chairperson of numerous educational organizations and operational response agencies & resources, Dion now serves as AERIE's SAR Branch Director where he coordinates the large group of professional researchers, authors, instructors and examiners.

Wes Podboy—Author

WES PODBOY is a 32-year veteran reserve deputy for the San Bernardino County Sheriff's Department. He is one of the founding instructors for the Sheriff's Department Basic Search and Rescue Academy and for the last 15 years served as the Course Coordinator.

Wes also serves on the County Incident Command System Management Team.

Wes served as one of the developers of the State of California Wilderness Medical Technician Trial Study. He has also taught EMT and AEMT at various educational institutions over the last 25 years. For his many years of dedicated service Wes is a recipient of the State of California Medal for Meritorious Service.

James Keck—Author

JAMES KECK is the Leader of the Search & Rescue Team for the Shawnee/Pottawatomie County Emergency Management Search and Rescue Team and has participated in many searches throughout Oklahoma. Previously he was a member of the Carroll County Emergency Management Team responsible for SAR, and other types of emergency response.

Jim has also served as a member of the Civil Air Patrol and worked in Emergency Medical Service for 10 years as a Paramedic. Jim is well respected for his years of experience educating SAR responders to serve their fellow citizens and continues to do so as an AERIE Instructor Trainer.

Gary Jenkins—Author

GARY JENKINS is a 25 year veteran Certified Safety Professional. As an experienced outdoors safety expert, Gary participates in avalanche prediction and crevasse rescue. After completing a rock climbing course at Colorado Mountain School, Gary became an avid climber. His accomplishments include successfully summiting Mount McKinley (Denali) in Alaska and all fifty-four "fourteeners" (peaks with peak elevations in excess of 14,000 feet) in Colorado.

Combining his outdoor safety expertise with his love of all things outdoors, Gary now looks to educate those recreationalists seeking safe fun in adrenaline raising adventures.

Julie Petaros—Author

JULIE PETAROS is a ten year veteran in Search and Rescue. Julie is a certified Flanker, Search and Rescue Technician, Flanker Trainer, Search and Rescue Examiner, and a passionate SAR Instructor. She has extensive experience training emergency response professionals in field operations and preparing them for field examinations. A love of working "in the field" and a desire to assist citizens in need, drives Julie to continue to learn and teach different areas and levels of SAR.

24591838R00254

Printed in Great Britain
by Amazon